Computers and Teaching

Computers and Teaching

Gregg Brownell

University of New Hampshire at Manchester

West Publishing Company

St. Paul • New York • Los Angeles • San Francisco

Copyediting and indexing: Barbara Hodgson
Design: Adrianne Onderdonk Dudden
Cover: Delor Erickson

Library of Congress Cataloging-in-Publication Data

Brownell, Gregg.
    Computers and teaching.

    Includes index.
    1. Education—Data processing.   2. Computer-assisted
instruction.   3. Computer managed instruction.   I. Title.
LB1028.43.B76   1987   371.3'9445   86–24621
ISBN 0–314–28487–1

The following publishers or authors have generously given permission to use extended quotations from copyrighted works: From "Jousting with Jargon," by Jean Fincher. Reprinted with permission from *The Computing Teacher*, November 1984, Vol. 12, No. 3. Published by the International Council for Computers in Education. From "Clerk brought NY courts into high tech world," by John O'Brien. Reprinted with permission of the *Democrat and Chronicle*, Rochester, New York. From *A Place Called School*, by John I. Goodlad. ©1984, McGraw-Hill Book Company. Reprinted with permission. From "Questions Teachers Still Ask About Kids and Computers," by Steven Mandell. Reprinted from *INSTRUCTOR*, October 1984. ©1984 by the Instructor Publications, Inc. Used by permission. From "Thinking Out Loud—Computer Use: A Question of Values," by Bruce W. Tuckman. Reprinted from *Educational Technology*, Vol. 24, No. 4. ©1984, Educational Technology Publications. Used by permission. From "The Talking Computer," by Murray Suid. First published in *The Teacher-Friendly Computer Book*. ©1984, Monday Morning Books. From "Computerphobia: What to Do About It," by Timothy B. Jay. Reprinted from *Educational Technology*, Vol. 21, No. 1. ©1981, Educational Technology Publications. Used by permission. From "Microcomputers in Mathematics Instruction," by Marilyn N. Suydam. Reprinted with permission of the National Council of Teachers of Mathematics, Reston, Virginia. From "Starting from Square One," by Norma C. Piper. Reprinted with permission from *The Computing Teacher*, Aug./Sept. 1984, Vol. 12, No. 1. Published by the International Council for Computers in Education. From "Don't Turn Off That Computer!" by Doris M. Kneppel. Reprinted with permission from *The Computing Teacher*, April 1985, Vol. 12, No. 7. Published by the International Council for Computers in Education. From "First Letter Fun." Used by permission: MECC (Minnesota Educational Computing Corporation). From an adding exercise by Catherine Oemcke. Reprinted with permission of Catherine Oemcke, Computer Literacy Teacher, Clark Lane Junior High School, Waterford, CT 06385. From "The Teacher and Computer Assisted Instruction," by Patrick Suppes. Reprinted by permission of the publisher from, Taylor, ed. *The Computer in the School: Tutor, Tool, Tutee.* (NY: Teachers College Press, ©1980 Teachers College, Columbia University. All rights reserved.) pp. 234–235. From "Software for Elementary and Middle Schools," by Twila Slesnik. Reprinted with permission from the 1984 Computers in Education Special Issue of *Popular Computing* magazine. ©by McGraw-Hill, Inc., New York 10020. From *Computers in Today's World*, by Gary G. Bitter. Reprinted with permission from John Wiley and Sons, Inc., New York. From "The 1986 Classroom Computer Learning Software Awards," by Holly Brady. Reprinted by special permission of *Classroom Computer Learning*, ©1986 by Peter Li, Inc., 19 Davis Drive, Belmont, CA 94002. From "Electronic Research," by Gwen Solomon. From *Electronic Learning*. ©1986 by Scholastic Inc. Reprinted by permission of Scholastic Inc. From

(continued following index)

To my parents, Donald and Dorothy Brownell,
in gratitude for the love, understanding,
and encouragement they have shown me.

Contents

Chapter 1   Computer Use and Our World

Introduction   4
Why Computers?   6
Why Computers in the Schools?   6
What Computers Do: An Overview   9
Computer Uses Today: A Sampling   11
    Business and Industry   11
    Government   13
    Education   13
    Science   15
    Medicine   16
    Entertainment   17
    Office Automation   17
Computer-Related Jobs   18
    Programmers   18
    Systems Analysts   19
    Management Positions   20
    Computer Operations   20
    Data Entry   21
    Training and Education   21
    Sales and Service   21
    Computer Science/Engineering   22
    Entrepreneurs   22
Computer Use Tomorrow   22
Conclusion   23
Key Terms   23
Questions   24
References/Further Reading   25

Chapter 2   Understanding Hardware

Introduction   28
Computers: A Short History   28
    Early Developments   28
    First Generation: 1951–1958   33
    Second Generation: 1959–1964   34
    Third Generation: 1965–1971   34
    Fourth Generation: 1972 to Present   36
Computer Systems   37
    The CPU   38

Peripherals 40
Auxiliary Storage 41
Input Devices 42
Output Devices 44
Other Hardware 46
Categories of Computers 46
Mainframe Computers 47
Minicomputers 48
Microcomputers 49
Communicating with the Hardware 50
Bits and Bytes 54
Conclusion 55
Key Terms 56
Questions 56
References/Further Reading 57

Chapter 3   Computer-Assisted Instruction: An Introduction

Introduction 60
Establishing a Context 60
Teachers as Professionals 60
The Transition to Computer Use 60
Computer-Assisted Instruction: Defined 63
Three Modes of Computer Use 65
Tutor Mode 65
Tool Mode 66
Tutee Mode 67
Control of the Computer-Student Experience 67
Conclusion 72
Key Terms 73
Questions 73
References/Further Reading 73

Chapter 4   Computer-Assisted Instruction: Examples

Introduction 78
Tutor Mode Examples 78
Drill and Practice 78
Instructional Games 83
Tutorials 90
Simulations 92
Tool Mode Examples 96
Word Processors 98
Spreadsheets 99
Data Base Management Systems 100
Tutee Mode Examples 101
Establishing a Future Context 101

Conclusion   104
Key Terms   104
Questions   104
References/Further Reading   105

Chapter 5   Using the Computer for Management

Introduction   108
Computer-Managed Instruction   108
    Who Manages Student Learning?   108
    How Does CMI Work?   109
    Example One   110
    Example Two   116
Teacher Utilities   123
    Managing Grades   123
    Other Applications   139
        Authoring Systems   139
        Readability   140
        Test Creation/Test Scoring Programs   140
Management Software for Administrators   141
What to Look For   141
Conclusion   142
Key Terms   142
Questions   142
References/Further Reading   143

Chapter 6   Software Evaluation

Introduction   146
Evaluating Software   146
General Criteria   146
    Cost   147
    Compatibility   147
    Target Group   148
    Subject Area   148
Specific Criteria   148
    Educational Criteria   149
        Prerequisite Skills   149
        Objectives   149
        Teaching Style   149
        Accuracy   150
        Pace   150
        Student Engagement   151
        Usefulness   151
        Grouping   152
        Stereotypes   152
    Technical Criteria   152
        Flexibility   152
        Use of Graphics and Sound   154

Documentation 154
Support 155
Error Handling 155
Management Information 156
Interactive Design 156
Screen Design 156
Bugs 157
Backup Copies 157
Reviewing Software: Hands-on Experience 158
Software Evaluation: Suggested Steps 159
Identify Need 159
Gather Information 159
Preview 168
The Software-Evaluation Form 168
Purchase 172
Conclusion 172
Key Terms 176
Questions 176
References/Further Reading 176

Chapter 7   Computer Literacy and the Computer Curriculum

Introduction 180
Why Is Computer Literacy Important? 180
Who Should Be Computer Literate? 182
Computer Literacy for Students 183
Knowledge 186
Performance 186
Computer Literacy for Teachers 187
Knowledge 187
Performance 187
Gaining Computer Literacy 189
Developing the Computer Curriculum 190
Components of a Computer Curriculum 191
A Curriculum for Computer Literacy 194
The Computer Curriculum: Specific Examples 204
Evaluation 206
Conclusion 210
Key Terms 213
Questions 214
References/Further Reading 214

Chapter 8   Logo: What and Why

Introduction 218
Theory and Practice 218
Piaget 220

Stages of Development   220
Sensorimotor Stage: Birth to Two Years   220
Preoperational Stage: Two to Seven Years   221
Concrete Operational Stage: Seven to Twelve Years   223
Formal Operational Stage: Twelve Years to Adult   223
Assimilation, Accommodation, and Schemas   225
More on Piaget   227
Piaget and Papert   227
Logo Characteristics   235
Logo Is Powerful   235
Logo Encourages Good Programming   236
Microworlds and Powerful Ideas   237
Logo Is Resonant with the Child's World   238
Logo, Students, and Teachers   238
Logo and Bugs   238
Conclusion   239
Key Terms   239
Questions   240
References/Further Reading   240

Chapter 9   Logo: Starting Out

Introduction   244
MIT Logo   244
Starting Logo: PRINT, and Editing: A Brief Tutorial   245
DRAW and NODRAW   247
FORWARD, BACK, LEFT, and RIGHT   248
A First Shape   250
HOME and CLEARSCREEN   251
Exercises   252
PENDOWN and PENUP   254
HIDETURTLE and SHOWTURTLE   255
SPLITSCREEN, FULLSCREEN, and TEXTSCREEN   257
Exercises   259
REPEAT   259
Exercises   262
Conclusion   264
Key Terms   264
References/Further Reading   265

Chapter 10   Logo: Expanding the Possibilities

Introduction   268
Procedures   268
What Is a Procedure?   268
Creating Procedures   270
Edit Commands   272
More on Procedures   272
Exercises   273

Managing Logo   274
    Working Memory   274
    Saving Procedures   275
    Reading Files   276
    Exercises   277
Subprocedures   278
    Exercises   281
Recursion   282
    Exercises   284
Teaching Logo   285
Conclusion   290
Key Terms   291
References/Further Reading   292

Chapter 11   Algorithms and the Teaching of Programming

Introduction   296
Syntax and Logic   297
Problem Solving   299
    Example 11–1   299
Algorithms   301
    Example 11–2   301
    Example 11–3   303
Flowcharts   304
Structured Programming   308
Structured Design   309
Conclusion   315
Key Terms   315
Questions   315
References/Further Reading   316

Chapter 12   BASIC: A Beginning

Introduction   320
Beginning BASIC   320
Getting to Applesoft BASIC   321
Variables and Constants   321
    Numerical Constants and Variables   321
    String Constants and Variables   322
    Exercises   322
Reserved Words, Commands, and Statements   322
PRINT, END, REM, and HOME   323
    PRINT   323
    END   323
    REM   325
    HOME   325
    Example   326

Exercises   327
Arithmetic Operations   327
LET   329
Example   330
Exercises   330
PRINT—One More Time   330
INPUT   333
Example   336
Exercises   340
Conclusion   340
Key Terms   340
References/Further Reading   340

Chapter 13   BASIC: Adding Options

Introduction   344
GOTO   344
IF–THEN   345
Example One   347
Example Two   349
Exercises   352
FOR–NEXT   352
Example   356
Exercises   360
READ, DATA, and RESTORE   360
Example   364
Exercises   369
Conclusion   370
Key Terms   370
References/Further Reading   371

Chapter 14   Computer Resources: Trends and Issues

Introduction   374
Types of Computers in the Schools   374
Computer Education and Cost   377
Managing Computer Resources: Four Models   378
The Computer Lab   378
Computers in the Classroom   379
Lab/Classroom   381
Mobile Lab/Classroom   381
Which Approach Is Best?   381
The Computer Coordinator   382
Trends and Issues   384
Hardware   384
Software   386
Equity   391
Conclusion   391
Key Terms   392

Questions   392
References/Further Reading   393

Appendix A: Relevant Periodicals   394

Appendix B: Organizations   396

Appendix C: Using an Apple   397

Appendix D: Software Manufacturers   401

Glossary   403

Index   415

Preface

As the twentieth century draws to a close, computers are becoming an important classroom resource for teachers. More and more, teachers are using computers as a tool to teach with, to offer instruction in a variety of subjects. At the same time teachers are being called on to teach students about computers—their history, how they function, and how they are used in society. To meet the need to educate teachers about computers and the use of computers in education, many schools and departments of education offer specialized computer education courses. This book is designed for students taking such a course. Its aim is to present a sound, readable, practical introduction to the topics taught to pre-service and in-service teachers preparing to teach with and about computers.

Purpose

One of the major strengths of this text is that it brings together a comprehensive body of current, relevant information about computers and teaching not readily available elsewhere. It does this in a way that makes the information accessible to the student by (a) being highly readable, (b) using many examples to illustrate the concepts presented, and (c) offering material and strategies actually used in the schools. Further, although the text is intended to impart practical skills and useful knowledge about educational computing, the theories underlying many of the practical applications presented are also addressed. In addition, because the field of computer education is not without its critics, and because those within the field often disagree, opposing views, where appropriate, are presented. The intent in doing this is to challenge students to decide what practices they will use in working with computers in the schools, and why they will use them.

Attributes

The text also contains a series of pedagogical features that aid in presenting the material covered in each chapter. Each chapter begins with a list of the topics addressed. This is followed by an outline of the material covered in the chapter. At the end of each chapter is a list of key terms, all of which are contained in the glossary. Except for the programming chapters, a set of questions aimed at focusing student attention on important skills and concepts is included at the end of each chapter. In place of end-of-chapter questions, the chapters on programming have sets of exercises included at appropriate points. Each chapter also contains a list of references and sources for further reading.

Features

The following features are also found in each chapter.

•A topical cartoon about computers or computers in education

•*Input/Output*: Material, taken from various sources, expressing the viewpoints of different people concerned with computers and education

•*Reactions and Research*: Examples of research findings about computers and education as well as material offering different individuals' opinions about and interpretations of relevant research and the use of computers in education

•*Computers in the Classroom*: Practical suggestions for using computers in the classroom

Structure and Content

The descriptions below present an overview of the structure and content of the text. Because a course of this type may be taught by instructors with any of various backgrounds, the text is structured to be a flexible resource. All the topics presented can be effectively covered in a one semester course, or, selected topics may be covered.

Chapter 1   Computer Use and Our World

The computer revolution is described. Arguments for and against schools devoting time to teaching with and about computers are presented. What computers do and how they are used by people is explained. The range of computer job opportunities available is outlined. A glimpse of what future computers may offer is presented.

Chapter 2   Understanding Hardware

The history of computers is traced. The components of a computer system are identified and described. Examples of peripheral devices and how they function are presented. Micro, mini, and mainframe computers are described. The concept of a programming language is introduced and the difference between low-level and high-level programming languages is explained. The terms *bit*, *byte*, and *encoding system* are introduced. How computers store data is explained.

Chapter 3   Computer-Assisted Instruction: Introduction

A discussion of the factors that affect the initial use of computers by teachers is presented, followed by a definition of computer-assisted instruction. A model for classifying software used in instruction is presented. The question of who controls the computer-student interaction, the student or the computer, is discussed.

Chapter 4   Computer-Assisted Instruction: Examples

Examples of tutor mode software, including drill and practice, instructional games, tutorials, and simulations, are presented. Examples of tool mode software, including word processors, spreadsheets, and data base management systems, are presented. The effects of future developments in the field of artifical intelligence as they may affect computer-assisted instruction are discussed.

Chapter 5   Using the Computer for Management

The term *computer-managed instruction* is defined. Examples of computer-managed instruction are presented, including management systems built into tutor mode software. Teacher utility software is identified and examples are presented, including an example of a grade-keeping program. Administrative uses of computers are identified and specific software is cited that will perform relevant administrative functions.

Chapter 6   Software Evaluation

The importance of teachers developing good software evaluation skills is emphasized. Criteria for evaluating software are presented. Steps involved in evaluating educational software are given. Sources of information about software are cited. Examples of software evaluation forms are presented.

Chapter 7   Computer Literacy and the Computer Curriculum

Reasons for helping students become computer literate are covered. Computer literacy is defined for both students and teachers. Suggestions about how students and teachers can gain computer literacy are offered. The relationship between the computer curriculum and helping students gain computer literacy is outlined. The process of developing a computer curriculum is covered. The components of a computer curriculums are introduced. Examples of different computer curriculum are presented. An example of how a computer curriculum might be evaluated is offered.

Chapter 8   Logo: What and Why

The connection between Logo, Jean Piaget, and Seymour Papert is presented. A review of relevant topics from Piaget's work is offered. Papert's interpretation and extension of Piaget's work are outlined. Ways in which Logo might affect cognitive development in children are presented. How Logo can be used to teach subject matter is covered. Attributes of Logo that reflect Papert's theoretical concerns are identified.

Chapter 9   Logo: Starting Out

The Logo programming language is introduced with appropriate examples and exercises. The editing commands ESC, CTRL–D, and CTRL–K are introduced. Other commands introduced are: PRINT, DRAW, NODRAW, FORWARD, BACK, RIGHT, LEFT, HOME, CLEARSCREEN, PENUP, PENDOWN, HIDETURTLE, SHOWTURTLE, SPLITSCREEN, FULLSCREEN, TEXTSCREEN, and REPEAT.

Chapter 10   Logo: Expanding the Possibilities

The concept of a procedure is introduced, as is the concept of workspace. The additional editing commands CTRL–P, CTRL–N, and CTRL–O are introduced. Other commands introduced are: POTS, PO, ERASE, GOODBYE, SAVE, READ, and ERASEFILE. The concept of a subprocedure is introduced, as is the concept of recursion. Examples of the various commands and concepts are presented. Relevant student exercises are included. Suggestions for planning a Logo project are given. The different types of learning styles that students may bring to working with Logo are presented. Attributes of Logo not covered in this introduction are cited.

Chapter 11   Algorithms and the Teaching of Programming

The responsibility of teachers to foster good programming habits is emphasized. The importance of syntax and logic as they relate to the development of a computer program is presented. General steps for problem solving are identified and applied. The concept of an algorithm is introduced. The function of pseudocode is illustrated. Flowcharts are introduced. Structured programming and structured design are covered. Structure charts are introduced.

Chapter 12   BASIC: A Beginning

An orientation to the different implementations of BASIC is presented. Numerical and string constants and variables are introduced. How BASIC performs arithmetic operations is covered. The following BASIC statements are introduced with examples and exercises: PRINT, REM, END, HOME, LET, and INPUT. The following commands are covered: RUN, LIST, SAVE, LOAD, and CATALOG. The writing of an algorithm as part of the process of developing a BASIC program is introduced.

Chapter 13   BASIC: Adding Options

The following statements are introduced, with examples and relevant exercises: GOTO, IF–THEN, FOR–NEXT, READ, DATA, RESTORE. Relational symbols are covered. Examples of using structure charts in the development of BASIC programs are covered.

Chapter 14   Computer Resources: Trends and Issues

The types of computers used in schools are reviewed and the relationship of cost to computer resources available in the schools is outlined. Several models for using computers in the schools are presented (computer lab, computers in the classroom, lab/classroom, and mobile lab/classroom). The role of a computer coordinator is presented. Trends in hardware and software are presented and discussed as to their possible effect on educational computing. Equity issues related to the use of computers in education are presented.

Appendix A: Relevant Periodicals

Selected periodicals dealing with computers in education are listed, as well as general interest periodicals that provide information on computers and computing.

Appendix B: Organizations

Organizations dealing with various aspects of computers in education are listed.

Appendix C: Using an Apple

Instructions are given for initializing a disk for an Apple II series computer, as well as information about a variety of system commands.

Appendix D: Software Manufacturers

Selected manufacturers of educational software are listed.

Hardware Considerations

Nearly all of the software used to illustrate the material in this text is available for Apple II series microcomputers. Much of the software is also available in versions for other machines. The chapters on programming contain examples written for Apple II series computers. This choice was made based on the fact that Apple computers are the type most commonly found in schools. Any correspondence from students or instructors regarding the use of this text would be appreciated. Correspondence should be sent to: Gregg Brownell, c/o Box 302, Newburyport, MA 01950.

Acknowledgments

There are many people whose help and support made this project a reality; they deserve a special note of thanks. Mary Gallagher served as a catalyst to get the project started and offered her knowledge and help as the initial proposal was developed. Dr. William Billingham made it possible to develop and teach the course on which this book is based. Vic Ferry offered his support while the content of the course was refined. Dan and Francine Perley offered personal encouragement and professional insight, both of which were invaluable and appreciated. The students in EDU 553 continually provided a source of lively discussion about the use of computers in education. Monique Leduc and John Hornyak were generous with both their encouragement and their technical help. The following people, over the years, helped to introduce me to the world of computers: Ed Mini, Ann Optis, Gail Tine, Marshall Kaplan, Penny Cooper, Rich Adelson, and Bob St. Laurent. Ron and Doris Seward offered encouragement throughout the project and were kind enough to loan me a printer for a prolonged period. Margi and Dick Gunn deserve extra thanks for their special help and support. Ray Hubbard did a fine job in providing many of the photographs in the text. The reviewers of the original manuscript, listed below, offered meaningful, informed suggestions for improvement; their help has been of great benefit: Steven Ross, Memphis State University; M. Mark

Wasicsko, Texas Wesleyan College; Richard Howell, Ohio State University; Ann Thompson, Iowa State University; Alvin Ollenburger, University of Minnesota-Duluth; John Wedman, University of Northern Iowa; Richard Warner, Trenton State College. At West, Clark Baxter has been a constant source of guidance and support. His professionalism and expertise have made this a truly enjoyable experience. Also at West, Nancy Crochiere has, in her competent, informed way, been a great help to me. Laura Carlson, at West, has been both patient and supportive during the production phase of this project. At the University of New Hampshire at Manchester, Lew Roberts and Jack Resch helped to make the completion of the final stages of this work possible. Karla Vogel has been supportive as a valued, competent colleague. My daughter, Sandy, has, on a daily basis, helped to keep things in perspective. Lastly, my wife, Nancy, has continually given freely of her time and energy—without her support this project could not have been accomplished. She is greatly appreciated both as a wife and as a friend.

Gregg Brownell

Computers and Teaching

1

Computer Use and Our World

TOPICS ADDRESSED

Why has there been a computer revolution?

Should the schools devote time to teaching with and about computers? What are the arguments for and against this possibility?

What do computers actually do?

How are computers used?

What computer-related job opportunities exist, and what background is needed to be employed in them?

What will the computers of tomorrow offer?

OUTLINE

Introduction
Why Computers?
Why Computers in the Schools?
What Computers Do: An Overview
Computer Uses Today: A Sampling
  Business and Industry
  Government
  Education
  Science
  Medicine
  Entertainment
  Office Automation
Computer-Related Jobs
  Programmers
  Systems Analysts

  Management Positions
  Computer Operations
  Data Entry
  Training and Education
  Sales and Service
  Computer Science/Engineering
  Entrepreneurs
Computer Use Tomorrow
Conclusion
Key Terms
Questions
References/Further Reading

Introduction

A large insurance company maintains a multimillion-dollar computer installation. The help that the computers provide to the organization is critical. The company will go out of business if its computer center is unable to operate for three consecutive days.

A blind student uses a computer to translate the work she does in braille into ordinary print materials for her high school teachers. The machine also allows her teachers to translate their instructions into braille. Another student uses a computer with a voice synthesizer to work with a series of lessons in language arts. The computer explains the lessons in understandable English and the student responds by typing on a keyboard.

A family shops and banks at home through a personal computer that is equipped to send information over ordinary telephone lines. The children in the family (and sometimes the adults) use the computer for entertainment by playing different types of games on it. Other uses include the preparation of letters, school assignments, and holiday mailing lists. The same family purchases a new car that has a computer built into the engine to aid the motor in operating efficiently.

Other computers monitor equipment performance in power plants and on ships, airplanes, and space vehicles. People in such diverse fields as medicine, business, government, the military, and education use computers routinely and in growing numbers. Today computers are part of life and will affect the

"The computer in my office says you don't have enough in your bank account for the down payment."

Figure 1–1 Computers are used in the home for a variety of purposes including education, entertainment, and to help with tasks such as keeping a budget.

quality of our personal and professional lives well into the foreseeable future. Faced with this reality, we raise the question, What, if any, responsibility does this imply for educators engaged in preparing the students of today for the world of tomorrow?

Figure 1–2 Computers continue to become more and more a part of everyday life. The question arises, what role should computers play in education?

Why Computers?

The situations described earlier did not exist thirty years ago. Indeed, some of the opportunities for computer use, such as the development of relatively inexpensive personal computers, could not be found even ten years ago. The revolutionary growth of computer power and availability has been spurred by the equally revolutionary growth in the amount of information available to people in various fields of endeavor. This growth is termed the Knowledge Explosion and the age it has catapulted us into is called the Information Age.

Take the field of medicine, for example. Today it is impossible for a doctor to keep track of all the developments in the medical community. In fact, it would be physically impossible for any individual to read within a year everything written about medicine during that year. Too much information is produced to allow that to happen. This is true in many professions. People therefore tend to gain a generalized understanding of their profession and then specialize in one particular area.

Along with the growth in the quantity of information came a need to manage information, to make it both available and useful. The vehicle for the management of information in the Information Age is the computer. This means different things in different fields. In education it might mean a computerized library search for articles related to the topic of a research paper. In business it could mean a computer program to analyze large amounts of marketing data to help predict market preferences.

Why Computers in the Schools?

Traditionally, one of the overall goals of schools has been to prepare young people to eventually take an active, supportive, and, it is hoped, fulfilling role in the perpetuation of the society. To accomplish this, children are taught skills that are thought necessary for survival in the society, such as reading, mathematics, reasoning, and a number of other subjects. Further, through interaction with peers and adults in a school setting, the learning of values and attitudes acceptable in the society, socialization, takes place.

Given this general view of what schools do and the reality that computers are increasing in importance in society, making a case that they should be a topic of instruction in the schools seems easy. This is in fact what has happened. Over the past several years, many schools have begun to teach with and about computers. Teaching *with* a computer involves using a computer to present part or all of the instructional material covered. Teaching *about* computers means presenting material about the history of computers, how they work, and what can and should be done with them. There is some debate, however, as to whether teaching with and about computers should be done at all.

Opponents of computer instruction argue that the computers available today are not the machines that young people will have to interact with when they are adults. Advances in computer technology tend to occur rapidly. The prediction is made that computers will eventually be part of our lives in much the same way that electric motors are now. We use electric motors in a variety of appliances, such as hair dryers, stereo turntables, and washing machines, but we do not need to know about the electric motors contained in those appliances in order to use them successfully. If this is the only type of contact people in the future have with computers, it would not make sense to give today's students information that will not be needed tomorrow.

Another point that opponents make is that the teaching of programming (the process of writing the instructions, or program, needed to have a computer do something) is not a wise undertaking. They hold that the vast majority of people who will use computers in their work, such as people in the business world, will not need to program them. Rather, someone else will have already programmed the computer for them so that using it is easy and straightforward.

Further, opponents propose that even teaching with computers may not be a good idea. This is based on a belief that much of the material available to present instruction on the computer is not very good and would hardly justify the cost of the equipment to use it or the time necessary to implement it. Lastly, opponents are concerned that, by introducing computer instruction into the curriculum, time needed for skills instruction in such areas as reading, mathematics, and writing will be taken away.

These are valid concerns. Proponents of computer instruction might respond that the analogy between computers and electric motors may not be appropriate. Electric motors are used to extend the individual's physical ability. Although computers can be used in the same way as electric motors, embedded into a device such as a car to improve its functioning, they offer more than that. Among other things, computers can be used to extend and enhance a person's mental ability; they can be used as machines to think with. For example, using a computer to manipulate and analyze a large amount of data, say data from a science experiment on population growth, may stimulate new insights into relationships among the data that would not otherwise be obvious.

Figure 1–3 Many schools have a computer lab where teachers and students work with computers to accomplish a variety of educational goals. Such labs can be as simple as the one shown here, with a number of computers placed on available tables. Other labs may incorporate special furniture and a wider variety of computer equipment.

In addition, a case can be made that the teaching of programming offers a concrete way to develop reasoning skills. Programming involves learning problem-solving techniques that may be beneficial in and of themselves, techniques that may transfer to other subject matter areas.

Also, although it is true that, initially, materials available for teaching with computers were not impressive, they have been steadily improving. Some excellent packages are currently being offered. When used as part of an overall instructional program, the quality of computer-based instruction can be high. As more powerful, less expensive computers become readily available, more sophisticated materials will be developed.

Proponents of computer instruction agree that computers will change over time. However, it is also true that computers and technology are becoming more and more a part of our lives. Therefore, the attitudes of students toward technology may need to be challenged and explored with regard to students' eventual roles as consumers, job-seekers, and voters. Early experiences with and information about computers can aid in fostering positive exploration of individual and societal attitudes about technology and its appropriate uses.

Lastly, instructional time is valuable. Certainly teaching with computers should not be a choice over current methods unless there is a reasonable

---

Input/Output

The computer field is filled with terms that are unfamiliar to most people. As you progress through this text you will learn many of the terms and concepts necessary for an understanding of what computers are, how they work, and how they may be used in the schools. The following excerpt is from an article by Jean Fincher entitled "Jousting with Jargon," which appeared in The Computing Teacher. *Although Fincher relates an experience with elementary teachers, she offers insights of value to teachers of all levels on how to deal with computer jargon and how to view computers in education.*

For some time I have felt sure that elementary teachers could step easily into using computers if the jargon barrier were removed. When my principal asked me to conduct a computer-orientation session for other teachers in our school, I jumped at the chance. With the exception of one teacher whose son owns a small home computer, these teachers had not used a computer.

I gave the workshop this title: "How to Start Using Computer Programs We Already Have." The orientation lasted just under an hour. I used computer terms only when I could not conveniently substitute more familiar words. Near the end of the orientation session, I handed my colleagues "cheat sheets" which gave concise directions for operating the computer with software. There were also a few cautionary statements regarding care and use of computing equipment. Finally, I encouraged them to enroll in further computer training.

A new sound began to be heard around the table in our faculty lounge—the sound of teachers critiquing computer software. Not a word about RAMs or ROMs, bits or bytes, interfaces, modems, loops or strings. Just teachers doing what good teachers always have done—analyzing resources available to them, accepting some, rejecting others, questioning some and speculating on possible improvement. Their approach is, "If it meets the learning needs of my students in my classroom, I welcome it. If it doesn't meet those needs, I don't want it." If enough such voices are raised in the world of teaching, the world of computing surely will hear and respond.

A recent incident in a city manager's office shows just how direct our approach to the computing world can be.

My husband had been asked to help plan the use of microcomputers in city offices. The city manager began the meeting by looking directly across his desk at my husband and announcing in a cordial but uncompromising tone, "My assistant and I have agreed to stop you any time you start using jargon."

We educators would do well to emulate that city manager. He made an effort to become informed about computer applications, but instead of feigning an understanding which he had not yet acquired, instead of feeling intimidated by technological wonders, he had the nerve to say simply, "Stop. Speak English."

(Fincher, 1984)

improvement in the quality of instruction owing to computer use. If this turns out to be the case, the computer may offer a way to strengthen instruction in those very skills about which some people are concerned. This possibility will be explored more fully in Chapter 3.

The discussion is by no means settled; educators will be debating the merits of teaching with and about computers for some time. It would be beneficial to consider the arguments on both sides of the question as you become more familiar with what computers are and how they are being used in education.

What Computers Do: An Overview

Basically, computers may be thought of as machines that process data. In this instance, data may be defined as facts. The temperature in a classroom, a student's grade, the price of an item in a grocery store, or the rate at which oil is flowing through a pipeline are all data that may be processed or manipulated in some way. The type of processing that may be done to the data depends on the outcome desired by the person using the computer. Processing refers to such operations as sorting, comparing, calculating, classifying, and summarizing. Once data is processed, the computer produces output from that processing. Data may be processed for two purposes. In the first instance, output may be provided to the person using the computer, called the user, as information. In this context, information is defined as data that has been processed into a form that is meaningful to the user. This output may be a printed report, or it may be information written on a video display screen. As outlined in **Figure 1–4**, data is input to the computer, processed in some way, and output to the user as information.

Imagine the superintendent of a large school district. As part of an analysis of trends in the district it becomes important for the superintendent to understand the performance of high school students on the verbal section of the Scholastic Aptitude Test. One way to do this would be to compare the scores on the test for the current group of students with the performance of other students over the past ten years. If 700 students had taken the test in each of the past ten years, the superintendent would have 7,000 pieces of data to consider. Without processing the data in some way, the individual facts, the scores, would be meaningless. Picture the superintendent sifting through 7,000 test scores and trying to make sense out of them!

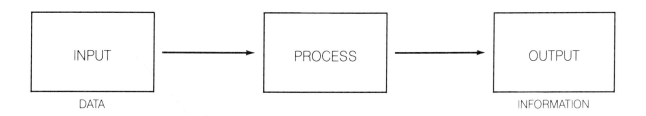

Figure 1–4 Data is input to the computer where it is processed and output as information.

Turning the data into usable information is fairly easy. The scores could be sorted by year and an average for each year could be calculated. A summary of this information could be graphed in a variety of ways to clarify the relationships among the data. Whatever form the processing took, the output would be information the superintendent could readily understand and use. **Figure 1–5** shows this.

Another manner in which output may be produced is for control purposes. A computer can monitor the flow of oil in a refinery pipeline. The data gathered are processed into output, which is used to automatically control the flow rate. This is similar to what happens in a thermostat in a home. The temperature of the home is controlled by the thermostat, which turns the furnace on or off, based on the temperature the thermostat registers. Computers are used for control purposes in a wide variety of settings, including power plants, submarines, commercial buildings, and homes.

Whenever coming into contact with any computer, large or small, remember that all it can do is accept input (data), process it, and provide output.

THE SUPERINTENDENT'S DATA PROCESSED INTO INFORMATION

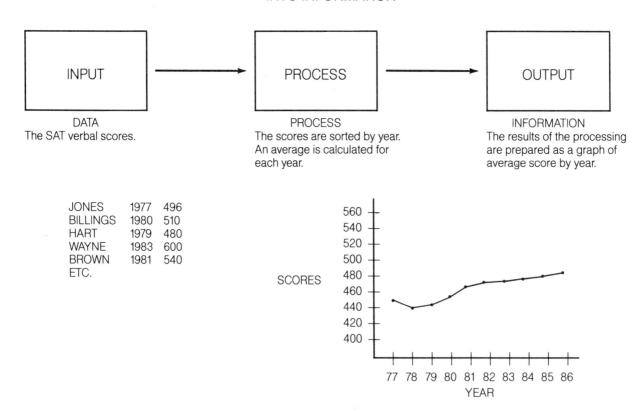

Figure 1–5 The test scores for all students over the past ten years are used as data. The scores are first sorted by year. An average score for each year is calculated. The results of this processing are reported as information to the superintendent. In this case the information is in the form of a graph.

Almost every area of human life has been touched by the computer. The following categories are offered to aid in organizing an overview of ways in which computers are being used today:

- Business and industry
- Government
- Education
- Science
- Medicine
- Entertainment
- Office automation

Uses in business include standard accounting functions, such as accounts payable, accounts receivable, and general ledger. Other common uses include computerized payroll systems, which may take as input time sheets showing hours worked and provide as output payroll checks and stubs, as well as a report to management detailing payroll statistics for the pay period.

Business and Industry

Different businesses use computers differently, depending on their particular business concern. Financial institutions such as insurance companies may use computers to keep track of policy premiums due and paid. Some insurance companies have automated some of their rating and policy-writing activities.

Banks make extensive use of computers in a variety of situations. Automatic teller machines have become standard in most parts of the country. These machines allow a customer to access an account at any time of the day or night without the aid of a human teller. Electronic funds transfer (EFT) allows banks and customers to move funds from one account to another. Funds may be transferred by a customer from one account to another within a bank or by a bank from one bank to another almost anywhere in the world. The concept of EFT is familiar to people who pay bills by telephoning their bank and telling someone what bills to pay from their accounts.

Many supermarkets and department stores are beginning to use point-of-sale (POS) terminals (**Figure 1–6**). These terminals are equipped to read the universal product code (UPC) symbol printed on many items. The symbol is read into a computer that has stored in it a description of the item and the item's price. The computer then records the information on a sales receipt and totals the cost of the goods purchased, including any applicable tax. The computer that this type of POS terminal is connected to usually keeps a running inventory of what goods are available. This enables the store management to maintain an adequate supply of merchandise. A sophisticated system of this sort would be able to automatically check a customer's credit rating to allow payment by credit card.

Debit cards look like credit cards but are used in place of cash, credit, or a personal check when goods or services are purchased. The debit card causes the amount spent to be subtracted from the person's bank account. EFTs, credit cards, debit cards, and POS terminals are helping to move us toward the long-

Figure 1–6 Many supermarkets use point-of-sale terminals to record transactions and track inventory.

predicted cashless society of the future. In a cashless society little or no hard currency will be used.

Companies that manufacture goods use computers in a variety of ways. In addition to typical business functions, certain types of computer uses are unique to companies that design and produce goods.

A company that produces stereo equipment may use a computerized system to track inventory of completed units. Further, since the assembly of various components is required to achieve the finished product, a careful inventory of parts on hand must be maintained and compared with production quotas. This assures adequate inventory for continued, uninterrupted production. Computer systems can be used to accomplish this.

Computers are used in some plants to monitor machine use as an aid in scheduling machine and employee time in order to better plan production schedules. Some companies make use of computer-aided design (CAD) and computer-aided manufacturing (CAM) in the production process.

CAD allows engineers to model a product on a computer and simulate the response of the product to a variety of situations. This allows the product design to be tested and refined before money is spent on actually manufacturing a version of the product under development. An example would be an engineer designing a new car. The design of the car could be accomplished by using the graphics available on a computer system. Once the car is designed, the computer could simulate different aerodynamic situations, allowing the engineer to observe the response of the car and improve the design as needed. Other components of the car, such as the suspension system, could be tested in a similar manner.

CAM refers to the use of computers in the actual manufacturing process and can mean something as simple as one industrial robot being programmed to perform welding tasks on a production line, or as complex as a fully automated manufacturing plant.

Government at all levels relies on computer processing to accomplish many necessary tasks. On the national level the Internal Revenue Service uses computers to process the millions of tax returns it receives yearly. By dialing a special toll-free number and entering a social security number over a touch-tone phone, taxpayers may access their computerized tax records and be told if they have a refund due. The Social Security Administration is another big user of computer power. The Defense Department and various military branches use computers for a variety of purposes ranging from personnel management to the control of sophisticated weapons systems.

Various state agencies, such as departments of education, transportation, welfare, and revenue, may use computers to manage data relevant to their purposes. One interesting use of computers has been in the management of various aspects of family court business at different court sites in the state of New York (see **Figure 1–7**). Desktop personal computers are used to keep track of such things as judges' schedules, vendors who supply the court with the many volumes of legal reference material needed for the court to function, and scheduling and notification of court appearance dates for people who have business with the court.

Government

Computer use in education ranges from instructional to administrative, and from preschool to graduate school. As mentioned earlier, computer instruction can be categorized as teaching about computers or teaching with computers. Many school districts have developed a computer education curriculum. One common concern addressed by such a curriculum is teaching about the history and functioning of computers. Hands-on experiences are also provided to help develop the skills associated with using a computer and with computer programming.

Teaching with a computer may involve the presentation of drill and practice sessions, tutorials, simulations, or instructional games. Word processors are computer-based electronic typewriters that make it easy to revise written work. Teachers may use computer-based tools such as word processors to enhance and enliven instruction. Many instructors use the computer for classroom administrative tasks, such as record keeping and grade averaging, as well as for tasks that involve material preparation. The computer, when coupled with an inexpensive printer, can furnish interesting, creative, and professional-looking graphics for bulletin boards and displays (see **Figure 1–8**). Teacher utility programs provide opportunities for teachers to create their own computer-based materials, such as tutorial lessons and drill and practice lessons. Such programs also allow the creation of, among others, customized materials, such as mazes, crossword puzzles, and word-find games.

Programming, the art of writing computer programs, is taught at the elementary, middle school, senior high school, and college levels for a variety of purposes. Programs are written in specific computer languages. Examples of

Education

Clerk Brought N.Y. Courts Into High-Tech World

State to Honor Seward for Computer Initiative

By John O'Brien
Democrat and Chronicle

Seven years ago, courts across the state were bogged down in a mountain of paperwork generated by an ever-increasing caseload.

In a clerk's office on the third floor of the Monroe County Hall of Justice, Ronald G. Seward decided to do something about it.

Seward, then the chief clerk of Monroe County Family Court, spent $5,000 of his own money to buy a personal computer and figure out a way to organize the reams of information into push-button technology.

While the system is still slow at times, court officials across the state now say Seward's initiative has saved time and frustration and has allowed judges to concentrate more on cases than schedules and paperwork.

"It was akin to somone who can't read all of a sudden realizing he needs bifocals—everything became more clear," said Charles L. Willis, supervising judge of Monroe County Family Court.

Seward, 61, will receive a special award tomorrow in Albany from the state Office of Court Administration, honoring him for the computer system he designed that is now in 130 courts in the state. Four other people also will receive the New York State Unified Court System's Merit Performance Award tomorrow.

"I had an incredible need as chief clerk," said Seward, now retired. "We were never ahead of the paper chase. There were 100 cases a day in and out of Family Court. Judges didn't know how many cases were assigned to them, or which ones were coming up on the calendar."

Seward bought an Apple personal computer in 1979 and spent many 20-hour days designing a way to organize cases until the first computer was installed in Family Court in August 1982.

From there, Seward's system was adopted by courts in all eight counties in the 7th Judicial District, and in 1983, his system went state-wide.

"His initiative was the key to time-saving in the courts," said Ronald M. Stout Jr., director of research and special projects for the state Office of Court Administration in New York City.

"Our caseload has been going up substantially in the past 10 years, and there has not been the same increase in staff levels to go with the population flow," Stout said. "Ron found a way to make us more efficient."

New York state is now considered the leader in the nation in the use of microcomputers to manage the mass of information generated every day in the courts. Stout and Seward said they have each talked with officials from several states about their programs.

The computer system allows clerks to sort out cases according to judge, then list them by types of cases and by how long they've been in the court system. The computers also can generate background on cases, and list an inventory of law books and cases at the disposal of judges across the state, Seward said.

Before the system became computerized, judges were often bogged down.

"Now, we can deal with the substantive problems in the court rather than the other extrinsic things." Willis said.

(April 30, 1986, Democrat and Chronicle, Rochester, N.Y.)

Figure 1–7 One innovative and effective use of computers was brought about by the initiative of Ron Seward, who at the time was the chief clerk of Monroe County Family Court in Rochester, New York. The changes introduced were so valuable that they were eventually adopted throughout the state.

popular computer languages currently taught in the schools are Logo, Pascal, and BASIC.

On the college level, computers are used to augment instruction across a wide variety of fields ranging from English, where word processing is gaining wide popularity, to the sciences, where computers are often used to record and analyze data. The simulation of complex experiments is another use of computers in this area. The benefits of computer use in higher education have been recognized by some colleges to the extent that all entering freshmen are required to purchase a computer for use during their college career.

Administrators at all levels of education receive computerized reports for some of the functions they perform, such as enrollment analysis for trend forecasting and grade reports for analysis of grading patterns. Some adminis-

Figure 1–8 Computers can be used to generate a variety of products for the classroom including posters and banners for bulletin boards.

trators make use of personal computers in much the same way that managers in business do for tasks such as word processing, statistical analysis, and modeling possible solutions to problems.

The business world also uses computers for educational purposes. Trainers in business and industry readily use computer-based training (CBT) materials to instruct company employees. A secretary using a word processor for the first time, a salesperson training to sell a new product, or an employee taking advantage of instruction in basic skills such as reading or arithmetic may find all or part of the instruction computer-based.

Scientific uses for computers stem back to the original development of the computer. Today computers are widely used in research and practical applications of research. Computers allow researchers to manipulate data in ways that would be impossible without the available speed at which computers can perform; some computers can perform more than 200 million operations per second. This type of power enables researchers to design experiments and look at data in ways that would otherwise not be open to them. Without computers the exploration and eventual colonization of space would be impos-

Science

Reactions and Research

John Goodlad, in his important study of the state of the schools in America, A Place Called School, *offers some observations and predictions about computers in the schools.*

Microcomputers, of course, are a new phenomenon in an area which writers have long been relating to our educational future. For decades they have predicted sweeping changes in the conduct of schooling as a consequence of startling advances in technology and their infusion into schools. But we found little use of calculators, computers, or even the earlier forms of electronic aids such as films, filmstrips, and television. The technological revolution appears to be sweeping around schools, leaving them virtually untouched, even while purchasing microcomputers is becoming the "in" thing for school districts to do.

Now, however, some predictions of change can be made quite confidently, given present trends. Increasingly, school districts will maintain computer-based information systems to provide employees with detailed information to explain the difference between their gross and net wages, to compile information about administrators, teachers, and students, to store test information, and so on. Using desk consoles located in their offices, principals will be able to call up more information about the student body than they know how to use. At a slower rate of increase, two-way systems will provide face-to-face communication between district superintendents and the principals in the schools. And there will be more settings like Irvine, California, where teachers-to-be in the University of California employ two-way video to observe and raise questions about classroom practices in the nearby schools. For children and youths to become functionally literate in their understanding and use of computers will be recognized as a necessity, not a frill. The far-sighted philanthropy of the International Paper Company Foundation, for example, in funding the purchase of microcomputers for schools will be replaced by the purchase of computers as a normal part of expenditures for public schools. These and more uses of technological advances will occur until they become virtually standard practice. But the role to be played in the instructional process remains ill-defined. Technology increasingly will provide educational delivery systems, however, whether inside or outside of schools.

(Goodlad, 1984)

sible. Some have observed that the two most significant developments of this century have been the development of the computer and the development of space travel.

Computers are used as an aid in the search for valuable mineral deposits. Photographs taken by satellite are enhanced by computer technology so that scientists can more accurately pinpoint likely locations of valuable resources. Weather forecasters use computers to help predict weather patterns and the probable course of dangerous storms (see **Figure 1–9**).

Medicine

Pharmacists use computers to keep their drug inventory up to date. Physicians sometimes use computers to aid in the diagnosis of disease. The computer can keep track of and cross-reference a wide range of symptoms and possible causes. Many physicians have automated their offices to help handle the large amount of paperwork they must generate for insurance companies. Hospitals use computers for a variety of business and medical purposes, including maintenance of patient records, billing, scheduling of tests, and coordination of the use of facilities such as operating rooms.

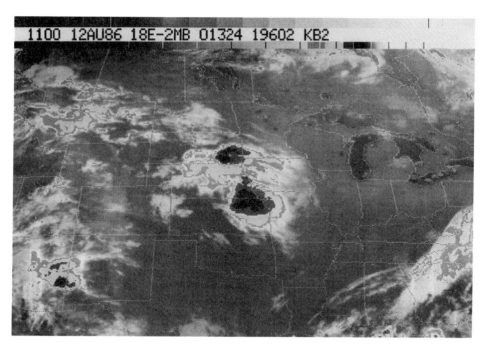

Figure 1–9 Weather forecasters use computers to track weather patterns and predict the course of dangerous storms. Computer-enhanced satellite photographs are used in this process.

Entertainment

As mentioned earlier, many families use computer games at home for entertainment. The design of the games and the colorful graphics that go with many arcade-type games are becoming art forms. Computers also play a large role in the production of some motion pictures. Special effects such as those in many science fiction movies can be generated by computer. Some of the effects seen in television commercials are generated through the use of computer graphics.

In the music world, computers have come to play a large part in both recording and performing. Music synthesizers making use of computer technology are capable of accurately reproducing the sound of almost any instrument and of creating original sounds. The incorporation of a musical instrument digital interface capability allows performers to connect various electronic instruments and recording devices to achieve a wide range of effects. With a good synthesizer, a digital drum machine, and the appropriate recording equipment, one talented individual can perform and record an entire musical composition with as many parts as desired.

Office Automation

The face of the workplace is changing. This includes the office environment, whether it is an office in a bank, a manufacturing firm, or a university. Computers, used as word processors, are taking the place of typewriters. The same computers are being used to transmit electronic mail, the function of sending messages from one computer to another across distances varying from a few hundred feet to thousands of miles. Reports and memos that otherwise would be put down on paper are being stored in and transmitted to computers. Pictures may also be transmitted in a similar manner. The office of yesterday is giving way to the "paperless" office of tomorrow.

These examples of computer use are by no means comprehensive. They do serve to illustrate the extensive and growing use of computers in our culture. This revolution of computer use is something with which we are all in contact. It offers us opportunities, as educators, to apply this new technology to our profession by teaching with computers. It also offers the challenge of preparing our students to interact with this technology as citizens in a participatory democracy and as job-seekers in the technologically rich employment climate of tomorrow.

Computer-Related Jobs

A wide variety of jobs associated with computers has developed over the past few decades. To gain an orientation to the types of possibilities available, the following descriptions are presented.

Programmers

Programmers write the instructions that tell the computer what to do. In professional programming, programs are written in the computer language best suited for the task to be accomplished on the computer. Examples of such languages are Pascal, COBOL, FORTRAN, BASIC, and C. **Figure 1–10** is an example of a portion of a COBOL program. Programmers take specifications that detail exactly what task or tasks the computer is to perform and code the program that will cause the computer to perform as desired. Once the program is written, the programmer must debug the program. Debugging is the removal of all the errors that might be in the program. After the program is debugged, it must be tested under conditions that approximate the way it will be regularly used by the company. Testing involves using the program to process test data similar to the real data it will eventually process. An example is a program written to produce payroll checks. Test data would consist of input data for fictitious employees. Such data might include hours worked, pay rate, and deductions. Testing is complete when the programmer is satisfied that the output produced by the program is correct.

Programmers need to be detail-oriented and have a highly developed capacity for working with logic. Business programmers, people who write computer programs to implement applications related to business problems such as the example cited earlier, need training in programming languages, program design, and business concepts. Good arithmetic skills are necessary, as well as an understanding of algebra, although a great deal of preparation in mathematics is generally not essential. A business degree with a specialization in this area, or an appropriate degree in computer and information systems is an asset in attaining employment. Although some entry-level jobs are still available to people with two-year degrees and those with no degrees, this is less and less the case.

Scientific programmers work on problems related to scientific applications of computer technology, such as writing a program to statistically analyze

```
PROCEDURE DIVISION.
P10-MAINLINE.
    PERFORM P20-INITIALIZATION.
    PERFORM P30-GENERATE-REPORT
            UNTIL END-OF-FILE.
    PERFORM P90-TERMINATION.
    STOP RUN.

P20-INITIALIZATION.
    OPEN INPUT INPUT-FILE
        OUTPUT REPORT-FILE.
    ACCEPT RPT-DATE FROM DATE.
    PERFORM P70-PRINT-HEADINGS.
    PERFORM P60-READ-DATA.

P30-GENERATE-REPORT.
    IF IN-DATE-EMPLOYED LESS THAN TEST-DATE
        IF IN-SALARY LESS THAN TEST-SALARY
            COMPUTE TOTAL-RAISES = TOTAL-RAISES + 1
            MOVE "UNKNOWN" TO SAVE-BRANCH-NAME
            PERFORM P40-SEARCH-TABLE
                    VARYING BRANCH-INDEX FROM 1 BY 1
                    UNTIL BRANCH-INDEX GREATER THAN MAX-TABLE-SIZE
            PERFORM P65-WRITE-DETAIL
        ELSE
            NEXT SENTENCE
    ELSE
        NEXT SENTENCE.
    PERFORM P60-READ-DATA.

P40-SEARCH-TABLE.
    IF TBL-BRANCH-NMBR (BRANCH-INDEX) = IN-BRANCH-NMBR
        MOVE TBL-BRANCH-NAME (BRANCH-INDEX) TO SAVE-BRANCH-NAME
    ELSE
        NEXT SENTENCE.
```

Figure 1–10 A portion of a computer program written in the COBOL programming language.

demographic data, or writing a computer program to control some aspect of the machinery on a space shuttle flight. Scientific programmers need a solid background in computer science as well as strong preparation in mathematics. A four-year degree in computer science is advisable for those seeking employment as scientific programmers.

There is a shortage of programmers that is expected to continue well into the future. Entry-level positions are the hardest to find but are available. Opportunities for people with a few years' experience are plentiful.

Systems Analysts

Specifications are written by systems analysts. After a user requests the computerization of some task currently performed manually or an upgrade of the way a job is presently done by computer, the systems analyst begins work.

Perhaps a manager of an accounting department wants a better way to accomplish weekly processing of accounts receivable in order to better track cash flow. The computerized solution to the problem may involve one program or a series of programs called a system. First the analyst studies the manual or computerized system that currently performs the task under consideration. Then the new system is designed. This would all be done in close consultation between the analyst and the user. It is the systems analyst's job to determine and deliver exactly what the user needs. After the system is designed and the specifications written, the analyst may work with the programmer, who uses the specifications to write the programs for the system. **Figure 1–11** is an excerpt from a systems analyst's specifications.

Systems analysts usually have several years of programming experience. The job requires highly developed communication skills and a good ability to work with a wide variety of people. Anyone subscribing to the stereotype that people who work with computers are incapable of working with people should watch a skilled systems analyst at work. Strong technical and business expertise is required as well as skill in working with people.

Management Positions

As in any work environment, management people who oversee the activities of others are needed at various levels. Managers usually have at least several years' experience in the computer field as well as good communication skills. Training and ability in management skills such as planning and organization are needed as well.

Computer Operations

The people who handle the machine we think of as the computer work in computer operations. This type of job includes responsibilities such as making sure particular programs are ready to run at the right time, mounting tape reels on the computer, and helping to assure maximum use of the computer equipment a company owns. Preparation for a job in computer operations can often be accomplished at a two-year college or technical school. Computer operators are in demand. Often a job in operations means working rotating shifts, some of which are at night.

```
Compute student average.
Print student name and student average.
If student average < 70
Then
    Print "STUDENT NOT PASSING"
Else
    Print "STUDENT PASSING".
Perform Get-Next-Student-Record.
```

Figure 1–11 A systems analyst's specifications often take the form of pseudocode—Englishlike statements that describe the instructions the programmer must write as a computer program. Above is an example of pseudocode. Specifications for a computer program can be quite lengthy—sometimes thirty or more pages long, depending on the complexity of the program to be written.

Data entry personnel are responsible for entering data into the computer. They work at a keyboard with a set of source documents, such as a stack of a few hundred time cards. Their job is to accurately and quickly transfer the information on the source documents into the computer. The main skill required is the ability to touch type. Data entry people are often evaluated on the amount of work they accomplish in a given time.

Data Entry

Business, industry, and the academic world are suffering a shortage of qualified people to teach about computers and computer applications. Because of this shortage many college-level teaching jobs that would normally require a Ph.D. in computer science are available to people with a master's degree in computer science. High schools need qualified people to teach courses about computer applications and computer programming, and many districts are interested in having a computer coordinator to oversee equipment acquisition and curriculum development.

Training and Education

Training related to computers is a lively field in business and industry. Many companies with medium- and large-scale computer centers have a department dedicated to providing training for their computer personnel. The computer field is fast-moving and almost constant updating of skills is the norm. Some companies exist solely to provide computer-training services on a consultant basis to clients.

A need also exists for training users on applications such as word processing and other functions available in the automated office mentioned previously. The need is so great that one community college obtained a grant to outfit a van with IBM personal computers and conduct training programs on site at the clients' location. The project was such a success that the college couldn't keep up with the demand for the program.

Preparation for working in this area usually requires a four-year degree in computer science or a degree in business with an appropriate concentration in computers. Experience in the computer field is desirable and sometimes required before teaching. Some positions may require a master's degree in computer science.

Opportunities are available in computer sales ranging from sales of services related to computer use (such as training) to sales of the actual machines. Retail outlets specializing in computer sales exist throughout the country. A career in sales requires a good background in business and marketing as well as some training related to computers. Often a successful background in selling is more important than a great deal of computer experience or training.

Sales and Service

Technicians trained to service computers are increasingly in demand as more and more people begin to buy and use computers. Many computer retail stores have service departments. Large computer companies hire service personnel with varying levels of expertise. Two-year colleges and technical schools can provide entry-level training for this field.

Computers in the Classroom

Early experiences with computers and computer education can often be presented concretely in a number of ways. Many people either work directly with computers (programmers, analysts, and so on) or use computer applications in their job (managers, travel agents, secretaries, etc.). It may be easy to locate a parent who is willing to come to class and talk about her job and how computers play a role in it. This can lead to a discussion of how the job was done before computers were used and how it may change as computers change. Such presentations can be used to generate new vocabulary and spelling words related to the computer curriculum. Students can be encouraged to write about the computer person they meet and the job the person does.

Artifacts of a computer society can be gathered and discussed. Computer printouts, punched cards, disks, printer ribbons, computer magazines, and so on can be located and brought to class. (A variety of computer devices are presented in chapter 2, Understanding Hardware.) A display or bulletin board can be set up by students, showing the objects gathered and explaining their use. Students might undertake such a project in conjunction with a social studies unit. Teams of students could be given the task of gathering as many computer-related artifacts as possible from the school building or the community. Using the objects gathered, the team generates a report containing their conclusions about the society that uses such devices.

Computer use in the school can be documented by arranging for students to take slides of computers being used in the school. Both instructional and administrative uses can be included. A slide show can be presented to another class as a way to share the students' findings.

Computer-related objects can be used to stimulate creative writing while teaching about the function of a computer artifact. Each student can choose an object and personify it, give it a name and have it explain its job. What does it do? What does it like and dislike about its job? What are its goals? Students might be asked to write first a serious response and then a funny response.

Activities that give students the opportunity to work with the concrete results of the computer revolution can help to impress on them the importance of computers in society.

Computer Science/ Engineering	Computers are designed by people who are trained in computer science or electrical engineering. A four-year degree is required in one of the two fields. A high level of mathematical training and logical ability is necessary.
Entrepreneurs	Many enterprising individuals have formed companies that provide computer goods and services. One of the all-time success stories in the business world has been the development of Apple Computer, Inc., from an enterprise started by two young inventors in a garage into a multimillion-dollar corporation. Possibilities still abound for people who see a need in the marketplace and have the energy, drive, and creativity to attempt to fill it.
Computer Use Tomorrow	The amount of growth and activity that has taken place concerning computers and the uses to which they may be put can correctly be called revolutionary. What is important to note is that we are just at the beginning of the computer revolution. We can expect, over the next few decades, to see equally revolutionary changes take place in this field; changes that will have a direct effect on the quality of our lives.

Two major developments should occur during this time. Both stem from an area of computer science called artificial intelligence. This term refers to a computer's ability to simulate what we commonly recognize as intelligence in humans. One promising area of artificial intelligence research has to do with the way human beings interact with computers. Currently, the common mode of interaction is through typing on a keyboard and receiving a typed response on a video display screen. Devices to allow spoken communication with computers exist but in a rudimentary form. It is predicted that the technology to speak and receive spoken responses from computers in a natural, unrestricted way will be developed over the next few decades. The possibilities that this will allow are intriguing. Imagine being able to dictate correspondence directly to the computer and then verbally correct errors.

Another promising area in this field is knowledge engineering. When programmed in a certain way, computers can become expert in a well-defined area of knowledge. These systems are called expert systems and they exist today. An expert system can be made to perform as good as or better than the humans whose expertise is tapped to provide the knowledge contained in the computer-based system. Such systems currently exist in such areas as medicine, finance, and geology. As further advances take place we can hope to see more powerful expert systems.

Conclusion

The use of machines to extend our physical and mental capabilities is a reality that is here to stay. The computer is the machine that can enhance both capabilities. It extends our physical ability when used to improve the functioning of other machines, such as automobiles. It extends our mental ability when used as a machine to think with. The effect of the computer revolution on our lives is real and growing. This offers educators the opportunity to provide tomorrow's citizens with the skills to survive in a computer-rich world and the background to form attitudes and make judgments about the use of such tools. This text offers information, skills, and concepts aimed at preparing you to take advantage of that opportunity.

Key Terms

BASIC
C
COBOL
computer
computer-assisted design (CAD)
computer-assisted manufacturing
  (CAM)
computer-based training (CBT)
computer program

computer revolution
data
debit cards
debug
electronic funds transfer (EFT)
electronic mail
FORTRAN
information
Information Age

input
keyboard
Knowledge Explosion
Logo
office automation
output
Pascal
point-of-sale terminal (POS terminal)
processing

program
programmer
programming
programming language
test
universal product code (UPC) symbol
video display screen
voice synthesizer

Questions

1. Explain the concept of the Knowledge Explosion and the Information Age.

2. Cite three arguments against the use of computers in the schools. Respond to these arguments as a proponent of computer use in the schools. What is your position on this issue?

3. Briefly explain what a computer does. Include an example in your explanation.

4. What is meant by the statement that computers may be used for control purposes? Give an example.

5. Choose any three of the following categories:

   - Business and industry
   - Government
   - Education
   - Science
   - Medicine
   - Entertainment
   - Office automation

   In each of the categories you have chosen, find one example of computer use not mentioned in the text.

6. Which computer-related job mentioned in the text appeals to you the most? Why? Which appeals to you least? Why?

7. Cite five ways you come into contact with computers in your own life.

8. What is an expert system? How do you feel about the idea that a computer may perform as well as or better than a human being who is an expert in a particular field?

9. Should teachers be concerned about providing opportunities for students to explore their attitudes about technology? Why or why not?

10. Name five ways in which computers may be used in education.

Bitter, Gary G. *Computers in Today's World*. New York, John Wiley & Sons, 1984.

Fincher, Jean. "Jousting with Jargon." *The Computing Teacher* 12, no. 3 (1984):18–21.

Goodlad, John I. *A Place Called School*. New York: McGraw-Hill Book Co., 1984, pp. 340–341.

Graham, Neill. *The Mind Tool*. St. Paul, Minn.: West Publishing Co., 1983.

Hopper, Grace. and Steven L. Mandell. *Understanding Computers*. St. Paul, Minn.: West Publishing Co., 1984.

Spencer, Donald D. *An Introduction to Computers: Developing Computer Literacy*. Columbus, Ohio: Charles E. Merrill Publishing Co., 1983.

Stern, Robert A., and Nancy Stern. *Computers in Society*. Englewood Cliffs, N.J.: Prentice-Hall, 1983.

References/Further Reading

2

Understanding Hardware

TOPICS ADDRESSED

What relevant early inventions and inventors preceded the development of computers?

What were early computers like? Who developed them, and for what were they used?

What are the characteristics of first-, second-, third-, and fourth-generation computers?

What is a computer system? How does the CPU play a role in a computer system? What are peripheral devices and what functions do they perform?

What differentiates the three categories of computers—mainframes, minis, and micros?

What are high-level and low-level programming languages?

How do computers store data? What are bits, bytes, and encoding systems?

OUTLINE

Introduction
Computers: A Short History
  Early Developments
  First Generation: 1951–1958
  Second Generation: 1959–1964
  Third Generation: 1965–1971
  Fourth Generation: 1972 to Present
Computer Systems
  The CPU
  Peripherals
    Auxiliary Storage
    Input Devices

    Output Devices
    Other Hardware
Categories of Computers
  Mainframe Computers
  Minicomputers
  Microcomputers
Communicating with the Hardware
Bits and Bytes
Conclusion
Key Terms
Questions
References/Further Reading

Introduction

This chapter presents a brief history of the development of computers, an introduction to the different components of a computer system, and an explanation of how computers operate. Familiarity with this material will help to put the computer revolution in perspective. It will also provide a good background for developing computer skills and working with students and computers.

Computers: A Short History

Early Developments

Although computers as we know them are relatively new, the story of their development starts with the need and desire of people to count and calculate. In fact, people have been computing and calculating for thousands of years. One of the earliest instruments to aid in calculation was the abacus, a device consisting of a rectangular box open on one side that contains strings of beads (**Figure 2–1**). The development of the abacus is thought to have taken place more than 4,000 years ago. The abacus is used to perform the arithmetic operations of addition, subtraction, multiplication, and division. It is still in use today.

Blaise Pascal, the famous French mathematician and philosopher for whom a modern computer language is named, built the first mechanical calculator in 1642 (**Figure 2–2**). Although it could only add and subtract, the principle of performing operations through the use of gear-driven wheels was used in calculators for more than 300 years.

The next occurrence related to the development of mechanical calculating machines took place in the late seventeenth century, when Gottfried Wilhelm von Leibniz developed a machine that could multiply, divide, and derive square roots as well as add and subtract.

Figure 2–1 The abacus has been used as an aid in calculation for centuries.

Figure 2–2 Blaise Pascal is credited with building the first mechanical calculator. The Pascaline, pictured above, could perform addition and subtraction.

The man often referred to as the father of the computer is Charles Babbage, who was an English mathematician during the nineteenth century. Babbage designed and built a model of a machine, called the Difference Engine, to be used in calculating mathematical tables (**Figure 2–3**). A second machine, the Analytical Engine, was also designed by Babbage. The Analytical Engine incorporated many of the ideas realized in the computers of today. It was to be programmed by the use of punched cards and was to have a memory area. Punched cards had originally been used by Joseph Marie Jacquard in 1801 in his invention of the automatic textile loom. Babbage died before the Analytical Engine could be built.

By 1880 the U.S. Census Bureau found that the manual tabulation of the data gathered during the census was taking too long. It took seven and one half

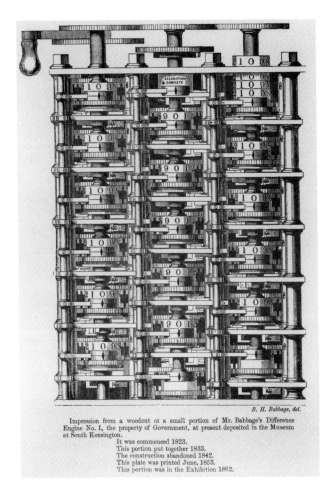

B. H. Babbage, del.

Impression from a woodcut of a small portion of Mr. Babbage's Difference
Engine No. 1, the property of Government, at present deposited in the Museum
at South Kensington.

It was commenced 1823.
This portion put together 1833.
The construction abandoned 1842.
This plate was printed June, 1853.
This portion was in the Exhibition 1862.

Figure 2–3 The Difference Engine, a drawing of which is shown here, was designed to be used in calculating mathematical tables. Charles Babbage, a nineteenth century English mathematician, was responsible for designing both the Difference Engine and the Analytical Engine.

years to manually complete the processing of the 1880 census. Herman Hollerith, working for the Census Bureau, developed a punched card on which data could be recorded and a tabulating machine to process the punched cards (**Figure 2–4**). Hollerith's version of the punched card was the forerunner of the punched cards used in twentieth-century computers. The success of his efforts were obvious when it took only two and a half years to complete the 1890 census. Hollerith eventually founded the Tabulating Machine Company, which, after merging with other firms, became International Business Machines (IBM).

The machines that followed Hollerith's were, for some time, mechanical. However, between 1937 and 1944, Howard Aiken of Harvard University, with financial assistance from IBM, devised and developed the Mark I (**Figure 2–5**). Also known as the IBM Automatic Sequence-Controlled Calculator, the Mark I was an electromechanical machine that made use of mechanical counters and electromechanical relays. The introduction of electricity into the computing process was important because electronic processes operate much faster than

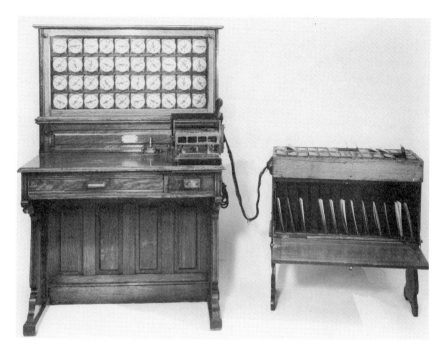

Figure 2–4 The Tabulating Machine, designed by Herman Hollerith, processed data stored on punched cards.

Figure 2–5 The Mark I computer was also known as the IBM Automatic Sequence-Controlled Calculator. It made use of mechanical counters and electromechanical relays.

mechanical processes. The Mark I was fifty feet long, eight feet high, and weighed five tons. It was capable of multiplying two twenty-three-digit numbers in about five seconds.

The early uses of computers were scientific and mathematical. By today's standards the ability of a machine to multiply two twenty-three-digit numbers

Figure 2–6 The ENIAC (Electronic Numerical Integrator and Calculator) was the first large-scale, general purpose electronic digital computer.

in five seconds is slow. Compared with the performance of a human being though it was (and is) fast. Early users of computers often were able to have a machine work out a complex set of calculations in a matter of hours that would have taken a person dozens of years to complete. This ability was an important aid to scientific inquiry.

John Atanasoff, a professor of physics at Iowa State College, now the University of Iowa, and Clifford Berry, a graduate student, were responsible for the first fully electronic digital computer in 1939. The Atanasoff-Berry Computer (ABC) made use of vacuum tubes instead of mechanical counters and electromechanical relays. A limitation of the ABC computer was that it was not general purpose, since it was designed to perform only a single function.

John W. Mauchly and John Presper Eckert, working at the University of Pennsylvania in 1946, developed the first large-scale, general purpose electronic digital computer. This machine was called the ENIAC, which stands for Electronic Numerical Integrator and Calculator (**Figure 2–6**). The computer was developed to help the U.S. Army to calculate trajectory tables for artillery. The computer weighed thirty tons and took up 1,500 square feet of floor space. It was capable of performing 300 multiplications per second. The programs, or instructions, for the computer had to be wired on boards. The increased speed of processing was due to the fact that the machine was electronic and not electromechanical.

The mathematician John von Neumann was responsible for introducing a concept important in the development of computers from the late 1940s to the present. Up until this point the computer did not store its instructions. Von Neumann introduced the stored program concept that, in future machines, allowed the computer to store, electronically, the programs that caused it to

Figure 2–7 The design of the EDVAC (Electronic Discrete Variable Automatic Computer) incorporated John von Neumann's stored program concept.

perform various functions. This helped to increase the speed at which a computer could perform. Instructions and data were stored using binary notation (1s and 0s).

The Electronic Discrete Variable Automatic Computer, or EDVAC, was created by Mauchly and Eckert in 1949 (**Figure 2–7**). It was important because it incorporated von Neumann's stored program concept.

The period of computer development from the early 1950s on is often divided into generations of computer equipment. The demarcation between one generation and the next is usually a significant invention in electronics that allowed revolutionary changes in the computers produced. In general, as computers developed, their components became smaller, and therefore the physical size of the computers became smaller. Along with this the speed at which computers process data became faster and their cost decreased significantly.

First Generation: 1951–1958

The UNIVAC I, again developed by Mauchly and Eckert, was the first commercially available computer (**Figure 2–8**). It was delivered to the U.S. Census Bureau in 1951 and is an example of a first-generation computer. It made use of vacuum tubes, which had certain problems associated with them. Vacuum tubes gave off a good deal of heat and were not reliable. Because of the heat generated by first-generation computers, they were kept in air-conditioned environments. The UNIVAC I could perform business functions. Businesses generally need to process large files and perform relatively simple calculations, whereas scientific users of computers require sophisticated calculating ability accomplished with great precision.

Figure 2–8 The UNIVAC I, an example of a first generation computer, was the first commercially available computer. Programs for the UNIVAC I could be written in a symbolic language, rather than as a series of 1s and 0s.

The ability to be programmed using a symbolic language was an important step in first-generation computers. Rather than writing the instructions for the computer in binary notation (machine language) as a series of 1s and 0s, the instructions could be represented by symbols that would be more readily comprehensible to the person doing the programming. The symbols were translated into machine language by the machine.

Second Generation: 1959–1964

The development of the transistor and its later application to computer technology was a major factor giving rise to second-generation computers (**Figure 2–9**). The transistor was much smaller and more reliable than the vacuum tube. It also gave off less heat. Magnetic core memory was used to store data and instructions during this period. A magnetic core is a tiny piece of metal that can be magnetized to denote an on or off (1 or 0) memory location in the computer. Other developments included the use of magnetic tape and magnetic disk for auxiliary storage (sometimes called secondary storage), which allows the computer additional storage space for data and instructions. During this period the development of high-level programming languages took place. These languages are more easily understandable by humans than the symbolic and machine languages that preceded them.

Third Generation: 1965–1971

The development of the integrated circuit was important to the production of the third generation of computers (**Figure 2–10**). Integrated circuits allow many circuitry components to be etched on layers of silicon. This further miniaturization of the electronics of the computer caused a reduction in the size of the

Figure 2–9 The Honeywell 200 is an example of a second generation computer. Transistors played a major role in the development of second generation machines.

Figure 2–10 The development of the integrated circuit was important in the creation of third generation machines. The IBM System/360, a third generation machine, was a very successful product for IBM.

Figure 2–11 Fourth generation machines, such as the Burroughs B7700, make use of large-scale integrated (LSI) circuits and very large-scale integrated (VLSI) circuits. VLSI circuits can contain up to the equivalent of 500,000 transistors on a tiny chip.

machines as well as an increase in the speed at which they could function. Operations performed by third-generation computers were measured in billionths of a second (referred to as nanoseconds).

Fourth Generation: 1972 to Present

There is some debate over whether or not a fourth generation of computers exists. Some hold the view that no truly revolutionary step has been taken beyond the third generation; that new computers are merely enhancements of third-generation technology. Others maintain that the development of large-scale integrated (LSI) circuitry technology and very large-scale integrated (VLSI) circuitry technology and its incorporation into the computer field is the point that marks the emergence of fourth-generation machines. Both technologies allow further miniaturization and increased speed. VLSI allows the equivalent of up to 500,000 transistors to be placed on a tiny chip (**Figure 2–11**).

The development of the microprocessor, the miniaturization of all the component circuitry needed for a computer onto a small chip, is also pointed to as denoting fourth-generation machines. This development allowed the introduction of the inexpensive microcomputers we see today.

Today, for a few thousand dollars, it is possible to buy a computer that will sit on a desktop and essentially perform the functions of a machine that would have cost several million dollars just fifteen to twenty years ago. The history of computers is such that more computer power in a smaller space has consistently become available for less money. The importance of the availability of more

Input/Output

Do students need computer knowledge as preparation for the job market? This question often arises when considering the place of computer education in the schools. Three educators addressed this issue as part of an article that appeared in the October 1984 issue of Instructor *magazine. The article is entitled "Questions Teachers Still Ask About Kids and Computers." The three experts are David Moursund, president of the International Council for Computers in Education; Dan Watt, a teacher and writer, author of several popular books on the Logo programming language; and Bonnie Brownstein, president of the Institute for Schools of the Future, in New York City.*

Will lack of computer knowledge hurt kids in the job market?

David Moursund: I guess I could imagine a situation where a high school has no computers and a kid who attends that school and who has a computer at home gets the edge on some of his classmates.

You know, the push to get parents to buy their kids a computer reminds me of the hype about having a set of encyclopedias in the house—except that parents don't just sit the kids down in front of the *World Book* before they can read and hope that the kids somehow figure out what to do with the books. Which is exactly what does happen when most parents bring a computer home. If there isn't any plan for helping the kid learn to use the computer—if you can't tie it in with the computer curriculum at school—then it won't do much good. However, if the child is getting good computer instruction at school—say he's learned to use it for word processing and he has access to the same programs at home—then he may have an advantage.

Dan Watt: I think there is truth in the idea that computers are going to be a part of most people's lives, and that people who have access to computers are going to have a better chance for success in the future. But I don't think the advantages are going to be of the type promised in the ads. Children are not going to pass or fail, be accepted by or be able to cut the mustard in the college of their choice, just because they do or do not have a computer at home. I think that access to computers—both for children and adults—is an issue for our society and should be addressed as a social priority. We have to make certain that all people have access not just to computers but to all technology that's transforming the way we work and think. Which parents spend money to buy their children an inexpensive computer is not the issue.

Bonnie Brownstein: I worry about what those ads say to the kids who are watching them. What about the really poor child whose school doesn't have a computer and whose parents will never be able to buy him a computer for home? The computer ads on TV tell him he won't make it in this world without a computer—no computer, no chance. That can be devastating to the eager child without access to computers. Both teachers and parents should be sensitive to this reaction in children and help them see beyond it.

(Instructor, 1984)

computer power is that the more powerful the computer, the more sophisticated the task to which it can be applied. The importance of the dramatic decrease in cost is that computers, as prices become lower, are available to more and more people. This is especially significant for educators. The advent of inexpensive computers that could perform in a fairly sophisticated fashion has allowed schools to begin to use this new technology.

The term computer hardware refers to the machine that is the computer as well as to the other physical devices connected to it. As mentioned previously, a computer must be given instructions in order to perform various tasks. The instructions it needs are called programs, or software. Both computer hardware and software are necessary for the computer to function.

Computer Systems

There are a wide variety of jobs to which a computer can be applied. Each job may demand a different piece of software to instruct the computer as to what must be done to achieve the desired function. A variety of software may be run on the same computer hardware.

Any one of a number of components may be called computer hardware. However, the piece of hardware that we think of as the computer, the hardware that actually does the computing, is called the central processing unit (CPU).

The CPU

The CPU, or processor, is the heart of the computer. As diagrammed earlier, a computer accepts input, processes it in some way, and produces output. The CPU is where the input is processed. Although computers can perform complex tasks, the job performed by the CPU is, conceptually, a simple one. It is from the relatively simple functions accomplished by the CPU that the complex tasks a computer can perform are derived. This is true in other areas as well. Understanding the letters of the alphabet is fairly easy, yet the same alphabet is used to produce both children's stories and Pulitzer prize-winning novels. The numerals 0 through 9 are another example: the same numerals can be used to represent simple addition as well as complex functions in higher mathematics. In much the same way, the basic operations of the CPU are the building blocks used to structure all the complex tasks that a computer can be programmed to do.

The CPU is made up of three parts: the control unit, the arithmetic/logic unit (ALU), and primary storage (**Figure 2–12**). Each part has a specific job to perform in the operation of the computer.

The control unit directs the operation of the entire computer system, including the flow of data and instructions input to and output from the CPU. It moves data into and out of the ALU for processing. Instructions that the

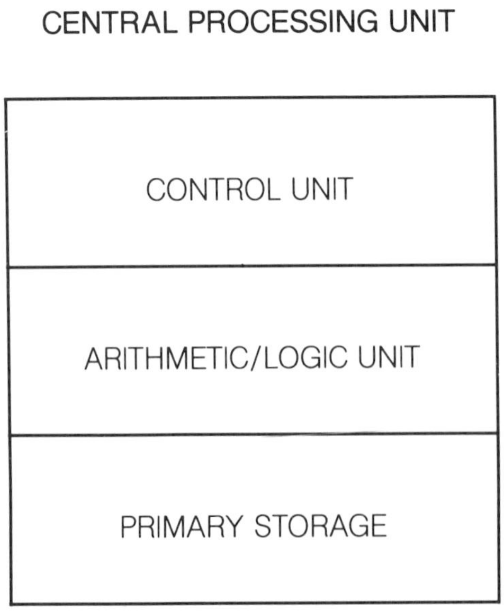

CENTRAL PROCESSING UNIT

CONTROL UNIT
ARITHMETIC/LOGIC UNIT
PRIMARY STORAGE

Figure 2–12 The central processing unit (CPU) is made up of the control unit, the arithmetic/logic unit and primary storage.

computer is to carry out must be brought from primary storage into the control unit before they can be executed. The main advantage computers offer human beings is that they can perform certain tasks very accurately and very quickly. The reason the CPU operates so quickly is that everything that happens within it takes place at the speed of electricity. The control unit's job is to manage this swift flow of data and instructions for the CPU.

The ALU is where arithmetic and logic operations are performed on the data managed by the control unit. The computer can only perform two types of manipulations on the data within it. It can perform arithmetic functions, such as addition, subtraction, multiplication, or division (hence the arithmetic portion of the name arithmetic/logic unit). It may also perform logical operations, such as comparing two numbers to see if one is greater than the other (therefore the logic portion of the name arithmetic/logic unit).

Arithmetic operations of the ALU are easy to understand and their utility is fairly obvious. If a teacher had a program in the computer to calculate her students' grades for a semester, it is apparent that some arithmetic operations would need to be performed by the ALU. The capability to perform logical comparisons is equally as important. Because the ALU can compare numbers, the teacher could use the computer to have the grades printed out from highest to lowest (or from lowest to highest). The ability to logically compare numerical data allows the sorting and classifying of such data to take place in a variety of ways (see **Figure 2–13**). Knowing the computer's ability to do this, a programmer could write a program that, in this case, would cause the grades to be sorted into the desired sequence.

The ability of a computer to perform logical comparisons goes beyond that of just comparing numbers. The ALU may also compare letters. A comparison

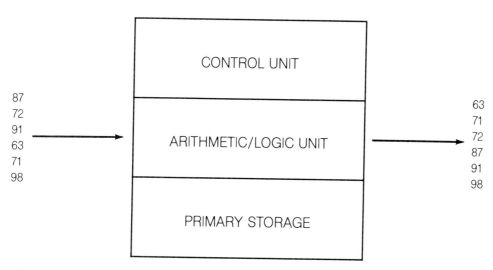

CENTRAL PROCESSING UNIT

Figure 2–13 The arithmetic/logic unit of the CPU performs arithmetic and logic operations on data. Here grades are sorted into ascending sequence.

CENTRAL PROCESSING UNIT

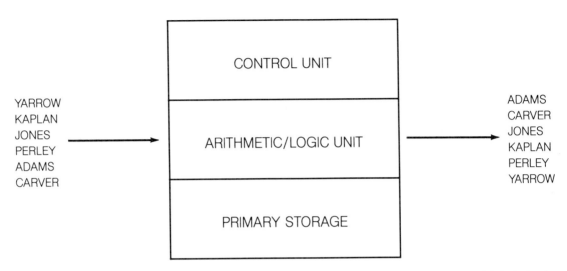

Figure 2–14 Alphabetic data can also be processed. Here a list of names is sorted into alphabetical order.

may be made such as "Is A less than B?" When the computer is initially designed, a decision is made to always treat letters as occurring in a particular order, such as the order of the alphabet. In this way A is treated as less than B and B is treated as less than C and so on throughout the rest of the alphabet. This allows the computer to do such things as alphabetize data (**Figure 2–14**). It also allows the computer to match data. If the computer needed to find information about a student named Jones, it could look through all of the data it had available about students until it found the data that had a name equal to the name it was searching for (Jones = Jones).

The primary storage of the CPU is where data and instructions being acted on by the computer are stored. Whenever the computer is processing some data within the CPU, it is necessary that it keep track of the data and instructions associated with the particular task, or job, on which it is working. It must also have available a place to store the intermediate steps involved in completing the job, as well as a place to store the result of any operations performed (until the result is output). Primary storage is the area where this is done. Because the computer can process a great amount of data quickly, and because the amount of primary storage is limited, once a particular task is completed and the results output, the same area of primary storage is used again. Primary storage is used over and over again for different tasks as the computer is processing data.

Peripherals

The CPU must have attached to it devices called peripheral devices, or peripherals, which enable it to accept input and produce output. A CPU plus all

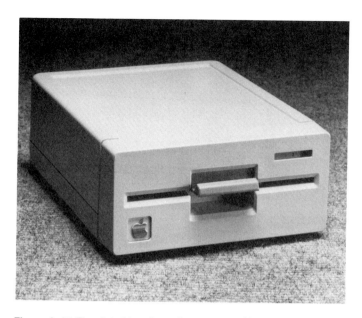 

Figure 2–15 The disk drive shown here uses a 5¼ inch floppy disk for a storage medium. This size disk is commonly used with the type of computers generally available in schools.

the peripheral devices attached to it is called a computer system. Most peripheral devices fall naturally into one of three categories: auxiliary storage, input, and output. The following is a sampling of various types of peripherals.

AUXILIARY STORAGE

The primary storage within the CPU is limited. Often more memory is required than the computer can supply in primary storage. In addition, this storage is usually volatile, which means that when the computer is turned off or the power is inadvertently interrupted for any reason, what is currently stored in primary storage is lost. For these two reasons auxiliary storage is necessary. Two types of auxiliary storage are common: magnetic tape and magnetic disk.

Auxiliary storage consists of a storage medium and a storage device. Magnetic tape is a storage medium and is similar to the magnetic tape used with a tape recorder. The magnetic tape, the storage medium, is mounted on a tape drive, the storage device. Magnetic tape usually comes on reels or, for small computers, in cassettes. Through the process of magnetizing small particles of metal on the tape, data may be stored, or recorded, on the tape. Another way to say this is to say that data is written to the tape. When needed, the data is retrieved, or read, from the tape.

Disk storage refers to the use of a magnetic disk as the medium for auxiliary storage. The disk has data read to and written from it by a mechanism called a disk drive (see **Figure 2–15**). Disk drives have certain advantages over magnetic tape; primarily, they are faster.

Auxiliary storage is used for both input and output purposes, since data may be read to or written from it.

Figure 2–16 A video display terminal (VDT) is connected to a CPU and is used to enter data into the computer through the keyboard.

INPUT DEVICES

The most common way to enter data into the computer is through a keyboard. What is typed is usually entered into the computer and displayed on a video display screen, sometimes called a cathode ray tube (CRT). The combination of the screen and the keyboard is usually referred to as a video display terminal (VDT), or terminal (**Figure 2–16**). The terminal is connected to a CPU.

Graphics tablets allow entry into the computer of such materials as charts or drawings (**Figure 2–17**). The user simply draws on the tablet surface and the image is input to the computer. Graphics tablets suitable for educational use, especially at the elementary school level, are available for under $100.

Devices called optical character readers (OCRs) are available that will read printed text and enter it into the computer (**Figure 2–18**). The text need only be typewritten or handwritten and does not have to be recorded with any special ink. Magnetic ink recognition devices (MICRs) are another type of input device used by banks to read data recorded on checks with a special magnetic ink. Bar code readers are familiar to shoppers in supermarkets and allow the information encoded on the universal product code (UPC) symbol to be entered directly into the computer.

Light pens enable a computer user to choose from a number of selections displayed on the CRT by touching the pen to one of the selections. The computer accepts the chosen selection as input.

Voice recognition systems are available. These allow the user to enter some commands to the computer verbally through a microphone. These types of systems, although available even for personal computers, are not yet sophisticated.

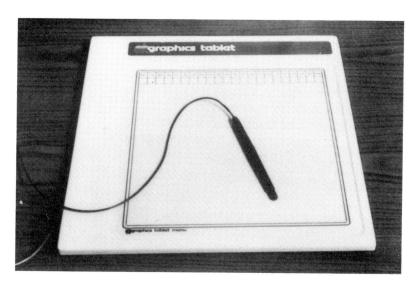

Figure 2–17 Graphics tablets come in a variety of sizes. They may cost under $100 or up to several thousands of dollars. Less expensive graphics tablets are sometimes used as input devices in elementary schools.

Figure 2–18 An optical character reader (OCR), left, can read typed or handwritten text directly into the computer. A light pen, right, allows a user to choose from a number of selections displayed on the CRT.

The punched cards mentioned earlier in the chapter are still around today, although their use is declining. When punched cards are used, they are run through a punched card reader to input the data stored on them into the computer.

Microfilm is a photographic storage medium that involves reducing printed material and transferring it onto film. The film may be stored on a roll or on a small rectangular piece of film called microfiche. Computer-input microfilm (CIM) allows the computer to input data from microfilm.

OUTPUT DEVICES

The CRT mentioned earlier as an input device is also an output device. The results of some process performed by the computer may be displayed on the CRT for the user. Depending on the CRT and the use to which the computer is applied, the display may be monochrome (black and white, green on black, or amber on black) or color. Many educational programs make use of the computer's color capability.

Printers are another widely used output device. It is often essential to have a paper copy of the information obtained from the computer. Paper copy is referred to as hardcopy, while the presentation of output on a CRT is called softcopy, owing to the transient nature of the display on the screen.

Printers come in various shapes, sizes, costs, and types. The individual letters, numerals, punctuation marks, etc. that printers produce are called characters. It is beyond the scope of this book to cover how various types of printers operate, but one distinction should be made. Dot matrix printers produce text by a series of tiny pins striking a ribbon that impacts a piece of paper. They produce output at a fairly fast rate. Daisy wheel printers produce output by having a fully formed character impact a ribbon and the paper. They are generally slower than dot matrix printers but produce a higher-quality formation of characters, called letter-quality print. Dot matrix printers have been undergoing improvements in technology that provide the option on some models of producing enhanced characters termed near-letter-quality. **Figure 2–19** shows examples of the different types of print.

EDUCATIONAL BACKGROUND

EDUCATIONAL BACKGROUND

EDUCATIONAL BACKGROUND

Figure 2–19 Above, from top to bottom, are examples of print from a daisy wheel printer, a standard dot-matrix printer, and a near-letter-quality dot-matrix printer.

Laser printers, which produce near-typeset-quality print, are available. They are more expensive than daisy wheel and dot matrix printers, although their price has been steadily dropping.

Plotters are special printers that are used to print charts, graphs, and other types of graphic materials.

Computer-output microfilm (COM) technology exists that enables computer output to be produced on microfilm and microfiche. Some businesses and organizations find this a desirable choice over storing bulky printed documents.

Reactions and Research

How computers are used in schools, and by whom, is an important issue in computer education. Computers are often a scarce resource in schools that serve minority students. In schools serving affluent students, computers may be in abundance. In the following article, Bruce Tuckman makes the point that a value judgment is made every time a computer is purchased and put to use in a school. Where the computer is placed and how it is used reflects the values and beliefs of those making the decisions.

A recent report issued by the Center for Social Organization of Schools at Johns Hopkins University provides some interesting insight into the use of microcomputers in the nation's elementary schools. Minority schools use their micros to provide drill and practice for *below-average* students, while predominately white schools, particularly those in low-income neighborhoods, concentrate their microcomputer use on teaching programming to *above-average* students.

Data were collected from over 1,000 elementary schools, and about half of the low-income primarily white schools reported an "intensive use" of microcomputers with above-average students compared to about one-quarter of minority schools providing such in-depth training for youngsters at the high end of the academic performance continuum. On the drill and practice use of microcomputers, clearly a remedial instruction service for poor performers, fewer than a tenth of the low-income white schools report an intensive involvement in comparison to a third of the minority schools reporting such involvement. Finally, instruction in computer programming occupied half of the white schools in contrast to a tenth of the minority schools.

We are dealing here with a difference that is significant in terms of both magnitude and import. Clearly, minority schools use their scarce and valuable computer resources to bring students at the low end of the academic performance continuum up toward the average, while schools teaching white youngsters of equally limited means focus on helping those at the *high end* move even further ahead,

particularly by providing them with potentially marketable skills.

MISSING THE POINT

Some months ago, I wrote a column suggesting that we be concerned about whether computers are made available to the few (to be read: "middle class") or the many (particularly meaning "the poor"). These new data tell me that I may have been missing the point on at least two counts. First, we cannot understand the process of technology in education by simply counting "how many computers" a school owns. We must look at how a school *uses* its computers (as was done in the Johns Hopkins study). Second, we are dealing with differences in values that seem to be based more on a cultural dimension than on an economic one. That is to say, black schools behave differently than white ones, even when the students in both are at a relatively similar economic level.

The first statement, about looking at the use rather than counting machines, is essentially a methodological caveat. Do not count computers, or any other instructional technology, for that matter. Look at the patterns of use, that is, who uses what and for what purpose? The second statement is the more difficult one to analyze or apply. What we need to know is (1) who makes the decision in a school or school district of how its computers are going to be used, and (2) whether the decision-maker (or makers) is (are) from the same culture as the students for whom the decision is made. Is the decision made by principals, superintendents, or boards, and are they, themselves, minority group members?

What I am asking is whether the decision to use computers to remediate the poorest students represents a value of the black culture and thereby reflects upon the conscious desire within that culture's value system to at least help more children get by, or does it represent a value of the white culture in dealing with black children, thereby reflecting a desire to minimize the possible "nuisance value'' of illiterate students? Of course, a third possibility exists, that being that minority schools have minority leadership in some but not all instances. In that case, it would be useful to compare the two subsets of minority schools to see whether computer use is similar in both, regardless of the culture of the decision-makers.

PREVENTING A TWO-TIERED STRUCTURE

I think that the study that I am proposing is important to do if we would like to keep this society from staying in (or, if you prefer, going back to) a two-tiered structure. It is important to know how and why computer-use decisions are made if we want to change the nature of those decisions.

In my judgment, the cause of minority students will be better served by using scarce computers more to teach programming to the better students than to remediate the poorer ones. And, if we want minority schools to change their strategy, we need to know on whose values it is currently based. Moreover, the current level of economic competitiveness both within and between countries means that upward mobility will require more and better technical skills, and that upward mobility is the route to weakening the caste or class system that minorities face.

MORE THAN JUST STATE OF THE ART

I think that this analysis points up another interesting aspect of the technological revolution and its impact on the schools. The use of technology is as much a matter of values and attitudes as it is of computer chips and programming languages; as much the business of philosophers and citizens as of hardware and software builders. The decisions that we make in this decade about how to use technology in the schools will have a profound effect on many generations of students to come. We had better realize now that every time we install a computer in a school and structure its use, we make a decision that reflects more than just the technological state of the art; *it reflects our deeply held beliefs*, in ways that we may not yet realize.

(Tuckman, 1984)

OTHER HARDWARE

Hardware other than that already mentioned exists that does not conveniently fit into the categories identified. A MODEM (which stands for modulator-demodulator) may be attached to a computer to allow it to pass information over a standard telephone line. This enables one computer to communicate with another computer at a different location. Surge protectors guard against transient surges in the electrical supply, which may cause the computer to malfunction or become damaged. Inexpensive surge protectors are available and are a valuable addition to any computer system, even a personal computer at home or in the school. A surge in the electrical supply can seriously damage computer hardware.

The point has been made that a computer system consists of the computer (CPU) plus any associated peripheral devices. **Figure 2–20** is a graphic representation of what might be the components of one computer system. As will be covered shortly, computer systems come in diverse shapes and sizes. The concept of what a computer system is (CPU plus peripherals), is true for any system of any size. The act of choosing the CPU and selecting other system components (of choosing what peripherals should be attached to the CPU) is called configuring the system. **Figure 2–21** is a photograph of a small computer system. This is one type of configuration you might see available for individual student use in a school.

Categories of Computers

Several factors may be used to denote different categories of computers; amount of primary storage, speed of processing, and number of peripherals that may be connected to the computer. The three categories traditionally used to define different groups of computers are mainframe computers, minicomputers, and microcomputers.

The amount of primary storage, or memory, a computer has is expressed in terms of bytes. A byte is roughly equivalent to a character. For our purposes

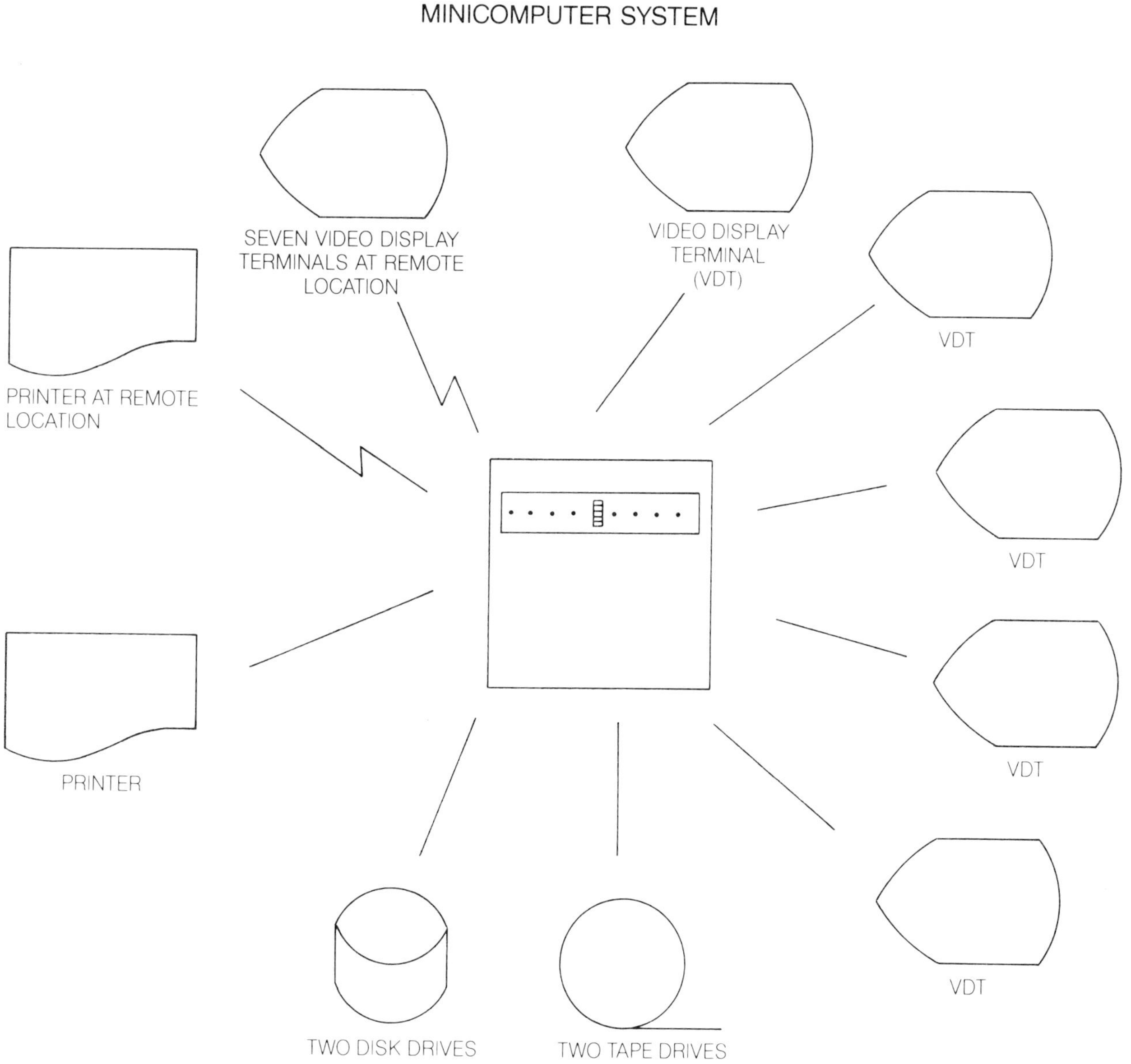

Mainframe Computers

MINICOMPUTER SYSTEM

SEVEN VIDEO DISPLAY TERMINALS AT REMOTE LOCATION

VIDEO DISPLAY TERMINAL (VDT)

VDT

PRINTER AT REMOTE LOCATION

VDT

PRINTER

VDT

VDT

VDT

TWO DISK DRIVES

TWO TAPE DRIVES

Figure 2–20 This example of a minicomputer system has a printer and seven terminals at a remote location that are connected to the CPU. Five more terminals, another printer, two tape drives, and two disk drives are locally connected to the CPU.

Figure 2–21 A typical configuration in a school setting might consist of the computer, a keyboard, one or two disk drives, and a CRT. The CRT is often called a monitor.

we can assume that one byte of storage will store one character of information, such as the letter A or the numeral 1. Primary storage in a computer may be measured in terms of kilobytes. A kilobyte is equal to 1024 bytes, or characters, of memory and is usually expressed as the letter K. Thus the notation 256K denotes a computer with 256 kilobytes of memory. Megabyte, which refers to 1 million bytes and is abbreviated MB, may also be used to describe the amount of primary storage available. A computer with 5 million bytes of storage could be said to have 5MB of storage (sometimes said to be 5 Meg of storage).

Mainframe computers are used by people who require sophisticated computer power with a large amount of primary storage ranging in some cases into forty or fifty megabytes. These computers are also among the fastest available and have the ability to support the connection of a great many peripherals. The only computers more powerful than the most powerful mainframe computers are those called supercomputers (**Figure 2–22**). These machines are usually used for scientific purposes and may have hundreds of megabytes of primary storage as well as the fastest processing times available.

Minicomputers

Minicomputers are smaller than mainframes, have less memory and slower processing speeds, and can support fewer peripheral devices (**Figure 2–23**). Minicomputers may have up to several megabytes of primary storage. Small to medium-sized businesses and academic settings, such as colleges, are examples of locations where minicomputers may be found. They may also function

Figure 2–22 The IBM 370, left, is an example of a mainframe computer. The Cray X–MP/4, right, is an example of a supercomputer; these computers are the most powerful available and are used for scientific work.

as part of a larger computer system by being hooked up to work in conjunction with mainframes.

Microcomputers

The term microcomputer, sometimes used interchangeably with the term personal computer, is used to describe the category of machine with the least amount of ability of the three categories mentioned. This can be misleading. Although microcomputers have less ability in terms of speed, number of peripherals supported, and amount of primary storage, they are still powerful machines.

In the computer field everything is relative. As mentioned earlier, some of the personal computers that are available today for a few thousand dollars are as powerful as the mainframes of twenty years ago. A personal computer may easily have 640K of primary storage. Some personal computers will support more than one megabyte of primary storage, and that figure is expanding rapidly as new microcomputers are developed and brought to market. By contrast just a few years ago the maximum amount of primary storage for a microcomputer was only 64K.

The trend of increased computer power for less money observed in the material on computer history has caused a blurring of the traditional mainframe, mini, micro classifications. As more powerful microcomputers become available and affordable, these categories may blur even further. This trend of more computer for less cost is beneficial for educators because it provides the

Figure 2–23 An example of a minicomputer is the 2350 System from Prime Computer. Minicomputers are frequently found in small to medium-sized businesses and also in colleges and universities.

opportunity for more sophisticated educational software to be developed on more powerful, more affordable machines.

In fact, the improvement in quality and drop in price of microcomputers to date is the reason microcomputers are the type most likely to be seen in schools. These machines may be used as stand-alone machines, meaning all functions and peripherals are exclusive to the one machine. A stand-alone microcomputer system typical of what may be seen in a school setting is shown in Figure 2–21. Microcomputers may also be networked, which means two or more machines are connected to share peripheral devices or primary storage. Theoretically, this allows a school to cut down on the number of peripherals, such as printers, that it buys. For various reasons, networking of microcomputers in the past has not always been successful. This is partly because earlier microcomputers were not really designed for networking. Innovations in microcomputer technology have provided the possibility of networking microcomputers effectively. However, there are questions that must be asked when the determination is made to provide a stand-alone or a networked environment in a school setting. Such questions include concerns about the availability of software that will run on a networked system and the security of information stored on such a system.

Communicating with the Hardware

The only way a person can communicate instructions to a computer is by using a programming language. It would be beneficial if we could tell the computer what we wanted it to do in a programming language that was as close to our

Computers in the Classroom

The following play by Murray Suid is a fun way to either introduce or reinforce basic concepts about computers and how they work. The play is recommended for K through 4 students.

THE TALKING COMPUTER

Ever feel as though the parts of your computer had minds of their own? Well they do in this play.

The play involves a large number of pupils and provides a good introduction to a computer's basic components as well. Costumes can be as simple as signs worn indicating the characters' names, or as elaborate as cardboard constructions.

Characters:

Byte	Main Memory	Printer
CPU	Microphone	Program
Mouse	Modem	Disk Drive
Screen	Light Pen	Speaker
Person	Keyboard	

Scene I. A science museum. A sign reading "Welcome to the Talking Computer Exhibit" hangs center stage. Note: **All Parts** *means that all characters except* **Person** *and* **CPU** *speak the given lines in unison.*

Person: This is the science museum's new talking computer. Since hearing is believing, I'll just turn it on.

All Parts: Hello. We are the parts of a computer. We're here to tell you what we do and how we work.

Person: That's great.

All Parts (*All parts shout out*): I'll go first because I'm the most important. You are not. I am. No, I am.

CPU (*blows a whistle and everyone quiets down*): That's better.

Person: Who are you?

CPU: I'm the Central Processing Unit or CPU for short. You might call me the computer's brain. I do the math and thinking work. I also tell the others what to do.

Person: I guess *you* are the most important part.

CPU: Not really. We're all important. Would your brain be much use without your heart, your skin, your ...

Person: I see what you mean.

CPU: To know how a computer works, you have to learn about *all* of us. Isn't that right, everybody?

All Parts: Sure! We're all important!

Person: So, who goes first?

All Parts: Me. Me. Let me. Let me.

CPU (*blows whistle again and waits for quiet*): You can see why a CPU is needed. Let's begin with you, Disk Drive. After turning the computer on, people often use you or your cousin Tape Drive.

Disk Drive: I knew I was the most important part.

All Parts: Boo. Hiss. That's not so. Boo.

CPU (*blows whistle*): Cut that out. Our guest doesn't want to hear bragging and arguing. Now, Disk Drive, just tell what you do in plain English. Okay?

Disk Drive: Okay. I'm something like a record player, only I play magnetic disks. (*Holds up a disk.*) Disks or tapes store words, numbers, pictures, and programs. A program is ...

Program (*interrupting*): Stop! Don't tell what I do. I'll talk for myself.

Disk Drive: Excuse me, Program.

Program: You're excused. Now, a program is a list of instructions a computer follows in doing a job. It's like the script for a play. But in this case the actors are the computer's parts. For example, a checkers program tells the screen how to make a checkerboard pattern. It also tells the CPU how to make moves.

Person: Can that program play chess, too?

Program: Nope. Every time you ask the computer to do a different job you need another program. There are thousands of ready-to-use programs for everything from doing math to drawing pictures. Plus, you can always write your own programs.

Person: I see why computers are so popular! With different programs, one machine can be used in lots of ways. But how does it work?

Program: Put the disk or the tape into the drive and, using the keyboard ...

Keyboard: Did I hear someone say *Keyboard?* That's me. My keys can send signals directly to the CPU. After you put a disk into the disk drive, you type the name of the program.

Person: You mean like checkers?

Keyboard: Yes. Then you push my *return* or *enter* key. That tells CPU what you want. Without me, nothing would happen.

Mouse: What about me, Keyboard?

Person: Who are you?

Mouse: I'm Mouse. I can do a lot of Keyboard's work, only faster. Plus, I can draw pictures.

Microphone: And what about me? Some computers let people use a microphone to tell CPU the job they want done. In the future I may be the main way people talk to computers.

Keyboard: We'll see.

Light Pen: Speaking about seeing, don't overlook me, Light Pen (*holds up package with bar code*). I can read bar code used in stores and libraries. Keyboard, Mouse, and Microphone can't do that! So there.

CPU: No bragging! What matters is that each of you can let the user talk to me in electrical code. In most computers, the code is made up of messages called *bytes*. Each byte stands for a letter, a number, or a symbol.

Byte: I work the way a finger code works. Suppose you want to send a message to someone across the room. First you both agree that one finger up is C, two fingers up is A, and three fingers up is T. Then you could send the word *cat* in this way. (*Byte holds up one finger, then lowers the hand, then raises the hand and holds up two fingers, then lowers the hand, then raises the hand and holds up three fingers.*)

Person: But there are no fingers inside the computer.

Byte: That's true. Instead, I'm made up of eight electrical signals. By using different ones, I can send 256 different messages. (*Byte moves fingers up and down to make different patterns.*)

Person: I could never make sense of all these bytes.

CPU: I'm made so I can figure out this kind of message quicker than you can blink your eye. When a user asks for a program stored on a disk, I instantly send a signal—using the same electrical code—telling Disk Drive to send the program to Main Memory.

Main Memory: That's me. I'm the place where programs stay while being used. I also hold some of the data—words and numbers—that the computer is working with.

CPU: After Disk Drive has done its job, I send another signal, using different bytes, to Main Memory. I ask it for the program's first instructions.

Byte (*running to Main Memory*): May I have the first instruction, please?

Main Memory: I send the first instruction, also in code, back to the CPU.

Byte (*running to the CPU*): Tell the screen to print a message saying that the program is ready.

Screen: I'm something like a TV screen. Without me, the computer couldn't tell the user anything.

Speaker: Really? In some computers, a speaker like me can talk to the user in a voice that sounds almost human. Why, in a few years electronic speakers may replace screens completely.

Screen: I doubt it. Can you *show* pictures and colors the way I can?

Speaker: No, but can you play music like I can?

CPU (*blows whistle*): Cut it out! The point is that my job is to take the program's instructions from Main Memory one at a time. I then make sure they're carried out.

Person: Do you always have the other parts do the work?

CPU: No. Sometimes I do it. Part of me does the math and thinking work. In a way, I send messages to myself.

Person: What happens next?

CPU: After I deal with the first job, I ask Main Memory for the next thing to do. In some programs, thousands of little jobs must be done before the big job is done. When the big job is finished, the result may be flashed on the screen or sent to the printer.

Printer: Like a typewriter I put words and numbers on paper. I can even print pictures.

CPU: Sometimes, the information is sent to the Modem.

Modem: My job is to change the code inside the computer into a different code that can be sent over phone lines to other computers.

CPU: But often the information will be stored for later use. In most computers, information can't be kept in Main Memory. When the computer is shut off, that erases everything. For safe keeping, information must be sent to the disk drive where it is put on a disk.

Person: Whew. You're really kept busy sending and receiving signals.

CPU: That's true. Most modern computers can move around a million or more messages each second.

Person: How do you do it so fast?

CPU: My main moving parts are electrical signals. Electricity travels at the speed of light. That's the fastest thing in the universe. Also, while I'm big in this play, I'm small in real life. I fit onto a tiny chip of silicon that's smaller than your fingernail. Many of the signals I send and receive travel less than a quarter of an inch. Since the trips are short, they don't take a long time.

Person: Well, all of you parts are amazing!

All Parts: Thanks. We like you, too.

Person: Shall I turn you off now?

All Parts: Yes, but before you do, we have one last message.

Person: What is it?

(*All Parts say nothing, but for three seconds they signal by rapidly moving their fingers up and down.*)

Person: Could you say it in English?

All Parts: Sure. This is THE END.

[This play appears in *The Teacher-Friendly Computer Book* (Monday Morning Books, 1984). (Suid, 1984)]

natural human language as possible. (It would be easiest if we could just use our own natural spoken language but that technology is not yet available.) Programming languages may be thought of as falling into one of two categories; high-level languages and low-level languages. A high-level programming language is designed to be easier for a human being to learn and use than a low-level language. Examples of high-level languages are Pascal, BASIC, Logo, and FORTRAN. Machine language and assembler language are examples of low-level languages.

In reality, all programs must finally be in machine language before the computer can perform that task outlined in the instructions. This is accomplished by using the computer to translate the instructions written in a high-level language into machine language. All this is done automatically and internally by the computer. The person who has written a program in a high-level language does not have to be concerned about the specifics of how the computer translates the program into the machine language the computer must use.

In general, translation may be accomplished through the use of an interpreter or a compiler (**Figure 2–24**). An interpreter translates one line of the program at a time into machine language and then immediately tries to do what the line of code has instructed it to do. A compiler translates the entire program into machine language and then, when the programmer tells it to, the computer executes the machine language instructions.

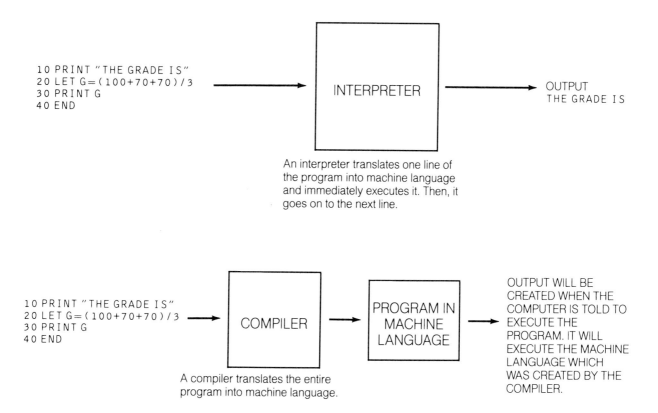

```
10 PRINT "THE GRADE IS"
20 LET G=(100+70+70)/3
30 PRINT G
40 END
```
INTERPRETER

OUTPUT
THE GRADE IS

An interpreter translates one line of the program into machine language and immediately executes it. Then, it goes on to the next line.

```
10 PRINT "THE GRADE IS"
20 LET G=(100+70+70)/3
30 PRINT G
40 END
```
COMPILER

PROGRAM IN MACHINE LANGUAGE

OUTPUT WILL BE CREATED WHEN THE COMPUTER IS TOLD TO EXECUTE THE PROGRAM. IT WILL EXECUTE THE MACHINE LANGUAGE WHICH WAS CREATED BY THE COMPILER.

A compiler translates the entire program into machine language.

Figure 2–24

Bits and Bytes

When a computer stores data or instructions, it does so in storage units that can only register as on or off. The primary storage of a computer consists of such units. Because each unit can only be either on or off, the state of each can be represented by a 1 for on or a 0 for off. The binary numbering system, or base two, can represent any number by using only the numerals 1 and 0. Binary notation (the use of 1s and 0s) is used to represent the state (on or off) of the storage units within a computer. One unit is referred to as a bit, which is short for binary digit. A bit is the smallest unit of information that a computer can address.

To represent the various letters (A through Z), numerals (0 through 9), and special characters e.g., ? and $, it is necessary to group bits together. A group of adjacent bits operated on by the computer as a unit is called a byte. The most common grouping of bits into a byte is eight bits to a byte. Another common system groups seven bits to a byte.

To have these groupings make any sense, there must be a predefined code to represent the various characters needed. An encoding system defines the meaning of different combinations of on-off locations within a byte. One common encoding system is the Extended Binary Decimal Interchange Code (EBCDIC). This system groups eight bits to a byte. **Table 2-1** shows the values for numerals 0 through 9 and letters A through Z in the EBCDIC system. The column labeled "EBCDIC Code" represents the state of the bits within the byte. The column labeled "Character" shows the character the computer would translate that information into. For example, if a byte contained the information 11000001, that would represent the letter A; 11110111 represents 7; etc.

Another common encoding system is the American Standard Code for Information Interchange (ASCII). This system groups seven bits to a byte (there is

Character	EBCDIC Code	Character	EBCDIC Code
0	1111 0000	I	1100 1001
1	1111 0001	J	1101 0001
2	1111 0010	K	1101 0010
3	1111 0011	L	1101 0011
4	1111 0100	M	1101 0100
5	1111 0101	N	1101 0101
6	1111 0110	O	1101 0110
7	1111 0111	P	1101 0111
8	1111 1000	Q	1101 1000
9	1111 1001	R	1101 1001
A	1100 0001	S	1110 0010
B	1100 0010	T	1110 0011
C	1100 0011	U	1110 0100
D	1100 0100	V	1110 0101
E	1100 0101	W	1110 0110
F	1100 0110	X	1110 0111
G	1100 0111	Y	1110 1000
H	1100 1000	Z	1110 1001

Table 2-1 EBCDIC Values.

also a different ASCII that groups eight bits to a byte, but it is not presented here). **Table 2–2** lists the byte values and their corresponding character values in the ASCII system for the letters A through Z and 0 through 9.

Computers are set up to use either ASCII or EBCDIC. Microcomputers use ASCII, while many mainframe computers use EBCDIC. The translation accomplished by the encoding system happens automatically and is of no concern to people who use computers, except for professional programmers. Even programmers seldom memorize such information. Rather, they refer to tables such as those presented here. After much use of such tables they may find they no longer need to refer to them.

It is possible to go on at length and in much greater detail about the information presented in this chapter. For our purposes that is not necessary. However, a good understanding of some of the basic concepts about computer hardware and the history of computers, as presented here, is a valuable aid in placing in perspective the technological change our society is undergoing. From the standpoint of teaching and learning, such a perspective helps in exploring attitudes about computers and computer use. Such information can also help in dispelling some of the stereotypes surrounding computers. Further, the information covered provides a valuable background for hands-on experiences with computers. There is, though, little need for any in-depth technical understanding about hardware in order to successfully and beneficially use computers in an educational setting. In fact, the trend is to make the hardware and software as simple to use as possible.

Conclusion

Character	ASCII Code		Character	ASCII Code
0	011 0000		I	100 1001
1	011 0001		J	100 1010
2	011 0010		K	100 1011
3	011 0011		L	100 1100
4	011 0100		M	100 1101
5	011 0101		N	100 1110
6	011 0110		O	100 1111
7	011 0111		P	101 0000
8	011 1000		Q	101 0001
9	011 1001		R	101 0010
A	100 0001		S	101 0011
B	100 0010		T	101 0100
C	100 0011		U	101 0101
D	100 0100		V	101 0110
E	100 0101		W	101 0111
F	100 0110		X	101 1000
G	100 0111		Y	101 1001
H	100 1000		Z	101 1010

Table 2–2 Values for the Seven-Bit ASCII System.

Key Terms

auxiliary storage
binary notation
bit
byte
central processing unit (CPU)
computer system
disk
disk drive
encoding system
first generation
hardware
high-level language
kilobyte
low-level language

machine language
mainframe computer
megabyte
microcomputer
microprocessor
minicomputer
networking
peripheral device
personal computer
second generation
software
supercomputer
third generation
video display terminal (VDT)

Questions

1. What role did the following people play in the early developments that preceded computers?

   - Blaise Pascal
   - Gottfried Wilhelm von Leibniz
   - Charles Babbage
   - Herman Hollerith

2. What were the Mark I, the ABC, the ENIAC, and the EDVAC?

3. Citing important characteristics for each generation, explain the differences between first-, second-, and third-generation computers. Do fourth-generation computers exist? Why or why not?

4. What is the difference between hardware and software?

5. Describe the three components of the CPU and explain what each one does.

6. What are peripheral devices? Into what categories might they be divided? Name two peripheral devices for each category and explain what each does.

7. Differentiate between mainframe computers, minicomputers, and microcomputers. Which are you most likely to find in schools?

8. How do computers of today compare with computers of twenty years ago? What generalization can be made about computer power, size, and cost over the past twenty to thirty years, and how has this had an effect on education?

9. How is a high-level programming language different from a low-level programming language?

10. What is a bit? What is a byte?

11. Decode the following using the EBCDIC values given in Table 2–1.

11000111   11010110   11010110   11000100
11010011   11100100   11000011   11010010
11100110   11001001   11100011   11001000
11100011   11001000   11001001   11100010

Once this is decoded, encode the message in the ASCII values given in Table 2–2.

References/Further Reading

Evans, C. *The Micro Millenium.* New York: Viking Press, 1979.

Mandell, Steven. *Computers and Data Processing Today.* St. Paul, Minn.: West Publishing Co., 1983.

"Questions Teachers Still Ask About Kids and Computers." *Instructor* 94, no. 3 (1984):83.

Spencer, Donald P. *Computers and Information Processing.* Columbus, Ohio: Charles E. Merrill Publishing Co., 1985.

Stern, Robert A., and Nancy Stern. *An Introduction to Computers and Information Processing.* New York: John Wiley & Sons, 1985.

Suid, Murray. "The Talking Computer." *Instructor* 94, no. 3 (1984):94–96.

Sumner, Mary. *Computers: Concepts and Uses.* Englewood Cliffs, N.J.: Prentice-Hall, 1985.

Tuckman, Bruce W. "Thinking Out Loud—Computer Use: A Question of Values." *Educational Technology* 24, no. 4 (1984): 36–37.

3

Computer-Assisted Instruction: An Introduction

TOPICS ADDRESSED

What factors affect the initial use of computers by teachers?

How does the transition to computer use occur?

What is computer-assisted instruction?

What modes of computer use are available to students?

Where does control lie in different types of computer-student experiences—with the computer or the student?

In what ways might it be desirable to bring students into contact with computers?

OUTLINE

Introduction

Establishing a Context

Teachers as Professionals

The Transition to Computer Use

Computer-Assisted Instruction: Defined

Three Modes of Computer Use

Tutor Mode

Tool Mode

Tutee Mode

Control of the Computer-Student
Experience

Conclusion

Key Terms

Questions

References/Further Reading

Introduction

This chapter begins by noting some of the concerns many teachers have when asked to integrate computers into their teaching. A model for understanding the types of computer activities available to students and teachers is then presented and discussed. The question of who is in control of the computer-student interaction is addressed. The topics covered here serve to set the stage for Chapter 4 which presents examples of the types of software used in education.

Establishing a Context

Teachers as Professionals

Consider the types of activities engaged in by the average teacher. Time is spent on a variety of tasks, including record keeping, material generation, content review, and the selection of appropriate instructional experiences. Contact time usually claims the greatest part of the day. Instruction may take place on an individual, small-group, or whole-class basis and may include lecture, demonstration, discussion, worksheets, tests, experiential learning, or some combination of these and other strategies. Besides all this, teachers frequently undertake additional responsibilities, such as committee work, coaching, and the organization of school clubs, plays, concerts, and other special functions. Further, it is necessary for most teachers to actively pursue and eventually earn a graduate degree. Teachers, much like any other professional group, are busy.

The Transition to Computer Use

Into this maelstrom of activity walks the principal or another supervisor one day and announces that all teachers should begin to use computers in their teaching. In some instances this happens with minimal support in the way of training and without much thought regarding such a seemingly drastic change in the educational environment. In other instances these questions are carefully considered. Teachers and administrators work together to define realistic goals regarding hardware and software evaluation, curriculum development, and teacher training. For some teachers, working with computers is an enjoyable experience from the start. For other teachers, however, integrating computers into their teaching is a new and, initially, unwelcome experience. Even in the case where care is taken to provide support for teachers, it is probable that for some, a transitional period involving stress and anxiety will occur. In the event that little or no support is offered, it can be guaranteed.

The source of this stress and anxiety is easy to trace. Most people who teach (and many who are training to become teachers) did not grow up in a computer-rich culture. Rather, when most teachers were forming attitudes and making career decisions, computers were a distant, somewhat mysterious phenomena. Computers may have touched the periphery of their lives by way of the monthly phone or utility bill, but aside from that, contact with computers was nonexistent. The notion that they would have to know enough about computers to use them in their daily interaction with students was not part of what the majority of teachers originally saw as their role in the classroom. This, coupled with the notion that computers are somehow mathematical, thereby stirring up

Campbell. ©1983 MARTHA F. CAMPBELL

*"I can accept and process data, but I have trouble generating
it on my own...."*

any latent math anxiety, tends to generate concern among many teachers who
are told that they should begin to use computers in their teaching. This situation is certainly not unique to education. Many people in business and government who have been asked to change the way they do their jobs experience a
similar period of transition as they integrate computers into their work (Sanders and Birkin, 1980).

The emotional reaction experienced during this transition is frequently coupled with other valid concerns about the idea of computerizing the classroom.
One concern is, Where do I find the time to master what I need to know to use
a computer? Other concerns are, Why bother to change what I'm doing? What
will the real benefits be? How will I, logistically, manage this new tool? How
much do I need to learn, and will I be able to learn it?

The most amazing aspect of this process is the facility that teachers quickly
gain in the use of the computer as an instructional device, provided they are
given the benefit of good, practical training that includes hands-on experiences. (This is an important point, and one that cannot be made too often; in
order to do things with computers, one must do things with computers—must
sit and work with the computer. No amount of verbal or written explanation
alone will accomplish this learning.) The subsequent loss of anxiety occurs
because teachers soon realize that they are in control of what the computer
does. They also realize that many of the early instructional uses to which
computers have been applied, and which are now readily available to school
personnel, are familiar to them. Rather than continuing to view the computer as
an imposition, many teachers find that they have another useful instructional

strategy that they, as managers of the learning environment, may make use of as they deem appropriate.

Take as an example a case study of one teacher we will call Edith, who signed up for a graduate course on microcomputers in the classroom taught on site in her district. Edith had twenty years of teaching experience and was quite vocal in her dislike of computers and the way they were being adopted in her school. She took the course, quite simply, because the district paid her to do so. Halfway through the semester, after several positive hands-on experiences, she began to become interested in what she might do with a microcomputer in her classroom. She felt in control of the machine and began to treat it as she would any other available resource. By the end of the semester she had found software appropriate for her teaching situation, had begun to use it with her students, and was extolling the virtues of computer-assisted instruction.

Not all such situations have as happy an ending, but Edith's experience points toward some important considerations regarding the initial use of computers by teachers. First, she became comfortable with the technology after she had the opportunity to use and control it. Second, she was shown, theoretically and experientially, that the concept of computer-assisted instruction was not alien to what she had spent the past twenty years developing as important, relevant teacher skills. Third, she applied what she already knew about instruction to her decisions about how she would use the computer to aid in her teaching.

It is important to emphasize here that were there no valid reasons for offering instruction with and about computers, it would be wasteful and time-consuming to incorporate them into our teaching. Why reinvent the wheel in a newer, shinier, more expensive form if functionally it does exactly the same job as the wheel currently in use? In Edith's case she had accomplished three things that to her justified the commitment of her time and energy: (1) she stimulated increased student interest; (2) she gained more efficient use of her time and her students' time by using the computer to generate examples for drill and practice, provide tutorial information, and keep track of student progress; and (3) she became adept at managing, within her profession, a potent tool that has spread, and will continue to spread, throughout our culture. This initial success in areas that are already part of her teaching repertoire will serve as a starting point for her investigation into other ways she may use computers. By overcoming her emotional and intellectual distrust of a new technology and incorporating it into her teaching, she became, in the short run, an innovator. Given her early predisposition against computers, she took one giant step for Edith and one small step for education.

In the larger sense, when Edith's experience is placed within the context of the types of innovation in education that may become available in the future owing to advances in computer technology, one could argue that what she did was hardly innovative at all. That would be a mistake. What is of significance is that the change Edith implemented was an innovation for her because it constituted a major change in the way she viewed her role as a professional. She changed from someone who was having technological change imposed on her to someone who was in charge of deciding how to use a new technology within her area of professional responsibility, someone who was still in control of her professional fate. As mentioned earlier, many people in business and industry have gone through a similar transition. For both pre-service and in-service teachers, as well as for people in business and government, the process is often quite similar. It is the process of adapting to the use of a new tool as it is applied to the needs of the job at hand. This leads us to a consideration of the types of instructional functions available on the computer that might be of interest to teachers.

Computer-assisted instruction (CAI) is defined in this text as any use of computers to provide instruction to students. Many people share this broad definition, but some do not. Coburn and others (1982) note that the term has gone through several changes in definition and has come to mean, for some, any application of computers to instruction. They, however, choose to adopt a more narrow definition, referring to CAI as, "computer applications applied to traditional teaching methods such as drill, tutorial, demonstration, simulation and instructional games" (p. 253).

Computer-Assisted Instruction: Defined

Choosing the broad definition allows us to view all educational computer use across one unified spectrum, which will, in turn, facilitate certain comparisons. Also, we will attempt to avoid any overt or implied value judgment regarding the range of teaching methods available to the practitioner. This approach is based on the recognition that for any given instructional situation, the teaching professional must choose the teaching strategy best employed. Such choices depend on the environment in which the choice will be implemented, as well as the teacher's previous training and individual preferences. No discussion of traditional versus nontraditional methods is attempted. Rather, a balanced approach to the types of instructional strategies used when students come into contact with computers will be favored.

Input/Output

Computerphobia: What to do about it
By Timothy B. Jay.

In the following excerpt from the article "Computerphobia: What to Do About It," Timothy Jay defines computerphobia, identifies possible causes, and suggests remedies. Certainly many teachers are perfectly comfortable with computers and use them to great advantage in their work. However, some segments of the teaching population (and the population in general) do experience what Jay identifies as computerphobia. It is probable that in time, the use of computers by people in education and other fields will be so commonplace as to make computerphobia a thing of the past. Young people, whose world has always been pervaded by computers, seem less likely to develop a fear of computers. This would seem especially true of students who benefit from a sound computer education curriculum. For now, though, the following points can be of value in dealing with a fear of computers, wherever it might arise.

Many instructors, whether they admit it or not, are afraid of computers. I validate my observation from discussions, either formal or informal, on the topic of computers and computer-assisted learning with administrators, teachers, students, and instructional technologists, who admit these fears. Computerphobia is but one branch of a larger technophobia in our society that has been engendered by our recent period of rapid technological growth and development. People either keep up or give up.

Computerphobia is unfortunate and uncomfortable. It must be overcome. Instructors need the sense of control, confidence, and authority that comes with understanding technology. Instructors need to use this technology as an effective and productive tool in educational settings. Most important of all, learners need to experience the creative, diverse, and motivated learning that is promoted by this technology when in the hands of knowledgeable instructors.

Before looking at the remedy for computerphobia, we have something to gain by examining the phenomenon in more detail. Understanding the etiology of computerphobia is part of the cure. Let us look at the symptoms and the causes of this electronic nightmare.

The Symptoms of Computerphobia. Computerphobia appears generally in the form of a negative attitude toward technology. The negative attitude takes the form of (a) resistance to talking or even thinking about computer technology; (b) fear or anxiety, which may even create physiological consequences; and (c) hostile or aggressive thoughts and acts, indicative of some underlying frustrations. We may see these resistances, fears, anxieties, and hostilities in some of the following:

- a fear of physically touching a computer;

- a feeling that one could break or damage the computer or somehow ruin what is inside;

- a failure to engage in reading or conversation about the computer, a type of denial that the computer really exists;

- feeling threatened, especially by students and others who do know something about computers;

- an expression of attitudes that are negative about computers and technology, for example: (a) feeling that you can be replaced by a machine, (b) feeling dehumanized, or (c) feeling aggressive toward computers (let's bend, fold, and mutilate those cards!). Such feelings are indicative of an underlying feeling of insecurity and lack of control; and

- a type of role reversal, whereby the person assumes the role of slave to technology rather than the master of a fine tool.

There may be other characteristics, but these are the ones manifest in many of those afraid of computers.

Causes of Computerphobia. The causes of computerphobia are diverse and may vary from individual to individual. I assume that there are both individual and institutional sources of these problems; therefore, I trace the causes back to simple beginnings, such as:

- a failure on the part of the phobic to "keep up" with technological advances that affect his or her life. This reflects a simple failure to keep up with readings in popular and professional literature about technological advances;

- the institution or organization for which a person works may have failed to take his or her job into consideration when planning to use this new technology. A recurrent theme in educators' stories is that administrators buy equipment without (a) planning for its use, (b) assessing teachers' attitudes, (c) evaluating job changes, or (d) finding out how the computer technology will affect a particular individual. A resulting feeling is having an "unknown force" about to "attack";

- a failure of institutions to provide incentives to educators to keep up with technology. These incentives take the form of time off, training, paying for courses at local colleges, and/or incentives to develop one's own courseware to further personalize the use of the computer.

The phobia develops because people and institutions have not assessed how the computer might affect a particular person.

Remedies for Computerphobia. The cure for computerphobia must come from sources within the phobic and from the support of the system in which he or she works. Basically, the cure must result in a change in the attitude and behavior of the phobic. Some of the following are suggested:

- individuals, on their own, can begin a course of personal education, doing readings about computer technology in terms of current hardware and software developments; and

- institutions must begin promoting computer literacy both with learners and instructors. Teachers need time off, monetary incentives, and encouragement to attend seminars and courses in computer technology and educational reform. A model for a computer seminar is presented in Figure 1.

Figure 1. A Model for a Computer Seminar

- A two to three day session, depending on the experience of the participants and the amount of introductory material to be presented.

- Participants should come from a variety of positions: administrators, teachers, students, and technologists. They should also have various levels of expertise, although most will be beginners.

- An introduction to the literature and philosophy of instructional technology.

- Reinforce the idea that they are "in control" of technology.

- Reinforce the idea that they do not need to be programmers or experts in electronics to use the technology.

- Provide hands-on experience with both hardware and software.

- Use both time-sharing and microcomputing systems, if possible. With either system, many computer neophytes have been extremely gratified by just touching the computer keyboard for the first time.

- Reinforce the idea that *they* are the experts in knowing how to instruct learners.

(Jay, 1986)

Taylor (1980) presents a valuable framework for viewing what can be done with computers in education at virtually any level. He categorizes the use to which computers can be put in education into three modes: a computer may be used as a tutor, a tool, or a tutee (student).

Three Modes of Computer Use

When the computer is used as a tutor, it may accomplish the following:

Tutor Mode

- Present material to the student
- Query the student
- Evaluate the response
- Choose the next instructional sequence to be presented based on the student's previous performance

These functions closely resemble some of those performed by a teacher or teaching assistant. The difference would lie in the use to which the unique abilities of the computer may be put in such a situation. Computers are fast and accurate and have an ability to keep track of greater amounts of data and information than do human beings. When the computer is used as tutor (the historical roots of which lie in earlier noncomputerized attempts at programmed instruction), it is theoretically possible to have available a wealth of information related to student performance. It is also possible to offer a wide range of instructional pathways down which a student might be led, as necessary, based on previous performance. This is called branching. For example, if a student incorrectly answered several questions about the natural resources of Brazil, the computer would branch to that part of the lesson on resources of Brazil and present that material before continuing on with new material. Thus, instruction is individualized for that particular student at that specific moment. Theoretically, instruction may be individualized to an extent not possible without a computer by having the tutorial branch to exactly the material needed by the student based on the response given. In reality, however, complex branching of this sort to the correct sequence of instructions for an individual student is difficult to program the computer to do. Few, if any, materials that exemplify the theoretical possibilities are available. This is especially true for the current generation of microcomputers, the most likely type of hardware to be used in school settings. This limitation is due in part to the infancy of the computer revolution and in part to the relative newness of the use of computers in educational settings. However, even though we are far away from achieving what might be possible by using computers as tutors, the simple branching available does have value as an adjunct to teacher-student interaction. As we shall see, when CAI is implemented, the value of computer-student interaction depends greatly on the quality of teacher-student interaction and the very human instructional decisions made by the teacher.

Applications to which the computer as tutor may be put include drill and practice, tutorials, simulations, and instructional games. These categories will be dealt with in more detail in Chapter 4, when specific software examples are considered.

In discussing his three modes of using computers in education, Taylor notes that the framework may be beneficial in understanding, at the outset, what may seem like a complex field. He encourages modification and extension of the framework as an aid in gaining new insights into the field and warns against becoming bound by his definitions. We'll accept him at his word as we place his three modes on a continuum to both clarify their initial meaning and aid in presenting another view of these types of computer-student interactions.

Table 3–1 represents a continuum on which have been placed Taylor's designations of tutor, tool, and tutee. Under the designation tutor, at the leftmost end of the continuum, are examples of the types of CAI that would qualify as tutor mode use. Under each of the other two modes appear examples related to the corresponding mode.

Tool Mode

In one sense, all computers may be viewed as tools used by people, regardless of the function to which the computer is applied. For Taylor, however, using the computer as a tool refers to providing, by means of the computer, an extension of human capabilities in a particular way: "In the tool mode, the computer provides a service that the user needs and more or less knows how to use. It is not primarily a teacher or tutor as in the tutor mode; it is not user-alterable and not a set of raw building components as might be provided under tutee mode" (p. 8).

One example would be a program to do statistics. A high school science class might gather information on some ecological problem and use the computer to turn their raw data into a series of meaningful graphs. A teacher might use the same program to process test grades in order to yield class statistics, such as mean, median, and standard deviation, or the same teacher might use a program to do an item analysis of a newly developed test.

One favorite use of the computer in the tool mode is as a word processor. The computer, when used to enhance the human ability to record symbols, can ease and enliven the revision and copying process that is so much a part of writing. Indeed, the case can be made that by separating the task of handwriting from the task of creating a written product, young children, who may not have mastered penmanship, can develop their writing and language skills more readily through the use of a word processor.

Tutor	Tool	Tutee
Drill and practice	Word processors	Logo
Instructional games	Statistical packages	Pascal
Tutorials	Spreadsheets	BASIC
Simulations	File management systems	PILOT
	Aspects of computer-managed instruction	Delta Drawing
		FORTRAN
		C

Examples given are not comprehensive.

Table 3–1 Modes of Computer Use.

As Taylor points out, the major use of computers outside of education is in the tool mode. The history of computers as tools in business ranges from early applications of accounting functions through modern-day sophisticated decision support systems that aid top-level executives in strategic planning (Thierauf, 1982). Some examples of tool mode uses are listed in Table 3–1. Included is a reference to some aspects of computer-managed instruction (CMI). This refers to using the computer for the management of teaching and record-keeping functions. CMI is the subject of Chapter 5.

Taylor's last designation, that of the computer as tutee or student, describes the use of the computer as something that can, in and of itself, be instructed to do something. The manner in which one currently tells the computer to do something is through a programming language. Computers understand one or more programming languages and a person who wants to give a computer a set of instructions to perform must do so in a programming language that the computer understands. For example, if a teacher wishes a student to add 5 + 2 and give the result, he or she may simply ask, "What is 5 + 2?" In a programming language—we'll use BASIC as an example—one way of having the computer add 5 + 2 and give the result would be by entering the following instructions into the computer:

Tutee Mode

```
10 LET A = 5 + 2
20 PRINT A
```

When this set of instructions, or program, is executed by the computer, the number 7 will be printed.

A variety of programming languages are available that allow students to communicate with the computer, including Logo, Pascal, and BASIC, all of which are widely used in education. The importance of teaching the computer to do something (programming), such as drawing a picture, drilling one on spelling words, or calculating interest on a bank statement, is that it forces the person doing the programming to thoroughly understand that which he or she is teaching the computer. Also, the programmer must begin to deal with how the facts and ideas being used to achieve the intended goal are manipulated into meaningful instructions for the computer. A shift begins to take place from the acquisition of information to the manipulation of information.

Table 3–1 lists several programming languages as examples of the means currently available for communicating with computers.

A case can be made that, based on the nature of an individual's interaction with a computer in any of the three modes, a person's experience is controlled to a greater or lesser degree by the computer. In **Table 3–2** two new designations have been added to the continuum. On the upper left is the label "Computer-Controlled Interaction" and on the upper right, the label "Human-Controlled Interaction." The intent is to still view this as a continuum but with the added distinction that different modes provide different mixes of human vs. computer control. For example, the tutor mode would, overall, be seen as

Control of the Computer-Student Experience

Reactions and Research

Microcomputers in Mathematics Instruction
By **Marilyn N. Suydam**
Ohio State University
Columbus, OH 43212

The following excerpt summarizes some of the research findings on using microcomputers to teach mathematics. Note that although many early uses of the computer in education were for math instruction, the variety of software available and the use of computers by teachers has been changing. There has been growth in the number of teachers who use tool mode software (such as word processors) with students. There has also been growth in the amount and use of programs aimed at developing problem-solving skills. Other areas in which more and more software is becoming available are language arts, social studies, and reading.

Many teachers are using microcomputers in their classrooms, trying out different programs and different ways of using them. Surveys indicate that most educational software is for mathematics, and thus microcomputers are used more frequently in mathematics lessons than in other subjects. Most of this software involves drill and practice for recalling previously learned facts, with no stress on higher-order skills. Few programs are designed to teach concepts or to develop problem-solving techniques.

What does research tell us about the effectiveness of using software programs for drill and practice in mathematics?

- Mathematics instruction supplemented by computer-assisted drill and practice is at least as effective or more effective in fostering achievement than instruction using only traditional methods.

- Administering drill and practice with a computer is less time-consuming than with conventional methods: many students learn more in less time.

The research evidence on other ways of using microcomputers is, as yet, scarce. However, we have some indication of the following:

- Using tutorial computer-assisted instruction can lead to higher achievement than using only traditional instructional methods.

- Extensive work on problem solving using the computer enhances an understanding of mathematics topics and aids in developing strategies.

- Teachers prefer microcomputer-managed instructional systems to nonmicrocomputer systems, whereas students have no preference; and no significant differences in achievement are found between students using either system.

- Higher gains in achievement result when a microcomputer is used for playing strategy games in geometry than when a computer is not used.

- Students at remedial levels demonstrate marked gains when they use computer programs for individualized work on their specific weaknesses.

BIBLIOGRAPHY

Burns, Patricia K. "A Quantitative Synthesis of Research Findings Relative to the Pedagogical Effectiveness of Computer-assisted Mathematics Instruction in Elementary and Secondary Schools." Ph.D. diss., University of Iowa, 1981. *Dissertation Abstracts International* 42A (January 1982):2946.

Crenshaw, Harrison M., II. "A Comparison of Two Computer Assisted Instruction Management Systems in Remedial Math." Ph. D. diss., Texas A. & M. University, 1982. *Dissertation Abstracts International* (May 1983):3467–68.

Haus, George J. "The Development and Evaluation of a Microcomputer-Based Assessment and Remediation Program for Mildly Mentally Handicapped Junior High School Students." Ph.D. diss., Indiana University, 1983. *Dissertation Abstracts International* 44A (September 1983):728.

Hersberger, James R. "The Effects of a Problem Solving Oriented Mathematics Program on Gifted Fifth-Grade Students." Ph.D. diss., Purdue University, 1983. *Dissertation Abstracts International* 44A (December 1983):1715.

Morris, Janet P. "Microcomputers in a Sixth-Grade Classroom." *Arithmetic Teacher* 31 (October 1983):22–24.

(Suydam, 1984)

---

providing more computer and less human control of a student's experience than the tool mode, while the tutee mode would provide the greatest level of human control. Further, within any given mode, specific types of activities may be seen as providing various degrees of computer or human control. For instance, within the tutor mode, drill and practice programs would be to the left of simulations, denoting that there is more computer control of the human-computer interaction in a drill and practice program than in a simulation.

Computer-Controlled Interaction *Tutor*	*Tool*	*Human-Controlled Interaction* *Tutee*
Drill and practice	Word processors	Logo
Instructional games	Statistical packages	Pascal
Tutorials	Spreadsheets	BASIC
Simulations	File management systems	PILOT
	Aspects of computer-managed instruction	Delta Drawing
		FORTRAN
		C

Examples given are not comprehensive.

Table 3–2 Computer-Controlled vs. Human-Controlled Interaction.

Comparing examples from each end of the spectrum will best illustrate. When a student sits down at a computer to work with a drill program on spelling words, the computer has loaded and running within it a series of instructions, the program. It, or, more specifically, the person who wrote the program, decides what words, in what order, the student will see. Also, it decides when the student will be permitted to respond and what form the response will take. Other than turning off the computer and walking away, the student has few, if any, options. All the decisions have been made previously. This must be the case because the computer had to be programmed to perform the drill and practice function. In turn, the student is being led through that program. When taken to the extreme, this notion of rows of children sitting in front of computers slavishly following instructions terrifies many people—and so it should if the end product of CAI were to accomplish such a goal. However, when a drill or other tutor mode program is written correctly, following sound pedagogical practice and used in conjunction with other instructional strategies, tutor mode experiences can be beneficial and desirable. They must, however, be recognized for what they are—a type of interaction in which the student has little or no control over the computer and only one of the types of computer-student interaction available.

For comparison, take an example of a student being asked to make the computer do something, say have the computer draw a tree. Aside from having to actively engage in problem solving, the student must, within the confines of the programming language used, control the computer. This is a vastly different experience from being controlled by the computer.

Another way to view the situation is to take the example of a person with excellent programming skills, perhaps a professional programmer. When that person sits down at a computer to write a program, the computer has no agenda other than what the person supplies to it in the act of writing the program. The human controls, to a great extent, what that agenda will be. On the contrary, when the same person sits down to work with the computer in the tutor mode, the machine has a full agenda previously supplied to it by some other programmer. The agenda will dictate how the computer controls the session when the program is run.

Tool programs are somewhere in the middle, since the use to which these programs are put is decided by the student, who chooses the tool to use, supplies relevant data, such as words or numbers, directs the use of the tool, and interprets, accepts, or rejects results.

Computer uses under the label "Computer-Controlled Interaction" are the types of experiences most closely associated with so-called traditional methods. We do not intend to demean these types of instructional interaction, whether between teacher and student or computer and student. Rather, we are saying that if students are to come into contact with computers as the source of these types of instruction, it may be wise to include other experiences for students in which they are more in control of the computer. This concern stems from two areas. First, given the growing importance of technology in today's world, it is disturbing that many people are mystified and uncomfortable when presented with issues surrounding various possible uses of technology (including different possible uses of computers). Such uses, more fully discussed in Chapter 1, may include applications related to medicine, education, resource management, transportation, and many other fields. Couple this situation with the possible misuses of technology and it does not seem far-fetched to want to socialize students in such a way that they thoroughly understand their role in relation to machines and technology. That role should be one of viewing the machine, no matter how sophisticated, as the idiot savant, or wise fool, it is. Wise in the sense that machines and technology may accomplish wonderful things. Fool in that a machine may do nothing until it is applied to some task by a human being. The ultimate responsibility for the use or misuse of any technology must always lie with the human who applied it to some function. A variety of experiences with computers, including experiences in which the student directly controls the computer, as well as relevant information about computers and technology, should aid in defining the computer's role. Second, in relation to the learning process, an argument can be made that it is beneficial to use computers to provide students with experiences in which they are active learners in control of their own learning. This position is presented in Chapter 8. The view adopted here is that teachers should use computers with students in a variety of ways reflective of the teacher's needs, the student's needs, and society's needs.

Instructionally, each type of tutor mode experience has educational relevance. As illustrated earlier, many teachers come to use computers in the classroom by adopting software in one of these areas. This is not surprising, since they provide common, known territory through which a new element of technology can be introduced to the teacher and into the classroom. Computers do have more to offer, however, than just the tutor type of environment, and educators owe it to themselves and their students to explore what some of those offerings might be. This is especially true of tutee mode uses.

As stated earlier, we have adopted a broad definition of CAI, such that everything portrayed in Table 3–2 would fall under the definition. In any of these categories, purposeful, meaningful learning may take place. The teacher, as the arbiter of that learning, must be aware of what goals are intended in any of the computer-student environments presented so far and should at some point be able to evaluate that learning as a basis for the formulation of future goals, strategies, and experiences. Viewing all three modes—tutor, tool, and tutee—as CAI allows ready comparison and contrast among the variety of CAI

Computers in the Classroom

STARTING FROM SQUARE 1
by Norma C. Piper

A lack of resources (too few computers, too little software) is a common problem in many schools. In Chapter 14 different models for offering and managing computer resources within a school are presented and discussed. But what about a situation in which a teacher is given one computer for a class full of students and asked to start teaching with and about computers? How can the individual teacher effectively manage this scarce resource? The following two articles offer nuts-and-bolts suggestions about how to manage a computer in the classroom. The first article also offers, for teachers just starting out, a few sources of information about computers.

What do you do when the principal puts a computer in your classroom? One computer, thirty 5th and 6th grade students, and no experience? Don't panic! There's a way out. Here are some do's and don'ts to help you.

First, buy a manual. I found *Creative Programming for Young Minds* by Leonard Storm [1] and *Kids and the Apple* by Edward Carlson [2] to be excellent. Each book is organized in lessons that are easy to follow and are ideal for classroom use. Don't depend on prepared software for your entire computer literacy unit. It is important to teach your students how to program. The interaction with the computer in doing even simple programming helps increase students' confidence and enhance self-esteem. A child learns by doing, and even young children can learn to program. They certainly do not write "professional" programs, but they do write programs that solve problems at their level.

I divided my days into eight half-hour periods:

	M	T	W	Th	F
8:30–9	(T)	(T)	(T)	(T)	(T)
9–9:30	1	8	15	5	(T)
9:30–10	2	9	16	6	12
10:30–11	3	10	17	7	13
11–11:30	4	11	1	8	14
11:30–12	5	12	2	9	15
1–1:30	6	13	3	10	16
1:30–2	7	14	4	11	17

This schedule provides 40 blocks of computer time every week for my class of 34 students. Each student is paired with a partner to make 17 groups. Each group is assigned two computer blocks per week. The other six blocks are reserved for me (T).

I use my blocks of time for computer programming instruction, for introduction of new software, or for individual students to save a new program on a disk.

My reserved blocks on Friday are especially helpful. If a few students miss their computer time earlier in the week due to an assembly or testing, they can move their time to Friday.

Students work together at the computer, one programming and the other editing, for fifteen minutes and then change places. When their time is up, the next scheduled group lets them know. If they are in the middle of typing in a long program, they can save it on a cassette tape or disk. The more experienced computer operators are available tutors.

A small paperback book called *Basic Fun* by Lipscomb and Zuanich [3] has some simple game programs that teach the use of computer language. My students have expanded these programs and have gone on to write some of their own.

A word of caution ... don't make the use of the computer a reward for finishing math or for good behavior. The computer is a tool for all students and should be treated accordingly. All children should be able to count on computer time each week. *You* will reap the reward.

Bibliography

1. Storm, Leonard. *Creative Programming for Young Minds.* Creative Programming, Inc. Charleston, IL 61920.

2. Carlson, Edward H. *Kids and the Apple.* Datamost, Chatsworth, CA 91311.

3. Lipscomb and Zuanich. *Basic Fun.* Avon Books, New York, NY 10019.

[Norma C. Piper, 5th/6th GATE Teacher, Covina-Valley Unified School District, P.O. Box 269, Covina, CA 91723.] (Piper, 1984)

DON'T TURN OFF THAT COMPUTER!
by Doris M. Kneppel

Have you ever walked down the hall of your school and noticed the computers sitting idle? Is there a way to keep those computers busy most of the day without the teacher's supervision? Take a peek inside this classroom and see for yourself.

John is at the computer looking perplexed. He glances over at Miss Johnson, who is working with a math group. John looks around the room and walks purposefully over to Janet who gets up and joins him at the computer.

John shows Janet what he's working on and a quiet discussion of the problem is underway. John's face clears and he is once more deeply involved in his work, never noticing that Janet has gone back to her desk.

All too soon the timer signals his turn is over. John saves his work on a disk, gathers his notes and looks for Kelly, whose turn is next. Kelly is with her math group so John writes her name on the board and signals Leslie that it's her turn. Leslie sets the timer and is quickly absorbed in the Logo program she began yesterday.

Suddenly she realizes her math group is being called. Leslie writes her name under Kelly's, and writes a "7" next to it. As the first math group leaves, Kelly, seeing her name on the board, erases it and heads for the computer.

What is being described here is a method of managing the rotation of children at the computer with a minimum of disturbance. It encourages peer help and appeals to the sense of fairness which many children have honed to a keen edge. Keeping the computer working this way assures each child of approximately 35 minutes of computer time a week.

In schools where the computer is rotated from room to room, its presence often threatens to disrupt lessons and is a distraction to children as they anxiously await a turn. There is frustration over missed turns and arguments about who has had more than their share of time. The situation can become so frustrating for a teacher trying to keep up with a tight teaching schedule that it sometimes seems that the only way to manage the situation is to turn the darn thing off!

There is a way, though, to manage computer time so it is always in use except when whole-class instruction is being given. For those schools where there is a computer in every room or those schools where the computer is wheeled in only occasionally, a system such as this will work.

It begins with a prominently displayed poster listing alphabetically the names of the children in the class. For minimum distraction, the computer is set up in a far corner of the room with its back to the class. Next to the computer is a kitchen timer. With appropriate solemnity the new procedure is introduced to the class. (It's interesting how intently children listen to any instructions involving the computer!) The "bare bones" ground rules are:

1. The order of turns follows the list of names as posted.

2. The timer is set for 10 minutes.

3. The child leaving the computer informs the next child listed on the name chart.

4. At the end of the day, the next child on the list writes his/her name on the board.

These four steps are simple, but will only work if all the "ifs" are taken care of as follows:

IF a child whose turn it is, is otherwise occupied (in a reading group, receiving individual help, out of the room at the moment, etc.), that child's name is written on the board by the child leaving the computer and the next child on the list is called. (For example, it's Jenny's turn but she's at a speech lesson. Jack writes her name on the board and calls Kelly. When Kelly is finished, she checks the board and looks to see if Jenny is back. If she is back, Kelly calls her to take her turn. If she is still out of the room, the next child is called.)

IF the teacher begins a lesson with the whole class, or calls his/her reading group, the child at the computer checks the timer to see how much time is left and writes his/her name on the board with the remaining time next to it.

IF a program requires two children to be together at the computer, both children have had their turns.

IF a child is absent, that child's turn is skipped.

IF the timer goes off at a point where the child needs another minute or two to finish the game or save a procedure, that's fine. (If the privilege is abused, you'll hear about it soon enough!)

IF a child needs help at the computer, s/he asks a friend who is not working with the teacher.

The children quickly learn that class and group lessons take precedence over one's turn at the computer, but since each child is assured of fair treatment, they react good naturedly.

Introducing this routine will take about 20 minutes, and if it is followed up by inviting questions, the children will come up with some "What if ..." questions that will help you refine and tailor it to your class.

Finally, it is advisable to monitor the new routine carefully for the first few days, offering reminders and reviewing the rules. The time spent during that first week will lay the groundwork that frees you from constant daily hassles and frequent settling of squabbles.

Don't turn off that computer—make it the willing partner it was intended to be!

[Doris M. Kneppel, 84 Cascade Way, Kinnelon, NJ 07405.] (Kneppel, 1985)

materials available in the light of both their purpose and the nature of the student-computer interaction used to achieve that purpose.

Conclusion

Both pre-service and in-service teachers are experiencing the computer revolution in much the same way as members of other professions. Individuals in a wide variety of fields, including educators, are being asked to apply computers to their work. Computer training is being offered to in-service teachers and is being required in programs for pre-service teachers. Taylor (1980) offers a framework for understanding the types of uses to which computers may be put in education. The manner in which a teacher chooses to have a student use a computer will dictate who controls the interaction: the student or the computer.

Key Terms

branching
computer-assisted instruction (CAI)
computer-controlled interaction
decision support system
human-controlled interaction

idiot savant
tool mode
tutee mode
tutor mode

Questions

1. What types of concerns might a teacher have in relation to the introduction of CAI into his or her school? How might the teacher deal with those concerns?

2. How, specifically, would you, as a teacher, respond to being told you should use computers in your teaching?

3. Analyze your response to Question 2. Which aspects of your response are emotional? Which are not? What values and beliefs underlie your response?

4. What is CAI, as defined in the text?

5. Based on what you know about computers and education so far, create your own definition of CAI. Compare your definition with those created by your classmates.

6. What is meant by the following terms as related to educational computer use: tutor mode, tool mode, tutee mode?

7. Which mode of computer use is most intriguing to you? Why?

8. Choose one mode of computer use and, in a paragraph, describe how you might incorporate software from that mode into a lesson (i.e., how would you incorporate tutorial software into a language arts lesson, or an instructional game into a social studies lesson?).

9. Briefly explain what Table 3–2 represents.

10. A parent explains that she does not want her child sitting mindlessly in front of a computer all day in your classroom. How do you respond?

References/Further Reading

Bitter, Gary G. *Computers in Today's World.* New York: John Wiley & Sons, 1984.

Coburn, P., P. Kelman, N. Roberts, T. Snyder, D. Watt, and C. Weiner. *Practical Guide to Computers in Education.* Reading, Mass.: Addison-Wesley Publishing Co., 1982.

Jay, Timothy B. "Computerphobia: What to Do About It." In Harper, Dennis O., and James H. Stewart. *RUN: Computer Education*, 2d ed. Monterey, Calif.: Brooks/Cole Publishing Co., 1986, pp. 94–95.

Kneppel, Doris M. "Don't Turn Off That Computer!" *The Computing Teacher* 12, no. 7 (1985):11.

Long, Larry. *Introduction to Computers and Information Processing.* Englewood Cliffs, N.J.: Prentice-Hall, 1984.

Piper, Norma C. "Starting from Square One." *The Computing Teacher* 12, no. 1 (1984):27.

Sanders, Donald H., and Stanley J. Birkin. *Computers and Management in a Changing Society.* New York: McGraw-Hill Book Co., 1980.

Suydam, Marilyn N. "Microcomputers in Mathematics Instruction." *Arithmetic Teacher* 32, no. 2 (1984):35.

Taylor, Robert P. ed. *The Computer in the School: Tutor, Tool, Tutee.* New York: Teachers College Press, 1980.

Thierauf, Robert J. *Decision Support Systems for Effective Planning and Control.* Englewood-Cliffs, N.J.: Prentice-Hall, 1982.

4

Computer-Assisted Instruction: Examples

TOPICS ADDRESSED

What are examples of tutor mode software for the categories of drill and practice, instructional games, tutorials, and simulations?

What are examples of tool mode software?

What functions do word processors, spreadsheets, and data base management systems perform?

What is an integrated software package?

What are some examples of tutee mode software?

How could the next generation of computers affect the use of computers in education?

OUTLINE

Introduction
Tutor Mode Examples
  Drill and Practice
  Instructional Games
  Tutorials
  Simulations
Tool Mode Examples
  Word Processors
  Spreadsheets
  Data Base Management Systems

Tutee Mode Examples
Establishing a Future Context
Conclusion
Key Terms
Questions
References/Further Reading

Introduction

The following is a discussion, with examples, of the different types of computer-assisted instruction (CAI) materials presented in the continuum shown in Table 3–1. No attempt is made to be comprehensive in the illustrations of the various types, since the amount of CAI software available is large and growing at a rapid rate. Nor is any attempt made to evaluate the software mentioned, since software evaluation is the main focus of Chapter 6. Further, although the commercial software presented is educationally sound and has gained some degree of use, the programs are not presented as ideals, or even as the best available within their category. Your instructor should be able to provide you with relevant hands-on experiences with software from any or all of the categories discussed. Such experiences will not only be informative in relation to the topic of CAI, but are also likely to stimulate ideas about potential teaching applications.

Tutor Mode Examples

Drill and Practice

For our purposes, the designation drill and practice will refer to any experience in which the student is presented with a number of problems, examples, or exercises aimed at either facilitating memorization or improving performance within a specific skill area. Further, the student should receive feedback on the responses given and perhaps, at the end of the session, a summary report on overall performance during the session.

Educators hold various views about the benefit derived by students from this type of instruction. Indeed, any educational environment restricted solely to drill and practice, whether computerized or not, is one that could easily be criticized as narrow and unsound. However, drill and practice exercises may be a valuable educational strategy when used to consolidate necessary skills. An example would be a drill on multiplication facts, after careful conceptual

"It's a <u>book</u>, Kevin. It has words and pictures in
it...you know...like on your computer."

© 1986; Reprinted courtesy of Bill Hoest and *PARADE* magazine instruction regarding multiplication as an arithmetic operation and in conjunction with other types of relevant experiences, such as physically grouping objects.

When drill and practice programs are carefully constructed and used as part of an overall program by teachers who realize both their positive and negative attributes, they can be well received and valuable. A computerized drill and practice package can offer a student the computer in the role of a patient, tireless, nonjudgmental presenter of material with the ability to adjust difficulty level as appropriate, based either on pupil performance or pupil (or teacher) selection. Further, the computer may, particularly if advantage is taken of the computer's ability to present graphics and sound, offer an engaging, interesting number of sessions to the student. The possibility of presenting a variety of examples related to the topic at hand—either the same series of examples presented in random sequence each time, or a selection of new, randomly generated examples—can help to maintain this interest.

Another possible plus is the feedback the student receives from the computer. If a student should respond incorrectly, that information can be immediately relayed to the student. This can serve to prevent a pattern of incorrect responses from developing before the student receives any information about his or her performance.

The first example of a drill and practice program is entitled *First Letter Fun* and is published by the Minnesota Educational Computing Corporation (MECC), which has its headquarters in St. Paul. MECC is a public corporation, owned by the state of Minnesota. Its mission is to provide educational computing products and services to schools in Minnesota, across the United States, in Canada, and other countries. MECC has an excellent reputation among educators for the collection of instructional courseware (educational computer programs accompanied by relevant printed materials), which it markets through various distributors. Two positive attributes of MECC courseware are the support materials provided and the fact that MECC courseware is the creation of practicing educators, of people who know about the practical as well as the theoretical aspects of actual learning situations in schools as they currently exist. (A two-disk set created by MECC for Apple II series microcomputers and distributed by Phi Delta Kappa national headquarters in Bloomington, Indiana, entitled *Computers in Teaching* is available. These disks, using portions of MECC courseware, introduce and demonstrate various topics relevant to the use of computers in teaching, including, among others, courseware options, classroom strategies, levels of skill, and materials to support lesson planning.)

First Letter Fun is for the preschool through first-grade level, and illustrates the basics of drill and practice software. The topic is reading readiness. The student sees an animated story on the screen. At certain points the story stops. An object from the story is enlarged on the screen and four letters appear in a box. (see **Figure 4–1**).

The student responds by typing the letter from among the four shown that matches the initial sound of the word represented by the picture, or by moving a hand-shaped pointer to the letter. If the correct response is entered, the correct spelling of the word appears below the picture (**Figure 4–2**).

Figure 4–1 A screen from *First Letter Fun*. The child may either type a letter on the keyboard or move the hand to point toward the desired letter.

If an incorrect letter is typed, that letter is crossed out on the screen (**Figure 4–3**).

A student is allowed to make three incorrect responses, after which all three incorrect letters are erased and the correct word appears under the picture. The word is displayed for a few seconds before the next example appears on the screen (**Figure 4–4**).

Four programs, each presenting ten unique pictures, are available for students. Care has been taken that incorrect letters for any given picture are generated randomly each time the picture is used and that confusing incorrect letters are avoided. (For instance, C for colt and P for pony will not appear with the picture of the horse, which is intended to elicit the correct response H for horse.)

The teacher may also choose to have the letters presented on the screen as upper or lower case. Although, since the letters appear only as upper case on the Apple keyboard, asking the student to match lower case letters on the screen with upper case letters on the keyboard may cause some difficulty.

Once a student has worked through all the exercises to be presented, the program gives a summary of the letters the student got right.

The second example of a drill and practice-type program is one written by a junior high school math teacher to provide addition practice for her students.

Figure 4–2 After the child chooses the correct response, the word associated with the picture is displayed.

Figure 4–3 When an incorrect letter is chosen the program responds by crossing it out.

Figure 4–4 If three incorrect responses are made, the incorrect letters are erased and the correct word appears below the picture.

Although teachers certainly do not have to write their own CAI materials, it shows what can be accomplished with some elementary programming skills. Also, it illustrates the point that teacher-produced software of this type does not have to be extraordinarily complex to yield beneficial results. Often what happens is that students, knowing the CAI material was produced by their teacher, take a great interest in interacting with the software and may in fact take an active interest in modifying or enhancing the program.

The program begins with a screen that has a picture of a rocket ship with the word ADD displayed on the ship. After a few seconds the screen automatically clears and the following directions appear:

```
THIS IS AN ADDING EXERCISE.
YOU WILL BE GIVEN 10 ADDING EXAMPLES.
DECIDE HOW DIFFICULT YOU WISH
YOUR PROBLEMS TO BE.

A.  VERY EASY
B.  AVERAGE
C.  DIFFICULT
```

The student then enters A, B, or C. Problems described as very easy yield sums not exceeding three places, average problems yield sums not exceeding four places, and difficult problems yield sums that will not exceed seven places. All problems are presented horizontally.

The student is then given ten problems, one at a time. If an incorrect response is entered, the machine responds as follows:

```
280 + 837 = 1217
THAT'S NOT CORRECT.
IF YOU DON'T SUCCEED, TRY, TRY AGAIN!
```

In the event of a wrong answer, there are a variety of responses available from which one is randomly selected and presented to the student. A different problem is then presented.

If a correct answer is entered, the screen clears and one of a group of several humorous pictures is displayed on the screen for several seconds. The screen then clears again and the next problem appears. Problems are presented randomly so that at any given level of difficulty, a variety of practice problems are offered. Once all ten have been attempted, the student may end the session or start the program again.

This program could easily have been expanded to repeat a problem that the student answers incorrectly and, in the event the problem is answered incorrectly twice, offer the correct solution.

The most positive aspect of this material is that it was home grown and therefore generated a good deal of student involvement. Also, since it was written by the teacher, aspects of the local environment could be included. (In this instance, the pictures presented when the students answered correctly played on the students' enjoyment of punning. In one picture a dog appears, wags its tail, and then the caption "That's nothing to wag about" is displayed.)

The quality of drill and practice programs has begun to improve in such areas as clarity of presentation of material, educational relevance, and potential for increased student involvement. Exploiting the strengths of the computer media, such as presenting engaging graphics or graphics and audio sequences, often aids in spurring student interest. The Sticky Bears series for young learners, published by Xerox, is a good example of software with interesting, meaningful graphics.

Instructional Games

Instructional games provide opportunities for students to receive instruction in a game setting. Instructional games (whether or not they are computer-based) are a type of educational strategy that (1) has as its purpose the achievement of one or more instructional goals or objectives; (2) presents a framework of rules within which the participants must function; (3) produces a winner as an outcome of the participants' interaction with the game; and (4) should, because of its "game" aspect, offer an engaging educational experience to participants.

Instructional games are often built into other types of CAI. For the purpose of consolidating learning, it is common for tutorial or simulation software to include an instructional game as part of the total package it presents. Often drill and practice programs will be presented in a game format. Because instructional games are often incorporated into other types of software, as well as existing as individual software packages, some people choose not to classify them as a separate category of CAI. For clarification purposes, and to present a clear definition of the characteristics of any instructional game, we will treat them as a separate category.

Educators have made use of noncomputerized instructional games for some time. Instructional games on the computer offer new opportunities for educa-

Input/Output

A number of individuals have, for many years, made contributions to the field of educational computing. One such person is Patrick Suppes, who, in his work at Stanford University, developed early examples of what CAI software could be. The following selection, from an article written more than twenty years ago, answers some questions about how computers will affect the schools. As you learn about computers in education, consider whether or not the following is true today, or will become true in the future. How does the vision of computer use outlined below compare with what you see in the schools and what you perceive as an ideal situation?

How will the computer change the teacher's role? Drill-and-practice systems will modify the teacher's role only slightly. What they will do is relieve teachers of some of the burden of preparing and correcting large numbers of individualized drill-and-practice exercises in basic concepts and skills and of recording grades.

The teacher will be more significantly affected by tutorial systems. Let us consider a concrete example: teaching addition and subtraction of fractions at the fourth grade level. The computer will provide the basic ideas and the procedure of how to add and subtract the fractions. The program will probably be written so that if a student does not understand the basic concepts on first presentation he will receive a second and possibly even a third exposure to them.

The new role of the teacher will be to work individually with all students on whatever problems and questions they may have in assessing and handling the new concepts. Tutorial systems allow teachers greater opportunity for personal interaction with students.

How will computer-assisted instruction affect teacher-administrator relationships? Teachers and administrators should be able to develop even closer relations in a setting where computers are used to aid instruction. The information-gathering capacity of the computer enables administrators to have a much more detailed profile and up-to-date picture of the strengths and weaknesses of each area of curriculum. As they develop skill in interpreting and using the vast amount of information about students provided by the computer, administrators and teachers should be able to work together more effectively for improvements in curriculum.

Is there a danger that the computer will impose a rigid and impersonal regime on the classroom and even replace teachers? Contrary to popular opinion, the computer's most important potential is to make learning and teaching *more* an individual affair rather than *less* so. Students will be less subject to regimentation and moving in lockstep because computer programs will offer highly individualized instruction. In our own work at Stanford, for example, we estimated that the brightest student and the slowest student going through our tutorial program in fourth-grade mathematics have an overlap of not more than 25 percent in actual curriculum.

The computer program is neither personal nor impersonal. The affect and feeling of the program will depend on the skill and perceptivity of those responsible for constructing it.

There seems to be little reason to think that computers will ever replace teachers or reduce the number of teachers needed. The thrust of computer-assisted instruction is to raise the quality of education in this country, not to reduce its cost. In any sort of computer-assisted instructional system used in classrooms in the near future, teachers will continue dealing with children on an individual basis and doing most of the things they are now doing during most of the school day with only slight changes.

Finally, we emphasize once again that no one expects that students will spend most of their school hours at consoles hooked up to computers. They will work at consoles no more than 20 to 30 percent of the time. All teachers everywhere recognize the help that books give them in teaching students. The day is coming when computers will receive the same recognition. Teachers will look on computers as a new and powerful tool for helping them to teach their students more effectively.

(Suppes, 1980)

tors. Good CAI in this area can offer the teacher some of the power to engage attention that is evident at any video arcade. Skills practiced and developed may range from simple math facts through the development of higher-order reasoning, analysis, and inference skills.

Facemaker, published by Spinnaker Software, is a software package that allows users to build a face by selecting, from a series of options for each category, a nose, mouth, eyes, ears, and hair (**Figure 4–5**).

The completed face may then be animated by pressing any of the following letters to achieve the result indicated. Each expression has a sound associated with it when animation occurs.

```
Press SPACE BAR
   for feature.
Press RETURN
   to choose.

  ⬡ MOUTH

  ⬬ EYES

  ⟫ EARS

  ⟩ NOSE

  ▚ HAIR

1 ① BUILD ② PROGRAM ③ GAME ④ CHOICES
```

Figure 4–5 A screen from *Facemaker*. Children build a face by selecting from options in each of the categories listed. The face may be animated with or without accompanying sound.

```
W—wink
F—frown
S—smile
C—cry
T—stick out tongue
E—ear wiggle
```

These movements may be activated one at a time, or the student may create a series of actions that will produce sustained animation. The game portion of this program consists of the computer selecting, initially, two actions that the face performs. The student must enter, in correct order, the appropriate letters for what the computer did. If the correct letters are entered, the computer repeats the last animation sequence, adding one more action. The player must continue to try and enter the correct letters for the animation shown until an incorrect sequence is entered. The score is equal to the number of expressions correctly repeated by the player. The object is to try for as high a score as possible.

The educational goal of the game aspect of this software is to provide practice in developing visual sequential and auditory sequential memory. Practice in developing visual sequential memory alone may be presented by turning off the audio portion of the animation sequence.

Math Blaster, published by Davidson and Associates, encompasses aspects of both instructional game and drill and practice CAI. The use of different types of CAI within one software package, as mentioned previously, is not uncommon and can lend variety and flexibility to computer-based materials.

Math Blaster provides instructional activities in five areas: addition, subtraction, multiplication, division, fractions, and decimals. A skill level ranging from 1 (lowest) to 5 (highest) may be selected for any of the areas available.

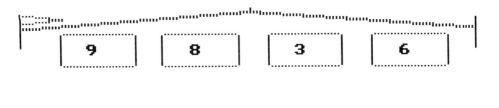

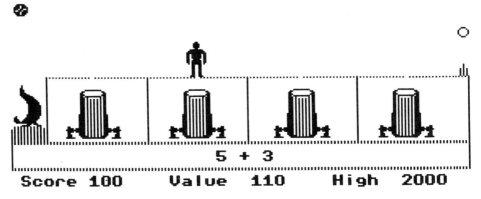

Figure 4–6 A screen from *Math Blaster*, a popular software package that includes aspects of both instructional game and drill and practice CAI.

Once an instructional area and skill level have been chosen, four activities are possible. The first is an automated flash card sequence (Look and Learn). The second and third are drills (Build Your Skill and Challenge Yourself), and the fourth is an arcade-type instructional game (Math Blaster). **Figure 4–6** is an example of the screen for the arcade game.

A math example appears in the box at the bottom of the screen. The student must solve the example, position the figure of the person under the correct answer, and then press the key that allows the figure to fall into the cannon directly below it. With accompanying sound effects, the figure is then blasted up to the correct answer. This progression continues until the balloon at the right of the screen has lowered itself to the bottom and is popped on the pin. Score is kept on the bottom line of the screen display.

Rocky's Boots, published by The Learning Company, is an excellent example of a learning game aimed at developing higher-order skills such as reasoning, logic, and analysis, as well as at teaching content related to computer literacy and science. This software package incorporates several excellent tutorial strands for concept introduction and learning how to play the game, as well as two strands of game activities.

In *Rocky's Boots* the object of the game is to create a machine. After learning how to build machines from component parts that are presented and identified as to function, the player is given the task of building a machine for a specific purpose.

Figure 4–8 shows a screen for the game. The machine to be built in this instance is one that will kick any figure that is not a circle displayed in the column to the right of the screen. The boot that will be hooked up to the machine is in the center of the screen. Remember, the student has previously

Some Favorites of Computer Educators

In a special issue on computers in education, Popular Computing *magazine asked five leading computer educators to describe three of their favorite software packages. The programs mentioned are primarily of use at the elementary and middle school levels.*

Richard Carter: *Anything as expensive as a computer ought to do things that can't be done in other ways. The ability to experiment is the hallmark of good educational software. It should function as a kind of intellectual playground, challenging a student's creativity and problem-solving skills.*

Green Globs is a math game that lets students try out, modify, and develop their ideas about how equations work. The computer draws eight randomly placed green spots on a standard coordinate grid displayed on the screen, and the student types equations which are immediately graphed on the grid. The object is to devise equations that, when graphed by the computer, will intercept the green spots. The program accepts almost any kind of equation—straight lines, ellipses, even equations with trigonometric functions. Through trial and error students quickly learn what parts of an equation control various aspects of a graph.

The Human Physiology Kit is actually a set of science lab tools that allow you to use a computer to collect and analyze data from the real world. With an electronic thermometer and a light meter, students explore heat and light phenomena in a variety of ways without getting bogged down in the tedious process of collecting and graphing data. The computer does that, leaving the students free to try a much wider range of experiments and perhaps do some "original" research.

The Milliken Word Processor, a writing tool designed for elementary school children, is suitable even for very young students to use because it has a simple command structure. Control keys move the cursor or delete characters without the need for frustrating switches from edit mode to write mode, and page breaks and format can be checked easily before the text is printed. Students can evaluate their work, reformulate their ideas, and make repeated changes without the laborious work of recopying every word.

Leroy Finkel: *These are my current favorites among the newer programs that not everyone has seen or that have not been widely reviewed. I prefer programs that allow changes to stored data or word lists so that they can be used in a variety of classroom situations.*

Create-a-Base is a productivity tool designed to teach middle school students how to use database programs. The program offers a blank database with nine fields available for the student to name, determine length, and identify as alphabetic or numeric before performing all the normal database functions of entering data, editing, sorting, searching, deleting, and printing. The package, which works well with younger or older students, too, includes a tutorial disk, a printed tutorial, and a guide for teachers. Students could also use the program at home to keep track of record albums, videotapes, and other such collectibles.

The Glass Computer teaches students what goes on *inside* a computer when a program is running. Graphic displays of inputting, outputting, and memory make the various operations clear. Students can run the program over and over at any speed to study programming concepts, including a limited subset of BASIC. Designed for grades 6 to 9 for use over six class periods, it is also appropriate for younger kids and for teacher training.

Word Spinning is a challenging crossword-puzzle, fill-in-the-word activity for one or two players that encourages word play and dictionary use. Each word entered is automatically checked against the built-in 38,000-word spelling checker, which also classifies words according to level of difficulty. The program makes effective use of graphics, helps develop both spelling skills and vocabulary, is fun to use, and with eight levels, can be used by a wide range of students both in school and at home.

Bobby Goodson: *My favorite software tends to be either versatile and open-ended or designed to make a very specific contribution to the learning process in one area. In either case it should be very well executed, taking advantage of the capabilities of a particular computer without going overboard on "bells and whistles."*

The Incredible Laboratory lets students create whimsical monsters by choosing from a list of available "chemical" ingredients. By trial and error the students learn the effects of each ingredient in combination with the others. By the second or third trial, they want to take notes and get organized. Drawing conclusions from available data is a natural outcome of the process. Used in the right context, where the stage is set for learning and the follow-up makes the learning real, this software can make a valuable contribution to education.

The Fact and Fiction Tool Kit is in a class by itself. The Story Maker portion of this package is a word processor, an illustrator, and a sketch pad that is easy to use and offers many creative possibilities. Students can choose from eight different type styles and can borrow illustrations from a prepared gallery or draw their own with a mouse or joystick. With this software the computer adds a new dimension to writing, especially for younger students.

Word Spinner is a "drill and practice" program that is definitely out of the ordinary. It provides

---

Figure 4–7 Several computer educators cite some of their favorite software packages.

word recognition and letter-combining practice in a fill-in-the-blanks format. The challenge lies in the large number of variations possible using just three- or four-letter words with two or three blanks. Word lists can be printed out as hard copy and used at home or when other children are using the computer.

Beth Lowd: *Software should allow kids to manipulate information in ways that were impossible before computers. The programs I have chosen put the user in control of what happens so that students of a wide range of ages and abilities can take charge of their own learning.*

Delta Drawing is an easy, friendly, aesthetically pleasing way to introduce teachers or kids to computers. Anyone can create computer graphics, erase, slide a drawing around the display screen, and print letters automatically. Single-key commands make it accessible to the young. The program can also make clear important computer concepts such as storage on disk, use of the printer, user control, saving programs, and using a program editor.

Rocky's Boots makes logic challenging and fun for students of all ages. The game tests their reasoning abilities with entertaining graphic devices such as moving objects, true/false sensors, and a visual flow of orange electricity to indicate where logic has broken down. Tutorials teach the basic moves; students can then set up any number of logical possibilities and test them against the rules of reason.

Survival Math has four simulations that require math skills for solving real-life problems. Hot Dog Stand calls for estimating ability; Smart Shopper Marathon deals with unit pricing; Travel Agent Contest requires planning and staying within a budget for a week-long trip; and Foreman's Assistant asks for detailed plans for purchasing materials needed to build a room onto a house, scheduling construction, and staying within a budget. The simulations ask students to make realistic use of math and emphasize planning, estimating, and problem solving.

Molly Watt: *The programs I have chosen fit the model that Seymour Papert calls microworlds. They provide a child with a territory to explore, a small piece of reality to learn about. Each deals with a different subject and allows a child to take on the role of writer or historian, rather than just learn facts about a subject. Such programs, of which there are more and more available, are patches of blue sky, making me excited about the future of educational computing.*

Quill is a language arts microworld designed to give writers ages 8 to 14 a "sense of purpose in their writing." Students create a library by writing up research projects and storing their reports on a disk to be shared by classmates. They index their work, update their research, even send electronic mail to classmates. Before writing they can use the program's planner to organize their ideas; then they can "publish" their work with the word processor.

Jenny of the Prairie is an adventure game featuring a plucky little girl separated from her wagon train. Her very survival depends on her preparations for braving winter blizzards on the prairie, gathering food, getting wood, and finding shelter. And all the time she must outrun wild animals, satisfy her thirst, and keep her wits about her. The program has three levels of difficulty and works well with one person or with groups of middle-school children.

Geography Search is a simulation game that provides a rare opportunity to take a field trip into history and learn something about sailing and geography as a crew member of an ancient ship searching for a new world. Using the computer as a data bank, crew members pool their observations about such matters as provisions and water supply, depth of the ocean, position of the North Star, and direction and velocity of the wind. Then, with the computer giving them data and tracking their position, they make decisions about setting their course, going ashore for food, and searching for gold. The program encourages groups of children to work together, pooling their knowledge to solve problems. It also strengthens their record-keeping, vocabulary, and research skills.

(Popular Computing, 1984)

Figure 4–7 Continued

worked through several tutorials to gain facility with moving the parts around the screen and to learn the concepts necessary for structuring machines. A completed machine is shown in **Figure 4–9**.

As each of the shapes travels through the column at right, "current" is turned on in one of the three sensors (diamond, circle, or triangle), depending on whether or not the object passing matches the sensor as to shape. The machine in this instance consists of a "not gate" hooked up to a circle sensor at the right and the boot at the left. The "not gate" will control when the "current"

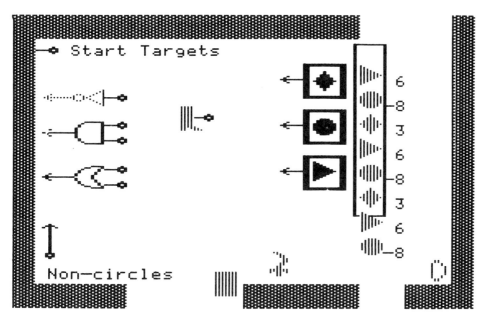

Figure 4–8 A screen from *Rocky's Boots* showing component parts the student may use to construct a machine.

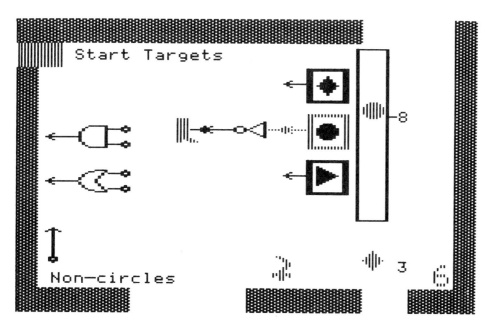

Figure 4–9 A completed machine in *Rocky's Boots*. The purpose of this machine is to kick any figure that is not a circle displayed in the column at the right of the screen.

flows. Because a "not gate" is defined as being "on," allowing current to flow to the boot, when an attached sensor is "off" and being "off," or disallowing current to flow to the boot, when an attached sensor is "on," this machine will boot all the non-circle shapes that pass by. Score is kept in the lower right-hand corner of the screen. If 24, a perfect score, is achieved, Rocky Raccoon comes out and does a dance accompanied by a tune.

This software package is of interest because of the higher-order skills it aims at developing, because of the quality of the software (graphics, etc.), and because it attempts, as part of the necessary rules that must be learned to play the game, to provide valid content instruction.

Where in the World Is Carmen Sandiego? published by Broderbund, is another instructional game. Its aim is to develop research skills and teach social studies concepts. The premise is that a member of Carmen Sandiego's gang has committed a crime and fled. The player assumes the role of detective and is supplied with a list of cities where the suspect may be. Working with clues about where the suspect may have fled, the player uses a copy of the *World Almanac and Book of Facts* to find the gang member. One copy of the *World Almanac and Book of Facts*, published by the Newspaper Enterprise Association, is supplied with the software. The player has only a limited amount of time to analyze clues and solve the crime.

Tutorials

The aim of a tutorial program is to instruct the student by engaging him or her in a dialogue related to the concept, skill, or information to be taught. Ideally, once the dialogue is begun, the course of instruction proceeds based on the student's response within the dialogue. Many tutorials have been computerized implementations of previous attempts in education and educational psychology to develop teaching machines and programmed instruction. As such, the intricacy of the dialogue established would depend greatly on the programmer's ability to foresee and make instructional provisions for the wide range of possible student responses. Because this is, realistically, impossible to do with current technology, the choice is usually made to restrict the student responses, for example, by using a multiple choice or matching format within which students must respond.

Theoretically, once a dialogue is established, the student will, at any given point in the tutorial, receive the instruction needed to continue progressing successfully through the material to be covered. If the computer should judge that the student has not mastered the material presented, the program will branch either to material needed to reteach the concept under consideration or to material aimed at presenting a prerequisite skill or concept.

As mentioned earlier, most tutorials, especially those available on microcomputers today, do not provide the type of complex branching that theory promises. This is partly due to the hardware limitations of contemporary microcomputers and partly due to the difficulty of writing complex tutorials. Further, the notion of the computer making this type of complex decision, regarding what will be taught, when and how, can lead us into the realm of artificial intelligence. This field deals with the idea that machines may be made to emulate what we view as human intelligence. The idea of applying artificial intelligence to education is quite different from what historically has been referred to as programmed instruction and is mentioned again at the end of the chapter.

Tutorials do exist as viable CAI materials and may be used to supplement instruction at a variety of levels. Tutorials on microcomputers offer instruction enhanced by graphic displays, animation sequences, and relatively simple but effective dialogues that provide immediate feedback to students regarding their progress. Within the limitations cited earlier, these programs may reteach material in a concise manner if student responses should indicate that a concept has not been grasped. More complex tutorials are sometimes used on larger computers in higher education and business.

One advantage of computer-based tutorials, and indeed of any CAI, is that the computer is a patient teacher, providing instruction through which a student may move at his or her own pace and often without embarrassment.

In the previously mentioned *Rocky's Boots*, the rules of the game, which incorporate important concepts related to logic, are presented in a tutorial format. At key points, practice examples are built into the tutorial to aid in developing the skills and concepts necessary to play the game. These examples are most interesting in that they provide for the graphic on-screen manipulation of the component parts of the machine to be built. This allows students to test concepts that have been introduced.

Computer Literacy, part of the PLATO Educational Software materials available for microcomputers and published by Control Data Corporation, is an example of a microcomputer-based tutorial. Instruction takes place in six areas, any of which may be selected from the program's main menu. The areas include the following:

- Review of Instructions

- Examples of Computer Uses

- Limitations of Computers

- The Nature of Computers

- Where Computers Came From

- How Computers Affect Us

Ample use is made throughout the program of techniques to involve the student in a dialogue. Concepts are presented clearly and concisely, and students engage in such activities as (a) an instructional game to illustrate conditional statements, a basic principle of computer programming, and (b) an interactive question-and-answer dialogue to reinforce previously presented concepts. Further, good use is made of computer animation to illustrate important points. **Figure 4–10** is an example of part of an animated sequence that illustrates the literal-minded nature of machines. The human has just requested the robot to mix two chemicals together, which the robot blithely did, with the resulting explosion.

The Milton Bradley Company publishes software packages, including packages on division skills, mixed numbers, and decimal skills, that make use of some aspects of tutorial CAI, as well as drill and practice and computer-managed instruction techniques. As an example, in the decimal skills package (see **Figure 4–11**), students are lead, step by step, through the addition of decimals. If an incorrect response is entered, the computer prompts the student with an appropriate hint; if two incorrect responses are entered, the computer fills in the answer and proceeds to the next step. This occurs during the instructional mode. Three modes are available: instructional, practice, and master. Criteria for each level may be set by the teacher, and the computer will

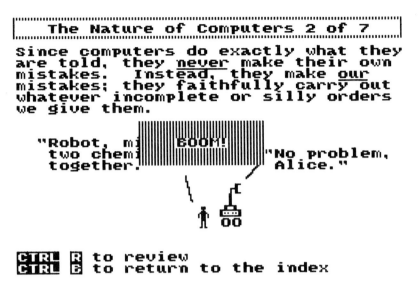

Figure 4–10 A screen from *Computer Literacy*. Alice has asked the computer-controlled robot to mix together two chemicals. The computer follows the directions without question. Unfortunately for Alice, the two chemicals create an explosion.

upgrade the mode of the examples presented on subsequent sessions if the student should demonstrate the teacher-defined criteria.

Simulations

A simulation is a model of an actual situation that is achieved by identifying variables relevant to the real-life situation and mathematically defining the relationships between those variables. This model of a real-world event, such as the experience of flying an airplane, can be programmed for a computer. An individual may then sit at the computer and work through the simulation of the real event, responding to the various conditions that might occur and seeing the effects on the situation being simulated.

Business people and scientists regularly use simulations for various purposes, as reported in Bitter (1984).

Simulation has been used successfully on mainframe computers for years. In simulation, a problem is reduced to mathematical terms. Then computations are done on the problem, including known and unknown conditions. The results predict an outcome that would not otherwise have been known. For instance, a company may plan to install a new inventory system. Before final installation the new system can be simulated to find out how it will work once it is operative. Inventory control over a period of several years can be simulated in a matter of hours. The company saves money by being able to alter certain aspects of a proposed system before time has been spent installing a faulty system.

The space program utilized simulation to predict the environment of outer space without actually requiring a human to experience each situation. Geological surveys are done by simulation to discover areas of the

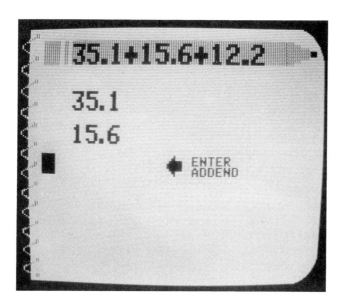

Figure 4–11 A sample screen from *Decimal Skills*.

world rich in certain minerals by reducing the known areas rich in minerals to mathematical formulas and applying these formulas to unknown situations. Simulation is now being used in innovative ways on mainframe computers as well as on smaller systems. (pp. 159–160)

One value of using simulations with students is that they may experience situations to which they might not otherwise be exposed. This can lead to an awareness of the important variables, and their relationships, operative within such situations. Also, the pressures and time constraints under which decisions must be made can be experienced, and practice can be gained with various individual or group decision-making processes. All this may be done in a safe manner; you can crash the flight simulator 100 times and walk away, not so with the airplane.

Of great importance in producing good simulations is the accuracy of the model that is used to define the real-world situation. The person who does the modeling for the simulation must have a valid handle on what happens in the real world and must discover, select, and relate accurate variables in a meaningful way. A simulation that did not accurately reflect that which it was supposed to simulate would be of little value.

Natural Selection is a combination tutorial and simulation published by the Education Materials and Equipment Company. From the main menu the student is offered three choices:

1. Gene Frequencies in Population

2. Changes in Moth Population in Industrial England

3. Experiments on the Effect of Pollution on a Moth Population

Gene Frequencies in Population presents some background information related to natural selection and offers a simulation of the relative frequencies of

Classroom Computer Learning's Ten Best Programs for 1986

Various periodicals and organizations present annual awards for and compile yearly lists of what they consider exemplary educational software. One such list is offered by the magazine Classroom Computer Learning. *Its selections for the ten best programs of 1986 are presented below. Do any of these programs sound as if they might be of use in your current (or future) teaching?*

Bank Street Musicwriter Students with little or no musical background will be able to compose music very quickly with this program, which is also sophisticated enough for advanced music students and allows experimentation with sound. Standard music notation is used to enter up to three notes at any one time.

A section of music fundamentals and a tutorial on how to use the major features make this ideal for beginners. Technical tips are given for advanced users. The menu-driven program is easy to use, and several sample pieces are included for the user's enjoyment. The documentation is clearly written and answers many questions before they are asked.

Mindscape, Inc. Commodore 64 [version tested] Atari 600/800XL. One disk with backup: $49.95. (Elementary-high school.) For a more detailed description, see the review in *Classroom Computer Learning*, January 1986, p. 24.

Bank Street Storybook Using this program and a joystick, Koala Pad, or mouse, students can create stories illustrated with full-color graphics and even simple animation. A built-in word processor allows placement of text anywhere on the screen. Stories can be printed out or displayed page by page on the computer screen. Several examples of stories are provided. In addition to a tutorial ac-

tivity with a step-by-step process for creating a story and pictures, there are also handy on-line tutorial files to provide help.

Mindscape, Inc. Apple II series [version tested] Commodore 64, IBM PC. One disk with backup: $49.95. (Intermediate-high school.) For a more detailed description, see the review in *Classroom Computer Learning*, February 1985, p. 14.

Cardiovascular Fitness Lab With this sophisticated package, students are able to monitor their own and fellow students' cardiovascular activity using a probe that can be attached to either an earlobe or a finger. Physiological data can be recorded on the screen or printed out. The user can explore how a heart functions under different conditions, following the suggested experiments in the guide. This program, in addition to being informative, demonstrates use of the computer as a scientific tool.

HRM Software. Apple II series [version tested] Commodore 64, IBM PC. One disk, interface box, heart rate sensor: $75.00 (Junior high-high school.)

ChipWits This program teaches programming concepts by having the user program robots (ChipWits) which then explore eight different environments. If they are programmed well, they survive; if not, they can be reprogrammed for another try. ChipWits are programmed in IBOL (Icon Based Operating Language), a picture language which is simple enough for children to understand, but complex enough to challenge adults. Critical thinking and problem-solving skills are developed and sharpened.

Brainpower, Inc. Apple Macintosh [version tested] Apple II series. One disk: $49.95 for Mac version, $39.95 for Apple. (Intermediate-high school.)

Geometric Supposer: Triangles A student is able with ease to explore, measure, and hypothesize

about the relationships in triangles, making constructions on the computer that the program remembers and can repeat on any other triangle. A student can thus check whether a construction is dependent on that specific property or whether the results can be generalized. This program will facilitate discovery learning in geometry and make students look at geometry in a totally different way. An extensive manual includes teaching suggestions and worksheets.

Sunburst Communications, Inc. Apple II series with 64K. One disk with backup: $99.00 (Junior high-high school.) For a more detailed description, see the review in *Classroom Computer Learning*, April/May 1985, p. 19.

Magic Slate An excellent program for people of all ages, easy to use with many sophisticated features. The program consists of three word processors: a 20-column format with large letters for very young or visually impaired students; a 40-column format with standard word processing commands and the ability to print in seven different type styles; and an 80-column format (requires an 80-column card) that delivers a powerful professional word processor. The 80-column version allows the user to edit two files in two windows at the same time. The excellent 200-page manual provides teaching ideas for primary grades through high school, as well as applications for the split-screen version. Reproducible handbooks for the 20- and 40-column versions are included.

Sunburst Communications, Inc. Apple II series. Two disks with backups: $89.95. (Primary-high school.)

Muppet Learning Keys This package includes the Muppet Learning Keys, which is a colorful alternate keyboard suitable for very young children, and one disk containing three programs that use the keyboard.

Figure 4–12 Several computer educators cite some of their favorite software packages.

The 14-by-15-inch keyboard, activated by touch, displays keys in alphabetical order, a natural order for children ages 3–7. Numbers are displayed on a ruler and colors appear as a paint set. The keyboard is sturdy and can be held in the child's lap.

Using the software that accompanies the keyboard, young students learn to recognize letters, numbers, and colors. In one program when the letter "A" is pressed, an alligator appears on the screen; when a "3" is pressed, 3 alligators appear; and when the color "red" is pressed, the alligators all turn red. Pressing the "go" button animates the characters on the screen. Students control the speed and level of difficulty of the tasks, making the program a tremendously powerful tool.

Varied graphics and sound keep both young and older children fascinated. A creative use of the computer's unique capabilities.

Sunburst Communications, Inc. Apple IIe [version tested] Commodore 64, IBM PCjr. Keyboard plus one disk: $69.95. (Primary.)

The Newsroom An excellent, well-designed program that allows students to create, edit and illustrate their own newspaper. Because of its complexity, the program does take some time to learn, but the end results are well worth the effort. Students become familiar with journalism as they create and organize their ideas according to the suggestions in the documentation. Included in the program are five different font styles and a library of cartoon-type pictures which can be added to the text.

Springboard Software, Inc. IBM PC and Apple II series [version tested]: $59.95. Commodore 64 and 128. Two disks: $49.95. (Intermediate-high school.) For a more detailed description, see the review in *Classroom Computer Learning*, September 1985, p. 34.

The Other Side The Other Side is a two-team computer learning game about global conflict resolution. Students experience how conflict evolves and the ways in which two opposing sides negotiate, and eventually compromise, to achieve a common goal. Players on the same side must learn to cooperate with each other, working together to balance long-term and short-term goals. This is the first piece of educational software designed to run on either a single computer or two computers set up in different locations. The program should instill in students a greater understanding of the complexities and subtleties of international peace negotiations.

Tom Snyder Products, Inc. Apple II series. One disk plus backup: $69.95. (Junior high and high school.) For a more detailed description, see the review in *Classroom Computer Learning*, April/May 1985, p. 20.

The Voyage of the Mimi This outstanding multimedia learning package, which includes video tapes, books and computer software, introduces students to scientific and mathematical concepts as they participate in whale research. Video tapes include thirteen, 15-minute dramatic episodes about the people and events on a research voyage to study the humpback whale in the Gulf of Maine. An additional thirteen, 15-minute documentary "expeditions" deal with scientific and mathematical concepts encountered in the drama. The themes of the four learning modules (software packages and student guides) are derived from the video programs: Maps and Navigation, Introduction to Computing with Turtle Graphics, Whales and Their Envionment, and Ecosystems.

The software emphasizes the use of the computer as a tool in solving or performing specific tasks, while the book *The Voyage of the Mimi* is an illustrated version of the video tapes with supplementary activities. The extensive guide includes lesson plans, background information, blackline masters, and charts. While each component is well done and could stand alone, together they make a superb learning tool. (The video segments continue to be broadcast over PBS stations nationwide.)

Holt, Rinehart, and Winston. Apple II series with 64K. The price of the entire package (video, books, and modules), including 25 copies of each of the 5 Student Guides, is $987.16; components can also be purchased separately. (Intermediate-junior high.)

(Brady, 1986)

Figure 4–12 Continued

various combinations of dominant and recessive genes over a period of years. The second choice, Changes in Moth Population in Industrial England, presents, using text, graphic displays, and animation, the case history of a moth population in England during the nineteenth century. The third choice, Experiments on the Effect of Pollution on a Moth Population, offers a simulation in which students may test their understanding of natural selection. In this section of the program, students are presented with the opportunity to modify or accept various parameters associated with natural selection pertaining to the moth population they have just studied. The computer then constructs a data table that shows the effects on the moth population for the specifications entered by the student. A graph of the table may then be obtained.

President Elect, published by Strategic Simulations, Inc., is a political simulation that allows the participants to contest any presidential election from 1960 through 1980. Participants may use actual historical candidates or may make up candidates of their own. Care has been taken to allow participants to manipulate many variables related to an actual presidential campaign. Such variables include determination of domestic and foreign conditions (gross national product, unemployment, inflation, war, or peace), foreign-trip scheduling for the candidate, expense management related to advertising of various types, decisions regarding campaign stops, and judgment about whether or not to debate. If the participant makes up his or her own candidate, the computer asks a series of twenty-five questions on issues to determine the candidate's ideological persuasion. If a simulation of any of the historical campaigns is chosen, the computer furnishes and uses historically accurate information for the variables. The following, from the rules documentation for the simulation (Strategic Simulations, 1980), illustrates the care that has been taken to attempt to make the simulation as realistic as possible:

> All candidates, in turn, express their desire to debate or not to debate. This expressed desire has nothing to do with whether the opponent is willing to or not; it merely indicates that the candidate has, during the week, indicated that he would be willing to debate. If a candidate is willing to debate but he knows his opponent is unwilling, he should still indicate his willingness, as he will receive a small sympathy vote for his frustration. (p. 5)

MECC offers a social studies-related simulation entitled *Voyageur*. This program attempts to model the experience of fur traders who traveled by canoe during the eighteenth century in the woods of northern Minnesota. The goal of the simulation is to travel from Grand Portage on Lake Superior to Rainy Lake in the shortest possible time with the greatest number of furs. Students choose various resources with which to load their canoe (i.e., clothes, gunpowder, wine, flour and sugar, tobacco, trading goods, and pemmican). Hazardous events that may have taken place on this type of trip during the eighteenth century are randomly simulated and students must respond to them. The effects of their choices are reported in status reports as they continue along their journey.

Tool Mode Examples

The use of the computer in the tool mode, as outlined earlier, provides the student and teacher with an extension of human capabilities in various areas. There are certainly times when this extension can yield a deeper understanding of concepts and relationships than might be arrived at without a computer. Tool software includes statistical packages that will automatically perform common statistical tests and generate graphs of user-supplied data. For example, using a statistical package during a project that requires data analysis, more time may be gained for analyzing and understanding data by allowing the computer to do the computations needed to prepare the data for analysis.

Reactions and Research

Computer Education Research: A Blinder for the Misguided
by **Twila Slesnick**

Twila Slesnick, in an article originally published in 1984, offers some cautions about the state of computer education research. In the following excerpt a summary of the research is also presented, as well as insights into the potential of computers in education. How does this author's interpretation of the research compare with the points made by Suydam in the Reactions and Research section of Chapter 3?

Use of computers in classrooms has been justified with claims of increased student achievement and revolutionary new content and instruction. These claims, however, are far from the truth and the most appropriate uses of computers in the classroom have made little headway.

For nearly three decades now, the use of computers in classrooms has been justified with claims of increased student achievement, new and vital curriculum content and revolutionary instructional methods. Examination of the research literature and some classroom observation reveals the true status quo—computers are having very little impact on the curriculum.

THE NATURE OF THE RESEARCH

Computer education research is notable for its abundance, its poor quality, and its inconclusiveness. In education there are many unquantifiable variables that might affect the outcome of a study, some of which cannot even be identified. Since it is virtually impossible to control all variables, it is difficult to identify causal relationships between treatments and outcomes.

There are other problems with the research as well. Populations are generally not selected randomly since researchers must often work with intact classes. The sample sizes are usually small, the duration of the studies is often too short for reliable results, and the Hawthorne effect (achievement as a result of being under concerned observation) is rarely controlled.

In addition to the methodological problems that abound, the literature is full of misleading summary articles. For example, a number of articles report that, in general, students learn more when using a computer. To many of us, this would indicate that computer-assisted instruction (CAI) is a viable alternative to traditional instruction. However, a closer look at the individual studies reveals that indeed students learn more, but only when CAI is used as a supplement to traditional instruction, not as a replacement for it. What is also missing from these articles is the fact that virtually any supplement to the curriculum will bring about increases in student achievement. . . .

SUMMARY OF THE RESEARCH

From the individual studies and summaries of the literature described above, and in spite of scattered individual studies which report conflicting results, the following points come across clearly:

1. In the majority of studies where CAI replaces traditional instruction, there is no difference in achievement between the two groups.

2. On the other hand, there is also no evidence that CAI is detrimental to achievement.

3. Drill and practice in arithmetic does indeed improve computational facility. It should be noted, however, that this is true whether or not a computer is being used.

4. In the case of drill and practice programs, there appears to be some evidence that rate of learning (or mastery of rote skills) increases with the use of CAI.

5. There appears to be some evidence that students retain less of what they learn through CAI although this area needs more investigation.

6. CAI is consistently found to be effective as a supplement to instruction. Again, however, this is true of virtually any supplement to the curriculum, whether or not it is computer-based.

7. Finally, use of the computer does seem to improve attitudes toward the computer, but not necessarily toward the subject matter under study.

THE TRUE REVOLUTIONARY POTENTIAL OF COMPUTERS

This all reflects poorly on the path we have chosen for computer education. But there is another path—one that leads to a new curriculum with new goals for students. If, for example, the computer were to assume a natural and unique position in the classroom, much extraneous content would disappear from the curriculum leaving a large gap into which curriculum developers could drop new and more appropriate topics and activities.

Let's take the mathematics curriculum as an example. We could painlessly eliminate pencil and paper computation from the cirriculum beginning with addition and continuing through calculus. The availability of calculators and computers obviates the need to teach mathematical skills that machines handle more efficiently. For example, in high school, students will still learn algebra, but instead of solving odd-looking equations using mysterious operations, they will give the computer equations to graph, and look for patterns until they can predict for themselves what a particular equation should look like. They will learn what physical event an equation models or how to match equations with physical phenomena.

The curriculum will have some brand new content, too. Computer science, a broad new discipline for both elementary and high school, might include programming, electronics, or the investigation of real world software tools like word processors, spreadsheets, computer-aided design programs, data base management programs and instrument-monitoring software.

Perhaps the most important new area of emphasis in both elementary and secondary mathematics will be the invention and study of algorithms. Its purpose will not be computation, but to encourage the search for patterns and the generalization of those patterns to other situations and other problems.

CONCLUSION

Our role as teacher is no longer simply to introduce new ideas and concepts. The long range goal of education must be to help students develop those skills and become familiar with those tools that allow them to take more responsibility for their own learning—both what they learn and how they learn it. These tools and skills will also be of critical importance in the world outside of the classroom.

Consequently, computer use in the schools should closely parallel use in society. Our goal should be to make the student more effective and efficient at acquiring knowledge. As the amount of available information increases, students can no longer afford to spend valuable classroom time learning obsolete skills for which a machine is better suited.

(Slesnick, 1986)

Also, the ability to quickly generate a graph of data, whether from a fifth-grade social studies project or a twelfth-grade biology project, may yield student insights not available without the readily obtainable graph.

Most important in relation to the use of a computer as a tool in this way, educators must distinguish between the teaching of computational skills and the teaching of skills related to data analysis. At some time and place students must master basic skills. Students should not, however, be tied to hand calculation when the object of a project is other than the teaching of some basic calculation skill. If the intent of the lesson is to understand the relationship between temperature and the volume of gas in a cylinder, time is better spent interpreting computer-generated tables and graphs related to the experiment performed than in doing hand calculations to turn raw data into tables and graphs. This assumes that the students have previously mastered the basic skills needed to do the hand calculations if a situation arises in which it is necessary or desirable to calculate by hand.

Spreadsheets, word processors, graphing programs, and data base management systems (sometimes referred to as file management systems) are other examples of tool software commonly used in the schools. Sometimes one software package contains several functions in an integrated fashion; such programs are called integrated software packages. *Appleworks*, published by Apple Computer and popular on Apple II series computers, and *Lotus 1–2–3*, published by Lotus Development Corporation and a favorite in the business world, are examples of integrated software packages. Word processors, spreadsheets, and data base management systems are described briefly below.

Word Processors

Word processors allow the computer to be used to enter and store text. A user sits at the computer and types in text to create a document. Mistakes are easily corrected because any error can be retyped correctly, or new words, sentences, or paragraphs inserted as desired, and the computer will automatically adjust the text in the rest of the document accordingly. In a similar fashion, letters, words, sentences, and paragraphs can be deleted. Also, text can be moved from one location in the document to another. The ability to manage the written word effortlessly makes editing and revision a task less tied to manual labor than when writing by hand or on an old-style typewriter. Some word processors have built-in spelling checkers. Others work with separate spelling checker programs. A program that checks spelling compares each word in a document with a dictionary contained within the program (an 80,000-word dictionary contained within a program is not uncommon). When a questionable word is located, it is presented to the user, who has the option of changing it or leaving it as it is (perhaps the word is spelled correctly but is not listed in the dictionary, such as a person's name). Sometimes the user has the option of asking the program for suggested spellings for the word. If the spelling of the word is changed, the user may elect for all identical occurrences of the misspelled word to be corrected at once within the document.

Word processors are used by teachers to manage instruction by creating materials and tests for the classroom. They are also used by students to create and revise written work in a variety of subject matter areas. Milone (1986) provides a series of word processor-based activities for the classroom. Popular word-processing and spelling-checker packages in the schools include *Bank Street Writer* and *Bank Street Speller*, published by Broderbund; *PFS:Write*, produced by Software Publishing; the *Milliken Word Processor*, published by Milliken; and *Apple Writer II*, produced by Apple Computer. *Sensible Speller*, a product of Sensible Software, is a popular spelling-checker program that works with a number of word-processing programs.

Spreadsheets allow a user to enter data in columns and rows and then define relationships between the data. Spreadsheets are a common tool in business in both their computerized and manual forms. An example of a simple computerized spreadsheet is given in **Figure 4–13**. The letters across the top of the spreadsheet refer to columns; the numbers down the side of the spreadsheet refer to rows. The intersection of a column and a row is termed a cell. For example, the intersection of column A with row 3 is cell A3, where, in this instance, the word Sales has been entered.

Spreadsheets

	A	B	C	D	E	F	G	H
1				Bake Sale				
2			Week1	Week2	Week3	Week4		
3	Sales		35.00	40.00	45.00	55.00		
4	Expenses							
5		Supplies	5.00	7.00	8.00	10.00		
6		Ads	3.00	5.00	5.00	3.00		
7								
8		Total	8.00	12.00	13.00	13.00		
9	Weeks						Total	
10	Profit		27.00	28.00	32.00	42.00	Profit	129.00

Figure 4–13 An example of data entered into a spreadsheet designed to track expenses and profits for a bake sale.

This spreadsheet has been set up to record the weekly sales, expenses, and profit of a class bake sale, as well as the total profit from the sale. The power of a spreadsheet comes from being able to set up relationships between the cells. In this instance, the profit for each week has been defined as equaling the week's sales minus the week's expenses. This can be expressed in terms of the cell names. For instance, the total expenses for Week1 appear in cell C8. A calculation has been set up for the spreadsheet such that the value in C8 will equal the value in C5 plus the value in C6 (C8 = C5 + C6). Therefore, whatever values are in C5 and C6 will be summed and the result automatically placed in C8. In a similar fashion the calculation of the week's profit has been set up by the expression C10 = C3 − C8. The ability to define relationships in this way allows the person using the spreadsheet to answer "what if" questions. This is so because anytime a new value is entered in a cell of the spreadsheet, all other values are automatically recalculated according to the relationships defined in the spreadsheet. If the teacher wanted to see how a projected increase in amount spent on ads would affect the week's profit for Week1 and the total profit, she would just change the number in cell C6 (Ads) and the amount in cells C8 (Total), C10 (Weeks Profit), and H10 (Total Profit) would all automatically be recalculated.

Spreadsheets are used by teachers for management purposes (to keep track of grades, expenses for trips, sales, accounts for clubs, etc.). They are also used to teach mathematical concepts and for training in business education courses. Large spreadsheet programs may provide for spreadsheets of up to 256 columns by 2,048 rows. Integrated software packages such as *Appleworks* and *Lotus 1–2–3* contain powerful spreadsheet programs.

Data Base Management Systems

A data dase management system (DBMS) is used to store and retrieve data in a variety of ways. A DBMS allows a user to build a file of related records called a data base. Each record is made up of a series of fields. **Figure 4–14** is an example of a record comprised of a series of fields. This is a record for an elementary school student. The fields that make up the record are Last Name, First Name, Street, City, State, Zip, Phone, Birthday, Mothers Name, Mothers Work Phone, Mothers Occupation, Fathers Name, Fathers Work Phone, Fathers Occupation, Brothers, Sisters, and Comments. For each student in his class, the teacher would enter the relevant data in each field. The entire set of filled-in fields would be the student's record. The entire set of records for the teacher's class (one record for each student) would be the class data base. A DBMS allows the user to create and store records and then manipulate the data in the records in different ways. For instance, if the teacher wants a list of all students with birthdays in a particular month, he would simply request the information from the DBMS and a report listing all those students would be provided. If the teacher needs a list of all parents employed as programmers, such a list could easily be generated.

The power of a DBMS lies in the flexibility it provides for storing and manipulating data. Data base management systems are used by teachers with students as tools to manipulate data in many ways, including recording data from experiments in science and social studies. The Computers in the Class-

```
Last Name _____   First Name _____
Street _____
City _____ State ____ Zip _____
Phone _____ Birthday _____
Mothers Name _____ Mothers Work Phone _____
Mothers Occupation _____
Fathers Name _____ Fathers Work Phone _____
Fathers Occupation _____
Brothers _____
         _____
Sisters  _____
         _____
Comments _____
         _____
         _____
         _____
         _____
```

Figure 4–14 An example of the screen layout containing the fields that make up a record for a student.

room feature for this chapter offers some ideas for using a DBMS to develop research skills. Popular data base management systems in the schools include *Bank Street Filer*, published by Broderbund; *PFS:File*, produced by Software Publishing; and the DBMS included in *Appleworks*, published by Apple Computer.

Tutee Mode Examples

The use of the computer as an object of instruction, as something that may be taught, will be dealt with specifically in Chapters 8 through 13. Examples of environments in which the computer may be used in the tutee mode are the previously mentioned programming languages of Logo, Pascal, and BASIC. These and other programming languages provide building blocks that the student may use to instruct the computer to accomplish a wide variety of tasks.

Establishing a Future Context

As outlined in Chapter 1, today's computers have specific strengths that may be used by society in a variety of ways. As Long (1984) states,

Today's computers can simulate many human capabilities, such as reaching, grasping, calculating, remembering, comparing numbers, and drawing. Researchers are working to expand these capabilities and, therefore, the power of computers to include the ability to reason, to learn, to strive for self-improvement, and to simulate human sensory capabilities. This general area of research is known as artificial intelligence (AI).

Computer systems with artificial intelligence can see, smell, feel, write, speak and interpret spoken words. To varying degrees, these artificial intelligence capabilities are possible with current technologies. (p. 468)

The notion that computers may, in the near future, be able to emulate those attributes we associate with intelligence in humans is frightening to some. It is

Computers in the Classroom

More and more, teachers are using tool mode software with their students. Gwen Solomon, in her article "Electronic Research," offers the following activities to help introduce students to both reference sources and data base software.

THREE RESEARCH ACTIVITIES

When students know their tools—both reference sources and software—they'll be able to make good use of computers in preparing research papers. Here are some activities that will introduce students to both.

1. Introducing Reference Sources.

To have students learn about traditional reference materials, have them create a chart covering the basic reference texts in the school library. Across the top of the chart, place the headings "Source," "Type of Information," "Arrangement," and "Special Features." Give students a list of basic reference sources in the library, and have them fill in the three remaining categories. A sample entry might look like this:

Source: The World Almanac

Type of Information: facts on people, place, science, sports, music, art, government and politics, literature, entertainment, business

Arrangement: by subject

Special Features: published yearly, summary of year's news, index by topic and name in front, quick index in back.

2. Creating a Data Base of Resources.

A variation of the above activity can be used to create a computer data base of library resources that students can use to start their research.

- Using a data base program, design a form with the fields used above: "Source," "Type of Information," "Arrangement," and "Special Features." You may also want to add a new field, "Location" for students to indicate where the source is stored. Locations might include various classrooms, the school library, or a public library. Students might also indicate the Dewey Decimal number or the Library of Congress number of the source, if the source is cataloged in that way.

- Create a list of topics that students can use to fill in the "Type of Information" field. Each entry must describe information the same way, in order for students to be able to search the file later. A list of topics might include these: *animals, art, automobiles, business, careers, entertainment, geography, government and politics, hobbies, literature, music, people, places, religions, resources, science and technology, sports, world records.*

- Assign each student a different resource, or resources, to catalog. Have them type the information on their resource into the data base.

- Then have the students do some practice searches on their data bases. For example, ask students to locate the resources they would go to for a biography of President Reagan. (They would search for every entry with "people" or "government and politics" in the "Type of Information" field.)

3. Using Data Bases for Note Taking.

After students have started their research, have them create and use some simple data base files to organize their notes. Using material collected on their topic, they can practice searching and sorting their file to come up with a rough outline for their research paper. Have them type up their outline using a word processing program.

A data base for research notes might use these fields:

- **Topic:**
- **Subtopic:**
- **Source:**
- **Page:**
- **Notes:**

A data base of sources that can be used in preparing a bibliography might use these fields:

For Books

- **Author(s):**
- **Title:**
- **City of Publication:**
- **Publisher:**
- **Year Published:**
- **Pages:**

For Periodicals

- **Author(s):**
- **Title of Article:**
- **Title of Periodical:**
- **Volume and Number:**
- **Pages:**

(Solomon, 1986)

important to remember that, no matter what level of artificial intelligence may be achieved, the computer will still be a creation of human beings to be used in the service of human beings. As Long (1984) notes: "Humans will always be the masters of computers. Any intelligence given a computer is the gift of a more intelligent human being" (p. 469).

Hardware is intimately related to software in that the limitations inherent in computer hardware dictate, to a great extent, what software may be written to make it perform various functions. As the quality of the hardware increases, the quality of the functions it may be programmed to perform increases.

Feigenbaum and McCorduck (1983) provide a description of current and possible future developments in the field of artificial intelligence that may greatly affect the level of functioning of computers and, in turn, the capabilities they offer to our world. They further relate these developments to the economic stability of world trade and present a picture of strong government support of AI research in several countries, most notably Japan. This governmental interest is aimed at achieving dominance in the world computer market by developing and controlling this emerging technology.

Because of important advances in hardware and software, the next generation of computers, the fifth generation, is described as capable of emulating human reasoning abilities. These machines will be capable of providing advanced expert systems. Feigenbaum and McCorduck (1983) define an expert system as

> a computer program that performs a specialized, usually difficult professional task at the level of (or sometimes beyond the level of) a human expert. Because their functioning relies so heavily on large bodies of knowledge, expert systems are sometimes known as knowledge-based systems. Since they are often used to assist the human expert, they are also known as intelligent assistants. (p. 258)

These systems (early versions of which already exist in such fields as medicine, engineering, manufacturing, resource engineering, and others) will provide more natural human-machine interaction, including communication through spoken natural language. They should offer capabilities beyond anything we might have dreamed of several decades ago. An example of an expert system from the medical world is offered in Chapter 14, "Computer Resources—Trends and Issues."

What might all this mean for education? Fifth-generation machines are scheduled to be introduced into the marketplace during the 1990s. If the history of cost as related to computing power should repeat itself, we might expect to see the price of these machines eventually drop to a level where acquisition by schools becomes a real possibility. The availability of a machine to which one could talk and show pictures, one that would respond in spoken natural language and that could be made to emulate human intelligence, perhaps by providing expert systems related to the educational needs of students, could be revolutionary. Imagine an expert system designed to reason through and present suggestions, as well as explain how it arrived at its suggestions, in the teaching of reading or mathematics, a system that could perform better than the best human reading consultant available. Imagine teachers trained to use such tools. Further, picture the types of CAI experiences that could be provided to students by coupling such expert systems with advanced graphics and instructional sequences tied into other media, such as video disc.

Would such machines eliminate the teacher from the classroom, causing widespread unemployment and dissatisfaction? Realistically, it does not seem so. Instead, as is the case with management in business, the teacher, as the manager of learning that most teachers currently are, would need to learn to use a new technology to further improve the learning environment. Would children be forced to interact with machines to the detriment of their interaction with human beings? Only if humans decided that would be the case, and few humans would be prone to make that decision. Rather, if the next generation of supercomputers should come about, with their corresponding quantum leap in potential for educational use, they must be seen for what they would be: devices with no intrinsic good or evil. The uses to which they are put would reflect the intelligence, sensitivity, and humanity of the race that created them. The ultimate responsibility would be ours, not the machines.

Conclusion

The amount and quality of software available for use in the classroom has been steadily growing. Taylor's (1980) model provides a way to view the types of software available. As hardware becomes more sophisticated, so will the software available for CAI become more sophisticated. We are actually at the beginning of computer use in society in general and the classroom in particular. Over the next few decades interesting developments should take place in both hardware and software development.

Key Terms

artificial intelligence (AI)
cell
data base
data base management system
  (DBMS)
drill and practice
expert system
field
fifth generation
file

instructional game
Minnesota Educational Computing
  Corporation (MECC)
record
simulation
spelling checker
spreadsheet
tutorial
word processor

Questions

1. Explain and give an example of each type of CAI software listed below:
   - drill and practice
   - instructional game
   - tutorial
   - simulation

2. What is branching, and how does it influence what can be done in a computer-based tutorial?

3. Write a lesson plan that includes the use of a drill and practice program or a computer-based instructional game.

4. Write a lesson plan that includes the use of a computer-based tutorial or simulation.

5. What does a word processor do? What is a spreadsheet? How might each be used in the classroom?

6. Explain what a data base management system is. From information in the text, cite one way a DBMS might be used in the classroom.

7. Write a lesson plan in which one of the following is used by students: a word processor, a DBMS, a spreadsheet.

8. Find a teacher who uses CAI in her teaching and interview her. Report your results to the class.

9. Define the following:

   - artificial intelligence
   - expert system

10. In what positive way might the fifth generation of computers affect education?

References/Further Reading

Bitter, Gary G. *Computers in Today's World.* New York: John Wiley & Sons, 1984.

Brady, Holly. "The 1986 Classroom Computer Learning Software Awards." *Classroom Computer Learning* 6, no. 5 (1986):31–32.

Feigenbaum, Edward A., and Pamela McCorduck. *The Fifth Generation.* Reading, Mass.: Addison-Wesley Publishing Co., 1983.

Long, Larry. *Introduction to Computers and Information Processing.* Englewood Cliffs, N.J.: Prentice-Hall, 1984.

Milone, Michael N. *Every Teacher's Guide to Word Processing.* Englewood Cliffs, N.J.: Prentice-Hall, 1986.

Slesnick, Twila. "Computer Education Research: A Blinder for the Misguided." In Harper, Dennis O., and James H. Stewart. *RUN: Computer Education*, 2d ed. Monterey, Calif.: Brooks/Cole Publishing Co., 1986, pp. 28–31.

"Software for Elementary and Middle Schools." *Popular Computing*, special issue, 3, no. 13 (1984):79–84.

Solomon, Gwen. "Electronic Research." *Electronic Learning* 5, no. 6 (1986):37–40.

Strategic Simulations, Inc. *President Elect Rule Book.* Mountain View, Calif.: Strategic Simulations, Inc., 1981.

Suppes, Patrick. "The Teacher and Computer Assisted Instruction." In *The Computer in the Schools: Tutor, Tool, Tutee*, edited by Robert Taylor. New York: Teachers College Press, 1980, pp. 234–235.

Taylor, Robert P., ed. *The Computer in the School: Tutor, Tool, Tutee.* New York: Teachers College Press, 1980.

5

Using the Computer for Management

TOPICS ADDRESSED

What does the term computer-managed instruction (CMI) mean?

What is the relationship between a management system and the teacher?

How does CMI function?

What are some functions a CMI component might provide when coupled with tutor mode software such as a combined tutorial/drill and practice program?

What is teacher utility software?

How does a grade-keeping program work?

What are some other examples of teacher utility software?

In what ways can administrators use the computer for management purposes?

What are important considerations when evaluating software for managing instruction?

OUTLINE

Introduction
Computer-Managed Instruction
  Who Manages Student Learning?
  How Does CMI Work?
  Example One
  Example Two
Teacher Utilities
  Managing Grades
  Other Applications
    Authoring Systems
    Readability
    Test Creation/Test Scoring Programs

Management Software for
  Administrators
What to Look For
Conclusion
Key Terms
Questions
References/Further Reading

Introduction

This chapter deals with applying the computer to the management of instruction. Three main topics are covered: computer-managed instruction, teacher utility software, and software for administrators. For a teacher, an understanding of how the computer can be used in the classroom to make the management of instruction more efficient, thereby providing more time for teacher-student interaction, will be valuable. Further, some idea of how administrators may use computers will be beneficial when working with supervisors and principals who use computers.

Computer-Managed Instruction

The term computer-managed instruction (CMI) refers to the use of the computer to "collect, analyze and report information concerning the performance of students in an educational program" (Gorth and Nassif, 1984). CMI software is used by the teacher to gather information about students' performance as a basis for planning and controlling instruction. When CMI software is used, the students' educational program may be computer-based, or it may not. For example, some CMI systems are geared to the use of textbooks for instruction, whereas others are incorporated into tutor mode software packages, such as tutorial, drill and practice, or instructional game programs. CMI software is used to collect information about students' performance, analyze that performance, and allow the teacher to generate reports in order to make instructional decisions about the students' program. One potential benefit of CMI software is that it can relieve the teacher of many of the clerical tasks associated with managing instruction.

CMI varies in its complexity. Systems exist that will manage instruction for a school's entire student population. Some CMI systems have been designed to run on mainframe and minicomputers, while others operate on microcomputers. CMI functions are often built in to individual software packages designed to run on microcomputers. The focus here will be on CMI as it is incorporated into tutor mode software running on microcomputers. This will offer an introduction to some of the functions CMI can provide, including the type of information gathered and how it may be used.

Who Manages Student Learning?

The answer to this question is simple: the teacher. Any decision regarding a student is made by the teacher, not by the computer. In this instance, as in every other instance of computer application in this text, the computer is used as a tool to assist the teacher. Because the computer can do certain, limited tasks quickly and reliably, it provides a convenient way for the teacher to store and analyze data, such as scores on different assignments, related to a student's progress. Such data is used by the teacher to make informed decisions concerning the student's progress and future instructional needs. It is the teacher who ultimately makes decisions about the student, not the computer. Although the time may come when computers can be programmed to make expert decisions about instruction, and perhaps even automatically create specialized instructional material for individual students, that day has not yet arrived in the typical classroom. Indeed, such totally automated management of instruction would dramatically change the role of the teacher. The desirability of such a dramatic change is open to debate.

How Does CMI Work?

CMI software provides a series of management options, often referred to as a management system. Sometimes such management options are built into tutor mode software. For example, a program that provides both tutorial sequences and drill and practice on addition facts may also allow the teacher to choose one of several instructional levels at which the student can proceed. The program may also, automatically, keep track of how many exercises the student answers correctly and report that data to the teacher on demand. In addition, as the student progresses through the computer-based material, the management system might automatically change the level of instruction if the student should do well (thereby offering a higher level of instruction) or poorly (offering a lower level). In some cases the management system allows the teacher to control instruction by changing the content of the lessons. For example, in a drill and practice program on addition, the teacher may be able to use the examples supplied with the program or supply his own. Sometimes other options related to the control of the software are offered by the management system.

Sometimes a software manufacturer will design a management system and then incorporate the same system into all or many of the programs the company produces. This allows the added benefit of only having to learn one management system, which can then be used with a variety of software.

CMI software that manages student data requires that a file of student records be created, either by the teacher or automatically by the computer as the software is used by the student. For instance, for a tutorial program, the teacher may create a file for each of her classes. Each file is comprised of one record for each student in the class. Each record is made up of data for a particular student. Each record may initially contain only the student's name. Later, data is added to each student's record, by either the teacher or the computer, as needed. For example, the teacher may enter the results of each student's score on a paper-and-pencil pretest. The computer might use this data to select the instructional level at which material will be presented. The computer may also, automatically, record the student's score on review exercises that are part of the tutorial. In this way the student's record becomes filled with data. The data contained in each record is processed by the computer to provide the teacher with information (reports) that will be of value in managing instruction. For instance, after the student has used the tutorial, the teacher might request a report of the student's progress. The report could include a listing of the tutorial sections completed; scores on review exercises attempted, showing how many were answered correctly on the first try and how many on the second try; and current instructional level. The overall process that takes place in the two examples given below follows this general pattern. A file of student records is created, meaningful data is recorded in the file, and the data is processed to provide valuable information to the teacher. The computer's ability to record and process data in this way makes it a beneficial tool in managing instruction.

CMI software is often menu-driven. The user is presented with a menu of choices and selects the option desired. The user is then prompted as to what needs to be done. If a teacher wants to add a student record to a class file (perhaps a student was just transferred into class), the main menu might offer the choice ADD/DELETE STUDENTS. The teacher would choose that option. This choice could lead to another menu, a submenu, that offered a series of options related to adding and deleting student records, such as ADD ONE STUDENT, DELETE ONE STUDENT, or DELETE ENTIRE CLASS. The teacher would choose ADD ONE STUDENT. The program then prompts the teacher as to exactly what data needs to be entered. For instance, it might ask the teacher to enter the name of the file to which the student record will be added. It might then ask for the student's name, identification number, and so forth.

The two examples of CMI we will look at are part of tutor mode programs. The subject matter of each program is language arts. Any CMI function, whether provided as part of a tutor mode program or offered as a separate, stand-alone program, is an example of the computer being used in the tool mode. Remember, however, that one piece of software may function in more than one mode, depending on the task being performed at a given time. An example is a tutorial program with a built-in management system. While instructing the student, the software is acting in the tutor mode. When the teacher uses the management system, for instance, to change options within the program and set instructional levels, the program is operating in the tool mode. As you read through the following examples, note the mode of software in use at any given time, tutor or tool, and identify the functions the software performs that characterize it as operating in tutor or tool mode.

Example One

Hartley Courseware publishes a program titled *Reading for Meaning with Mother Goose 2.* The software is designed for use with students in grades three and four. The instructional intent of the software is to teach reading comprehension skills. The content read by students consists of Mother Goose rhymes, the assumption being that the rhymes will be both familiar and of interest to students. Five sets of rhymes are available, and each set consists of five

Reprinted by permission: Tribune Media Services

3. Its fleece was white as snow.
   The word fleece means ___.
         a. its head
         b. its feet
         c. to run away
         d. its coat of wool
   answer:

Figure 5–1 A screen from *Reading for Meaning with Mother Goose 2*. The student enters the letter of the answer selected.

rhymes. First, a student is presented with a rhyme. An illustrative picture is shown on the screen in conjunction with the text of the rhyme. The student may have the computer play an accompanying tune for most rhymes if the teacher has chosen to have this option available and has instructed the student in how to do this. After reading the rhyme the student is presented with a series of questions (see **Figure 5–1**). Each question will be one of six possible types in relation to comprehension skills: main idea, detail, inference, sequence, pronouns, or word meaning. The student answers the question. The child may go back and look at the rhyme while answering a question, as long as the teacher has activated that feature of the program. If a correct answer is given, a box appears on the screen, with a phrase aimed at reinforcing the correct response. In the event an incorrect answer is entered, the student is asked to try again. If an incorrect answer is entered, the correct answer is given and the student proceeds to the next question (see **Figures 5–2** and **5–3**). The teacher chooses how many times the question may be answered incorrectly before the correct answer is given. At the end of the session the student is told how many questions were asked and how many were answered correctly the first time.

A management system is provided for teacher use that offers six options, as shown in **Figure 5–4**. On entering the manager the teacher is presented with a menu from which the option desired may be chosen. The teacher can change a lesson, do student planning, run lessons, catalog the disk, turn the sound on or off, or print out the contents of a lesson. Each option is discussed below.

The teacher may choose to change the content of the rhymes, the questions asked, or other textual information. The graphics portion of the program may

Figure 5–2 If an incorrect answer is entered the computer crosses it out and asks the student to try again.

Figure 5–3 If a second incorrect answer is entered the computer crosses it out and displays the correct answer.

```
                    〈29 FREE SECTORS〉

         DO YOU WANT TO:

              1-CHANGE A LESSON
              2-STUDENT PLANNING
              3-RUN LESSONS
              4-CATALOG DISK
              5-SOUND ON/OFF
              6-PRINT A LESSON

         WHICH?
```

Figure 5–4 The six options for the management system in *Reading for Meaning with Mother Goose 2.*

not be changed. A teacher might opt to rewrite an entire lesson, using a new rhyme, or change one or more of the questions associated with any of the original rhymes. When a new question is entered, the teacher is asked to identify which of the six categories of question type it belongs to: detail, main idea, inference, sequence, pronouns, or word meaning. This is necessary because the computer keeps track of the number of questions in each category per rhyme and the number of correct answers the student gives in each category.

The teacher can also choose from among several design options for the lessons. As stated earlier, the number of tries the student is allowed before the correct answer is given is set by the teacher. The teacher can choose whether or not the student will be allowed to see the nursery rhyme again while answering questions. The teacher can elect to have the lesson stop if the student answers fewer than a given percentage of some minimum number of questions on the first try. For example, in a twenty question lesson the teacher may set up the program so that at least eight questions will be presented, but if the student has answered fewer than 50 percent of the first eight questions correctly, the lesson will stop. The minimum number of questions to be presented and the percentage that determines whether the lesson must stop are selected by the teacher. If the student does well, perhaps answering correctly on the first try the first fifteen questions in a twenty-five-question lesson, the lesson can be set to stop after the first fifteen questions. The teacher controls this by deciding how many consecutive questions must be answered correctly on the first attempt. The teacher also controls whether or not any questions missed in the lesson are presented again at the end of the lesson. These options provide flexibility in planning and controlling the content and flow of the program.

The student planning part of the management system for the program allows the teacher to either view on the screen or print out on a printer the data kept

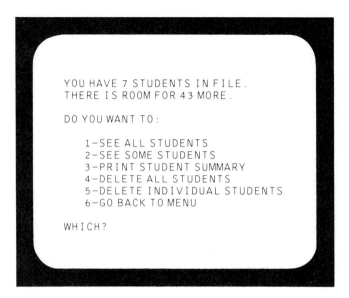

Figure 5–5 A menu used by the teacher when working with the student planning portion of the management system. If option 2 is chosen, SEE SOME STUDENTS, the type of information in Figure 5–6 is presented.

by the program on each student's use of the software. After choosing to work with the student planning portion of the management system, the teacher is first given the option of deleting all students in the file. If N is entered in response to this option, the teacher is then presented with a menu as shown in **Figure 5–5**. If the teacher chooses option 2, **SEE SOME STUDENTS**, a screen is presented that shows what set of rhymes each student has worked with (see **Figure 5–6**). The teacher then selects which students' records are to be viewed. For each student, a screen (or output on the printer) gives the set of rhymes used, the percentage answered correctly on the first try, the number of screens (or frames) in the lesson, the number of questions in the lesson, how many questions the student attempted, and how many were answered correctly on the first try. Also included is a list of the number of questions in the lesson for each question type and how many of each type were answered correctly on the first try. **Figure 5–7** shows a student record for one lesson.

The teacher also has the option to display, either on the screen or on the printer, all the individual records for all students. A summary of all students may be chosen and is in the form shown in **Figure 5–8**, where each student's name, lesson completed, and percentage correct are given. The program will store a maximum of fifty student records. Therefore, it will be necessary for the teacher to delete (erase) either all student records or individual records from time to time. This would be done if new students had to be added to the system but the maximum number of records were already stored on the disk. The student planning menu (Figure 5–5) provides two functions to accomplish this: DELETE ALL STUDENTS, or DELETE INDIVIDUAL STUDENTS.

Other options provided from the main menu shown in Figure 5–4 allow the teacher to run the lesson from the manager, catalog the disk (be presented with

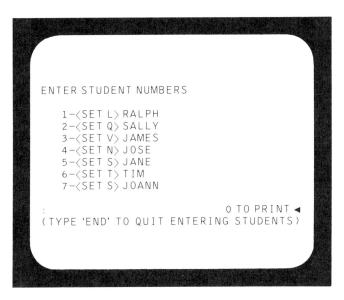

Figure 5–6 This screen shows which set of rhymes each student has worked with. By selecting a student number, the teacher may view a record of the student's performance. This information is shown in Figure 5–7.

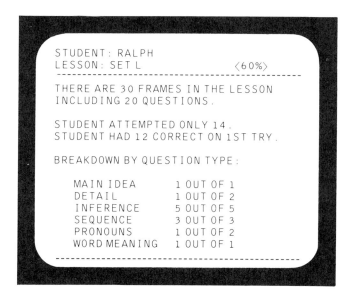

Figure 5–7 A report of one student's performance.

a list of the information [files] on the disk), choose to enable or disable the sound portion of the program, and print out the content of any selected lesson.

The management system provided with the program does a reasonable job of allowing the teacher to change lesson content and lesson flow. It also offers a simple but meaningful record-keeping function. The options available are straightforward and easily learned and used by the teacher.

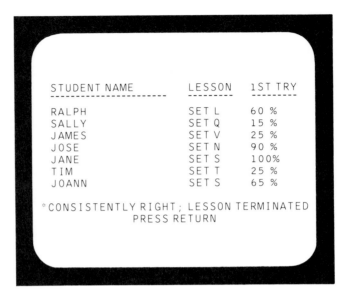

```
STUDENT NAME          LESSON    1ST TRY
--------------------- --------- ---------
RALPH                 SET L      60 %
SALLY                 SET Q      15 %
JAMES                 SET V      25 %
JOSE                  SET N      90 %
JANE                  SET S     100%
TIM                   SET T      25 %
JOANN                 SET S      65 %

*CONSISTENTLY RIGHT; LESSON TERMINATED
             PRESS RETURN
```

Figure 5–8 The teacher may choose, from the menu presented in Figure 5–5, to see a performance summary for all students. Such a summary is shown here.

Example Two

Milton Bradley publishes a series of language arts programs, including the following titles: *Building Better Sentences: Combining Sentence Parts*, *Building Better Sentences: Creating Compound and Complex Sentences*, and *Reading Comprehension: Main Idea and Details*. Each program includes a tutor mode component as well as a management system for the teacher (the Student Record Manager) and a set of worksheets correlated to specific lessons. The Student Record Manager is also included in other software published by Milton Bradley. The program *Building Better Sentences: Combining Sentence Parts* will be considered here.

Building Better Sentences: Combining Sentence Parts is most suitable for middle school and junior and senior high school. It provides tutorial information, practice with sentences, and mastery testing in five skill areas. These areas are (1) identifying subjects and predicates, (2) identifying complements, (3) compounding subjects, (4) compounding predicates, and (5) compounding complements.

The program is developmental and aimed at providing students with the skills needed to use a variety of sentences in their writing. It is suggested by the publishers that when the software is used, the five skills be covered in the order listed. The software also offers a cumulative review section in which students are asked to combine pairs of two sentences by compounding subjects, predicates, or complements. The student's score on the review section determines the amount of time earned to play an arcade-type computer game that is part of the software and that is used as a reward for successful completion of the review section.

Students can access any skill lesson in one of three modes: instructional (I), practice (P), or mastery (M). The teacher determines what level the student needs to work at by administering and scoring a paper-and-pencil pretest that comes with the software. Of course, a student might do so well on the pretest

Input/Output

As part of a special issue on computers and education published in mid-October of 1984, Popular Computing *asked eight prominent individuals who were active in education to respond to a series of questions about computers and education. The respondents were as follows:*

- *John G. Kemeny, professor of mathematics and president emeritus of Dartmouth College, co-inventor of the BASIC programming language*

- *Andrew R. Molnar, program manager in the Division of Science Education Development and Research at the National Science Foundation*

- *Patricia Graham, dean of the Harvard Graduate School and Charles Warren professor of history of American education*

- *Patricia Sturdivant, associate superintendent for technology in the Houston Independent School District*

- *Joseph Weizenbaum, professor of computer science at the Massachusetts Institute of Technology*

- *Seymour Papert, professor of mathematics and education at the Massachusetts Institute of Technology and creator of the Logo programming language*

- *Terrel H. Bell, U.S. Secretary of Education from 1981 to 1985*

- *Representative Timothy E. Wirth, a congressional supporter of grants to public schools for the purchase of computer equipment and the training of teachers*

One question, presented below, dealt with the future of computers in the classroom. Although all of the responses are of interest, notice especially the replies of Terrel Bell and Timothy Wirth. Both deal with the use of the computer as a management tool that may relieve the teacher of burdensome clerical tasks and allow more time for teacher-student interaction. As you work with the material in this chapter, consider whether or not you believe this will be true. Also, consider how you react to some of the other comments about the future of computers in the classroom.

How integral to the classroom is the computer going to become? What is the likely impact of this on teachers and on children and on the effectiveness of education itself?

Kemeny: I will not teach a mathematics class unless I have a computer in the room. In high school and college the use of computers in the classroom will be as common as the use of blackboards. The coming of good, inexpensive personal computers was the major step that was holding things up. Five years from now there will be better ones cheaper than those of today, but I think the big jump has occurred now that you can buy personal computers for less than $2000.

Molnar: One of the new educational imperatives is the computer. It used to be that you couldn't have a school unless you had books and a library; now you can't have a school of excellence without having a computer or a computer-based system. As the proliferation of knowledge occurs, if we're to take advantage of it we must be able to use it. So in addition to human memory we now need intellectual tools to cope with it. Such tools are coming about as knowledge systems and databases provide *syntheses* of the literature rather than document retrieval.

Graham: Some people are saying you can't have a school of excellence these days without computers. I don't believe that. The real question is what are you going to use the computers for? It's important to recognize that books can be salacious literature of the most dubious sort for children; on the other hand they can be powerful learning tools. I feel the same way about computers.

There's a big difference between saying computers have the *capacity* to enhance children's learning and that they automatically *will* enhance children's learning. We think it's a hard question to figure out how children truly can learn more as a result of using microcomputers. We're investigating that in five or six different projects. I'd say we're skeptical of the hoopla but cautiously optimistic about the long-term potential of the microcomputer to enhance learning.

Sturdivant: I think computers are going to do a number of things for students. They're going to make kids more autonomous learners. Because they're not regurgitating text from a book but are dealing with lots of information and having to analyze it and synthesize it, they're going to be more capable of dealing with the information explosion. We can't project what kinds of facts kids are going to need for everyday life in 10 to 15 years so the best that we can do is to prepare them with strategies for dealing with information, to give them good study skills, teach them how to scan, teach them how to get the information to make decisions. We're emphasizing procedural things, step-by-step problem solving so that students will be better prepared to think critically. I think kids are going to get more and more attuned to simulation and problem solving and they'll be better able to deal with the world because they'll be able to simulate the conditions of a problem and evaluate what strategy they should use.

Weizenbaum: Considering that the schools are in fairly desperate trouble, there's great danger of putting in a technological "fix" that will make it appear that something is being done, while nothing is being done to address the actual problems that give rise to this "rising tide" of mediocrity and illiteracy. In other words, computers just may be a powerful distraction that will leave the original problems— money, teachers, time, and energy—untouched. The other thing is that the computer uses up valuable resources.

If things are going very badly in inner-city schools, then it's important to ask in what ways they are going badly and why. If one starts out by assuming that the computer is the solution to it all, then one is never going to ask these two questions.

There's a lot of talk about lack of motivation in schools and then it's pointed out that when computers are used, kids *are* motivated, they like to come to school, they like to play with the computer, they stay after hours. I don't know to what extent this is true. But if the intention is to increase motivation, there are lots of other things that could be done. For example, suppose we showed pornographic movies every day at lunchtime or gave out small samples of heroin once a week or once a day. Of course we don't do these things because it isn't just motivation as such that we want, we want a *relevant* motivation, a motivation to read, for example.

Papert: Many children fall in love with written language because they see it as something their fathers do. For children who don't have this kind of relationship, something else is needed. The problematic personality isn't the one that can't eventually adapt to the written language but the one for whom our culture has not provided any mode of access; they don't have any way of making contact with it. The computer is a catalyst, a bridge; it's a matchmaker to get them together, and once together they don't need a matchmaker anymore.

Bell: Teaching is a labor-intensive industry. As in a lot of other industries where machines have taken on a lot of the drudgery work, I think that the computer at long last is emerging as that equivalent in education. Take today's English teacher. If you're meeting 30 students in a class and teaching five periods a day in a typical high school, you have 150 papers to mark. We know from the word-processing software we have now—spelling, punctuation, grammar—that what teachers have to spend hours going over can be done with a computer. Test scoring, analysis of tests, and printouts that show each student's learning needs will relieve hours and hours of teacher toil. This is the kind of detail work where computers have fantastic potential.

Wirth: The electronic day and age is going to partially solve the teacher availability problem. You can have *more* teacher-student interaction because teachers have to spend less time on a lot of mundane chores that can be done electronically. Some people will make the assumption that computers are going to replace teachers or replace the learning system—but that's not true at all. But it will demand increasingly sophisticated teachers to manage the interaction of computers and teachers. We may even wind up with what the NEA (National Education Association) calls "master" teachers, which is going to require a great deal of teacher retraining. Proposed legislation addresses the need for teacher retraining.

(Ebisch and Immel, 1984)

---

that the teacher decides no instruction is necessary for that student on that particular skill. Once the teacher has graded the pretest, a class record sheet is filled out that lists the student level for each skill. This sheet will eventually list the dates on which relevant computer lessons are completed. A record of the dates when associated worksheets are completed and the paper-and-pencil posttest score for a given skill are also kept on this form. **Figure 5–9** shows an example of a class record sheet.

Student record sheets are also provided. It is suggested that students record on this sheet the results of the pretest, the scores earned for each computer lesson, and the posttest score. An example is shown in **Figure 5–10**. Each entry represents the number correctly completed compared with the total number of exercises. For example, 5/10 means five of ten exercises were completed correctly.

This software presents a comprehensive management system, some of which is accomplished manually and some of which is computerized. To some teachers, the entire system may seem restrictive or too rigid. The publishers are sensitive to this, however, and encourage teachers to use the system in whatever way best fits their particular teaching style and the individual needs of students.

The Student Record Manager keeps track of a student's progress through the material. The teacher initially sets a level of I, P, or M for each skill for each student. A level of I will cause the computer to prevent a student from working on the computer lesson for that particular skill. Instead, a message will appear on the screen, telling the student to see the teacher before progressing further.

STUDENTS' NAMES	SKILL 1 Identifying Subjects and Predicates						SKILL 2 Identifying Complements					SKILL 3 Compounding Subjects						SKILL 4 Compounding Predicates				
	Pretest Score	Computer Session	Practice Sheet #1	Practice Sheet #2	Practice Sheet #3	Posttest Score	Pretest Score	Computer Session	Practice Sheet #1	Practice Sheet #2	Posttest Score	Pretest Score	Computer Session	Practice Sheet #1	Practice Sheet #2	Practice Sheet #3	Posttest Score	Pretest Score	Computer Session	Practice Sheet #1	Practice Sheet #2	Practice Sheet #3
1 Amy	M	X	X	X	X	M	P	11/9	11/8	11/9	M	P	X	11/12	11/13	11/3	M	P	11/14	11/14	11/14	X
2 Marie	M	X	X	X	X	M	M	X	X	X	M	P	11/8	11/8	11/9	11/9	M	P	11/10	11/10	11/14	11/11
3 Tom	P	11/8	11/9	11/9	11/8	M	P	11/10	11/9	11/10	M	I	11/13	11/12	11/12	11/13	M	I	11/14	11/13	11/14	11/14
4																						

M = Mastery (5 out of 5 or 4 out of 5)
P = Practice (3 out of 5 or 2 out of 5)
I = Instruction (1 out of 5 or 0 out of 5)
X = no instruction necessary
11/7, 11/8, etc. = date assignment completed

Figure 5–9 An example of a class record sheet from *Building Better Sentences: Combining Sentence Parts*. For each skill category, the student's initial skill level and subsequent performance are recorded on this sheet.

Tom Loganberry

ACTIVITIES	Pretest Score	Computer Lesson	Practice Sheet #1	Practice Sheet #2	Practice Sheet #3	Posttest Score
SKILL 1: Identifying Subjects and Predicates	2/5	4/5	7/10	8/10	13/10	4/5
SKILL 2: Identifying Complements	3/5	4/5	5/8	11/12		5/5
SKILL 3: Compounding Subjects	2/5	5/15	2/3	2/3	3/3	4/5
SKILL 4: Compounding Predicates	1/5	4/5	1/3	2/3	4/4	5/5

Figure 5–10 An example of a student record sheet. A student may use such a sheet to keep track of individual performance in each skill area.

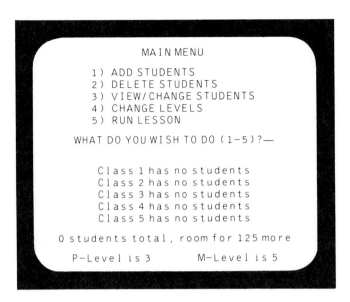

Figure 5–11 The teacher accesses the Student Record Manager through this main menu.

Then the teacher can give the student any extra needed instruction in preparation for working on the skill at the computer. A level of P allows the student to access the computer lesson for that particular skill. Under the practice option, the student receives tutorial instruction and does the practice exercises, both on the computer and with print materials (worksheets). When the student is ready, the Mastery Quiz is given. If the score on the quiz meets the criteria set by the teacher for mastery, the manager automatically changes the student's record for that skill from P to M and allows the student to go on to the next skill. Remember, the manager will cause the skills and their associated lessons to be presented in order. When the lessons are run under control of the manager, a student must be at the mastery level on skill 1 (identifying subjects and predicates) before being allowed to work on skill 2 (identifying complements) and so on.

The teacher accesses the Student Record Manager through the main menu screen, shown in **Figure 5–11**, for the purpose of viewing or changing student records. This menu exhibits the options available, the number of student records for each class, the total number of student records currently stored in the manager, and the number of new records that can be added. It also displays the criteria for the practice mode and for achieving mastery. The P level score is used only as a reminder to the teacher of the criteria she has set that will separate students at the I level from students ready for practice (P level). The M level criteria determines the score necessary on the Mastery Quiz for the student's record to be changed from P to M.

The first option, ADD STUDENTS, allows the teacher to begin building a file of student records, or to add students to an existing file. The manager will hold records for five classes. A total of 125 student records may be maintained by the manager. **Figure 5–12** shows an entry for adding a student to a file. Notice that the teacher has entered the student's name, the class number, and an instructional level for each of the skills for which instruction is available.

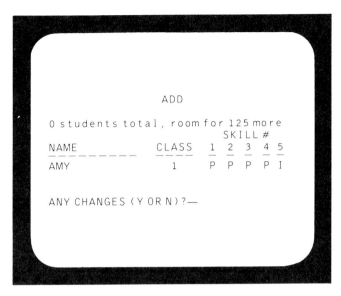

```
                        ADD

     0 students total, room for 125 more
                              SKILL #
     NAME            CLASS   1  2  3  4  5

     AMY               1     P  P  P  P  I


     ANY CHANGES (Y OR N)?—
```

Figure 5–12 An entry for adding a student to the file. This student is a member of class 1.

The second option listed on the main menu allows the teacher to delete either individual students or entire classes from the manager. The teacher simply chooses the class needed and then either deletes all students in the class by selecting that option from a menu or selects, from a display of all students in the class, the individual student record to be deleted. These choices are shown in **Figure 5–13**.

Option 3 allows the teacher to view student records and elect to change the data in each record, as desired. The teacher simply selects the student record to be changed. The program then prompts the teacher for changes in name, class, and skills 1 to 5. If the entry for class is changed, the student's record is deleted from the current class and automatically entered in the file for the new class.

Option 4 is used to change the practice level or the mastery level. **Figure 5–14** shows the screen presented when option 4 is chosen. A new criteria for either or both levels is entered on this screen.

The final option, RUN LESSON, allows the teacher or the student to run a lesson without the program using the Student Record Manager. This option is used when there is no need for the management system. For instance, the teacher may wish to review a lesson or may not need management information for a student. (Perhaps the teacher feels that a lesson will provide a student an informal review of material previously mastered.) Also, lessons may be selected in any order when this option is used; it is not necessary to follow the manager-imposed sequence of skills when lessons are selected without control of the manager. This option also provides access to the review sections of the program.

Figure 5–15 is a flowchart showing how the manager controls instruction. **Figure 5–16** is a flowchart showing a way to integrate print materials with the software. Flowcharts are pictorial representations of instructions and are introduced in more depth in Chapter 11 as aids to programming. For now, read

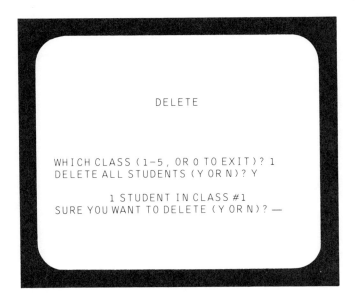

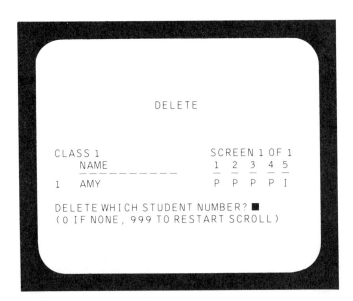

Figure 5–13 The teacher's options for deleting student records. The records for an entire class may be deleted. (top), or individual student records may be deleted (bottom).

these flowcharts from top to bottom, following the arrows. The instructions are contained as text in the symbols shown. A diamond-shaped symbol represents a question. If the question is answered yes, follow the arrow labeled yes out of the symbol; otherwise, follow the arrow labeled no.

The type of CMI outlined in the two examples just presented can take a variety of forms. The underlying functions performed are usually based on several principles. Student records are created and maintained. Student per-

CHANGE LEVELS

ENTER NEW LEVELS
(PRESS RETURN IF NO CHANGE)

PRACTICE LEVEL IS 3 —
MASTERY LEVEL IS 5

Figure 5–14 If the teacher chooses to change levels, the screen above is presented. Either the practice or mastery level may be changed.

formance is automatically recorded by the computer as students use the software. The management system may adjust the level of instruction automatically during a computer session, based on criteria set by the teacher. The teacher may have the option of changing lesson content as well as a variety of design options, such as the content of reinforcers, the reinforcement schedule, acceptable achievement levels, number of examples presented, and the flow of the lesson.

Teacher Utilities

Teacher utility software includes programs that allow teachers to automate some of the myriad tasks they perform, such as grading, generating materials for instruction, determining the readability level of material, sending communications to parents, and tracking expenses for special projects. Specialized programs are available for many of these jobs. Word processors, data base management systems, and spreadsheets are also used by teachers to accomplish some of these functions. A detailed example of a program to manage grades is presented below. This is followed by general descriptions of several other applications for which teacher utility programs are available.

Managing Grades

One task that teachers at all levels must perform is grade keeping. This involves maintaining accurate student records, numerical grade calculation, and grade determination (what constitutes an A, B, C, etc., if grades should need to be expressed as letters). It also involves viewing grades in different ways. For example, what is the class average on a test, and how are the grades for the test distributed? The computer is an excellent device for storing student

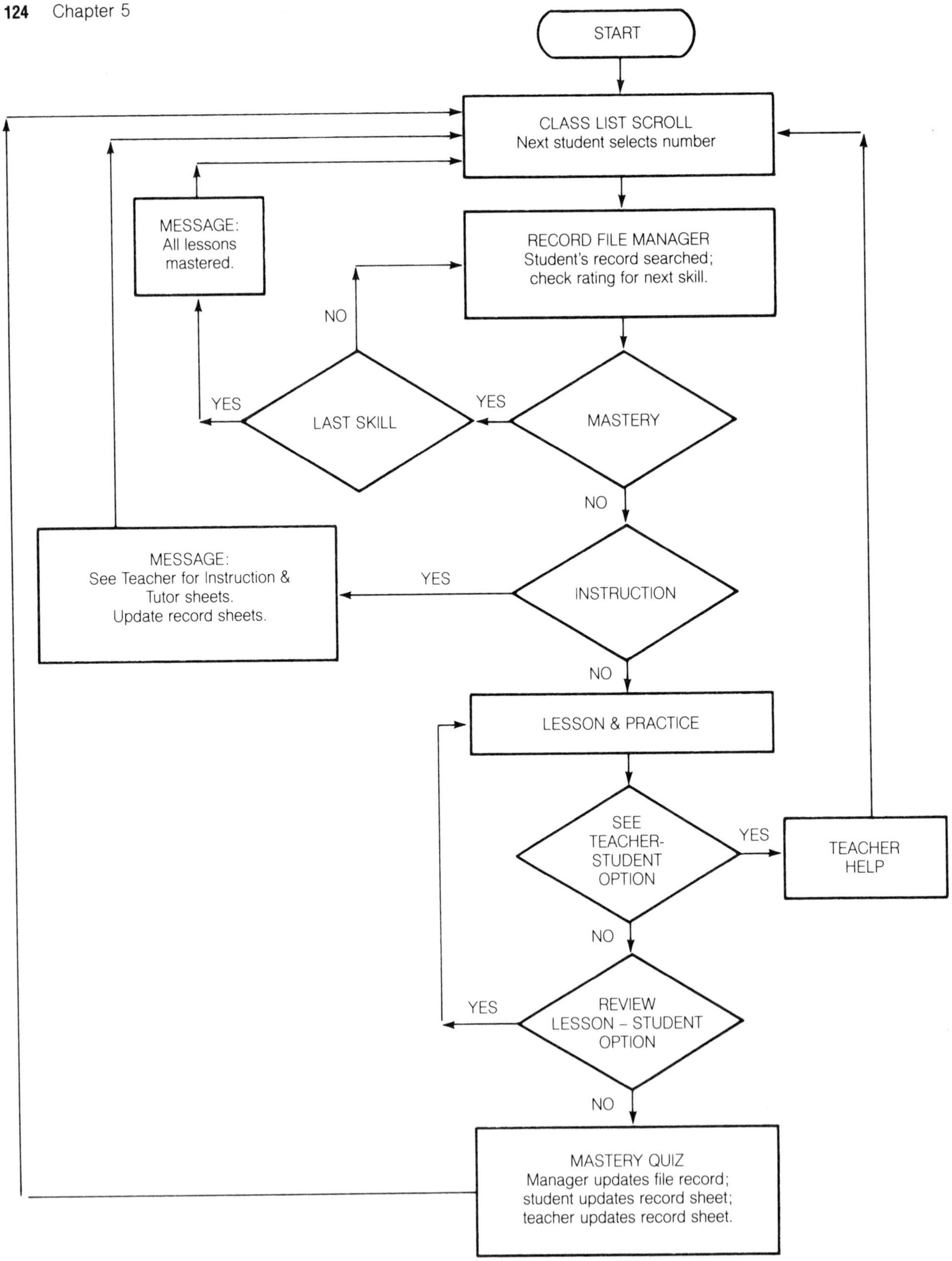

Figure 5-15 A flowchart depicting how the manager controls instruction.

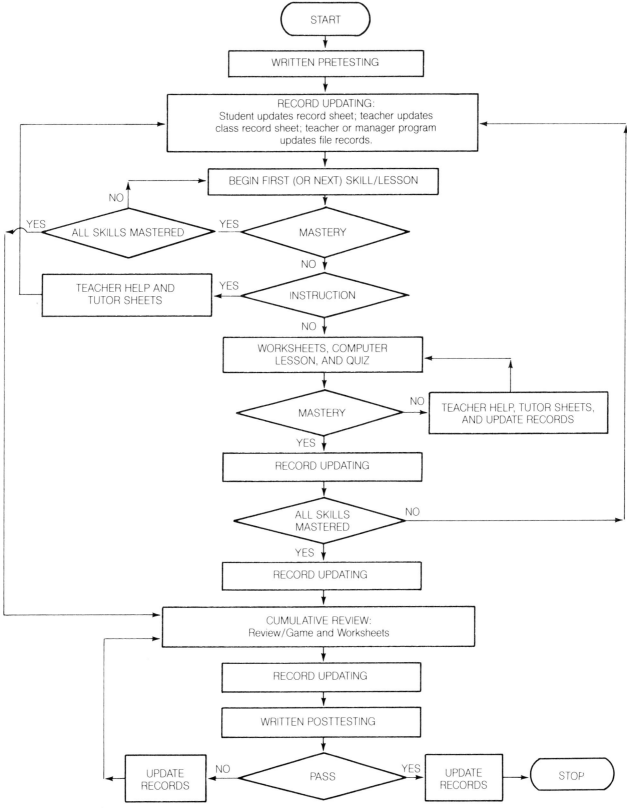

Figure 5–16 A flowchart showing a way to integrate print materials with the software.

Reactions and Research

Germundsen and Glenn (1984) conducted a study to investigate some of the positive and negative aspects of using a computerized grade-keeping system in a junior high school. Their main concern was how teachers, students, and parents react to the use of a computerized gradebook in the classroom. Specifically, they were interested in four areas: (1) Does such software save teachers time in record keeping? (2) Is computerized grading more useful to teachers than a traditional gradebook? (3) Do teachers, students, and parents perceive that computerized grading improves student class performance? and (4) Does such a system provide parents and students with easy-to-understand, useful information?

Six teachers, 214 students, and 107 parents participated in the study, which lasted for fourteen weeks. The teachers taught English, math, social studies, and science. The computerized gradebook Gradepoint, developed by Paul Rogne, was initially introduced to the students, who were shown how to interpret information generated by the system. Class reports generated by the Gradepoint software were then posted each week by the teachers. At various times during the semester, progress reports were sent home to the parents and provided to the students. Teachers completed a fifty-two-item questionnaire about how they used the grade-keeping system and their perceptions of its effectiveness. Students completed a sixteen-item questionnaire about the effectiveness of the printed reports they received from the grade-keeping program, as did their parents. The teachers were interviewed at the end of the study for additional information about their perceptions of the usefulness of the computerized system. The researchers summarize the findings as follows.

The results of the study indicate that the computer gradebook has the potential of being an effective teacher utility—however, there are important issues that a teacher must consider before deciding to use such a program. These issues are discussed in the examination of student, parent and teacher reactions.

STUDENT REACTIONS

Students felt that the information provided by the computer gradebook was useful. When compared to a traditional gradebook, 87 percent of the students liked the computer system better. Ninety-six percent felt that the computer printouts used by the computer gradebook were easy to understand and 97 percent of the students said that they looked at the reports generated by the computer gradebook at least once a week. Further, 95 percent said it was easier for them to keep track of how they were doing in class because of the reports they received.

Did using the computer gradebook in classes encourage students to try harder in their work? Forty-nine percent claimed that the new computer system made it easier for them to try harder and 84 percent said they would like to see an electronic gradebook used in their other classes.

PARENT REACTIONS

Parents also felt that the computer gradebook was a better system. Ninety-seven percent believed that the computer system was better than the traditional grade reporting system because of the information provided. In fact, 90 percent of the parents sampled wanted more progress reports and suggested that at least two reports be sent home each marking period.

Twenty-nine percent thought that the better reporting system helped their children try harder in school. Some parents noted, "With this reporting system, he evaluates his own progress and sets new goals when needed without me saying anything! Great!" Or, "After a report she generally does her homework right away and I'm more aware [of it]."

Did parents feel that the system should be used throughout the school? Ninety-one percent said they wanted other teachers to use the system. As one parent noted, "All classes should be required to send these reports home. I notice only a few do it."

Students and parents seem to really like the new system because it provides more information than the traditional gradebook system. With a computer gradebook a teacher can provide reports quickly and as frequently as a class, student or parent desires. These reports provide information that both parents and students see as important and useful. But how did the teachers feel?

TEACHER REACTIONS

All six teachers felt that the computer gradebook was more useful than the old method of keeping grades. They believed that parents and students liked the computer gradebook system better because all six teachers had received positive comments from parents concerning the information that had been sent home as progress reports. Four of the teachers felt that the new reporting system helped some students try harder in class and keep up with their assignments.

The computer gradebook, however, did not save time for the majority of teachers. Setting up the gradebook, learning the various options, entering the grades and updating student scores still took time. Moreover, these activities had to be completed at school if the teacher did not have a computer at home. In fact, all felt that additional computers would be needed in the school when more teachers began to use such teacher utility programs.

IMPLICATIONS

What do the results of this pilot study mean? Probably the most revealing finding is that using a computer gradebook does not result in an immediate saving of time for the teacher. It takes time and energy to learn how to use the new system effectively. In addition, the supplemental reports to students and parents may generate additional telephone calls and conferences. These, too, may take time. On the other hand, the computer gradebook has the potential to transform gradebook numbers into a meaningful student profile for teachers who are looking for a way to provide specific information to both parents and students. Looking at grading from a larger perspective, then, the computer gradebook may indeed offer savings of time over the long run.

Students and parents liked the use of the computer gradebook. Students liked being able to know how they were doing in class and parents appreciated receiving information on their child's progress. Whether this additional information can help students become better students cannot be determined at this time—however, feelings are quite positive about the potential of the gradebook information in helping students.

In this age of high technology, teachers need also to be reminded of the human touch that is necessary to bring the technology to its highest potential. Two examples illustrate this point. First, students often approach the teacher's desk and ask, "How am I doing in here?" What are such students really asking? If the teacher's reply is to say, "Go check the computer printout on the bulletin board," the human touch needed in the lives of students may be missing. And second, parents may appreciate feedback from the teacher via the computer printout—however, as one parent noted on a returned survey, "I like the system only if the teachers are looking at the reports and are seeing them as an extension of the kids." Or, "We would rather have a personal call when our child is not doing well." Technology can go only so far in meeting the human needs so closely associated with the teaching/learning process.

Finally, this study raises important questions for the administrator. First, if parents and students want all teachers to use computer gradebooks, should all teachers be required to use such a system? What about inservice training? Findings from the teacher questionnaire indicate that the best inservice is one colleague helping another. How could such a program be established and implemented? Second, entering grades means that a computer or several computers must be made available to teachers. How will the school district meet that need? These are still unanswered questions.

Wisely used, a computer gradebook system can provide useful information to the teacher, the student and the parent. As one teacher noted, "It makes me look more efficient." If a teacher can *be* more efficient, the time allocated for purposeful instruction may increase and educational goals may be met.

(Germundsen and Glenn, 1984)

---

records and calculating grades, since grade keeping involves data storage and data processing, things at which the computer excels.

Any grade-keeping program must provide a way to create and store student records. It must also provide a simple way to delete student records. The data stored should be easily accessed by the teacher for purposes of viewing records on the screen or printing out a hardcopy report. It should be a simple task to enter grades for students and to change a student's grade on any test, quiz, or assignment that has been entered previously. Beyond these basic functions it is often valuable for teachers to have the option of sorting grades so that a rank ordering of student performance, perhaps from lowest to highest, can be viewed. Further, teachers often assign different weights to tests and assignments, so a function that allows assignment of weights to grades is valuable. The ability to perform different statistical tests, such as calculating the mean and standard deviation of a set of data, is also valuable. The option of producing a graph showing grade distribution is often desirable.

Depending on the teacher's preferences, many or all of these functions may be essential. Grading programs vary in their level of sophistication. One program may allow the teacher to assign weights to scores by giving a number to each assignment and having the total for all assignments equal 100. For instance, if there were six assignments, the weights might be 10, 10, 20, 20, 20, and 20. Other programs allow choices for assigning weights, perhaps by total points or proportional values. Some programs provide no statistical information; others automatically calculate meaningful statistics. A good

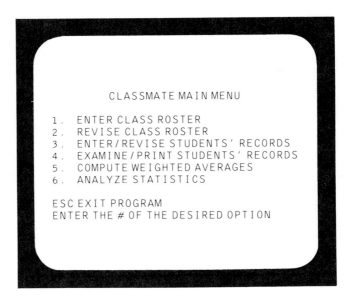

CLASSMATE MAIN MENU

1. ENTER CLASS ROSTER
2. REVISE CLASS ROSTER
3. ENTER/REVISE STUDENTS' RECORDS
4. EXAMINE/PRINT STUDENTS' RECORDS
5. COMPUTE WEIGHTED AVERAGES
6. ANALYZE STATISTICS

ESC EXIT PROGRAM
ENTER THE # OF THE DESIRED OPTION

Figure 5–17 The main menu for *Classmate.*

example of a fairly sophisticated grade-keeping program available for microcomputers is the *Kalamazoo Teacher's Record Book,* published by Hartley Courseware. Another popular program is *Classmate*, published by Davidson and Associates. An overview of the functions provided by *Classmate* will serve to introduce this type of software.

The main menu for *Classmate* is shown in **Figure 5–17**. Options available from this menu include entering a class roster or revising an existing roster, entering or revising students' records, examining or printing students' records, computing weighted averages, and analyzing statistics. When option 1 is chosen, ENTER CLASS ROSTER, the submenu shown in **Figure 5–18** appears. From this menu the teacher may choose to create a new class roster by entering each student's name and ID code. This roster will later be used to enter data for each student. Once the roster is created, it may be automatically sorted by the computer. The teacher can choose to have the roster sorted by student name or by ID number. Option 3 is used to save the newly created roster to a file on disk. The file is given a name by the teacher. Option 4 allows the teacher to view the roster, either on the screen or as hardcopy printed out on a printer. **Figure 5–19** is a printout of a sample class roster. This program also allows the teacher, by choosing option 5, to create a new file from a roster that has already been created. For example, if a teacher needed a new file for her class at the beginning of a semester, so that grades for the new semester could be entered, it would not be necessary to retype all the students' names and ID numbers. The teacher would simply use option 5 to create a new file from the previous semester's roster. Only the names and ID numbers of the students would be contained in the newly created file.

Option 2 from the main menu, REVISE CLASS ROSTER, causes the submenu shown in **Figure 5–20** to be presented. The options on this screen allow the user to manipulate the information on the roster in various ways. The teacher chooses which file he wants to work with and loads it into the computer's

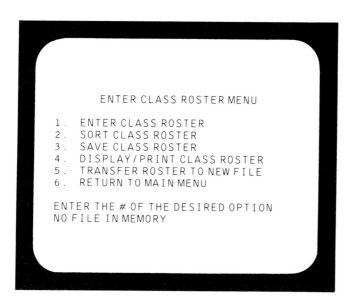

ENTER CLASS ROSTER MENU

1. ENTER CLASS ROSTER
2. SORT CLASS ROSTER
3. SAVE CLASS ROSTER
4. DISPLAY/PRINT CLASS ROSTER
5. TRANSFER ROSTER TO NEW FILE
6. RETURN TO MAIN MENU

ENTER THE # OF THE DESIRED OPTION
NO FILE IN MEMORY

Figure 5–18 When option 1, ENTER CLASS ROSTER, is chosen from the main menu, the ENTER CLASS ROSTER MENU appears.

PERIOD ONE ROSTER

4/16/84

ADAMS, WALKER	0133	_____
BAILEY, KATHLEEN	3356	_____
BELL, ALEX	2431	_____
BROWN, HAROLD	3984	_____
DAVIDSON, JEFF	3050	_____
EVANS, ROGER	2294	_____
GRAHAM, BARRY	2746	_____
HALL, JUDY	3806	_____
JOHNSON, CHRISTY	6666	_____
MARINO, ANTHONY	2258	_____
MITCHELL, SCOTT	6027	_____
MURPHY, ERIN	6645	_____
OTSUKA, HIROKO	4463	_____
RASKIN, EDDIE	7155	_____
ROSENBLOOM, SARAH	3012	_____
RUBIN, ELLEN	5736	_____
SCHAEFFER, CATHY	1838	_____
STUBENRAUCH, LONNA	3240	_____
SUMMIT, ERIC	0127	_____
WANG, MARK	9588	_____

THE TOTAL REGISTER IS 20

Figure 5–19 A printout of a sample class roster.

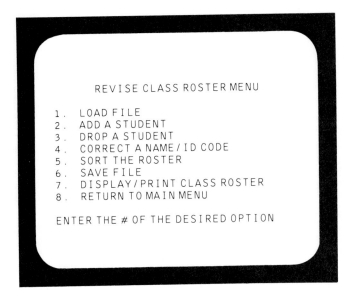

Figure 5–20 The choices presented to the teacher for revising a class roster.

memory by using option 1. Choices 2 through 4 allow the teacher to either add or drop a single student or correct the name or ID code for any student on the roster. The option of sorting the roster is again presented (on this screen it is choice 5). Once the roster has been changed as desired, it may be saved as a file on disk by using option 6. The roster may be printed out or displayed on the screen by choosing option 7.

After a roster has been created, the teacher enters data about each student, as needed. This is accomplished by selecting number 3 from the main menu, ENTER/REVISE STUDENTS' RECORDS. The submenu presented for this choice is shown in **Figure 5–21**. From this screen the teacher would first load the file containing the desired roster. Three types of data may be kept for each student: grades (for tests, quizzes, or assignments), attendance data, and comments. When option 2 is chosen, the teacher may enter any of three types of marks for each student in the class: percentage grades (98), letter grades (A, B−, etc.), or any of several special marks provided, such as EXC (which means excused from the test and has no effect on the student's average). When this option is used, the teacher enters the title for the test or assignment and then enters the grade for each student. When entering attendance records (option 3), the teacher enters the title for the attendance period (i.e., MONTH1). Up to ten attendance periods may be entered for each roster. The number of days absent during that attendance period is then entered for each student in the class. Option 4 allows the user to revise a student's marks or attendance record. Option 5 lets the teacher change the title of a set of marks or an attendance period. In addition, an entire set of marks or the attendance records for any attendance period may be deleted.

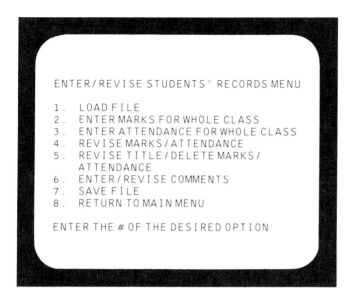

Figure 5–21 The options available for entering and revising student records. Grades, attendance data, and comments may be entered, revised, or deleted.

Figure 5–22 From this menu the teacher may enter or revise comments for students. Comment codes, as presented in Figure 5–23, are used to store comments.

```
CLASSMATE'S Comment Codes
CODE    COMMENT
AF      ADMIT FORM ON FILE
AN      ABSENCE—NOTE ON FILE
AU      ABSENCE—UNEXCUSED
BK      BOOK OWED
CA      CLASSWORK—AVERAGE
CB      CLASSWORK—BELOW AVERAGE
CS      CLASSWORK—SUPERIOR
CU      CUTTING
DR      DISCIPLINARY REFERRAL
EC      EXTRA CREDIT
GF      CONFIDENTIAL FILE IN GUID. OFF.
GO      STUDENT ORG. MEMBER
GR      GUIDANCE REFERRAL
HA      HOMEWORK—AVERAGE
HB      HOMEWORK—BELOW AVERAGE
HS      HOMEWORK—SUPERIOR
HU      HOME CONTACT CARD UP TO DATE
LE      LUNCH ELIGIBILITY FORM ON FILE
LN      LATENESS—NOTES ON FILE
LU      LATENESS—UNEXCUSED
MR      REFERRAL TO MEDICAL ROOM
OR      OUT OF ROOM PASS USAGE
PC      PROGRAM CHANGED
PI      PARENT CONTACTED—INTERVIEW
PL      PARENT CONTACTED—LETTER
PP      PARENT CONTACTED—PHONE
PR      PERMANENT RECORD CHECKED
RC      REPORT CARD NOT RETURNED SIGNED
TA      TRIP AUTHORIZATION FORM ON FILE
TF      TRANSPORTATION FORM ON FILE
```

Figure 5–23 A list of the comment codes initially available in *Classmate.* The teacher may change the comment codes.

Option 6, ENTER/REVISE COMMENTS, provides the useful function of including comments in each student's record, as desired. The submenu for this option is shown in **Figure 5–22.** Because space on the screen (and sometimes in the computer's memory) is at a premium, comment codes are used to record comments. The teacher may create her own codes or use the ones suggested by *Classmate.* **Figure 5–23** shows the codes specified by *Classmate.* To work with comment codes, the teacher chooses either option 1, ENTER/ADD COMMENT, which allows new comments to be entered for each student, or option 2, REVISE COMMENT. The latter choice lets the teacher change any comments previously entered for any student on the roster. Option 3 prints out a list of suggested comment codes.

Choice 4 from the main menu, EXAMINE/PRINT STUDENTS' RECORDS, lets the teacher print out on a printer or display on the screen either individual student records or the records for the whole class. The teacher may also choose to view class performance on an individual test or assignment rather than class records for all students for all assignments. A list of all missing

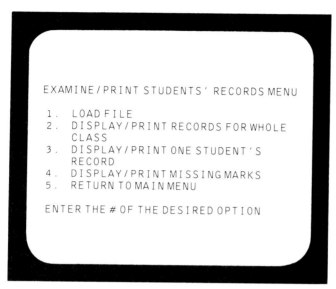

Figure 5-24 The choices available for the teacher to examine or print out student records.

```
            COMPLETE RECORDS
                                   4/16/84
ADAMS, WALKER                   0133
S-1 CH1 CH2 S-2 CH3 S-3 CH4 MID
C   68  68  C   75  D   77  66
M-1 M-2
3   0
COMMENTS BK HA EC

BAILEY, KATHLEEN                3356
S-1 CH1 CH2 S-2 CH3 S-3 CH4 MID
C+  73  59  ABS 66  C   65  69
M-1 M-2
0   1
COMMENTS CA

BELL, ALEX                      2431
S-1 CH1 CH2 S-2 CH3 S-3 CH4 MID
C   73  77  C+  80  C   88  74
M-1 M-2
7   3
COMMENTS HEARING PROBLEM-SEAT NEAR FRONT HA CA

BROWN, HAROLD                   3984
S-1 CH1 CH2 S-2 CH3 S-3 CH4 MID
ABS 79  ABS D   73  C+  59  81
M-1 M-2
4   0
COMMENTS LN PC

DAVIDSON, JEFF                  3050
S-1 CH1 CH2 S-2 CH3 S-3 CH4 MID
EXC CUT 61  C   77  F   53  79
M-1 M-2
3   3
COMMENTS HB
```

Figure 5-25 An example of the first page of a complete records printout for an entire class, including grades, attendance data, and comments for each student.

assignments for any class may be printed, or displayed, as well. **Figure 5–24** shows the submenu from where these choices can be made. **Figures 5–25** and **5–26** show, respectively, a portion of a sample printout of the complete records for an entire class and a sample of a missing-work printout for an entire class. Notice the use of comments and titles in these examples.

Option 5 from the main menu, COMPUTE WEIGHTED AVERAGES, offers the possibility of having the computer calculate and print weighted averages for each student in a class or for a selected student in a class. The teacher controls which numerical values will be associated with each letter grade (i.e., A = 95, A− = 90, etc.) and may choose to have all assignments, tests, and quizzes count equally or be assigned different weights. The computer will

```
                MISSING WORK
                MISSING MARKS      4/16/84

        BAILEY, KATHLEEN
        S-2
        ABS

        BROWN, HAROLD
        S-1 CH2
        ABS ABS

        DAVIDSON, JEFF
        CH1
        CUT

        EVANS, ROGER
        S-2
        ABS

        HALL, JUDY
        S-3
        ABS

        MARINO, ANTHONY
        S-1
        ABS

        MURPHY, ERIN
        S-3 MID
        ABS ABS

        RASKIN, EDDIE
        S-1 CH1
        CUT ABS

        WANG, MARK
        CH1
        ABS
```

Figure 5–26 A missing-work printout for a class.

compute either an average rounded to the nearest percent or an average that is not rounded, based on teacher preference. **Figure 5–27** shows a sample printout of weighted averages. Each student's name and ID are given, as well as the title for each test, quiz, or assignment and the associated grade. The weighted average is shown, as is the rounded average. Following the rounded average is the letter grade the average translates into, a code specifying either N for needs improvement, SAT for satisfactory, or EXC for excellent, and the grade translated into a four-point scale, where 1.0 equals D, 2.0 equals C, and so forth. The codes N, SAT, and EXC are based on the following: An average equal to or less than the numerical score the teacher has chosen to represent a C– will automatically cause an N to be printed. A score above C– but less than the teacher-assigned numerical equivalent for an A causes SAT to be printed. An A or above (A+) will produce an EXC. At the end of the printout, cumulative information for the entire class is displayed as well as the weights assigned to each test, quiz, and assignment.

```
               AVERAGES FOR FIRST QUARTER
                                        4-16-84
   BELL, ALEX                      2431
   CH1 CH2 CH3 CH4 FQE EXC
   66  60  79  60  71  EXC

   WEIGHTED AVERAGE IS    67.83
   ROUNDED AVERAGE/GRADE  68 (D/N/1.0)

   DAVIDSON, JEFF                   3050
   CH1 CH2 CH3 CH4 FQE EXC
   72  66  81  70  72  EXC

   WEIGHTED AVERAGE IS    72.17
   ROUNDED AVERAGE/GRADE  72 (C-/N/2.0)

   HALL, JUDY                       3806
   CH1 CH2 CH3 CH4 FQE EXC
   81  72  86  75  84  A

   WEIGHTED AVERAGE IS    81.8
   ROUNDED AVERAGE/GRADE  82 (B-/SAT/3.0)

THE # OF STUDENTS IN THE CLASS IS 10
THE # OF PASSING (65 & UP) IS 10 FOR A PERCENTAGE OF 100%
THE # FAILING (BELOW 65) IS 0 FOR A PERCENTAGE OF 0%

         TESTING INSTRUMENTS AND THEIR WEIGHTS
CHAPTER ONE TEST                CH1         15
CHAPTER TWO TEST                CH2         15
CHAPTER THREE TEST              CH3         15
CHAPTER FOUR TEST               CH1         15
FIRST QUARTER EXAM              FQE         30
EXTRA CREDIT ASSIGNMENT         EXC         10
```

Figure 5–27 A sample printout of weighted averages. This printout includes the student's name, ID, the title for each test, quiz, or assignment, and the associated grade. A weighted average plus a rounded average and the equivalent letter grade are also shown. A code specifying N for needs improvement, SAT for satisfactory, or EXC for excellent is displayed, followed by the grade translated into a four-point scale. At the end of the printout is cumulative information for the entire class, plus the weights assigned to each test, quiz, or assignment.

The last option on the main menu, ANALYZE STATISTICS, offers the choice of displaying, for any assignment, quiz, or test, the class average, the number of students present and absent, the number of students who passed and the number who failed, and the percentage of passing and failing grades. Further, the teacher may choose to have a distribution of the marks displayed or printed. **Figure 5–28** shows a sample of the distribution information that may be obtained.

A good deal of information can be generated by this type of program. Many teachers find that it takes an initial investment of time to learn how to use a grade-reporting program and to set up their files. A program such as *Classmate* attempts to simplify the process by being menu-driven and by presenting clear documentation that explains what the program can do. Once the files are set up and a transition has been made to keeping records on the computer, many teachers find that they save a considerable amount of time when grades are due. This time can be better spent by the teacher on instruction and preparation for instruction.

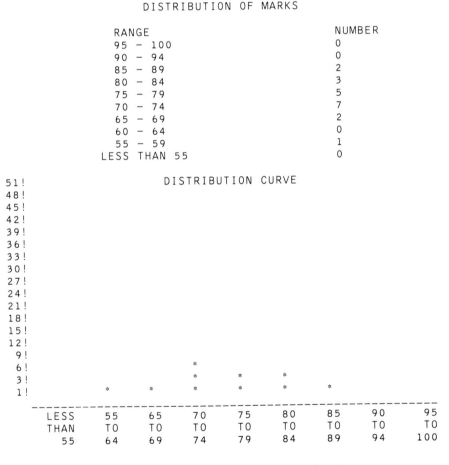

Figure 5–28 Class grade distribution information displayed in two formats.

Computers in the Classroom

Sometimes students can become highly motivated by taking on responsibility for management tasks related to their own instruction. Upper elementary students can use a word processor to prepare weekly or monthly reports on their progress for parents. Aside from accomplishing goals in the computer curriculum, this also provides practice in language arts. Practice in math skills can be part of this activity if students need to calculate weekly or monthly averages. Graphing programs can be used to plot and track individual or group performance. Data base management systems might be used to keep a file of students' performance in each of several subject areas. A monthly report could be published showing top performers in each subject, students with most improvement, etc. Spreadsheets could be used to store individual student grades and perform simple calculations to arrive at averages, even allowing for weighting of different tests, quizzes, and assignments.

Any discussion of individual student performance in a group situation should only be done after careful consideration of the students involved. Sensitivity to students' attitudes and feelings should be paramount. Although students are often acutely aware of how they perform in relation to other students, experiences such as those mentioned earlier should not be used to single out poor performance. Instead, reports to parents can be kept confidential between students, parents, and teachers; graphs can be generated of whole class performance over time; individual students can generate graphs of their own performance; and so on. The final determination of what is appropriate rests with the person who knows both the children involved and the educational environment in which they live and learn. Naturally, that person is the teacher.

Despite the variety of ways in which children can participate in these activities, using the computer for management purposes in the classroom is intended to be of primary benefit to the teacher. Sometimes finding instructional programs and management systems that adequately fit into the educational environment created by the teacher takes a bit of research. The following article by Jane Dundas Smith appeared in the April 1986 issue of Electronic Learning. *It contains some good points related to CMI as it is available with reading software in general and with three software packages in particular. As discussed in the next chapter, choosing software based on a single review is not a good idea. Yet if you had to choose one of these software packages for your classroom based solely on this review, which one would you choose? Why? How is your decision influenced by the management functions provided?*

Reading instruction does not change very quickly. New trends in reading theory lead slowly, if ever, to changes in reading textbooks and classroom teaching. But with computers, things have been different. Five years ago, hardly any of the textbook publishers sold software with their reading textbooks. Now, they all do. And for some schools, particularly those with reading programs that stress mastery of individual reading skills, this software may soon be indispensable.

For this buyer's guide, we asked six leading textbook publishers to provide us with their textbooks and the software they sell with them. Three agreed to—Houghton Mifflin, Macmillan, and Holt, Rinehart & Winston. Their products are reviewed below. The three others— Ginn, Harcourt Brace Jovanovich, and Scott, Foresman— are all releasing new reading series with software late this spring.

USING THE SOFTWARE

The software sold with reading textbooks consists of two types. There are management programs that test students on specific reading skills, and there are instructional programs that reinforce skills taught in reading programs. Although the features and the organizational structure of these packages may differ, the content of the programs consists largely of drills and tests on individual reading skills like distinguishing fact from opinion, and understanding context clues. If your reading curriculum is based on a skills model (reading equals mastery of all objectives) then you would probably find a management program useful.

Most of the available programs emphasize comprehension skills, but programs covering vocabulary and word analysis skills are also available. The drills or tests usually supplement skills taught through reading lessons and in practice workbooks. Computer programs in reading provide excellent drill and practice, but none of these software programs include anything that approaches instruction. In short, what is provided on computer is not substantially different in content from what is provided in workbooks and other supplementary materials. However, using software can be more efficient if it provides immediate feedback, motivating graphics, and tracks student performance.

Probably the most compelling reason to purchase textbook-correlated software is the efficiency of data management such a system offers. Reading instruction often requires teachers to individualize student work. Without a computer this is a record-keeping nightmare. With a good data management, storage, and retrieval program, the job is much easier. A good management system will score diagnostic tests, correlate weak areas to existing instructional materials (methods must still remain the teacher's area of expertise), keep records of students' progress, and produce reports and summaries of students' work.

FEATURES TO LOOK FOR

It's important to keep in mind that some textbook-correlated software is generic enough so that it will work with a number of reading series. So, if your school has adopted one reading textbook, you needn't feel that your only choice is software from the same publisher. An exception is the Macmillan software. It is too closely tied to the Macmillan readers to be used with other texts, but the other programs reviewed here could supplement a number of reading texts, depending on what you teach in your curriculum. Here are some features to keep in mind as you look at textbook-correlated software:

- **Ease of Use**—Software that evaluates student skills and stores data on student progress frequently requires lead time for teacher training before it can be used successfully in the classroom. An easy-to-read manual is a big plus in this process as is the availability of someone who can do staff training in the use of the system.

- **Automatic Record Keeping**—As students use the software, the program should record, in a single report, how each student performed. If teachers have to write or type results into each student's record file, the software will organize a teacher's records, but it is questionable whether the system will really save the teacher any time.

- **Prescriptions**—Comprehensive management systems for reading programs promise that they will provide student "prescriptions" on the basis of tests given at the computer. What this means is that every objective in which a student is weak will be listed, and possibly, if a list of materials is in the computer program, the weaknesses will be correlated to the list of instructional materials. However, this is not a prescription in the clinical sense, and it would be a mistake to rely on these too heavily. Teachers still need to evaluate student performance and decide what type of instruction will be best for each student.

Teachers also need to be aware that these prescriptions will only cover the skills evaluated by the software. If your school's approach to reading is more holistic, as more and more programs are, teachers must direct students to activities that will help them integrate the discrete skills these software programs reinforce. Here again, practice is slow to catch up with current reading theory.

SOFTWARE FOR THREE READING SERIES

Houghton Mifflin

Instructional Software: *Microcourse Reading* (Apple IIe, IBM PC/PCjr. PC XT, Digital Rainbow 100, 100+) levels 3–8, $798

Management Software: *The Classroom Answer* (Apple II series, TRS–80 III 4, IBM PC. Commodore Pet. CBM 4000, 8000) $324

The *Microcourse* series provides tests and drills on 252 isolated reading skills, organized into four content areas: comprehension, word structure, word attack, and study skills. Resource books are available for the last two. Of the programs reviewed here, this series provided the largest selection of print and software materials, as well as a comprehensive and readable manual. The comprehension section is broken down into three subsections: literal, inferential, and evaluative comprehension. Within these categories 66 separate skill areas are covered on 13 disks. For each skill there is a pretest, drill, and a post-test. These menu-driven programs could be used with any reading series, as the exercises are not text-dependent.

The programs are very easy to use and require minimal training of students. The teacher assigns the skill to be practiced; students enter their name, the skill number, and begin. There is a minimum of disk switching, and students can use simple commands to exit the program or to skip a section. The management program evaluates student work, and a final summary screen provides information on all work done in that session. The results must then be written on the Student Progress Record (one copy of the booklet is provided with the program). The system will, however, hold the summary screen for the two most recent sessions in memory for the teacher to access on a special command. This is not so much a data storage system as it is a "fail safe" procedure in case one forgets to record scores. Teachers can generate prescriptions for students from the pretests and post-tests. There is, however, no software to do this task. A class record form is also provided, for teachers to fill in by hand.

Macmillan

Instructional Software: *SERIES r Vocabulary Comprehension Computer-Assisted Instruction* (Apple II series) grades 1–3, $220 each; grades 4–6, $330 each

Management Software: *SERIES r Instructional Management System* (Apple II series and Chatsworth or True Data optical-card reader) $597.10, plus $76.45 for each grade-level disk

Macmillan's data management system is similar to Holt's, but it is designed solely for the Macmillan SERIES r reading program. The software will score the SERIES r assessment tests, make prescriptions based on the results of the assessment test, score student records (up to 35 on a disk), and produce printed test reports, student summaries by objective, and class reports. The management software will require some training for teachers, particularly those without a computer background. The manual is clear, and not as hefty as some others.

In addition to the management software, the Macmillan program comes with a set of computer-assisted instructional materials for each textbook level. For the sixth-grade textbook there are three disks to test students on the vocabulary from each story in the textbook and three disks to test student comprehension of these stories. These menu-driven drills are not lessons relating to the stories, but a means of assessing students' knowledge of the vocabulary and story content. Typically each story has five comprehension questions, few of which attempt to assess higher-level thinking skills. The program automatically saves a record of student performance. This program, unlike the Holt and Houghton-Mifflin programs, is totally text-dependent. This direct tie to the reading text provides for a more direct integration of the computer into the daily curriculum.

Holt

Instructional Software: *Reading Skills Extender* (Apple II series, IBM PC) levels 3–8, $1294.80; levels 3–6 $863.20, multiple-copy discounts available

Management Software: *CLASS II Reading Testbank* (Apple II series, IBM PC, automatic scoring device optional, but recommended.) $1296; for subsequent purchases of program in the same district, price is $696

The Reading Skills Extender is a series of grade-specific programs that accompany each level of the textbook series. Typical content includes drill and practice on major comprehension skills such as identifying the main idea, cause and effect, finding details, sequence, etc. It also covers study skills such as using a glossary, outlining, and using reference books.

These menu-driven instructional programs come with a built-in management system that is much simpler than *CLASS II*. The teacher's class list and each student's assignment are entered on the system. Students sign on and off, and the computer gives them their skills assignment and a summary report for teachers that is printed out before the student leaves. Only the most recent report is retained in memory.

These programs are not dependent on the reading textbook, but they do come correlated to the skills introduced in Holt's reading series. There is quite a bit of diskette shuffling involved in the set-up of this program. This may be a drawback in some classroom situations.

CLASS II (The Computerized Learning and Scoring System) is the data management program that serves not only Holt's reading program, but the English, math, science, and social studies programs as well. *CLASS II* provides test administration, scoring, and item analysis. It also prints reports of test results and student progress toward mastery of specific objectives. Student disks provide information for 40 students; each student record will indicate up to 100 objectives mastered and 50 objectives not yet mastered. Curriculum disks allow teachers to display, edit, or enter objectives, up to 500 on a disk, and the disks are copyable. Because of the customizing features, *CLASS II* is usable with any instructional program, provided you are willing to put in time to adapt it to your curriculum.

CLASS II is a comprehensive data storage, management, retrieval system. It will provide teachers with a lot of information relating to skill mastery, but teachers will need training to use it.

Directory of Publishers

Ginn and Co., 191 Spring St., Lexington, MA 02173 617/863–7711

Harcourt Brace Jovanovich, Orlando, FL 32887 305/345–3000

Holt, Rinehart & Winston, 383 Madison Ave., New York, NY 10017 212/872–2000

Houghton Mifflin, One Beacon St., Boston, MA 02108 617/725–5000

Macmillan, 866 Third Ave., New York, 10022 609/461–6500

Scott, Foresman, 1900 East Lake Ave., Glenview, IL 60025 312/729–3000

Jane Dundas Smith is the Assistant Principal of Fontana (CA) Junior High School. She was formerly the Reading Specialist for the Fontana Unified School District.
(Smith, 1986)

Selected examples of other teacher utility software follow.

Other Applications

AUTHORING SYSTEMS

Authoring languages, such as PILOT, allow teachers to create computer-based educational materials. Such languages would best be categorized as an example of the computer being used in the tutee mode, since the teacher is actually programming the computer using a specialized high-level programming language. Menu-driven authoring systems, such as a product called *TAS: Teacher*

Authoring System, published by Teach Yourself by Computer Software, would be classified as tool mode software because no programming is required of the teacher. Rather, the teacher chooses from a series of options, which are usually presented in menu format. Data is entered in response to prompts displayed on the screen. The *TAS* package consists of (a) an authoring program that teachers can use to create tutorial lessons; (b) a presentation program, which teachers use to create and offer drill and practice lessons to students; (c) a file maintenance program that helps teachers to maintain a catalog of lessons created; and (d) a student records program, which is used to maintain data on student progress. Such an integrated authoring system provides the teacher with the ability to create computer-based lessons and then couple those lessons with a CMI-type program to maintain student records that contain relevant data on student performance with specific lessons.

Another type of software consists of program shells (sometimes called skeleton programs) that allow teachers to specify the content of a lesson or instructional game, such as choosing the examples to be used in a math game that offers practice with division. Diversified Learning Materials publishes a series of programs called *Arcademic Drill Builders* which are essentially program shells of this nature. Included in this series are instructional games that offer practice in various areas. *Wiz Works* offers practice in sequencing and can be used for practice with spelling words or math facts. In *Meteor Mission* students are required to fill in the missing answer. It may be used with such content as fractions or abbreviations.

READABILITY

Software is available that offers the convenience of having the computer calculate the readability level of written material. Depending on the program used, readability will be calculated according to one or more of the many standard formulas, such as the Dale-Chall Index, the Fry Index, the Flesch Index, and the Spache method. Berta-Max Software publishes the *Readability Estimator*, a menu-driven program that calculates readability for the following methods; Dale-Chall, Flesch, Fog, Fry, Smog, and Wheeler-Smith. Micro Power and Light publishes *Readability*, which computes scores according to nine scales; Dale-Chall, Flesch, Fry, Flesch-Kincaid, Fog, ARI, Coleman, Powers, and Holmquist.

TEST CREATION/TEST SCORING PROGRAMS

Software to create a variety of teacher-made tests on the computer is available to teachers. The creation and scoring of tests may be functions supplied as part of a comprehensive CMI system. Individual programs, not part of a comprehensive management system, may be used to create and score tests. Such programs are classified here as teacher utilities. The tests created can often be used by a student at the computer, in which case the computer will usually score the student's responses, or they may be printed out for future use by students. Shenandoah Software offers a series of three programs, *Exams, Examiner*, and *Records*, collectively called *The Instructor's System*. *Exams* is used to create and store test items for multiple-choice and true-false tests. *Examiner* is used to give tests on the computer and will grade the student's test. *Records* is a record-keeping program used to store, calculate, and display information about students' grades. Results from tests designed using *Exams* and administered using *Examiner* may be transferred by the computer to the *Records* program for inclusion in the student's record. *Exams* and *Examiner* may be used independently of the *Records* program.

A variety of software is available to help administrators. Addison-Wesley publishes a series of programs for school administrators, including *Equip*, a program to keep an inventory of school equipment, and *Purchase*, a program to automate the paperwork and record keeping necessary for preparing school purchase orders. *Bursar* is a program to maintain data on funds generated by extracurricular activities, such as sports teams and clubs. K–12 Micro-Media offers the *School Attendance Manager* to track student attendance and the *School Discipline Manager*, which keeps data on discipline problems and allows such reports as an individual student's discipline record or a list of discipline problems by teacher. A host of other applications are available, including a program published by the Minnesota Educational Computing Corporation that helps to select optimal bus routes, called, appropriately, *Bus Routes*. Programs are available that can generate report cards for an entire school; other programs assist administrators in class scheduling and some of the bookkeeping tasks that must be performed by schools. Some schools and school districts buy off-the-shelf software for specific applications such as those mentioned here. Others have specialized all-encompassing systems especially designed for them. In a large district a full-time staff of programmers and analysts may design and maintain the programs used for the administration of the district. Some building administrators use spreadsheets and data base management systems to automate the tasks they must perform, such as budgeting and scheduling. Other school professionals may use the computer for various purposes. For example, a librarian might use software designed to track overdue books and generate past-due notices. Other programs are available to produce cards for the card catalog as well as labels for books.

Management Software for Administrators

Chapter 6 offers information on software evaluation, much of which will apply to evaluating software that provides management functions. Briefly, any software that offers management functions should be easy to use and useful. The applications offered should be meaningful to the teacher or administrator who will use the program. It should provide for easy generation of a variety of information both on a screen display and on a printer. The software should be flexible. This is especially important with this type of software. If the program does not fit into the way the user chooses to do things, it should not be adopted. For example, if it is important to the teacher to be able to vary the numerical equivalent of different letter grades and to award pluses and minuses (A+, B−, etc.), a program that does not allow this should not be adopted. Otherwise, the user falls into the trap of letting the limitations of the software dictate how the task will be performed. This should never be allowed. Software should be adaptable to the needs and desires of the user. An educator should not have to change the way she prefers to do something just because a particular software package does not allow it.

What to Look For

Conclusion

CMI software, teacher utilities, and software for administrators and other professionals in education can all be used to perform necessary tasks in education. Although it may cost in terms of time, effort, and money to adopt the use of the computer in one or more of these areas, the ultimate results are, to many educators, worth the initial investment. Such results can include an increase in the amount and type of information available for decision making, as well as an increase in the time available for instruction and teacher preparation. Letting the computer do what it does best—store and manipulate data—can free educators to do what they do best—make decisions about the instructional needs of students and find ways to meet those needs.

Key Terms

authoring system
computer-managed instruction (CMI)
flowchart
grade-keeping program
management system

menu-driven
PILOT
program shell
skeleton program
teacher utility

Questions

1. What is CMI software, and how might it be used by a teacher?

2. Describe the general process performed by a CMI package that manages student data. What role does file creation and maintenance play?

3. Identify and explain at least five functions that a management system that is part of a tutor mode program might provide.

4. Discuss the various tasks a grade-keeping program can perform. Be specific and give examples for each task mentioned in your answer.

5. What are three examples of teacher utility software? Choose one of your examples and explain how you, as a teacher, would use it.

6. What are some applications of computer use for administrators?

7. Choose one category of professional educator other than a principal or a regular classroom teacher (i.e., school counselor, nurse, school social worker, speech therapist). Speculate as to how this professional might use the computer for management purposes.

8. Use a grade-keeping program to set up a file of fifteen students. Explore the functions available in the program. Print out examples of the reports generated by the program. As a teacher, would you find the program of use? Report your findings to the class.

9. Form a group of four. Each person is to do number 8, but each should investigate a different grade-keeping program.

10. Choose a tutor mode program that has a management system. Locate a copy of the program and spend time using it. What is your reaction?

11. Locate a program you would classify as a teacher utility. Spend time working with it. Report your findings to the class.

12. How much of a teacher's job involves record keeping? List all the record-keeping tasks you can think of. Which of these tasks might it be worthwhile to automate?

References/Further Reading

Ebisch, Bob, and Richard A. Immel. "Trying to Predict the Future. Guide to Computers in Education." *Popular Computing* (special issue), October 1984, pp. 32–44.

Germundsen, Richard, and Allen D. Glenn. "Computer Gradebooks: Implications for Teachers." *The Computing Teacher* 12, no. 2 (1984):13–15.

Gorth, William Phillip, and Paula M. Nassif. "A Comparison of Microcomputer-Based, Computer Managed Instruction (CMI) Software Programs (with an Evaluation Form)." *Educational Technology* 24, no. 1 (1984):28.

Kinzer, Charles K., Robert D. Sherwood, and John D. Bransford. *Computer Strategies for Education: Foundations and Content-Area Applications.* Columbus, Ohio: Merrill Publishing Co., 1986.

Kohl, Herbert. "Classroom Management Software: Beware the Hidden Agenda." *Classroom Computer Learning* 5, no. 7 (1985):18–21.

Smith, Jane Dundas. "Managing Reading: Software for Use with Reading Textbooks." *Electronic Learning* 5, no. 7 (1986):24–28.

6

Software Evaluation

TOPICS ADDRESSED

Why should teachers develop software-evaluation skills?

What criteria should be considered when evaluating software for classroom use?

What steps can be followed when evaluating software?

Where can information about educational software be found?

What is the value of a software-evaluation form?

What are some examples of software-evaluation forms?

OUTLINE

Introduction
Evaluating Software
General Criteria
  Cost
  Compatibility
  Target Group
  Subject Area
Specific Criteria
  Educational Criteria
    Prerequisite Skills
    Objectives
    Teaching Style
    Accuracy
    Pace
    Student Engagement
    Usefulness
    Grouping
    Stereotypes
  Technical Criteria
    Flexibility
    Use of Graphics and Sound

    Documentation
    Support
    Error Handling
    Management Information
    Interactive Design
    Screen Design
    Bugs
    Backup Copies
Reviewing Software: Hands-on Experience
Software Evaluation: Suggested Steps
  Identify Need
  Gather Information
  Preview
  The Software-Evaluation Form
  Purchase
Conclusion
Key Terms
Questions
References/Further Reading

Introduction

The amount, availability, and quality of educational software have been growing at a steady rate. Although the overall quality of programs has improved over time, there is no guarantee that a particular program will be educationally sound and appropriately designed for use in a school setting. As always, the ultimate responsibility for the educational materials used with students rests with the classroom teacher. Even when the teacher does not directly select materials, it is still her responsibility to evaluate them as they are used, on a daily basis, with students.

Often, however, the teacher will be responsible for selecting many of the materials she uses in her classroom, especially computer software. In fact, for most teachers, skill in the selection of educational software will be essential. It is much more likely that teachers will select and have their schools purchase various types of commercial software than it is that teachers will design and write their own software. This is simply a matter of practicality. Even a teacher with excellent programming and design skills cannot match the time and resources a software company can invest in the development of a product. It may take a cumulative total of 50 to 100 years of employee hours (and in some cases much more) to produce and refine a sophisticated software package. An individual teacher can't match the time put in by thirty persons over a two- or three-year period. Although some valuable programs may be created by teachers, the vast majority of teachers primarily use commercially prepared software.

This chapter presents some guidelines for teacher evaluation of educational software. Once the guidelines are presented, a process for evaluating software is described. Examples of software-evaluation forms are cited and sources of information about software are presented. The emphasis is on providing practical information about software evaluation.

Evaluating Software

Teachers, implicitly or explicitly, are always involved with the evaluation of educational materials. A teacher may be asked to serve on a committee to review new reading texts. An administrator may ask a teacher to, individually, review and evaluate new materials. Even when not formally reviewing materials, teachers are always noting what works and what doesn't work during their interaction with students. In their professional reading, teachers come across new ideas and suggestions for classroom implementation and must judge the potential effectiveness of those ideas. Evaluation, then, is not new to teachers. In fact, many of the criteria for evaluating other types of educational materials apply to the evaluation of computer software, and therefore are already familiar. Other criteria, though, owing to the unique properties offered by the computer, will be new.

General Criteria

Before citing specific criteria for the evaluation of individual software packages, several general criteria should be considered in relation to any software purchase.

"No, B.C. does not mean 'Before Computers'."

One teacher, after doing research on software evaluation and available software-evaluation forms, was astounded to find that many forms did not list the cost of the software as an evaluation category. Cost is obviously an important practical consideration. It is a waste of time to evaluate and recommend for purchase a software package that costs more than a school or district can spend. Also, cost may be a factor in deciding which of a number of packages is adopted. If it is a choice between spending $500 on one software package that will serve a small group of students, or spending the $500 on a variety of packages that will serve a wider range of students, the consensus may be that the money will be better spent buying a range of software. Of course, there may be times when the more expensive package is the appropriate choice. The fact remains that without cost information, an informed determination cannot be made.

Cost

Any software purchased must be compatible with the hardware available in the school. If a piece of software is designed to run on an Apple IIe computer and is not available in a version to run on the IBM computers owned by the school, the software is incompatible with available hardware and should, naturally, not be purchased. Further, even within a given hardware model, the computer must be configured, or set up, with the correct options to run a particular software package. Most programs will specify what computer and what computer configuration is needed for the software to work. For example, if the computer specified is an Apple IIe, further information about the computer configuration might include the following: Apple IIe, 128K, 80-column card, two disk drives, color monitor, printer.

Compatibility

In this instance the Apple IIe must have 128K of memory as well as an 80-column card, which allows text to be displayed in eighty columns across the screen. The computer must be connected to two disk drives. A monitor capable of displaying information in color must be part of the system. Also, a printer must be connected to the computer. It should be assumed that the software was designed to make use of all of the peripheral devices specified in the configuration. It may be that there are two disks that must be available to the computer at all times while the software is running. It could be that the software requires that students differentiate, based on color, between objects on the screen. Although the software may run correctly with a monochrome monitor, students asked to choose a red circle from three circles displayed on the screen will be confused when, on a monochrome monitor, they are presented with three circles of the same color (perhaps green or amber).

Target Group

Software evaluation and selection should be preceded by identifying the target group that will use the software. For what age or grade range is the software intended? Some software can be used, for different reasons, across a range of grades or ability levels. A program in language arts may be used as enrichment in grade 4 and for remediation in grade 6. However, software publishers, in seeking expanded sales, may take unwarranted liberties in their grade-level designations. A program billed as appropriate for grades 3 through 7 may, in reality, be too difficult for an average third-grade student and too simple for a seventh-grade student. For this and other valid reasons a piece of educational software must be used, hands-on, by the teacher as part of a competent evaluation.

Subject Area

A preliminary decision must be made as to what area (or areas) of the curriculum the software will affect. Depending on the software, one content area or several may be enhanced. A drill and practice package that covers state capitals will have obvious use in social studies. A simulation that traces the voyage of Columbus might readily lend itself not only to lessons in social studies content, but also to work in reading and language arts, or perhaps even science. The relationship of the software to the overall curriculum must be considered. The evaluation process will be affected if the intention is to use the software for multiple purposes because all possible applications of the software will need to be considered during the review process.

Specific Criteria

Once the general criteria are dealt with, specific criteria regarding particular software must be considered. They are divided into two categories: educational criteria and technical criteria. As you read this section, notice the criteria in which, by thinking about and evaluating other types of educational materials, you have already developed expertise.

PREREQUISITE SKILLS

What prerequisite skills are necessary for the student to successfully interact with the software? One obvious area to consider is reading level. Is it specified? If so, is the method used to identify reading level given (i.e., what formula was used to compute reading level, Fry, Dale-Chall, etc.?). If the software requires computational ability, what number facts or operations must the student have mastered? What are the prerequisite facts or concepts related to a given subject area, such as science, that the student must know? For example, if a piece of software simulates the path of Halley's comet when it passes by Earth at different periods in time, is there any particular information about astronomy with which the student must be familiar?

OBJECTIVES

Are the educational objectives for the software stated clearly and explicitly? This information should be contained in the written material that accompanies the software. Specific objectives may be stated, such as: The student will be able to list three alternative strategies for selecting provisions for a trip by wagon to the West in 1840. Or, more general goals may be stated, such as: The student will understand factors affecting travel by wagon in the West during the middle of the nineteenth century.

Whichever form this information takes, it is important that the educational outcomes of the software be identified and explained.

TEACHING STYLE

Each teacher, over a period of time, develops her own teaching style. Depending on the teacher's professional experience, the reading she has done, her natural propensities, and her current teaching situation, her instructional style takes on a unique character. Most teachers develop preferences over time for certain types of materials and methods. One teacher may opt for an approach that emphasizes the affective as a spur toward intellectual growth. Another may see himself as running a tightly ordered, teacher-centered classroom, while a third teacher may develop strategies that are highly student-centered. Another teacher may consciously and uniquely blend these and other strategies to create her teaching environment.

The teacher's job is to match the teaching style of the educational software selected to his teaching style. For instance, simulations assume that vicarious experience and emotional involvement can aid in learning content. A teacher who disagrees with these assumptions would probably be uncomfortable using a computer simulation with students. As software is reviewed, the type of educational interaction it will provide (i.e., instructional game, tutorial, etc.) must be considered as it relates to the environment the teacher has created in the classroom. Of course, teachers are not bound by their past experiences and may use the introduction of a computer into their classroom as an opportunity to experiment with new strategies. A well-written computer simulation may interest a teacher in working with a variety of simulations, both computer-based and otherwise. A good drill and practice program may provide a teacher who dislikes drill and practice with the opportunity to see its positive educational applications.

ACCURACY

Software must be accurate in each of two ways. First, the content conveyed by the software must be accurate in relation to the discipline covered. For example, a tutorial program on the use of metaphors must contain accurate definitions and present valid examples. A simulation program presenting a space shuttle launch must present a valid model of that experience. Second, the software must be free of spelling, punctuation, and grammatical errors. Any educational program must receive at least as much attention in its preparation, regarding accuracy, as a good textbook. This point may seem trivial, but it is not uncommon to find errors in the accuracy of computer materials. A colleague, reviewing a program that contained samples of software offered by a major publisher, reports that within the first several screens, spelling errors appeared. This did little to ensure the teacher that any great care had been taken in the preparation of the software.

PACE

When working with a computer program, the speed at which screens are presented should be controlled by the person using the program. This is often done by prompting the user to hit a specified key (perhaps the space bar) when ready to move on to the next screen. If a response is required, such as the answer to a question, the machine waits until the user enters the response. In this way the flow of material, by screen, is controlled by the user and not the machine. A program that paused only for a specified number of seconds per screen and then moved on automatically would disallow individual differences between students in reading rates, attention span, and so on.

Pace also refers to the concept load of the material. With computer-based material, as with other educational materials, the rate at which concepts and facts are presented should match the instructional level of the student served. Further, the options available for instruction will also affect pace. Based on a student's response, software will, ideally, allow the student to branch to material best suited for instruction at that moment. The software may do this automatically or may offer suggestions to the student or the teacher. For example, in working with a reading tutorial on comprehension skills, the student may enter the skill level at which he is currently operating. After presenting some reading strategies (reading for main idea, finding supporting details, and so on), the program may present a series of exercises. If the student does poorly on the exercises (according to preselected criteria contained in the program), the software might automatically present tutorial material designed to reteach the concepts. In other instances the program may suggest that the student try a different skill level. In the same way, if the student does well on the material, he may be prompted to try a more difficult level. The degree to which the program allows or does not allow branching will, naturally, affect the pace of the program. In the best of all worlds, programs would allow for adequate branching such that all students always receive the ideal instruction required. As mentioned in Chapter 3, programs that will run on the types of hardware most educators use do not allow sophisticated branching.

STUDENT ENGAGEMENT

One prime concern related to classroom planning and management is, Can the student run the software by herself? A product is of little value if the teacher has to stand next to the student while the software is used. Ideally, the student should be able to run the program successfully with minimal instruction from the teacher. There may even be a special set of instructions (documentation) for students.

Further, the length of time it takes a student to run the program is important. Because students are individuals, the teacher must consider how long different students may need to run the software. One desirable feature is that a student be able to stop the program, save her work, and continue at a later time. One sure way to frustrate students (and teachers) is to have a student work for awhile, run out of time, loose all the work completed, and have to start at the beginning of the software during the next computer session.

Another consideration is, Will the software be of interest to students? Although education and entertainment are not necessarily the same thing, any degree of motivation cleverly designed software elicits from students can be beneficial. Materials that are educationally sound and that motivate students are desirable. Yet teachers should not have unrealistic expectations about computer-based materials. Even the best-designed software usually has a life span for students. It is unwise to expect students to continue to be highly motivated by a program after they have worked with it a number of times. This may not be the case, however, with some types of software that can maintain interest over a prolonged period of time (e.g., programming languages, tool mode software, some educational games, and some simulations).

USEFULNESS

Any adoption of computerized materials costs in terms of teacher time, the school budget, and, initially at least, student time to learn how to use the software. The teacher must consider carefully what the computer-based materials can accomplish that other materials and methods cannot. There must be some gain the teacher can identify that will justify the expenditure of resources necessary to adopt computer-based materials. Perhaps the software provides experiences and opportunities for decision making not available to students any other way, such as in computer-based simulations. Maybe the software allows adequate coverage of material by means of a tutorial or provides an opportunity for practice, such as a drill and practice program, while freeing the teacher for other tasks. The program might quickly garner student interest while accomplishing a meaningful instructional objective, as with an instructional game. The opportunity to learn a computer language might yield tangible results related to thinking skills. Whatever the case, the teacher should be prepared to determine what it is about the software that makes it worth the effort of incorporating it into the curriculum.

GROUPING

In managing instruction, teachers may have students work independently (alone or in groups) or may choose to work with students individually or in small or large groups. The teacher should ask, In what situations can the software be used? When students are working independently, does the design of the software allow it to be used by more than one student at a time? If the teacher is working with students, is the software appropriate for use by one student, a whole class, or a small group? For example, in most instances, a drill and practice program will be used by one student at a time, as will a word processor (of course, a group-composed story, or some other legitimate activity, may cause a word processor to be used by several students at a time, although one student may be chosen to actually enter text). An instructional game may, however, require two or more players. A programming language may be used cooperatively by more than one student to solve a problem, or a spreadsheet may be used cooperatively by several students to record and analyze data from an experiment. Considering what options are available for a particular piece of software will aid in classroom management and planning when the time comes to integrate the software into the curriculum.

STEREOTYPES

Teachers must be sensitive to the presentation of stereotypes in computer-based educational materials, just as they are sensitive to stereotypes in other instructional materials. Ethnic groups, the aged, and women are some of the groups that come to mind when confronting this issue. The unfair representation of any segment of society has no place in materials used in the classroom.

Technical Criteria

FLEXIBILITY

The more options the user of a program has for controlling the functioning of the program, the more flexible the program is. For example, if a program uses the sound capabilities of the computer, it is best if the user has the option to turn the sound off. The ability to avoid graphics sequences by choice, perhaps by choosing the appropriate option on a menu, is another example of flexibility. Often software will present graphics sequences, either as reinforcement or as an integral part of the content presentation. Although such sequences can be colorful and amusing, they may wear thin after repeated use. Computer programs, unlike many other educational materials, may be used repeatedly by students. Hence the problem of graphics sequences becoming boring may not be a function of poorly designed animation. Rather, the sequences may become tedious because they are viewed over and over again. Other areas in which flexibility is desirable include the ability to select one from a number of available skill levels, the ability to vary the order of presentation of exercises in a drill and practice program, and the ability to selectively present material

Input/Output

The role of the computer in the schools has been developing and changing for awhile. Different people concerned with computers in education have varying opinions about how computers should be used in schools. The following commentary by Arthur Luehrmann, a valuable contributor to this field for a considerable length of time, offers insight into the way schools might view computers.

The New Trend: Ed-Teching the Computer

Until a year or two ago, the computer came into the school with a well-defined, specific mission. Today, the mission is becoming vague, hopeful, even wishful and dangerously unrealistic.

Back in the middle and late seventies, a school had a computer, if at all, for only one reason. Some teacher who had managed to get hold of a computer made a universal discovery: Kids were fascinated by the computer, wanted to learn about it, take control, and use it to express their ideas.

At first, the teacher made valiant efforts to relate the computer to the subject being taught. Usually, that meant doing math activities on the computer: finding prime numbers or printing the Fibonacci series. Within a few years, however, the teacher began to identify "computing" as a new subject.

A cooperative administration, impressed by the eagerness of students to sign up for a class that featured the computer, approved a formal nine-week unit about the computer; later, it grew to a regular class in computing. The teacher was soon arguing for additional computers to support growing enrollments. Parents of students in computer classes became advocates of budget items to buy computers.

The decision to buy was a simple one back then. The computer teacher demonstrated the near impossibility of handling 30 kids with only one or two computers. Any units purchased would obviously be put to immediate, visible use throughout the day. On the other hand, at about $2800 a pop back then, no administrator was likely to buy dozens of computers on a whim.

That healthy tension between a clear, specific classroom need and fiscal reality kept everyone honest. The teacher had to show exactly what the computers would be used for; the administrator had to evaluate obvious benefits against equally obvious costs.

Changed decision making.

This healthy tension prevailed until about two years ago. As Henry Jay Becker's surveys (*School Uses of Microcomputers*, Johns Hopkins University, Baltimore, MD 21218) reveal, the computer teacher has become less and less involved in a school or district's decision to buy and use computers.

There are several reasons for this. First, computer prices are about a third what they used to be; the decision to buy is less agonizing and, therefore, gets less scrutiny. Second, hundreds of millions spent on personal computer advertising has softened up the public, including school leaders. Third, the computer teachers today are not far from having their own immediate equipment needs satisfied, so they are less vociferous now, on average. Fourth, as the sheer number of computers in a district gets big, there is a natural tendency to put someone "higher up" in charge.

Enter the ed-tech folk.

Especially dangerous, I believe, is a trend these days to base planning and purchasing on a view of the computer as nothing more than the latest in *educational technology:* a sexy way to mechanize instruction in traditional subjects. According to this ed-tech view, computers are important *only* to the extent that they make teaching "regular subjects" better and cheaper, saving money or improving test scores. (That may be why the ed-tech specialists seem eager to integrate the computer throughout the curriculum, whether or not the teachers are clamoring for it.)

Not surprisingly, this view is strongest when an existing ed-tech department inherits responsibility for computer policy. One sees this happening in larger school districts, in some education agencies, and even in schools of education.

Computer as piano.

The ed-tech image of the computer misses the whole point of what has been happening in the classroom during the past ten years. In the view of any seasoned computer teacher, a computer is no more a piece of educational technology than is a piano, a typewriter, or a miscroscope. A student can learn wondrous things from each one of these machines, but only through mastering the skills of using it. However, as educational technology pianos, typewriters, and microscopes are flops: None of the machines delivers instruction; none makes teaching cheaper; none improves basic skills.

Despite claims to the contrary, computers also have largely failed to do these things. Therefore, to promote school computers as mere educational technology is courting disaster. A naive public may believe these claims today, but it will look for results tomorrow, and, not finding much, will dismiss computers as "just one more technological fix that didn't work"—like instructional TV, language labs, and programmed instruction.

Wise school leadership today can avert that unnecessary disaster. Don't sell the public on the computer as a way to save money or improve test scores. That hasn't often happened, nor is it likely to. Instead, go visit the successful computer class. Watch what goes on between kids and computers. Listen to the computer teacher. Then ask yourself if such learning belongs in your schools. If so, tell that to the public. They'll get their money's worth.

Arthur Luehrmann is founding partner of the firm Computer Literacy in Berkeley, CA. (Luehrmann, 1985.)

from a tutorial. Another example of flexibility is the option to select criteria for successful completion of an instructional game (e.g., choosing the number of points participants must score to win the game). In general, the more flexibile a program is, the more likely it is to meet the individual needs of students.

USE OF GRAPHICS AND SOUND

The graphics and sound capabilities of computers can be exploited to increase student involvement. Although the warning offered about the repetition of graphics sequences still stands, it must be noted that the clever use of graphics and sound can do much to motivate and engage students. Depending on the program content and grade level, graphics and sound may or may not be appropriate. Especially in software designed for the elementary grades, engaging sequences of animation may be a clue to a carefully prepared, well-designed product. There are no guarantees, however, that well-designed graphics automatically means good software.

DOCUMENTATION

The printed materials, such as manuals, that accompany commercially prepared software are referred to as documentation. The quality of the documentation that comes with software can be an important factor in judging the software's worth. Good documentation will be well written, easy to understand, and thorough. It should explain, for the novice user, how to start the software. It should outline in clear terms the process the user must go through to use the different options offered by the software. For instance, a piece of software designed to allow teachers to create a variety of tests (multiple choice, true-false, fill-in-the-blank) should have documentation that explains the options available from each menu in the program. The documentation should show actual examples of the screens with which the user will work. Any special conditions necessary for using the software must be identified. For example, if there is a maximum permissible length for any question entry, perhaps 200 characters, the documentation should state it. Instructions for setting up a variety of printers for use with the software should be included, as should clear, unambiguous instructions for printing out different test formats.

The conditions for good documentation would apply to any type of software (business, recreational, educational), but documentation for educational software should offer additional information. This might include suggestions for use in an educational setting, perhaps even lesson or unit plans for integrating the software into the curriculum. The need for identifying prerequisite skills and for clearly stated objectives was cited previously. This information should appear in the documentation. Depending on the type of software, background information related to the development of the product might be presented. For example, the appropriateness of any simulation will depend greatly on the model that the designer of the software uses to create the simulation. The documentation for a simulation might contain an explanation of the model, including appropriate bibliographical citations. This allows the teacher to consult various references as desired and supports the validity of the simulation.

Other materials such as worksheets, puzzles, suggestions for bulletin boards built around the software, and suggestions for evaluating students' work may prove useful. When reviewing educational software, the teacher considers the accompanying documentation in two ways. Once for its clarity and completeness in making possible the practical use of the software. For example, questions such as What must be done to get the software to run? and What options are available within the program? should be clearly answered in the documentation. In addition, consideration is given to the supplementary educational materials provided to help integrate the software into the curriculum (lesson plans, background information, etc.).

SUPPORT

Good support for any software product is invaluable. Support is available from one of two places; the dealer who sold the software (either a retail computer store or a distributor) or the manufacturer of the software. The dealer or manufacturer supports the software product by making people available to answer questions, which may or may not be covered in the documentation, about the normal use of the software ("How do I get a screen to print out on my printer?") as well as to help solve problems that may arise with the software ("I was running the program and it just stopped!"). These people should also be able to provide technical information to users ("The documentation says that your word-processing program produces standard ASCII files, but they won't work with my other programs that need standard ASCII files. Do I have to do something to convert them?").

Many distributors and retail computer stores cite their support of the products they sell as an important consideration in doing business with them. This can be quite true. A dealer who courteously and knowledgeably supports his customers is a good one with whom to do business. However, many software packages are available, and it is difficult for salespeople or a small support staff to have in-depth knowledge about all of them. Good software support from a dealer may mean that a member of the staff will find out the answers to the customer's questions (by asking the software manufacturer) and pass on the information. Even this level of support can be a comforting service.

Some software manufacturers offer toll-free help lines that purchasers can call to receive needed information. The availability of such direct help is certainly beneficial. It also says something positive about the company's commitment to its customers. Sometimes such help is available free from the manufacturer but the customer must pay for the phone call.

ERROR HANDLING

When entering information into a program, it is possible that the user will enter something incorrectly. For instance, the program may request that a number be entered, but the user may enter a word by mistake. In another case the program may allow the user to enter data that are in the correct form but that the program cannot process. For example, the program may erroneously allow the teacher to enter forty-two sets of scores for students when, in fact, the program is only capable of processing thirty-five sets of scores. In either case the software should be designed to gracefully trap the error and return meaningful control to the user. In the first case, if the user enters a word when the program expects a number, the program may simply place a message on the screen that reads, "That is not a number. Please enter a number." The program would then wait for the user to enter a number. In the second case, if the user attempted to enter more scores than the program could process, the program might present a message that stated, "I can only handle thirty-five sets of scores." The program might then allow one of several options. The user could either change the maximum number of scores the program could process (perhaps to forty-five), have the program process the thirty-five sets of scores already entered, or exit the program.

A poorly designed program may not be able to gracefully trap errors. Instead, it might cease running and display a meaningless message, such as BREAK IN 6578 (meaningless unless you wrote the program). There is no excuse for commercial software that is this poorly designed.

MANAGEMENT INFORMATION

As covered in Chapter 5, various types of educational software may include a management component. Depending on the way the software is used, a management component may or may not be of value. The ability of software to report what the student has done and how she has progressed through the material can be of great interest to the teacher. However, software that does not automate management, or some aspect of management, may be every bit as valuable as a product that does. The teacher must decide if a management component is necessary. Another consideration, if management information is available, is how easily such information can be accessed. Is it possible to quickly print out a report for one or more students?

INTERACTIVE DESIGN

One strength computers offer is that they can involve the user actively in the learning process, can present some information and then require the user to react before continuing. In this way computer software can be, to a greater or lesser degree, interactive. Software that is highly interactive is much more desirable than software that requires the student to sit passively in front of the screen. Teachers should be sensitive to the degree of interaction that software offers.

SCREEN DESIGN

Screens should be laid out so that they are uncluttered. Text material should be presented clearly and unambiguously; graphics should be crisp and sharp (within the limitations of the hardware). The idea is that nothing on any individual screen should distract from the purpose of the screen. For example, on a combined tutorial and drill and practice program for addition facts, one teacher noted that the designers of the program had invented their own stylized characters (type faces) to represent letters of the alphabet, numerals, special characters such as +, and so on. Some of the characters were virtually unreadable, even by adults. Because the intent of the software was to teach addition, the students did not need the added confusion caused by trying to decipher the stylized characters.

BUGS

Errors within commercial programs should simply not be tolerated. It is surprising to many educators that sometimes software manufacturers market and sell programs that they know are not ready to be sold, that contain bugs that may cause the program to fail or data to be lost. Attempted justifications for this practice usually center around the highly competitive nature of the computer industry. Sometimes manufacturers claim that they are under much pressure to keep up with the market and release new software before their competition does. Further excuses include the fact that developing software is a complicated undertaking and can be a highly complex task. Neither one of these excuses is valid. A software manufacturer, especially a manufacturer of educational materials, has a responsibility to produce an honest product. The practice of marketing unfinished products should be no more acceptable in the computer industry than it is in any other industry. Programs that contain bugs should be avoided until the manufacturer releases a newer, bug-free version of the product.

BACKUP COPIES

A backup copy of software allows uninterrupted use if the original copy should become damaged (computer programs stored on floppy disks are especially prone to damage if they are mishandled). Backup copies can be obtained in a variety of ways. Sometimes software manufacturers include a backup copy with the original purchase. At other times they may sell a backup copy of the software to the original purchaser for a nominal fee (five to ten dollars) when the purchaser returns the damaged copy of the original software. Other companies make their software so that it can be freely and easily copied by the consumer for the purpose of storing a backup copy against the time when it may be needed. Some companies, however, do everything possible to prevent consumers from making a copy of the software they purchase. Their fear is that the consumer will make multiple copies and distribute them to friends, theoretically costing the company sales. The company may also fear that, in the worst case, the purchaser will make copies and sell them. These two viewpoints about copy protection are quite different, and each says something specific about the way a company views its customers. When the management of a company makes it a policy to freely allow its software to be copied for the purpose of making a backup copy, they are saying, in essence, that they trust the people who buy their products. When a company's management establishes a policy that attempts to prevent customers from copying the software they have purchased, they are saying that they do not trust their customers to abide by the understanding that they may make a copy for backup purposes only. The software industry is divided on this question, and people can become quite heated in discussing which approach is best for a company to take. An interesting outcome of these two viewpoints is that an industry has developed that specializes in creating utility programs that will copy supposedly uncopyable programs. Software manufacturers respond to these utility programs by designing more intricate copy-protection schemes. This, of course, leads the people who sell the copy utility programs to devise new ways to copy programs protected by the new protection schemes.

Reactions and Research

The issue of software protection is a crucial one for educators and software manufacturers. Tolman and Allred (1984), in their National Education Association publication The Computer and Education: What Research Says to the Teacher, *cite a survey study aimed at exploring the concerns of software producers about this issue. The following excerpt from their work summarizes the findings:*

SOFTWARE PROTECTION

The illegal duplication of software has become a major issue in the use of microcomputers in education. The way this problem is handled will have a marked influence on software availability. Hoover and Gould (41), after a survey of software producers to explore their concerns about this issue, contended there is much misunderstanding and little clarity about software protection rights. Respondents' opinions ranged from beliefs about mistreatment of software producers to beliefs about inadequate protection of users.

In this survey, the authors randomly selected 68 publishing houses from among 451 that produce software for the Apple microcomputer. Results included the following:

1. Preview: Seventy-five percent of the respondents do not allow preview of software prior to purchases. Fifteen percent allow preview and 10 percent did not respond to this item.

2. Return option: Forty-five percent allow preview after purchase, with a return option.

3. Copy protection: Sixty percent reported that software was not copy-protected.

4. Backup copies: Seventy-two percent provide no backup copies. Six percent provide one backup without additional charge. Twenty-two percent provide backup copies with additional charge.

5. Negotiability of special multicopy prices: Eighty-two and one-half percent indicated willingness to negotiate special prices for purchase of multiple copies or a licensing agreement to make multiple copies of programs.

6. Illegal duplication of products by schools: Thirty-five percent of the producers consider illegal duplication of software by schools to be a serious threat to profits. (41)

The survey authors considered willingness to negotiate special multicopy prices to be the most significant finding of the study. They also expressed dismay that so few software producers were willing to allow schools to preview their products; they suggested that this may be due to the producers' assumption that buyers make copies of programs and then return the originals for refunds.

Problems of the software industry will not be easily resolved. Schools want to buy software, but because of limited budgets they prefer to preview a product before investing in it. Software companies want to sell their product, but they must also protect their huge production investments and marketing costs. A partial solution might be greater adherence to legal and ethical codes on the part of school systems in order to earn the trust of software producers and to encourage more liberal sales policies such as preview privileges and backup copy allowances.

(41) Hoover, Todd, and Gould, Sandra. "The Pirating of Computer Programs: A Survey of Software Producers." *Educational Technology* (October 1982). 23–26.

(Tollman and Allred, 1984.)

Regardless of how a teacher or administrator feels about the issue, it is most important that a legitimate backup copy of the software be available. It is not realistic to expect to spend anywhere from fifty dollars to several hundred dollars for a computer program and then have to pay the same amount again to replace it if the disk it is on becomes damaged.

Figure 6–1 presents an overview of software evaluation criteria.

Reviewing Software: Hands-on Experience

In reviewing software, there is no substitute for hands-on experience; the teacher must sit at the computer and run the software. A series of steps for evaluating potential software purchases is outlined below. Although second-hand material (reviews, catalogue descriptions) can be of value in learning

Criteria for Software Evaluation

General

    Cost
    Compatibility
    Target Group
    Subject Area

Specific

Educational Criteria	Technical Criteria
Prerequisite Skills	Flexibility
Objectives	Use of Graphics and Sound
Teaching Style	Documentation
Accuracy	Support
Pace	Error Handling
Student Engagement	Management Information
Usefulness	Interactive Design
Grouping	Screen Design
Stereotypes	Bugs
	Backup Copies

Figure 6–1 A listing of the criteria to be considered when evaluating software.

about programs that may be of potential benefit, it is vital that the reviewer work with the software before a decision is made. There is no substitute for experiencing what the software actually does as opposed to reading about what it does. An analogous situation would be the difference between reading a synopsis of a movie and seeing the movie. The viewing of a movie is a visual and auditory experience. A written description does not provide the same experience as seeing the movie. This may be even truer with software, which can require interaction on the part of the user as well as provide a series of visual and auditory experiences.

Software Evaluation: Suggested Steps

Software purchases may be considered for a variety of reasons. A teacher might identify an area in which software would be of benefit in the curriculum and then seek out a program to fill that need. Or, he might become aware of a particular software product that sounds interesting; maybe another teacher raves about a program she is using. Perhaps the computer education curriculum requires students to gain experience using computers in certain ways. Such uses include learning a programming language, using the computer as a word processor, or using the computer for tutorial or drill and practice. Good software may need to be purchased for any of these reasons.

Identify Need

Once a need has been identified, the next step is to gather information about available software. For instance, if a teacher wants an instructional game to help teach a language arts unit on parts of speech, he may consult a variety of software catalogues to see what is available. Software catalogues are pub-

Gather Information

lished by software companies and software distributors. If the teacher has already identified a particular package in which he is interested, he can start by consulting software catalogues to get preliminary information about the program. **Figure 6–2** is an example of several catalogue descriptions taken from the Sunburst Communications catalogue. These descriptions are from the section that covers software related to problem solving. Notice that the descriptions are fairly thorough, including information about what publications have recommended the software, who designed it, hardware required, and what teaching objectives it covers.

One suggestion should be offered about descriptions of software in catalogues: be cautious. Not all catalogues offer thorough, accurate descriptions. In the best case the description of what the software can do will be accurate and complete. In the worst case the description will have little resemblance to reality. What this means is that catalogues are a good starting point for information about software but should be supplemented by other sources.

Software reviews are an excellent source of information. Reviews may appear in periodicals that deal with educational computing in particular or the computing field in general. Appendix A lists computer-related magazines and journals. **Figure 6–3** is a software review that appeared in *Electronic Learning*. This review is of a magazine on a disk published by Scholastic Inc. The magazine is called *Microzine*. Notice that the review provides information about price, backup policy, preview policy, and necessary hardware. Further, the software is described, applications for the software are suggested, and overall comments are included from the reviewers. The reviewers are identified at the end of the article. Identifying a reviewer's background lends credibility to the review.

The Educational Products Information Exchange (EPIE) Institute offers *The Educational Software Selector (TESS)*. EPIE is an independent product-evaluation agency supported by consumers. *TESS* is published yearly and contains product listings that outline a variety of information about educational software, including sources for reviews. *TESS* also contains information about software suppliers. **Figure 6–4** shows an entry from *TESS*.

EPIE also offers the *Micro Courseware Evaluation PRO/FILES* kit. *PRO/FILES* are in-depth analyses and evaluations of educational software. **Figure 6–5** is an example of a *PRO/FILE* evaluation. Information about the software producer, hardware configuration needed, topics covered, and possible uses is presented. The software receives an overall rating in the area of instructional design and another rating in the area of software design. Detailed descriptions and accompanying evaluations are offered for program content, teacher and student use, and management system provided. Also, goals and objectives, contents, methods and approach, and evaluation and management information are summarized in a table. *PRO/FILES* are available on a subscription basis. The starter kit contains 500 *PRO/FILES*, plus an additional 200 *PRO/FILES* that are provided during the subscription year. In each succeeding subscription year an additional 200 evaluations are provided. Software review products from EPIE have a solid reputation among educators.

Information about software is also available from EPIE electronically over Compuserve, an electronic information service that makes a variety of data bases and computer software products available to its subscribers. Customers

Code Quest

Strategies in Problem Solving

Grade level: 4-adult

Designed by: Mary Anne Hermann, Marge Kosel and Jon Sweedler

- AWARD WINNER—Council for Exceptional Children Software Search, Gifted Category
- RECOMMENDED FOR PURCHASE IN *Booklist, Popular Computing, Instructor* and *The Best of Educational Software for Apple II Computers*, Gary G. Bitter and Kay Gore, Sybex Inc.

What is the mystery object? Six clues lie embedded in a series of codes composed of letters, numbers or pictures. This teacher-created program sharpens thinking skills such as discrimination, classification and rule formation as students decode the hidden clues and form hypotheses on the identity of the mystery object.

A special option lets students or teachers create their own mystery objects and clues.

Teaching Objectives:
1. To develop the skills of discrimination, classification and pattern identification.
2. To provide practice in solving problems of varying complexity.

Contents of package: one diskette, backup, teacher's guide.
For 48K Apple II+, IIe, IIc.
No. 1147–DG $59
No. 114710–DG: Computer Lab Pkg. $177

Corvus Network Compatible!

Fun House Maze

Strategies in Problem Solving

Grade level: 4–adult

Designed by: Donna Stanger and Lon Koenig

- RECOMMENDED FOR PURCHASE IN *Electronic Learning, MicroSIFT* and *The Best of Educational Software for Apple II Computers*, Gary G. Bitter and Kay Gore, Sybex Inc.

A journey through a surprise-packed three-dimensional maze gives students practice in developing and testing problem-solving strategies.

Teaching Objectives:
1. To provide practice in pattern recognition and identifying multiple solutions.
2. To build skills in problem solving.

Contents of package: one diskette, backup, teacher's guide.
For 48K Apple II+, IIe, IIc.
No. 1149–DG $59
No. 114910–DG: Computer Lab Pkg. $177

Corvus Network Compatible!

Color Keys

Strategies in Problem Solving

Grade level: 4-adult

Designed by: Donna Stanger and Scott Clough

- RECOMMENDED FOR PURCHASE IN *The Best of Educational Software for Apple II Computers*, Gary G. Bitter and Kay Gore, Sybex Inc.

A thought-provoking game that improves students' command of analysis, synthesis and problem-solving strategies. Students use a key as the basis for "coloring in" answers to problems. 41 levels of difficulty provide a challenge for a wide range of students.

Teaching Objectives:
1. To provide practice scanning and transferring information.
2. To build skills in analysis and synthesis.

Contents of package: one diskette, backup, teacher's guide.
For 48K Apple II+, IIe, IIc. Color monitor required.
No. 1164–DG $59
No. 116410–DG: Computer Lab Pkg. $177

Corvus Network Compatible!

NEW AND IMPROVED!
Memory Castle

Grade level: 5-adult

Designed by: Rochester School District, Rochester, MN

- RECOMMENDED FOR PURCHASE IN *Family Computing* and *Computer and Software News*

An exciting, colorful adventure game that helps your students remember instructions and follow directions.

Inside the *Memory Castle*, students are given instructions . . . "go to the shieldroom, then to the cemetery to the grave of Sir Gray, then to the kitchen. . . ."

To help them play the game successfully, your students are introduced to a special strategy designed to improve their memories. Once they have mastered this strategy, they will be amazed at the power of their minds . . . and so will you!

Teaching Objectives:
1. To help students learn ways to improve their memories.
2. To teach students to work with exact information.

Contents of package: one diskette, backup, teacher's guide.
For 48K Apple II+, IIe, IIc. Color monitor required.
No. 1240–DG $59
No. 1376–DG: Computer Lab Pkg. $177

Corvus Network Compatible!

FREE REPLACEMENT! *Memory Castle*—APPLE VERSION ONLY—has been improved with all new graphics, and the program now features some animation. Programs purchased prior to June 1, 1985 may be returned for exchange. Use the order form in the center of this catalog.

Note: Computer Lab Packages contain 10 diskettes and one teacher's guide.

(Sunburst, 1986)

Figure 6–2 Catalogue descriptions taken from the Sunburst Communications catalogue.

MICROZINE, VOL. 1, NO. 3

An Interactive Mystery, an Electronic Library, a Game of Tag, and More, in This Latest Microzine Volume

Hardware: Apple II micros, (48K); IBM PC in future.
Source: Scholastic Inc., 730 Broadway, New York, NY 10003.
Price: $39.95 per issue; $148 for one-year subscription (6 issues).
Backup: On an individual basis; contact company.
Preview: No policy.
Description: by now, *Microzine* subscribers know not to expect just an ordinary magazine in the mail. The latest "issue," like its predecessors, offers several programs that require the active participation of its audience. On two sides of a floppy disk, *Microzine Vol. 1, No. 3* has users browsing for books, solving a mystery, playing tag, and commanding a robot.

"What's Inside," the first title on the table of contents, gives you an overview of each of the five *Microzine* programs. Additional information can be found in the program manual, along with tips for operation. Here, briefly, is what they are all about.

- "Mystery at Pinecrest Manor" is an interactive mystery that challenges you to make choices and decisions that will lead you to a solution. The program begins with an invitation from your uncle to spend a weekend at his island manor home. Once there, you discover that your uncle's rare Egyptian statue has been stolen, and the other five guests at the manor are suspect. Together with the friend you've brought along as your assistant, you read through the Suspect File and search the manor and grounds for clues to identify the thief.

- "Tag" is a game of dexterity played in ten rounds of increasing challenge. The object is to tag five "top-hatters," and avoid getting zapped by an Electric Net. With each new round, the speed of the game increases, and you receive more points for each top-hatter you tag.

- "Bookstore" is a data base containing the title, author, and a short description of 200 books in 10 categories, specially selected for students. You can "browse" through the titles under each category, or do a search under one or more of seven fields, such as the kind of book, main character, or time period.

- In "Amazing Robot," you use Logo-like commands to maneuver a robot through several types of mazes and courses called "Screen Worlds." This program also allows you to write, combine, and save procedures.

- "Computer Stuff," the last program, is used for two things: to change your disk drive set-up (from one to two drives, or vice versa); or to initialize a data disk. Data disks can be used to save robot procedures, or for storage of any other *Microzine* program in this or future issues.

Applications: Though each of these programs will be of particular interest to different age groups, the manual, ability required of the user, and time to complete the program are all within the range of students in grades three and above.

Because the programs do appeal to a wide range of users, *Microzine* may be best suited to the school Learning Center or Computer Room. Except for "Tag," there are no time constraints on any of the activities, and the users can take as much time as they want to complete an activity.

If necessary, however, all programs can be completed within thirty minutes, which makes them equally suitable for the classroom. Many good problem-solving programs are not used by teachers simply because they take too long.

"Amazing Robot," for example, could be used in a programming class as an introduction to Logo, to practice using commands, and to learn to write procedures. "Mystery at Pinecrest Manor" could be used to supplement a reading lesson in differentiating the important parts of a story—for example, the main and supporting characters and the main idea.

There are many possible applications for "Bookstore." Whether as an aid for writing book reports, a lesson on categorizing books, or simply to spark an interest in reading, this program would be a nice classroom addition or library activity. A librarian would also find "Bookstore" an excellent way to introduce students to annotated bibliographies or to locating books in the library. Many libraries are also beginning to use electronic card catalogs, and "Bookstore" would be a good introduction to this concept on an elementary level.

The Teacher's Edition of *Microzine* includes a Scope and Sequence chart, and the manual includes some ideas for follow-up activities.

Comments: This *Microzine* volume not only demonstrates how the computer can be used to develop different skills—in problem solving, reading, and programming, for example—but allows the user to experience a number of different types of programs firsthand. The computer, used alternately for interactive fiction, for arcade-type entertainment, as a programming tool, and as a data base that can store and retrieve information in different ways, becomes, in effect,

Figure 6–3 A software review from *Electronic Learning.*

an important object of instruction in its own right.

Each of the *Microzine* programs is enhanced with excellent graphics, and a manual formatted to allow users to scan for appropriate information. Directions are clear, and feedback is meaningful.

Whether to practice problem-solving and logical thinking skills in solving a mystery, to find a good book, or to understand the myriad uses of the computer, this volume of *Microzine* has something for everyone.

Reviewed by: Ann Dana,

Microcomputer Consultant, Hinsdale Junior High; Carol Haynes, Learning Center Director, Prospect School; Linda Accardo, Reading Teacher, Hinsdale Junior High, Hinsdale, IL.

(Electronic Learning, March, 1984)

Figure 6–3 Continued

Where does it fit into the curriculum?

What does it do?

Is it copy protected or networked?

What does it include?

Which hardware does it use?

Where can I find reviews and are they favorable?

BASIC SKILLS

Arithmetic, Mult'n/Div'n

1) TEASERS BY TOBBS: PUZZ/PRB SOLVG　　**Rel.:** 12/82
Cat. No.: 133–1　　　　　　　　　**Author:** O'Brien, Thomas
Types: Educat'l game, concept devel't　　　**Grades:** 4–10
Uses: School for main curric.
Scope: Mult. topics, one year.　　**Grouping:** Indiv., small group.
Description: Two programs give students practice in logically solving addition and multiplication problems. Both programs offer 6 levels of difficulty. A grid and a character called Tobbs appear on screen. The grid presents a series of math problems, each with a missing number. Students decide which number can't be, might be, or must be the correct solution. No record-keeping. Is copy protected. Network version available.
Components: 2 programs, diskette, teach'g guide, back-up diskette.
Configurations:
Apple II + /IIe/IIc, 48K, 5″ dsk dr, Applesoft, DOS 3.3.
Atari 400/800/600XL-1200XL, 16K, 5″ dsk dr, DOS.
TRS-80 Mod III/IV, 32K, BASIC.
IBM PC/PCjr, 64K, 5″ dsk dr, PC-DOS.
Comm. 64/128, 64K, 5″ dsk dr.
Availability: Sunburst Communications, $59 on disk.
Reviews: CCL 9/83 (+), CHI 06/83 (+), CLMC 6/83 (+), CRC 6/83 (+), MR 6/83 (+), MSFT 06/83 (+), MTCH 2/84 (+).
*EPIE Eval.: Highly recommended.

When published?

Where can I buy it?

What does it cost?

How does EPIE rate it?

Figure 6–4 An entry from *The Educational Software Selector* (*TESS*), published by the Educational Products Information Exchange (EPIE).

---

of Compuserve access the information network through a computer terminal or a personal computer set up to function as a computer terminal.

Other data bases of educational software information exist, such as RICE (Resources in Computer Education), developed by the Northwest Regional Educational Laboratory (NWREL) of Portland, Oregon. RICE contains more than 3,000 listings of available educational software, including information about programs and software producers. NWREL also runs MicroSift, a data base that additionally includes software-evaluation information provided by educators.

Computer Literacy

Understanding Computers

Encyclopaedia
Britannica

October 1983

HARDWARE CONFIGURATION (*used for analysis)

Apple II	48K	DOS 3.3 Printer optional
Apple II Plus*	48K	DOS 3.3 Printer optional
TRS-80 Model III	48K	

COMPONENTS

4 Diskettes, Back-up Diskettes (not for circulation)
107-page Teacher's Guide, 106-page student Workbook

	PRICE
Without back-up diskettes	$306.00
	$266.00
Package of 5 workbooks	$ 24.95
Package of 25 workbooks	$100.00

PRODUCER

Encyclopaedia Britannica
Educational Corporation
425 North Michigan Avenue
Chicago, IL 60611
312–347–7000
800–554–9862

CURRICULUM ROLE

Computer Literacy
Comprehensive

COPYRIGHT

1983

AUTHORS

EduSystems, Inc. (ESI)

USERS SPECIFIED BY PRODUCER

Junior high school students
Individuals
Pairs
Small groups

CONTENT TOPICS

History of the computer
Using the keyboard
Computer applications
Computer hardware
Computer programming
Software evaluation
Computers in society

OVERALL RATING OF INSTRUCTIONAL DESIGN	8/10
OVERALL RATING OF SOFTWARE DESIGN	7/10

ANALYSTS' SUMMARY

UNDERSTANDING COMPUTERS is a high-quality computer literacy course for junior high school students. The program's 106-page student workbook and four diskettes effectively introduce students to the history of computers, use of the keyboard, computer applications, programming concepts, and software evaluation. In addition, it provides information and learning activities that can make students intelligent consumers. The quizzes and activities on the diskettes are highly interactive. The workbook prepares users for work on the computer with informational text and clear explanations of the on-screen activities. The reading level of the workbook makes the program best suited to average and above-average junior high students.

Each of the six chapters begins with a reading assignment in the workbook. In chapter one, this is followed by a computerized introduction to the keyboard. The other chapters are followed by a short on-screen quiz which includes some remediating feedback. Included in each lesson are three student activities that incorporate both the workbook and the computer. The teacher coordinates pre- and post-instructional activities and discussion sessions. Each chapter ends with a brief computerized quiz, too brief to be adequate as a basis for evaluation of student learning. The program reports how many items were answered correctly, but this record cannot be saved on the diskette. It must be recorded in the workbook.

For each chapter, a brief summary description, objectives, and the sequence of activities are presented. For each activity within a chapter, the manual provides a description, objectives, background information for classroom implementation, sample frames, and answer keys (where needed). Instructional suggestions are also offered, although many of them involve classroom discussions that go beyond the program's content presentation. Teachers, therefore, should be familiar with the program and knowledgeable in other computer uses and issues not directly addressed in the content.

RECOMMENDATIONS TO THE PRODUCER

1. Include in the teacher's manual and the workbook directions for operating the computer, instructions for on-screen and workbook coordination and a list of recommended readings.
2. Provide students with the option to exit at any time.
3. Correct program errors (see "Technical Quality/Warranty").

Figure 6–5 An entry from PRO/FILES, published by EPIE.

CONTENT DESCRIPTION

UNDERSTANDING COMPUTERS consists of a 106-page student workbook, a 107-page teacher's manual, and four diskettes. The computer activities relate to reading assignments found in the workbook and, to a lesser extent, to teacher-student discussions. Readings vary in length (3–8 pages) and are accompanied by pictures. Individual assignments will take 10–20 minutes, depending upon the activity and the user. Group activities may take longer, requiring an additional 2–3 hours per week. Many activities can be undertaken by an individual or a small group, and the teacher's guide provides grouping options.

The workbook is divided into six chapters. Picture symbols at the beginning of each activity inform students of the type of activity they will be encountering. Chapter 3 contains eight activities, five of which are computer-based. Each of the other chapters consists of six activities, five requiring use of the computer.

The diskette for Chapter 1, "Introduction and History," includes an exercise in keyboard use, a game to develop keyboard proficiency, an interactive demonstration of computer functions, a computer history puzzle, and a randomly-generated quiz on the entire chapter. The computer activities for Chapters 2, 4, 5, and 6 consist of 10-item quizzes based on the chapter readings, three opportunities per chapter to apply concepts and principles presented in the reading, and randomly-generated chapter overview quizzes. In each of these chapters, the initial quiz provides explanatory feedback, but the overview quiz only indicates whether an answer is right or wrong. An appealing graphic is displayed as a reward for good performance on the end-of-chapter quiz. For Chapter 2, "Computer Applications," the on-screen learning activities include a data-processing exercise, a computational exercise, and a process control simulation. In Chapter 4, "Computer Programming," the student uses a simplified graphics language to generate "angle art," practices flowcharting to control the movements of an on-screen robot, and has a choice of seven different exercises on BASIC language programming. The computer-based application exercises for Chapter 5, "Software," include data-base manipulation, software evaluation, and software design. In Chapter 6, "Computers in Society," the student is provided with a choice of six word-processing activities. These are followed by a computer crime-solver simulation and a self-correcting, chess-like game, "Hexapawn." Chapter 3, "Hardware," begins with the same type of quiz as the chapters described above. However, following two computer-based hardware review activities and a workbook puzzle on hardware, there is an additional reading assignment and a quiz. The chapter ends with a chapter overview quiz.

CONTENT EVALUATION

The content of UNDERSTANDING COMPUTERS is highly appropriate for the needs of junior high school students. The program will help fill the "computer information gap" at this particular educational level. Its broad scope and sound instructional design make the program unique when compared to other computer literacy programs. Junior high users are provided with essential terminology, concepts, and principles in each reading selection. The short, multiple-choice quiz that follows checks for recall of the material. When the student's response is incorrect, the explanatory feedback is often detailed and very helpful. In addition, users are presented with very engaging hands-on experiences which provide opportunities to apply what has been learned. Each of these computer-assisted activities is carefully described in the workbook.

The program guides the student through the logic of computers and programming. It provides important building blocks for the user who may want to explore computing in further detail. Students will become not only computer literate, but also smart consumers.

Figure 6-5 Continued

TEACHER AND STUDENT USE DESCRIPTION

The program is designed to be a course in itself, however, it is imperative that the teacher know the content and understand the program's format. S/he must have a good working knowledge of computer capabilities and must be able to instruct students in the use of the microcomputer.

Students begin the program by reading a workbook selection and then discussing its key points with the teacher. The user determines whether the next activity is in the workbook or on the computer by finding the picture symbol of either a book or a computer terminal (or, sometimes both). To use an on-screen activity, the student selects the appropriate chapter from a menu and is then notified what disk to use. Once that disk is loaded, a menu presents a list of the chapter activities and the student types in his/her choice.

After selecting the initial "Check Your Understanding" quiz, the user answers the questions on-screen, but must return to the workbook to record his/her score. The teacher then initiates appropriate follow-up activities suggested in the teacher's guide before the class goes on to the other computer-based activities.

MANAGEMENT SYSTEM DESCRIPTION

End-of-chapter quizzes are provided as a means of evaluating student performance. Each "follow-up" quiz randomly presents 10–12 questions from a pool of 20 questions. The user's score is presented at the end of each quiz, but the report cannot be saved on the diskette. A place is provided in the workbook to record each score.

There is a score-keeping system for the computerized game, "Hexapawn." The system keeps track of the number of games the player has won, the number of games the computer has won, and the total number of games played. The record cannot be stored for later use.

TEACHER AND STUDENT USE EVALUATION

The teacher's guide provides helpful information on the sequencing of activities, instructional strategies, and follow-up activities. This provides an excellent structure for presenting the content. In spite of this, planning for teacher-initiated discussions and activities is a must. The teacher must also assume responsibility for demonstrating how to operate the computer. The only operating instructions are on a small card in the disk binder.

The mix of workbook-based, computer-based, and classroom-based activities allows for a wide variety of activities—each of them presented in its most appropriate form—and the activities themselves hold students' interest and deliver the program content clearly and effectively.

There are some minor problems with the program's operation. Display of opening titles and credits is uncomfortably long. The numbers that identify activities in the workbook do not correspond to the numbers that identify disk activities. Finally, completion of each computer-based activity is not formally announced on the diskette. The teacher must make sure that students move smoothly from activity to activity.

MANAGEMENT SYSTEM EVALUATION

The system for evaluating student performance is inadequate for a program of this scope and breadth. The ten questions randomly encountered by the student in each chapter are insufficient as an indicator of what has been learned. Recordkeeping is left to the students. The teacher must retrieve the quiz scores from student workbooks. The scores do not indicate the content areas in which each student is experiencing difficulty. This makes planning for remediation a difficult task.

Figure 6-5 Continued

INSTRUCTIONAL & SOFTWARE DESIGN

Goals & Objectives

- Goals and objectives are well supported by contents

Developer's Rationale

"Understanding Computers introduces junior high students to the world of computers. Students learn by reading, by discussing, and, most important, by doing!"

Development Evidence

None

Learner Objectives

Sample chapter objective from the Teacher's Manual:

"Students will learn some things to look for when evaluating software."

Student uses a 7-question form to evaluate a piece of software

Sample activity objective from the Teacher's Manual:

"Students will learn that the computer follows their instructions without questioning whether or not the instructions are reasonable."

Student completes a flowchart to control a robot's movements

Contents

- Six chapters consisting of integrated workbook and computer-based activities

User Appropriateness

Content and approach suited to average and above-average junior high students

Graphics are juvenile for a junior high audience

Accuracy and Fairness

Numbering of workbook activities does not correspond to numbering on the diskettes

Clarity

Workbook picture symbol is used for Activity 2–2, but it is really computer-based

Directions, examples, and demonstrations within the program are easy to understand

Support Materials

Well-designed student workbook is essential for program implementation

Methods & Approach

- Highly motivating approach enhances presentation of content

Technical Quality/Warranty

3 programming errors: Activity 4–5 (subactivity 2) is inoperative; in Activity 6–3, pressing the space bar makes letters move inappropriately; in Activity 5–3, a student name file cannot be displayed

90-day trial period includes free replacement; $25 thereafter

Documentation/Teacher's Guide

Annotated workbook provides information necessary to implement the total program

User Control

Menus provide choice of activities

Student can view instructions at the beginning of an activity only and cannot exit at will

Feedback

Always immediate; remediates in quizzes following chapter readings

Correct: "That's right. A bar code identifies an item."
Incorrect: "No. A printer is an output device. It's used to display the result of the computer's work."

Graphics

Some are embedded in content; others reward quiz performance

Medium resolution, poor color quality

Audio

Beep indicates incorrect entry

Limited use of music (Ch. 1) and synthesized voice (Ch. 6)

Random Generation

Used to present end-of-chapter quizzes and some learning activities

Evaluation & Management

- Evaluation of student performance does not adequately cover the program content

Tests

Overview quizzes serve as end-of-chapter tests; each one includes 10–12 items chosen from 20-item pools

Insufficient in scope

Branching

None

Records/Management

Individual quiz scores cannot be saved; they must be recorded in the workbook

Quiz scores do not indicate the source of the student's difficulty

One game keeps a record of the highest score

Figure 6–5 Continued

Catalogue descriptions, reviews in journals and magazines, and evaluations from agencies like EPIE are all important sources for information about educational software. Asking colleagues about their experiences is another way to gain valuable information. A district's computer coordinator, or a school's computer teacher, can also assist teachers in finding and choosing software.

Preview

When a promising program has been selected, a preview must be arranged. Some retail computer stores, software manufacturers, and software distributors allow a preview period before purchase. Others offer a preview period after purchase. A preview period allows the teacher to test the software and, if it is found to be unacceptable, return it at no cost. Some stores allow the teacher to preview software before purchase, but only in the store. If none of these options is available, the teacher may be able to find a colleague in another school or another district who has a copy of the software that can be borrowed for review.

When previewing software, the teacher should first read the documentation. The software should then be run one or more times while the teacher considers it both from the perspective of a teacher and from the perspective of a student. How will students react to the program? What, educationally, does the software offer? She should try to make the software fail by entering incorrect data, by typing in what the program does not expect. For instance, if the prompt says, "Enter a number," she should purposely enter a word. During the entire process, from reading the documentation through running the program, she should be sensitive to the criteria for evaluation outlined earlier.

The Software-Evaluation Form

It is a good practice to fill out a software-evaluation form as part of the review process. The form can serve to focus a reviewer's attention on many of the criteria worth considering when evaluating software. **Figure 6–6** is an example of a form developed by a principal for use within his district. His prime concern was that the form be usable by a practicing teacher. In reviewing available forms he found some to be ten or more pages long. In his school (and district) the intent was to encourage classroom teachers to become involved in evaluating and selecting software. Because instructional and preparation time is at a premium for teachers, and the principal was sensitive to that fact, one of his main objectives was to make the form a reasonable length. This particular form covers some of the criteria cited earlier and provides the reviewer with the opportunity to include areas not specifically mentioned on the form by entering comments. This form can also be used as a management tool by administrators to coordinate and control software purchases. Once the evaluator completes her work, the building administrator reviews the form, adds her comments, and sends it to the computer coordinator. The coordinator will choose to approve or not approve the purchase. If the purchase is approved, the coordinator will then order the software.

Kayser and King (1984) offer a one-page form, presented in **Figure 6–7**. Their form is divided into sections on Cost of the Program, Subject Area Content,

Evaluator's Name _____ Position _____

School_____ Date of Evaluation _____ Date of Report _____

Software Program Title _____

Producer/Publisher_____

Copyright _____ Price _____

Curriculum Relationship(s) (Check more than one as necessary.)

☐ Mathematics   ☐ Reading   ☐ English   ☐ Business   ☐ Science

☐ Social Studies   ☐ Other (specify) _____

- -

☐ Drill and Practice   ☐ Tutorial   ☐ Educational Gaming

☐ Computer Language   ☐ Other (specify) _____

Content Description

_____
_____
_____
_____

Time needed for the full program: _____

Does this software meet the goals/objectives specified by the publisher?

Comment: _____
_____

Grade level appropriateness _____

Is the material presented accurate and technically correct?_____
_____

Is the program "user friendly"? _____ Are the instructions clear? _____

Can students readily understand the format, cues, and manuals?

Comment: _____
_____

Figure 6–6 An example of a software evaluation form. This form was developed by a principal.

Can an average student use the program independently? _____

Does the program allow more than one student to participate at the same time? _____
_____

What is the recommended optimum number of students who could reasonably participate in using this
software at one time? _____

Will the program improve/accelerate learning in a selected area? _____

Please describe any weaknesses you found:

_____
_____
_____

Is a trial or "return within ___ days" available so that hands-on assessment can be made without a bind-
ing purchase obligation? _____

Would you recommend purchase of this software? _____

Please note: All software must run on either Apple II, Apple IIe, or Franklin Ace 1000 computers, depending on what is available at your facility. Please specify computer designation for the software
reviewed: _____

Evaluator Signature _____

Administrative Review Section

Site Administrator Comment (From faculty or department requesting purchase): _____
_____

Signature _____ Date _____

Computer Coordinator Action:

☐ Approved for purchase   ☐ Not approved for purchase

Signature _____ Date _____

Additional Notes _____
_____

(Ferry, 1984)

Figure 6–6 Continued

Name of Program _____

Publisher/Author _____

Address _____ Telephone _____

Cost of Program	Enter (Dollar Amounts)
A. Hardware	$_____
B. Software	$_____
C. Cost of Lab (if needed)	$_____

Respond to each question by rating the program on a scale of 1 to 5, where 1 is a low rating and 5 is an excellent rating.

Subject Area Content

A. Are the stated objectives met? 1 2 3 4 5
B. Does the program fit into your curriculum? 1 2 3 4 5
C. Is the author's approach and style similar to yours? 1 2 3 4 5
D. Is the subject area content pedagogically sound? 1 2 3 4 5
E. Is the development of concepts clear and concise? 1 2 3 4 5
F. Does the program use correct grammar and punctuation? 1 2 3 4 5
G. Does the program offer a learning experience that couldn't be achieved using paper and pencil alone? 1 2 3 4 5

Ease of Using the Program

A. Is the documentation, internal and external, adequate? 1 2 3 4 5
B. Are the directions easy-to-follow and free of computerese? 1 2 3 4 5
C. Is the method of user input simple? 1 2 3 4 5
D. Does the program allow the user to recover from errors easily? 1 2 3 4 5
E. Will the user feel at ease while running the program? 1 2 3 4 5
F. Does the program allow the user to enter different parts of the program at will or to stop at any time? 1 2 3 4 5
H. Is it easy for the user to correct mistakes? 1 2 3 4 5
I. Is it difficult for the user to "crash" the program? 1 2 3 4 5
J. Are the instructions for ending the program and/or for starting over clear? 1 2 3 4 5

K. Does the program clearly indicate when the student should input an answer? 1 2 3 4 5
L. Does the program state the proper form for answers? 1 2 3 4 5
M. Can the sound be controlled? 1 2 3 4 5
N. Can a user operate the program without a lengthy training session? 1 2 3 4 5
O. Does the program employ effective audible responses to user input? 1 2 3 4 5

Instructional Range

A. Does the program cover the topic thoroughly? 1 2 3 4 5
B. Are there pauses where they are needed? 1 2 3 4 5

Screen Formats

A. Are the layouts on the screen attractive? 1 2 3 4 5
B. Are graphics used to enhance the quality of the screen's appearance? 1 2 3 4 5
C. Does the screen scroll appropriately? 1 2 3 4 5
D. Is the text presented in readable blocks? 1 2 3 4 5
E. Do the screens employ variety effectively? 1 2 3 4 5
F. If diagrams are used, are they effective? 1 2 3 4 5
G. Does the user have control over the rate of presentation? 1 2 3 4 5

The Programmer's Philosophy

A. Does the program branch to easier or harder material automatically? 1 2 3 4 5
B. Does the program give the user some control over the pace, topics and difficulty level? 1 2 3 4 5
C. Does the amount of interaction between the student and the computer stimulate student interest? 1 2 3 4 5
D. Does the program provide a summary of student performance? 1 2 3 4 5
E. Does the program help the student to find his/her errors? 1 2 3 4 5
F. Is the program designed to make it more difficult for the student to misuse it than it is to learn from it? 1 2 3 4 5
G. Does the program address the integrity and intelligence of the student at which it is aimed? 1 2 3 4 5
H. Does the program use the computer creatively and effectively to teach some worthwhile objective? 1 2 3 4 5

(Kayser and King, 1984)

Figure 6–7 A second example of a software evaluation form.

Ease of Using the Program, Instructional Range, Screen Formats, and The Programmer's Philosophy. When entering information on this form, the respondent answers each question by rating that aspect of the software from 1 to 5, 1 being the lowest rating and 5 the highest.

The form that appears in **Figure 6–8** is used by the California Library Media Consortium for Classroom Evaluation of Microcomputer Courseware, to solicit reviews of software from educators. The consortium publishes reviews of software by educators based on actual classroom use. Ann Lathrop's article "Microcomputer Courseware: Selection and Evaluation," (Lathrop, 1986) from where this form is taken, outlines the software-evaluation process and highlights the role that librarians have in being critical evaluators of software for use in library media centers and classrooms.

Whatever form is used, either one from the many that are available or one developed locally, the results of the evaluation will be recorded by the reviewer. Also, after software has been reviewed, it is a good idea to keep a copy of the completed forms on file for future reference by other teachers. Access to such locally generated information is often of great value to teachers.

Purchase

If a decision is made to purchase the software evaluated, it is a good idea to review the software again, some time after it has been received and put into use. After using a program for awhile, teachers are apt to be much more knowledgeable about its strengths and weaknesses. Also, after using the software in the classroom, teachers may have some interesting things to say (either positive or negative) about the support they receive from the software vendor. This information can be valuable in relation to future purchases.

Conclusion

By gaining some skills in evaluating educational software the teacher is certainly fulfilling his responsibility as an instructor in the twentieth century. Historically, teachers have been responsible for evaluating the materials they use with students. Evaluating educational software is simply an extension of that function. Further, by communicating the results of evaluations to other teachers and to software developers, educators can play a part in assuring that future generations of software improve in quality. The materials used by teachers should be developed in response to the real-life needs of teachers and students, with input from practitioners as well as from theorists and software designers.

CALIFORNIA LIBRARY MEDIA CONSORTIUM FOR
CLASSROOM EVALUATION OF MICROCOMPUTER COURSEWARE 1983

Program title _____

Title on package/diskette _____

Microcomputer(s) brand/model _____ Memory needed _____K

Language _____ BASIC (or _____) Version/copyright date _____ Cost_____

Publisher _____

Peripherals needed: _____Disk drive(s) _____Cassette _____Printer (Other _____)

Other materials/equipment needed _____

Backup copy available? _____

* * * * * * * * * * * * * * * * * * * *

Reviewed by_____ Grade level/subject you teach _____

School/district _____

Address/phone _____

May we use your name in the published review? _____

PROGRAM TITLE_____ SUBJECT AREA(S) _____

SUGGESTED GRADE LEVELS   K   1   2   3   4   5   6   7   8   9   10   11   12   College teacher use

TYPE OF PROGRAM (check all that apply)

____ drill/practice   ____ problem solving   ____ game   ____ word processing
____ simulation   ____ tutorial (teaches)   ____ testing   ____ classroom management
____ demonstration   ____ educational game   ____ utility   ____ authoring system

SCOPE (check one)

____ one or more programs on single topic   ____ one program in an instructional series
____ group of unrelated programs   ____ multi-disk curriculum package

EVALUATION CRITERIA

YES   NO   N/A

GENERAL DESIGN: ____ EXCELLENT ____ GOOD ____ WEAK ____ NOT ACCEPTABLE
____ ____ ____ Creative, innovative, effective use of computer
____ ____ ____ Well-organized curriculum design
____ ____ ____ Free of programming errors
____ ____ ____ Free of excessive competition or violence
____ ____ ____ Free of racial, ethnic, or sex stereotypes

EASE OF USE: ____ EXCELLENT ____ GOOD ____ WEAK ____ NOT ACCEPTABLE
____ ____ ____ Simple and complete instructions
____ ____ ____ Screens are neat and attractive
____ ____ ____ Speed and sequence of paging can be controlled
____ ____ ____ Technically easy to operate
____ ____ ____ Any sound is appropriate and can be turned off

CONTENT: ____ EXCELLENT ____ GOOD ____ WEAK ____ NOT ACCEPTABLE
____ ____ ____ Factual material, grammar, and spelling are correct
____ ____ ____ Word lists, problems, and speed can be modified
____ ____ ____ Interest level, difficulty, typing, and vocabulary are appropriate
____ ____ ____ Provides easier or harder material in response to performance
____ ____ ____ Responses to errors are helpful, avoid sarcasm or scolding
____ ____ ____ Response to student success is positive, enjoyable and appropriate
____ ____ ____ Avoids clever graphics that make it "fun to fail"

MOTIVATIONAL DEVICES USED: ____ EXCELLENT ____ GOOD ____ WEAK ____ NOT ACCEPTABLE
____ graphics for instruction   ____ color   ____ game format   ____ sound   ____ timing
____ graphics for reward   ____ scoring   ____ random order   ____ personalization

DOCUMENTATION AVAILABLE: ____ EXCELLENT ____ GOOD ____ WEAK ____ NOT ACCEPTABLE
____ none   ____ instructions appear on screen
____ instruction manual   ____ suggested classroom activities
____ teacher's guide   ____ instructional objectives
____ student worksheets   ____ workbook   ____ tests

Comments:

Figure 6–8 This software evaluation form was designed by the California Library Media Consortium for Classroom Evaluation of Microcomputer Courseware to solicit reviews of software from educators.

OVERALL OPINION * * OVERALL OPINION * * OVERALL OPINION

_____ Great program! I recommend it highly!
_____ Pretty good/useful. Consider purchase.
_____ OK, but you might wait for a better one.
_____ Select only if suggested modifications are made.
_____ Not useful. I don't recommend purchase.

INSTRUCTIONAL CONTENT AND OBJECTIVES

• What are the objectives of the program and how does it achieve them?

• What learning outcomes are expected?

• What classroom management, testing, or performance report capability is provided and how easy is it to use?

   How many students/classes can be handled by program?

   Is it possible to make backup copies of student records?

• Describe any special strengths of program.

• Comments/concerns/questions.

• Suggestions to author/publisher.

BRIEFLY DESCRIBE STUDENTS AND THEIR RESPONSE TO PROGRAM

Grade level/subject

Behavior observed that indicates learning took place

Enjoyment, boredom, or other reaction expressed

Any problems experienced

Any quotes you want to share

PLEASE USE ANOTHER SHEET IF YOU HAVE ADDITIONAL COMMENTS
***** THANK YOU FOR YOUR HELP *****

(Lathrop, 1986)

Figure 6–8 Continued

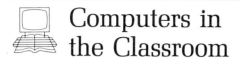

Computers in the Classroom

Parental involvement in a child's school experience can be of benefit to the child and the teacher. The following two letters from Electronic Learning *are aimed at both informing parents about and involving parents in their child's computer activities at school. The second letter is also used to gather information about computer use at home.*

Teachers might also involve parents and children in generating a software-evaluation form. Perhaps parents could assist their child in evaluating software and making suggestions about possible adoptions. Many parents use computers at work. Teachers may find some parents a ready source of expert information about computers.

LETTER 1: A MONTHLY NEWSLETTER TO PARENTS

Dear Parent:

Your child has probably told you that classes are learning about computers at school. I thought you might like to hear more about your child's use of computers, so with this letter, I'm beginning a series of notes to keep you up to date.

Your child is learning to use the following computer(s):

We're using the computer in many different ways in our classroom. We do so by using different types of *software programs*—the lists of instructions (on cassette or floppy disk) that tell the computer what to do. Your child is learning to use several of these programs; I have listed them below, along with the skills that they are helping your child develop:

Your child appears to be enjoying learning about the computer in school. You can support that learning at home by:

- Showing an interest in what your child is learning;

- Taking our adult education computer classes *(include necessary information here);*

- Volunteering through our school's Parent-Computer Connection program *(or whatever; include necessary information here)*

I plan to send letters home on a monthly basis to help you become an important part of your child's involvement with computers. Please excuse this form letter. It's the only way I can send you and other parents this kind of information on a regular basis.

Send me your comments and suggestions!

LETTER 2: A QUESTIONNAIRE FOR PARENTS

Dear Parent:

As you know, your child has been learning about computers at school. I would like to offer you the opportunity to be a part of those computer activities—even if you don't know that much about computers yourself. If you are interested in participating, please answer the following questions:

I know something about computers and would like to participate in the school's computer program.
1. Do you own a computer, or do you use one in your home or office? If so, which brand?

2. Would you be interested in contributing your time or expertise? The following are areas where we could especially use assistance:

- Helping instructors set up equipment and answering technical questions during afternoon in-service workshops;

- Helping school staff organize our computer program in various ways (for example, setting up data bases in the school library);

- Speaking to students on careers in computing, or on the use of computers in business and other professions.

3. If you are unable to help yourself, could you recommend another source of information or guidance?

I don't know very much about computers, but would still like to participate in the computer program.
1. Would you be interested in assisting our computer coordinator one or more mornings/afternoons a week, or with our school's annual Computer Fair?

2. Would you be interested in taking a parent-child computer literacy course?

Please return this letter to me at the above address or send it along with your child. Thanks for your interest and participation in our program. Either I or another member of the staff will be in touch with you soon.

(Electronic Learning, 1984)

Key Terms	backup copies	flexibility
	bugs	interactive design
	compatibility	*PRO/FILES*
	documentation	*The Educational Software Selector*
	Educational Products Information	*(TESS)*
	Exchange (EPIE)	
	error handling	

Questions

1. Locate three educational software catalogues. Find a description for the same piece of software in each catalogue. Compare the descriptions and comment on the similarities and differences between the content of the descriptions. Also comment on the similarities and differences in the format of the descriptions in each catalogue.

2. Choose a piece of educational software. Use the format of one of the evaluation forms in the book to evaluate the software.

3. For the same software used in number 2, use a different evaluation form from the text and review the software again.

4. Discuss the specific criteria for software evaluation given in the text. Which five criteria do you consider most important? Why?

5. Design your own evaluation form and use it to evaluate a piece of software different from that reviewed in numbers 2 and 3.

6. Write a short unit (approximately five lessons) to introduce the concept of software evaluation to students in either grade 5 or grade 6. As part of your unit have children evaluate at least one piece of software. Either design an evaluation form for them to use or have them design one as part of the unit.

7. Describe what, to you, would be the perfect educational software package.

8. Respond to the position taken by Arthur Luehrmann in the Input/Output selection for this chapter. First summarize his viewpoint and then state how and why you agree or disagree.

9. Locate two sources where a local school can arrange a preview period for educational software. What is the policy of each source?

10. Choose an educational software company and write them a letter asking for information about how they develop software. Address such questions as the following: Where do they get their ideas? Do they field-test their programs? How long does it take to develop software? How many people are involved and what are their jobs? What is the company's policy about copy protection and backup copies?

References/Further Reading

Accardo, Linda, Ann Dana, and Carol Haynes. "Software: Reviews, Microzine, Vol. 1, No. 3." *Electronic Learning* 3, no. 6 (1984): 88, 90, 92.

Educational Computer Courseware 1986. Pleasantville, N.Y.: Sunburst Communications, 1986, p. 4.

Ferry, Victor. K–12 Software Evaluation Form. Unpublished, 1983.

"In-service Workshop, Part VIII: Classroom Tips, SkillsMaster 2: Letters to Parents." *Electronic Learning* 3, no. 8 (1984): 4h.

Kayser, Roger, and George King. "Seven Steps to Buying Better Software." *Electronic Education* 3, no. 6 (1984): 14–15.

Lathrop, Ann. "Microcomputer Courseware: Selection and Evaluation." In Harper, Dennis O., and James H. Stewart. *RUN: Computer Education*, 2d ed. Monterey, Calif.: Brooks/Cole Publishing Co., 1986, pp. 149–151.

Luehrmann, Art. "The New Trend: Ed-Teching the Computer." *Electronic Learning* 4, no. 4 (1985): 22.

Micro-Courseware PRO/FILE & Evaluation. EPIE Institute, New York, 1983.

Microgram. EPIE Institute, New York, 3, no. 5 (1985): 2.

Tolman, Marvin N., and Ruel A. Allred. *The Computer and Education: What Research Says to the Teacher.* Washington, D.C.: National Education Association Professional Library, 1984, pp. 23–24.

7

Computer Literacy and the Computer Curriculum

TOPICS ADDRESSED

Why has the question of computer literacy arisen?

Is computer literacy the same for everyone?

What is a definition of computer literacy for students? for teachers?

How might computer literacy be gained by students? by teachers?

How may a computer curriculum be developed?

What are the components of a computer curriculum?

What are some specific examples of different computer curriculums?

How might a computer curriculum be evaluated?

OUTLINE

Introduction
Why Is Computer Literacy Important?
Who Should be Computer Literate?
Computer Literacy for Students
  Knowledge
  Performance
Computer Literacy for Teachers
  Knowledge
  Performance
Gaining Computer Literacy
  Developing the Computer Curriculum
  Components of a Computer Curriculum
  A Curriculum for Computer Literacy

The Computer Curriculum: Specific
  Examples
Evaluation
Conclusion
Key Terms
Questions
References/Further Reading

Introduction

The term computer literacy is widely used today by educators and the general public. It means different things to different people; sometimes it seems to have no concrete meaning. In some people it causes interest and excitement, while in others it elicits strong negative reactions. Many school districts have begun to teach with and about computers based on a perceived need to offer their students the opportunity to become computer literate. Critics have charged that adding a computer literacy component to the curriculum takes time and emphasis away from other areas. Also, critics observe that by the time today's students are adults, computers will have changed so much that the skills and information learned now may be of no use in the world of tomorrow.

In this chapter computer literacy is defined from two perspectives: that of a teacher and that of a student. Opportunities for teacher training in relationship to computers are outlined. The rationale for teaching a computer curriculum are presented and discussed. An overview of the process many school districts go through in arriving at a computer curriculum is offered. Lastly, examples of computer curriculums are presented and analyzed.

Why Is Computer Literacy Important?

The statement is often made that computers are taking over society. Indeed there has been phenomenal growth and expansion in the computer market over the past few decades. During the late 1970s and early 1980s people in unprecedented numbers began to make use of computers. One reason for this was the advent of dependable, powerful, and relatively inexpensive microcomputers. These machines began to show up in homes, schools, and offices. People became aware that computers were proliferating throughout society and began to wonder what, if any, value computers could add to their lives.

Large computers have been used in business since the 1950s. But with the advent of powerful microcomputers, a revolution in the amount and type of computer use occurred. Two things are unique about the growth of the microcomputing industry and the revolution in computer use which it spurred:

© 1985, G. B. Trudeau. Reprinted with permission of Universal Press Syndicate. All rights reserved.

180

(1) computer power was made available to individuals who previously could not afford it and (2) organizations began to use computers in new ways.

In business, industry, government offices, nonprofit organizations, and other institutions, microcomputers began to show up in a variety of settings. These organizations had previously made use of mainframe and minicomputers, which were usually kept in special locations and tended by highly trained specialists. As microcomputers were integrated into the daily activity of these institutions, computers, quite literally, began to show up on individuals' desks. Computers became an intimate, and often indispensable, part of the way a person did her job. Individuals began to feel ownership of the computer as it was used to do word processing and data analysis and to store and retrieve files. Computers had come out of a remote location and become the property and tool of the individual.

The lower cost and increased capability of microcomputers allowed smaller organizations the opportunity to adapt computers to their needs. Microcomputers began to be used routinely in law offices, doctors' offices, retail establishments, and other places of business. Individuals such as writers, artists, coaches, and consultants in various fields also began to use computers. School systems, some of which had used mainframes or minicomputers for administrative jobs, and occasionally instructional tasks, started to make microcomputers available to students and teachers.

Microcomputers also began to appear in homes (**Figure 7–2**). People started to use computers for entertainment, word processing, managing household accounts, keeping household inventories, and education. Computers in the

Figure 7–1 Above, left, is an example of an older computer, the CDC 1604. Newer machines, such as microcomputers, are, to a great degree, responsible for the public's interest in using computers. A variety of microcomputers are available today. The Commodore Amiga is shown above right.

Figure 7–2 With the advent of inexpensive microcomputers, many people began to apply computers to various tasks at home.

home began to be used to access other, larger computers that could provide a variety of services, including, but not limited to, stock market information, UPI wire releases, shopping services, sophisticated entertainment software, airline reservations, and electronic libraries.

Who Should Be Computer Literate?

The revolution of computer power had the effect of creating a great deal of interest in society in general about what computers are and what they can (and can't) do. Quite naturally, people became concerned that there were things they needed to know about computers, since computers were becoming such an integral part of society. These circumstances led to the evolution of the idea that an individual in a society permeated by computers must become computer literate, must know how to deal with computers. In other words, to survive (and, it is hoped, flourish) in a culture that uses computers, a person must know some things about what computers are and how they may be used.

This is a good beginning point in trying to understand what computer literacy might be. In general, one may say that computer literacy is a state in which an individual has an understanding of what a computer is and how it works, and is comfortable and effective in making a computer accomplish a necessary task. In reality, however, a good definition of computer literacy will be specific to the situation in which the computer-literate individual must function. A certified public accountant, a Hollywood screenwriter, and a secretary will all need different skills and information to be comfortable and effective in their interaction with computers; each will need something different to become computer literate. The same is true for students and teachers.

Input/Output

The following excerpt is from an article by Wallace Judd entitled "A Teacher's Place in the Computer Curriculum," which appeared in the October 1983 issue of Phi Delta Kappan.

A number of factors are falling into place today. Foremost among them is the fact that the new computer technology is available at the individual level. Trains traveled 50 and 60 miles per hour long before automobiles could. But only with the advent of the motorcar could individuals take advantage of the increased speed of transportation. Giant arc lights illuminated the streets of San Francisco 10 years before Edison invented the incandescent light bulb. But the gigantic arc lamps could illuminate only such large areas as whole plazas and squares, whereas a light bulb was small enough to replace a single candle.

Similarly, the giant computers of the Sixties and Seventies could compute pi to 100,000 places or keep track of millions of insurance policies. But for all their computational power, they had relatively little effect on daily life. Only when microprocessors became widely available could their influence on everyday life become pervasive.

The Teacher's Role

I was a schoolteacher for a total of seven years in three districts. In one district I was director of a media center. To support reading, we used tape recorders, movie projectors, filmstrip projectors, tachistoscopes, and a variety of materials for these machines. One day I asked a fairly successful, older teacher whether she would like to try some new materials we had just received. She told me that she wouldn't have a machine in her classroom. She offered a variety of reasons. Someone has to run them, they break down, and they're just not worth the bother. She would probably feel just the same way about a computer.

But a teacher who won't have a computer in his or her classroom is like a ditch digger who won't learn to use a steam shovel. Like a steam shovel, a computer is a tool. It can increase the power a teacher can apply to a learning situation, but it does not replace the teacher. In a competitive world, ditch diggers who refuse to adapt are going to go out of business.

A teacher is still needed to motivate students. Whatever array of math games a teacher may have in the classroom, there will be times when students need to be motivated to use them. A teacher will need to pace student use of the computer, to mix practice with conceptual advances, to intersperse periods of personal contact with periods of intense concentration. A teacher knows when to push a lazy student and when to ease up on a student who is having family problems. These are the personal dimensions of teaching that a computer can never replace. They are also the dimensions of teaching that will increasingly distinguish the excellent teacher from the average teacher.

Several years ago I visited a kindergarten classroom right after the noon recess. When a child came in crying, the teacher picked her up, put her on her lap, and, with the rest of the children watching and listening, asked a series of questions. What made you feel bad? The other children wouldn't let you play with them? Remember that story we read about the ugly duckling? How did he feel? What happened at the end of the story? How did the other ducklings feel then? With this short sequence of sympathetic questions, the teacher persuaded the child to explain her feelings and involved the rest of the class in the event. The lesson was as much about reading as about how to treat others. By drawing the parallel between the child's feelings and those of the ugly duckling, the teacher showed the child and the class that the stories they read were relevant to their own feelings.

This anecdote illustrates one important function of the teacher: linking the skills students learn in the classroom to the real world. This cannot be premeditated or planned into a curriculum. Yet it is essential that students learn how the skills they are learning in the classroom can be used in the world outside. A computer can deliver many skills to students, but only teachers can connect those skills to the contemporary world.

Of course, teachers will still need to select curriculum materials—a task they must perform even more judiciously than before, for computer programs will not only organize the material and provide opportunities for practice, but in many cases they will also present new concepts. And teachers will still need to guide and encourage students' efforts to explore subjects in more depth. At least in the early years of the computer revolution, teachers will continue to be the main source of materials to enrich a subject.

(Judd, 1983.)

A prime concern for educators is that students be prepared to become productive members of the society in which they will live. The ideal of education is to pass on the skills and information necessary for all students to pursue their lives as contributing, fulfilled members of society. So, for students, any definition of computer literacy must take into account that they are being prepared for a world of the future. For young children, this world may be as far off as thirteen to seventeen years, depending on whether or not they continue their

Computer Literacy for Students

Figure 7–3 The availability of relatively powerful, inexpensive microcomputers opened the door for computer technology to be applied to education throughout the country (and throughout the world).

education beyond high school. Although it is impossible to say exactly what the world of the future will be like, one can say that it will be a world that depends to a great degree on computers. It will be a world in which computers will affect everyone's life.

Many educators feel a strong responsibility to prepare students for such a technologically sophisticated world. This is obvious in the statements of philosophy about computer education presented on the following pages. These philosophies are expressions of educators' concerns about preparing students for a future world. They provide a meaningful background on which to present a definition of computer literacy.

Figure 7–4 presents such a statement from a computer literacy curriculum developed by teachers. The teachers in this district obviously feel strongly that part of their responsibility is to direct the way children come into contact with computers. They believe that children, as adults, will eventually be users of computers and that they must develop both a positive attitude toward computers and a set of skills related to their use. Further, the statement addresses the issue of the societal implications of computers and implies that students must gain some background information about computer technology as an aid in forming opinions about appropriate and inappropriate uses of this technology as it grows and expands.

Figure 7–5 presents a different statement of philosophy from teachers in another district. Again, this statement is part of an overall computer curriculum designed by teachers for districtwide implementation. This statement addresses the issue of living in a computer-oriented society and calls for students

---

PHILOSOPHY

Our statement of philosophy concerning computer literacy is based on the message that we are getting from today's newspaper headlines:

- Computers now play a major role in our society.
- This is only the beginning.
- Computer education for all children is of highest priority.

The growing importance of computers in the world of work makes it clear that knowledge in this area is a necessity. As with any technology, computers are not good or bad in and of themselves. They can be misused, inappropriately used, even neglected. But their potential is enormous and our children surely will learn to live in a computer-pervaded world whether or not the school plays a major and guiding role in that learning.

We, in Regional District #13, believe that our schools must become a major force in the direction of that learning and that we are all challenged as teachers and school administrators to respond to the needs of our students for computer literacy and computer skills. Today's students, as adults, will be users of computers.

Beyond an acquaintance with the role of computers in society the student must obtain a working knowledge of how to use them, including the ways in which one communicates with and commands their services in problem solving. Students must have the opportunity to use computers in order to feel comfortable and confident about them.

We believe that our school program should provide opportunities for our students to interact with computers, understand simple programming, have a knowlege of computer components, have an awareness of the impact and limitations of computers, and to develop a positive attitude toward computers.

Based on this rationale we submit the following statement of philosophy of computer education:

Recognizing that the computer is and will be both a major subject and tool of education, it is the obligation of the educational community to insure that students achieve computer literacy and are provided with the opportunity to achieve computer mastery. The computer, as both topic and tool, should be an integrated element of the total curriculum and organization for instruction.

(Regional District #13, 1983, p. 1)

Figure 7–4 A statement of philosophy concerning computer literacy. This statement is a preface to one district's computer curriculum.

to be educated in the limitations, capabilities, and possible uses of computers. The main concern of these teachers is that students understand that technology in general and computers in particular exist as tools to be applied by humans. These teachers are concerned that the computer as a tool be used to stimulate originality. They also emphasize the importance of human relationships in any type of technological education. The impression is strongly given that their intention is to be sure their students do not become less human as they work with technology.

These philosophies are similar to what many districts are expressing as a justification for implementing a computer curriculum. The overall goal of a computer curriculum is to help students become computer literate. Computer literacy for students consists of two components: knowledge (information) and performance (skills). To become computer literate, students must work with a computer (to gain performance skills) as well as with information about computers. The act of working with a computer will also help to present, concretely, some of the knowledge components of computer literacy for students.

STATEMENT: This syllabus is the product of a committee of teacher volunteers charged to draft a K–12 computer education program. It is designed to be a beginning of the process in which education broadens basic curriculum to include technological influences on society.

PHILOSOPHY: As technology increasingly affects our lives, students will be directly or indirectly involved with computers. We believe that it is essential to educate students to function in a computer-oriented society. Computer education includes becoming familiar with the capabilities, limitations, and uses of computers.

We believe computers are tools which can be used to stimulate originality and depth in student learning. Because the student alone must ultimately control what is done with technology, we must build an environment which supports creative solo learning built on disciplined study. Therefore, we believe that it is essential to recognize the importance of the teacher in the technological setting.

In designing the computer education curriculum for the Waterford Public Schools we realize the primary importance of human relationships in technological education.

(Waterford Public Schools, 1983, p. 1)

Figure 7–5 A statement of philosophy from another district regarding computer education.

Knowledge

Students must be:

- familiar with the components of a computer system (hardware and software) and how they work and interact.
- informed about the history of computing.
- aware of the current and projected uses of computers in society and the possible implications of those uses.
- knowledgeable about job opportunities associated with computers.

Performance

Students must be able to:

- use the computer for instructional purposes by using computer-assisted instruction software of both the tool and tutor type, both with teacher direction and, when presented with appropriate documentation, alone.
- write simple programs in two computer languages.
- engage in problem solving by breaking a complex problem into modules, generating a solution for each module, and combining the solutions to solve the problem.

This definition is in keeping with all of the concerns expressed so far about computers, education, and society. Its intent is to provide students with information and skills that will be of value when coming into contact with tomorrow's world as well as the world of today. The computers of twenty years from now may well be very different from those currently available. Still, students will need to make decisions about technology and will function, as adults, with the attitudes about computers and technology that begin developing today. Further, problem-solving skills developed through learning to correctly program a computer will aid in understanding the machine and in developing what may prove to be a valuable, transferable skill. Learning about today's hardware and becoming comfortable in using hardware and software at school is good preparation for working with computers as adults. Also, using computer software for instruction in different content areas may offer the benefit of increased student motivation.

Teachers should, in most areas, have more in-depth knowledge about computers than do students. They must also have a wider range of knowledge related to their professional concerns. The following definition restates most of the points listed in the definition for students and adds several more: Computer literacy for teachers consists of two components: knowledge (information) and performance (skills). To become computer literate, teachers must work with a computer (to gain performance skills) as well as with information about computers. The act of working with a computer will also help to present, concretely, some of the knowledge components of computer literacy for teachers.

Computer Literacy for Teachers

Teachers must be:

Knowledge

- familiar with the components of a computer system (hardware and software) and how they work and interact.
- informed about the history of computing.
- aware of the current and projected uses of computers in society and the possible implications of those uses.
- knowledgeable about job opportunities associated with computers.
- familiar with opinions and research, pro and con, related to the use of computers in education.
- knowledgeable about the different types of software available for education.
- capable of stating and identifying valid criteria to be used in evaluating educational software.
- aware of the relationship between programming a computer and learning problem-solving skills.

Teachers must be able to:

Performance

- use the computer for instructional purposes by using computer-assisted instruction software of both the tool and the tutor type with students in a classroom setting.
- write simple programs in two computer languages.
- engage in problem solving by breaking a complex problem into modules, generating a solution for each module, and combining the solutions to solve the problem.

Figure 7–6 Teachers should have adequate training in using computers with students and using computers to perform management and other professional tasks.

■ take a piece of educational software and, with appropriate documentation, sit down at the computer and use the software.

As stated in this definition, it is necessary that teachers, as professionals, be aware of the potential pluses and minuses of using computers in education. They should also be familiar with the research and theory behind the main uses of computers in education. Further, it is of great importance that teachers be acquainted with the types of educational software available and with criteria for evaluating educational software.

The definition also states that teachers should be able to write simple programs in two computer-programming languages. There is often great confusion when discussing teachers and programming. It would not be desirable, necessary, or, in many instances, possible to turn teachers into programmers. (To become a competent professional programmer takes quite a bit of time, training, aptitude, and experience.) Besides, there is simply no need for teachers to become programmers. There is, however, a need for teachers to understand what programming is and how it relates to problem solving. To do this it is necessary that teachers be exposed to the rudiments of at least two of the more popular programming languages used in education. This can be accomplished by learning how to write a few simple programs in each language and definitely requires hands-on experience at the computer. The overview of BASIC and Logo presented in this book is an example of the type of introductory material to which teachers should be exposed. Writing a few programs helps a teacher to understand the way the computer works and provides concrete experiences of controlling a new technology. Depending on interests and job responsibilities, some teachers choose to gain in-depth experience in programming a computer, but this is certainly not necessary for all, or even many, teachers.

COMPUTER LITERACY (1 day)
Date: Friday, May 3
9:00 am–3:30 pm

Designed for the beginner, this hands-on workshop will cover the essentials of hardware and educational software. You will learn how to evaluate software and ways to integrate the computer with your curriculum. Also included is a brief history of computers.

INTRO TO LOGO (offered twice)
Dates: Thursday, May 2; May 9; May 16
3:45–5:30 pm
Friday, May 10
9:00 am–3:30 pm

Learn the Logo language by doing. Eighty percent of the time will be spent on the computer. Also includes a short introduction to Logo theory. No prior computer experience is assumed.

INTRO TO BASIC (1 day)
Date: Friday, May 17
9:00 am–3:30 pm

Designed for the beginner who wants a practical introduction to the BASIC programming language, the workshop will be 80 percent hands-on. No prior computer experience is assumed.

Figure 7–7 Some examples of computer education workshops available to practicing teachers.

Lastly, teachers should be comfortable enough with the computer so that they can take a piece of educational software that is new to them and, given well-written documentation, use it. This ability comes from a conceptual familiarity with computers in general and hands-on experiences with the different types of educational software available.

Gaining Computer Literacy

For students, computer literacy is gained as part of a current or developing computer curriculum in their school. Prospective teachers may learn about computers and education in one or more undergraduate courses. Even in the case where undergraduates have had the benefit of computer instruction in high school, such courses serve the purpose of enhancing computer skills and introducing issues related to educational computing.

In-service teachers may attend workshops in educational computing, examples of which are presented in **Figure 7–7**. Conferences lasting from one day to one week (and sometimes longer) are presented by various organizations concerned with computers and education (see Appendix B). In-service teachers may take graduate coursework in educational computing. The needs of some teachers are met by one course; others opt for a number of courses. **Figure 7–8** presents a series of courses for a concentration in educational computing. This

---

Computer Education Field of Study

The Computer Education Field of Study is designed to meet the needs of elementary and secondary teachers and administrators who wish to develop a better understanding of the varied uses of computers in Education. The concentration requires 12 s.h. of computer education courses and a minimum of 6 s.h. in Math Education.

EDU 553 The Microcomputer in the Classroom, is required and a prerequisite for all additional courses in Computer Education.

Courses in Computer Education

EDU 553   The Microcomputer in the Classroom
EDU 554   Computer Programming: Logo
EDU 576   Microcomputers and the Curriculum
EDU 577   Educational Computing—Theory and Practice
EDU 578   BASIC for Teachers
EDU 579   Pascal for Teachers
EDU 580   Microcomputer Applications—Productivity Tools

EDU 530   Modern Mathematics in the Classroom I, and
EDU 532   Special Mathematics Workshop I
are recommended for elementary school teachers completing the Computer Education Concentration.

EDU 531   Modern Mathematics in the Classroom II, and
EDU 533   Special Mathematics Workshop II
are recommended for secondary school teachers completing the Computer Education Concentration.

(From the 1985–1987 Graduate Catalog, Eastern Connecticut State University)

Figure 7–8 A concentration in computer education designed for classroom teachers and administrators. The required six semester hours in math education in this program would not be found in many programs.

particular program was designed for practicing classroom teachers and administrators. In this program, students take a total of twelve credit hours of graduate-level educational computing courses as a concentration within a master's degree program. Other programs exist that are aimed at training educators to design and produce educational software. Still other programs are aimed at training researchers in educational computing. In addition to more formal instruction, many interested teachers read extensively about computers and education.

Developing the Computer Curriculum

Owing to the types of concerns expressed in the philosophies cited earlier, many districts have gone through a process of developing and implementing a computer curriculum. Once the need has been identified, a committee is usually set up to investigate the feasibility of teaching with and about computers. This committee may be composed solely of teachers. In other instances it may be made up of a mixture of teachers and other education professionals, such as counselors, reading consultants, and building administrators. In any case, teachers will probably be well represented on such a committee. The scope of the committee's concern will be identified. For instance, the committee may be charged with developing a curriculum for grades K through 12, or may be asked to provide a curriculum for grades 5 through 8, or some other set of grade levels. Some districts develop such a curriculum for a narrow range of grade levels, such as 4 through 6, and then implement the program one grade level per year and evaluate the program at the end of each year. The information gathered from the evaluation is used to improve the existing curriculum and to help plan the curriculum for the next range of grade levels.

The first order of business for the committee is to identify what other schools are doing. It is important to know what national, regional, and local trends are in relation to computers and education. It is also important to become aware of the possible positive and negative effects of introducing computers into the schools. Only by gathering valid information can the individuals on such a committee proceed intelligently. After such information is gathered, discussed, and analyzed, recommendations are formulated. There is usually some mechanism, such as periodic progress reports, to keep the rest of the district informed about how the project is proceeding. When all work is completed, a formal presentation of the committee's proposal is usually made to the school board for approval and funding.

In reality, the impetus for a computer curriculum may develop over a period of time. A district may have individual teachers who begin to use computers in their classrooms. The district may support research and training activities for teachers before any formal curriculum is in place. Over a period of years the actions of different teachers and administrators can lead to a sophisticated program of computer education. **Figure 7–9** outlines the occurrences over thirteen years that led to the development of computer education as it exists in Mahopac Central School District in Mahopac, New York. Note the various committees and individuals involved in different aspects of the development of the program.

A thoughtful approach to developing a computer curriculum will include the following information:

- Statement of philosophy justifying the program
- General, overall description of the program, including a narrative description and a scope and sequence chart
- Time line for implementation of the curriculum
- Specific description of the program at each grade level, including goals and objectives for each grade level and perhaps suggested materials or activities to achieve the stated objectives
- Program for teacher training to prepare teachers to implement the curriculum, including a software evaluation component
- Budgetary implications of the proposed curriculum
- Statement as to possible personnel needs
- Statement regarding space needs
- Mechanism to periodically evaluate the success of the curriculum and a way to modify it based on such periodic evaluations

Components of a Computer Curriculum

CHRONOLOGY OF THE INCREASING INVOLVEMENT OF
THE MAHOPAC CENTRAL SCHOOL DISTRICT
IN EDUCATIONAL COMPUTING

Date	Activity or Event
9/73	One year sabbatical given to a math teacher to investigate the feasibility of offering a computer science course in the high school.
9/74	In-service computer workshop given to Mahopac teachers.
9/74	Teachers completed computer literacy courses.
9/74	Teachers given professional days to attend computer workshops and meetings.
9/79–6/81	Northern Westchester Putnam Teachers Center housed in the Mahopac School District. Mahopac was part of the teacher center.
9/79	A district computer coordinator (K–12) was appointed.
9/79	District obtained a Computer-Assisted Instruction system with a CAI lab in every building with Suppes software on the CCC terminals. Teacher assistant hired for each lab.
7/82	Director of Staff Development appointed to assist in teacher training.
7/82	Science teacher wrote software for science curriculum during summer.
9/82–11/82	Released time provided for teachers during the school day for computer training. All Logo teachers were given four ½ day training sessions (grades 1,2,3,4).
11/82, 83, 84	Presentation on Mahopac's Computer Program at NYSAED's Conference.
2/83	Logo Committee created.
2/83, 2/84	Set up a booth showing Mahopac's Computer Program at the Technology Fair in Albany.
6/83–present	Summer Computer Day Camp Program.
7/83	Five teachers wrote social studies software.
9/83	District study conducted to research the effects of 1, 2, or 4 computers in a classroom.
9/83–present	Advanced Placement Course in Pascal offered at High School.
2/84	Director of Curriculum and Staff Development appointed to assist with technology concerns.
5/84	English, Technology and Communications curriculum (ETC) written.
9/84	Educational Computing Committee for grades K–12 formed with representatives from all levels.
9/84	Offered a computer science program for students who previously attended an off-site center.
9/84	Mahopac becomes a pilot school district for Syracuse University—offering two 3 credit courses on "Digital Structures" and "Computer Organization."
9/84	Learning Technology Center launched at Junior High School. Staffed with teachers and teaching assistants.
9/84	District participates with BOCES in a software review project.
2/85	Nassau Presentation on Educational Computing given by Mahopac's Superintendent, Assistant Superintendent, and Director of Computer Education.
3/85	Mahopac was chosen by the NYS Center for Learning Technology to be videotaped for a staff development presentation. Presentation was aired on Channel 13 on March 5th, 1985.
6/85	Keyboarding Research Study completed.

(Mahopac, p. 32)

Figure 7–9 Important events that led to one district's sophisticated involvement with computer education.

This process is similar to other curriculum development projects that take place in schools, with a few important exceptions. Schools have generally felt some pressure to "catch up" to the computer revolution and so have felt the need to incorporate computers into the schools quickly. This "jump-on-the-

Reactions and Research

Computer-based materials may be used by individual students, by pairs of students, or by students working in small groups (triads, quads, etc.). Trowbridge and Durnin (1984) report the results of an experimental study to investigate unsupervised learning by individuals and groups using computer-based materials. The computer activities involved the manipulation of pictures of batteries, wires, and bulbs on the computer screen. The activities were simulations of science experiments aimed at developing reasoning skills and a conceptual understanding of current flow through a completed circuit. The investigators observed students working alone, in pairs, in triads, and in quads. The subjects were fifty-eight seventh- and eighth-grade students. Data about student interaction with the computer and about student cognitive and social interaction with other students were recorded. Achievement data were also recorded, as were data to describe the global aspects of each group during each session (i.e., error frequency, response quality, cooperation, competition). The findings indicate there may be some advantages to using interactive computer-based materials with students in pairs and triads.

This study has shown that small group usage of highly interactive computer based learning materials has certain advantages over individual usage. On the whole, verbalizations among pairs, triads and quads were relevant to the learning material and socially supportive. We found no evidence for any detrimental effects among students working in pairs or triads. Quads, however, seemed to be too large, in general, for all four members to maintain high levels of interactivity with either the program or with other members of the group. On post-session achievement measures of individual competence, no differences were found among individuals and members of groups.

Students working in groups seemed more likely to interpret program questions as the authors of the materials had intended. Often, discussion about multiple interpretations would converge to the correct interpretation. On the other hand, individuals working alone were more likely to misinterpret program questions and to pursue incorrect paths through the material than students working in groups. Individuals showed a greater willingness to go back and review material that gave them trouble, however, which may explain why we found no inferiority of individuals' performance on achievement measures.

A comparison of achievement between those students who had used the materials and a control group who had not indicated clearly that students had learned some elementary ideas of electric current flow by using the computer simulation. In addition, these students had no difficulty at all applying their knowledge to a task involving actual physical equipment.

CONCLUSION: Teachers and school administrators who are considering the use of computer based learning materials in the classroom need to examine the desirability of more than one student working at the computer. With the limited availability of computers in schools, teachers may wish to consider the advantages of having students work in groups.

While it is difficult to measure gains directly attributable to social interaction, a student working with one or two others at the computer typically verbalizes his or her own thoughts so frequently that an inference of cognitive gain is not unreasonable. Furthermore, performance is generally unimpaired.

Our conclusions suggest that the use of computer based learning materials should not be restricted to individuals alone. On the contrary, many benefits are to be gained by having pairs, and, under some circumstances, groups of three working together.

(Trowbridge and Durnin, 1984.)

---

bandwagon" syndrome is best avoided. Taking the time to develop a curriculum carefully should always yield better results than moving too quickly. Also, bringing computers into the schools requires money, often a lot of money relative to what a district may have to spend. A carefully proposed plan will include recommendations about approximate costs for hardware and software. Recommendations about personnel may be included, particularly if it is feasible to hire a computer coordinator. Further, hardware takes up space, so recommendations as to space usage may be offered (i.e., should each classroom be equipped with one or more computers or should computers be kept in a centralized lab). Recommendations about where software should be stored and how it should be evaluated may also be included in the plan.

A Curriculum for Computer Literacy

Most computer curriculums will address five general topics:

1. Information about the history of computing

2. Instruction about and experiences with the various components of a computer system, including hardware and software and how they work and interact

3. Information about the social implications of computer use, including the effect of computers on the current and future job market

4. Instruction about and experiences with two or more programming languages, with specific attention to developing problem-solving skills

5. Instruction about and experiences with tutor-type computer-assisted instruction (CAI) software (i.e., tutorials, drill and practice, etc., in support of instruction in other content areas) and instruction about and experiences with tool CAI software (i.e., word processing packages)

As with any curriculum, topics may be introduced in a simplified form at an early level and expanded on at a later grade level. The teaching of programming languages may be done in the primary or elementary years as an aid in teaching problem solving and developing a generalized awareness of computers. During later years, specifically in high school, different languages may be introduced as subjects for vocational education or as preparation for college-level work.

Figure 7–10 presents the scope and sequence chart from the educational computing program in the Mahopac Central School District, mentioned previously, as well as the justification for the program. Notice that these educators are concerned with both educating students about computers and having students use computers as they learn other subject matter areas.

The point is made that the role of the teacher in implementing the plan is one of both manager and user of educational computer programs. This role is new for many teachers, and to be successful at it they must be supported by administrators who understand and value it. Further, the importance of training for teachers, both initial training and the availability of ongoing programs, is addressed. This type of administrative and instructional support for teachers is invaluable in making such a program a success. Lastly, a sensitivity to the time constraints a teacher is subject to is evident. The administrators in the district have made a commitment to teachers to provide release time for training.

The program provides all the curriculum components outlined earlier. Care is taken at the elementary level to provide experiences for all students in appropriate areas. Junior and senior high school programs build on this base and offer more extensive experiences for students at these levels. The senior high school offerings are quite sophisticated and are offered in conjunction with a large university (obviously not an option for every district).

The curriculum starts as early as kindergarten by helping children become oriented to and aware of computers. Notice also the introduction of Logo as the programming language taught at the elementary level. Computers are used to teach word-processing skills beginning in the earliest grades. Teacher-selected software is used to support learning in other content areas, beginning at the elementary level. Specific software packages have also been adopted at different grade levels for particular instructional areas. Computer Curriculum

Introduction

The advent of the computer is causing a learning revolution which we will look back upon as being the most important event in the history of modern education. Historically, the field of education has been "conservative" in its approach to utilizing computers as an educational tool. The early use of computers in schools centered on student accounting, school business functions, and personnel record keeping. Many limited computer systems and programs were initiated in the 50's and 60's. Led by B.F. Skinner of Harvard and Patrick Suppes, the CAI (Computer-Assisted Instruction) movement was supported for a time with Federal funds. The early computers were used primarily for business and governmental purposes. Now all of that has changed. Several radical technical advancements have been made over the past 8 years which have been recognized and utilized in the schools of the Mahopac Central School District. The adoption of the BASIC language allowed computers to react immediately to program input. The use of CRT television-like screens provided a new access media. The development of chips offered miniaturization and low-cost computing. The impact of all these advances and others is only now beginning to be felt. It appears that American Education is finally entering the age of the computer.

The computer, its programs, and everything about the electronic media is a creation of human beings. However, because of the machine's seemingly lifelike qualities (the ability to immediately respond to written or spoken English as well as the capabilities of sorting, comparing, calculating, retrieving, selecting, and presenting data) the learner sometimes experiences a phenomenon that is new to the field of education—the feeling that the learning is taking place without the intervention of other human beings. The impact of this methodology is being studied in the Mahopac schools in an effort to improve present learning.

Educators may no longer deny learners access to the new media. This is the time for our national political leaders, school superintendents, college presidents, principals, teachers, and parents to exercise their educational leadership by recognizing that the Learning Revolution is with us. We must place Educational Computing where it belongs—in the hands of students and teachers in order to remain in the mainstream of American Education.

What We Are Doing in Mahopac

The Mahopac Schools have adopted a dual approach to educational computing which focuses on both Computer Education and Computer Curriculum Applications. We believe that Computer Education is required for all pupils in order to assist them in better understanding the role and function of computers in living and in society. We have therefore provided mandatory learning experiences for our students in all grades.

The Educational Computing Curriculum may be conceived of as being in 2 parts: the elementary school curriculum and the secondary level school curriculum. The elementary curriculum for pupils in grades K–6 has three major goals as follows:

1. To provide each student with the skill to control the computer in order to use it as a tool for learning.
2. To provide each student with the ability required to use instructional software and applications programs (e.g., word processing, and graphics) which may enhance the learning process.
3. To provide each student with computer experiences which will improve individual thinking and problem solving skills.

The secondary curriculum for pupils in grades 7–12 has three major goals as follows:

1. To provide intensive word processing experience as part of the writing program for each student.
2. To offer increased learning opportunities through instructional software and applications programs.
3. To provide all students with the option of studying computer languages (i.e., BASIC, APL, Pascal, and/or assembler).

The use of educational computing applications to facilitate learning within the adopted curriculum constitutes the current major thrust of the school district. One observes from the variety of disciplines listed on pages six and seven, that the computer is being used extensively to provide and to supplement instruction on the elementary, junior high, and high school level. The Mahopac Schools have pioneered in efforts to provide viable teaching and learning alternatives for both pupils and teachers in classrooms and laboratories.

A key factor underlying our success has been a continuing emphasis on staff development and support. We have found that teachers and administrators need time to assimilate new ideas and concepts. The process of change in educational computing is especially threatening unless the following factors are present:

1. The role of the teacher as a user and manager of computer programs is clarified.
2. The new role is valued by the school administration.
3. Hardware is purchased according to a district plan.
4. Practitioners are involved in the screening and selection of software.
5. Competent instruction is initially provided for staff and thereafter made available on a continual basis, as needed.
6. There is a school district and building commitment to provide released time for the training of teachers.

(Mahopac, 1985, pp. 3–4)

Figure 7–10 The scope and sequence of the educational computing program in the Mahopac Central School District, Mahopac, New York.

**EDUCATIONAL COMPUTING
CURRICULUM SCOPE AND SEQUENCE PLAN**

The educational computing curriculum in the Mahopac schools is a multidimensional series of experiences offered in various programs at appropriate grade levels.

Computer Education

							Grade Level						
	K	1	2	3	4	5	6	7	8	9	10	11	12
Orientation to and awareness of Computers & Software	X	X											
Computer Languages													
Logo			X	X	X	X							
Introductory BASIC							P				X	X	X
Adapted Introductory BASIC											X	X	X
Advanced BASIC										X	X	X	
Introductory APL												X	X
Advanced APL												X	X
Pascal (advanced placement course)												X	X
Project Advance (a program in cooperation with Syracuse University)													
Digital Structures (3 cr.)													X
Computer Organization & Assembly Language (3 cr.)												X	X

Legend
X = Currently Offered
P = Projected

Figure 7-10 Continued

Curriculum Applications of Educational Computing for Learning

	K	1	2	3	4	5	6	7	8	9	10	11	12
									Grade Level				
Business Education													
Data Processing (Course No. 233)											X	X	X
Word Processing (Course No. 235)													
Office Procedures (Course No. 229)													
Accounting (Course No. 213, 214)													
English													
Developing Word Processing Skills	X	X	X	X	X	X	X	X	X	X	X	X	X
ETC Program (English, Technology & Communications, Grade 7)													
Language Arts													
Library													
Library Search & Retrieval Program (BRS)					X	X	X	X	X	X	X	X	X
Library Skills Software	X	X	X	X									
Mathematics													
Math Software	X	X	X	X	X	X	X	X	X	X	X	X	X
Science													
Elementary Level— Classrooms with teacher-selected software	P	P	P	P	P	P	X	X	X	X	X	X	X
Junior High Level— Laboratory with a teacher-developed, monitored and updated learning system. Offers tutorial instruction, simulations, drills and practice, test-taking, and teacher utilities													
Astronomy Software													
High School Level— Teachers prepare computer generated randomized Regents-type test questions													
Classrooms with teacher-selected software													

Legend
X = Currently Offered
P = Projected

Figure 7–10 Continued

Curriculum Applications of Educational Computing for Learning (Continued)

	K	1	2	3	4	5	6	7	8	9	10	11	12
Social Studies													
Elementary Level—													
Classrooms with teacher-selected software	P	P	P	P	P	X	X	X	X	X	X	X	X
Junior High Level—													
Laboratory with a teacher-developed, monitored and updated learning system													
High School Level—													
None													
Other Programs													
Computer Curriculum Corporation CAI													
Individualized basic skills program for remediation, reinforcement, and enrichment in Reading, Math, Language Arts, and a variety of other disciplines.	X	X	X	X	X	X	X	X	X	X	X	X	X
Guidance Information System (GIS)								X	X	X	X	X	X
Discover (Career and Guidance Education)								X	X	X	P	P	P
Computer Summer Day Camp	X	X	X	X	X	X	X						

Applications for Administration/Management

Word Processing in school offices
High School Attendance
High School Scheduling
Scoring of tests
Central Office business functions

Legend
X = Currently Offered
P = Projected

(Mahopac, 1985, pp. 5–7)

Figure 7-10 Continued

Corporation's computer-assisted instruction materials are used for individualized instruction in basic skills and for remediation and enrichment at all levels in such areas as reading, math, language arts, and other disciplines. Some software is teacher-developed. A computer camp is offered for all ages over the summer. As you review the scope and sequence of this program, notice the components of the program in place at the time of this writing and the components that are proposed for future implementation. Also, remember that this is a sophisticated program that has developed over a period of years in a district with a good variety of computer equipment available.

Figure 7–11 is an overview of a computer curriculum presented in Beverly Hunter's book *My Students Use Computers: Learning Activities for Computer Literacy* (1983). Hunter's book presents a curriculum for computer literacy for grades K through 8, along with a wealth of activities for implementing the curriculum (see the Computers in the Classroom section of this chapter for an example).

The suggested curriculum in Figure 7–11 is divided into the following six strands:

1. *Using and developing procedures.* Computers need procedures, or specific sets of unambiguous instructions, to operate. This strand develops students' ability to write procedures and use them to solve problems.

2. *Using computer programs.* Children learn to use programs for learning in different content areas and to select and use appropriate programs to help them perform specific tasks they may need to accomplish.

3. *Fundamental concepts about computers.* Students learn fundamental concepts about what computers are and how they operate.

4. *Computer applications.* Students learn how computers are applied in different areas of society and become familiar with general ideas about how applications are built and what they comprise.

5. *Impacts of computers on society.* This strand helps students to investigate the ways computers affect individuals and groups and provides information about the advantages and disadvantages of computers. The roles of individuals who work with computers are investigated, as well as possible computer-related careers. Here, and elsewhere in the curriculum, the subject of ethics is addressed as it relates to computer use and information processing.

6. *Writing computer programs.* Students learn to write, test, debug, and modify computer programs as an outgrowth of previous work with procedural thinking skills.

There is a strong component in this curriculum aimed at developing an awareness of how computers are used, how computer applications are developed, and what the impact of computers may be in society. Much time is taken to develop skills for using and selecting software as an aid to learning and to personal productivity. These skills could be of great value in adult life.

The curriculum seems to emphasize development of procedural thinking skills as a prerequisite to learning how to program a computer. Care is

Strands	Grades K–2	Grades 3–4	Grades 5–6	Grades 7–8
	TEACH STUDENTS TO:			
Procedures	• Follow a procedure for a familiar task • Modify a procedure • Show different procedures can produce the same outcome • Find and correct errors in a procedure • Describe procedures used to perform a task	• Help to develop a procedure involving repetition, decision making, and variables • Find and correct errors in a procedure • Develop a procedure, demonstrate that it works • Use procedures to perform new tasks	• Apply procedures skills to new problems • Note differences between procedures for people and procedures for computers • Break problem into subproblems: plan procedures and subprocedures • Develop procedures for organizing data	• Apply procedures skills to new problems • Choose the best aid for solving a problem: calculator, computer, pencil?
Using Programs	• Use computer drills and games • Operate equipment; load and run programs • Recognize the computer needs instruction	• Read documentation that describes programs and tells how to use them • Select and operate programs without teacher's help • Select and use a program to solve a specific problem	• Use simulations as an aid in learning • Demonstrate learning from a simulation • Retrieve information from a computer data base • Apply skills in using equipment, programs and documentation	• Use word processor to improve writing • Use more complex simulations • Use new methods to retrieve information
Fundamentals	• Understand that computer instructions are contained in a program	• Understand that the computer is a general purpose machine	• Recognize tasks for which computer speed is needed • Recognize tasks requiring repetition • Recognize tasks requiring large amounts of data	Apply knowledge of fundamentals to new situations
Applications	• Discover computer applications in homes and neighborhoods	• Know about computer applications in school and local government • Compare fictional and real computers	• Understand 1 or more ways information retrieval is used in diverse fields • Understand how scientists might use computers	• Recognize uses of Word Processor • Recognize uses of computer in business and manufacturing • Recognize use of computer systems in large organizations • Recognize main components of computer systems
Impact	• Follow rules for using equipment and programs	• Follow rules for using equipment and programs	• Understand reasons to restrict access to data bases and programs • Understand advantages and disadvantages of particular uses of information retrieval	• Become aware of new social issues created by computers • Appreciate social dependence on computers • Understand effects of computer failures • Understand the kinds of computer skills needed in diverse careers • Become aware of computer professions
Writing Computer Programs	(Note: For grades K–6, objectives and activities related to computer programming are reflected in the Procedures, Using Programs, and Fundamentals strands.)			• Modify programs • Code programs • Write documentation • Test and debug programs • Plan and develop programs

(Hunter, 1983, pp. 12–13)

Figure 7–11 An overview of the computer curriculum presented in Beverly Hunter's book *My Students Use Computers: Learning Activities for Computer Literacy.*

taken to develop procedural thinking skills by engaging in specialized activities beginning in the early years.

In general, the orientation of this curriculum is toward a sort of social implications approach coupled with developing skills in writing procedures, selecting and using software, and writing programs. Social implications in the sense that students learn about a variety of computer applications in society and also study how the use of computers may affect society. Tool mode uses of computers are covered in the curriculum, as are tutor mode uses. Computer programming, specifically slated for grades 7 and 8, is addressed in the Procedures, Using Programs, and Fundamentals strands for grades K through 6.

Hunter's book provides a carefully constructed curriculum complete with engaging activities tied to specific objectives. Her book can be a valuable resource for practicing teachers and for those preparing to teach.

Computers in the Classroom

The following sample activity is from Beverly Hunter's book My Students Use Computers. *It is designed to be used in grades K through 2 and to implement objectives associated with the Procedures strand of Hunter's suggested curriculum (see Figure 7–11). The statement, Procedures 1, 3, 4, under the objectives section of the activity, refers to specific objectives for the Procedures strand in grades K through 2. Those objectives are as follows:*

1. Execute a procedure (follow step by step instructions) for a familiar task (or a new task), and be able to show the end result of having executed it. . . .

3. Demonstrate that different procedures can be used to obtain the same outcome.

4. Find and correct errors (such as the wrong sequence of instructions) in a procedure that involves fewer than ten steps and does not involve decision making. (Hunter, 1983, p. 14)

SAMPLE ACTIVITY: ZEEP007 THE ROBOT

Objectives

Students give step-by-step instructions to an imaginary robot, ZEEP. They discover that a procedure is a sequence of carefully defined steps to accomplish a task, and that different procedures can be used to get the same result. Students find and correct errors in simple procedures. (Procedures 1, 3, 4)

Prerequisites

No prerequisites for this activity

Materials

No materials needed

Time for Activity

One or more class periods

Teacher Preparation

Read the section on the Procedures strand in Chapter 3 for tips on teaching procedural skills.

Teacher

1. Introduce the idea of ZEEP007 to the students in the following manner:

   I have a friend named ZEEP007. ZEEP is a little robot. He looks something like R2D2 from *Star Wars*. ZEEP is a very nice, friendly fellow. He does chores for me. But he doesn't know how to do anything unless I tell him exactly how to do it. One day I gave ZEEP instructions to go to the kitchen and peel me a banana and bring it to me. Can you guess what he did? He brought me a banana peel! "ZEEP," I asked, "where is the banana?" "I followed your instructions," ZEEP said.

Have the students talk about robots they have seen in movies and TV. These robots seem to be very "smart," but they can only do what they have been told to do by the person who built them or instructed them.

Some questions to ask the class:

- What is a robot?" *(A machine.)*

- Does a robot have a brain?" *(No. People do. Animals do.)*

- "Who controls a robot?" *(Human beings.)*

2. Tell the students they are going to play ZEEP. One student will be ZEEP and the others will take turns giving ZEEP instructions. The first task will be to get ZEEP to go from his seat to the chalkboard and erase the chalkboard.

Have discussion about what ZEEP will understand. Does he understand "Walk to the chalkboard," or must he be told: "Take one step forward, turn right, etc."? Have students decide on a set of words that ZEEP understands, such as the following:

Stand
Turn *(halfway around, all the way around, etc.)*
Stop
Lift *(right arm, left arm, left foot, right foot)*
Grasp *(object)*
Move *(arm, hand, etc.)*
Front, back
Right, left
Up, down

Encourage the students to think out the first few steps in their procedure before giving any instructions to ZEEP. What will they tell him first? Second? etc.

3. Have a student volunteer to be ZEEP. Remind him or her that ZEEP only does exactly as told—no more, no less.

Have one student give the instructions to ZEEP; ZEEP should follow them exactly. Interrupt only if ZEEP isn't playing by the rules of the game. If ZEEP doesn't understand an instruction, perhaps he makes a strange noise or says in an electronic-sounding voice "I-DO-NOT-UN-DERSTAND."

If students playing ZEEP are having difficulty with the idea of doing only and exactly as they are told, then the teacher should play the role of ZEEP in order to demonstrate that the instructions must be executed exactly.

The activity will be more instructive (and more fun) if there are errors, "bugs" in the procedures ZEEP tries to follow. So don't try to have the students get it right the first time.

Use the students' bugs as opportunities to discuss important ideas about procedures. For example, does ZEEP go on erasing and erasing without end? How does he (or she) know when to stop erasing the chalkboard? Does he get to go back to his seat, or is he left standing, facing the chalkboard? Does he keep the eraser in his hand, or is he instructed to put it back on the shelf?

4. After one procedure for getting ZEEP to do the task has worked successfully, challenge the students to come up with a different set of instructions that will accomplish the same task. Does it matter what order the instructions are given in? *(Sometimes yes, sometimes no.)*

5. Have students suggest another task for ZEEP, and carry out the activity as before.

6. Ask:

- What have we learned about procedures? (A procedure is a set of instructions. *The steps must be clear. The instructions must be in the right order.*)

- What have we learned about robots? *(We must tell them exactly what to do.)*

Related Activities

Variations of the ZEEP game can be used for classroom management procedures such as hanging up coats in the morning, going to lunch, getting to the bathroom, using the activity center, etc.

Other tasks include tying shoes, jumping rope, getting lunch money ready, putting library books on desk, copying from the chalkboard.

(Hunter, 1983, pp. 54–56)

The problem of aligning specific instructional objectives with particular activities and materials that will accomplish those objectives is an old one for educators. The Educational Products Information Exchange (EPIE) Institute, mentioned in Chapter 6, provides a resource for educators to do this while maintaining local control over the development of curriculum objectives. **Figure 7–12** presents a conceptual schematic of their developing Integrated Instructional Information Resource (IIIR), which matches curriculum objectives with a wide range of relevant educational materials. Educators enter their

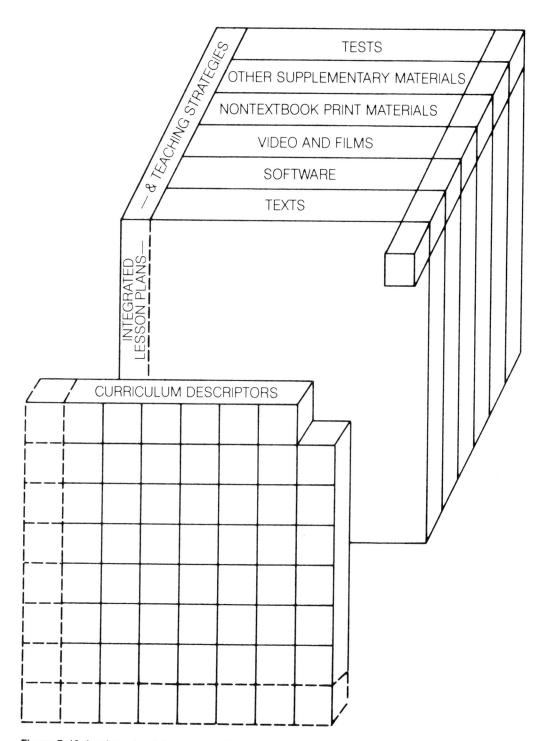

Figure 7-12 A schematic of the Integrated Instructional Information Resource (IIIR) offered by the Educational Products Information Exchange (EPIE) Institute.

curriculum objectives into the IIIR and can then examine and align the appropriate textbooks, tests, software, and other instructional resources with their local curriculum. Of special interest in relation to this discussion is the capability of matching quality educational software to specific curriculum objectives. The IIIR is part of EPIE's Curriculum Alignment Service for Educators (CASE).

The Computer Curriculum: Specific Examples

After viewing the computer curriculum as a whole, the focus now shifts to specific examples at particular grade levels. The examples below are from two districts engaged in developing their computer education offerings. **Figure 7–13** presents an overview of one district's proposed curriculum for grades K through 6. The recommendation is made to pursue computer education both as computer literacy (which here means learning about computers) and computer-assisted instruction (which, in this document, means the use of the computer to aid in teaching other content areas). Notice that the recommendation is made to start to use computers in teaching content beginning in kindergarten. Learning about computers is scheduled to start in the fifth grade. The committee has been quite specific in identifying the number, duration, and type of lessons in the curriculum, as well as who will be responsible for offering instruction. Also, they have specified from where in the school's overall plan of study the instructional time should be taken to allow implementation of the computer curriculum. In this instance, time will be allotted from time currently devoted to language arts and mathematics. Although some educators may not agree with taking time from these areas to teach about computers, addressing this issue shows sensitivity to the fact that the teacher has available a finite

---

Proposed K–6 Elementary Program Description

The committee recommends that computer-assisted instruction (K–6) and computer literacy (grades 5 and 6) be the focus of the proposed computer program for teachers and students.

The committee recommends the introduction of systemwide computer literacy programs beginning in grade 5. Every student in the fifth grade will receive two class periods of computer literacy a month for a total of 18 sessions throughout the school year. These classes will include lecture and teacher demonstration of new skills to be taught. Additionally, students may be assigned to the computer on a daily basis for 15 minutes to allow students hands-on experience with new concepts on Apple microcomputers.

The classes would be taught by the fifth grade teachers as a team or individually by members of the team. Supervision of daily use of computer time would rest with the classroom teacher. Student assistants could be named as needed.

Time for the computer literacy program will be taken from Language Arts/Mathematics instructional time as appropriate. (Grades 5 and 6)

Time for computer-assisted instruction will be alloted within the appropriate subject area. (K–6)

Computer use time may be made on an individual basis at each school for students to come to school early or remain after school with appropriate arrangements and prudent supervision.

(Waterford, 1983, p. 4)

Figure 7–13 An overview of a K through 6 computer education curriculum.

number of hours each day with students. Once the decision is made to offer a computer curriculum, the time for computer education will have to be taken from somewhere.

In **Figure 7–14** the goals and objectives for computer instruction for grades 5 and 6 are presented. Students are to become aware of different types of

---

Computer Curriculum for Grades 5 and 6

1. GOAL: Elementary students will develop computer awareness.

The students will:

OBJECTIVES: 1. be introduced to some different types and uses of computers
    a) microcomputers
    b) minicomputers
    c) main frame computers
    d) applications and careers
    e) computer development
  2. be introduced to Apple hardware and available software

2. GOAL: Elementary students will participate in Computer Assisted Instruction.

The students will:

OBJECTIVES: 1. turn computer on/off
  2. gain keyboard knowledge and typing skills
  3. boot a diskette
  4. find the catalog of a diskette
  5. run a prepared program from a diskette

3. GOAL: Elementary students will develop computer literacy.

The students will:

OBJECTIVES: 1. be introduced to BASIC programming definitions

a) PRINT	m) VARIABLE-STRING VARIABLE
b) NEW	n) GO TO
c) ERROR STATEMENT	o) FOR—NEXT
d) LIST	p) IF—THEN
e) CONTROL	q) INPUT
f) RESET	r) OUTPUT
g) END	s) READ
h) GR	t) DATA
i) PLOT	u) ROM—RAM
j) HLIN	v) SAVE
k) VLIN	w) DELETE
l) TEXT	x) LOAD

  2. be introduced to simple uses and programming on an Apple microcomputer
    a) IMMEDIATE MODE
      1. PRINT–TEXT & MATH FUNCTIONS
    b) PREDICT OUTPUT OF A GROUP OF STATEMENTS OR COMMANDS
    c) DEFERRED MODE
      1. ENTER, EDIT, & RUN A GROUP OF NUMBERED STATEMENTS OR COMMANDS

(Waterford, 1983, p. 5)

Figure 7–14 The goals and objectives for a fifth- and sixth-grade computer curriculum.

computers as well as various computer applications and careers. They will use a computer to run prepared software and will begin instruction in BASIC programming.

This district continues the program into the eighth grade. The curriculum for seventh and eighth grade is given in **Figure 7–15** as a set of goals and a series of subskills. The goals are similar to the goals seen before related to computer education. Again, the committee has dealt with the specifics of when instruction will take place. At grades 7 and 8, a computer literacy course will take the place of a study hall. The subskills are identified as to level. Students will, theoretically, be introduced to some concepts and experiences, practice others, and master still others. Note that at grades 7 and 8, all the work is identified as being at the introductory and practice levels. This may be a function of the time available for instruction or may reflect the committee's view that mastery will occur at higher grade levels after more in-depth experiences.

Figure 7–16 presents objectives and activities for a third-grade computer curriculum developed by another district. The overall curriculum for this district fits within the framework of the definition of computer literacy mentioned earlier. In this instance, activities to achieve intended goals have been included in the plan. Notice that, while instruction is primarily aimed at teaching computer concepts, there is ample opportunity in these activities to teach other subjects, such as language arts and art. For example, for the objective "The student can describe realistically what a computer can and cannot do for humans," students are asked to design a fantasy machine to perform some task for a human being. They then present their machine to the class and discuss whether or not a computer could be part of their machine. (In addition to teaching about computers, this helps to develop vocabulary as well as listening and speaking skills and could lead into a writing activity.) Under the heading "Creativity," the students use computer programs to create pictures. Some students then demonstrate their creations to parents, administrators, or other teachers.

Being sensitive to the fact that these activities are aimed at third-grade students, it is obvious that instruction about computers need not be dry and pedantic. It can in fact be lively and humanistically oriented. People created computers, people use computers. Instruction aimed at computer literacy can be warm and human and can strive to improve the quality of each student's life. The best uses of computers are those that make us more, not less, human.

Evaluation

The district cited in Figure 7–16 evaluated the computer curriculum yearly, as it was implemented. The evaluation instrument, designed by teachers, was given at the end of the school year to all students engaged in computer instruction. Examples from the instrument are shown in **Figure 7–17**. Part I of the instrument deals with general background information about what students have done, at home and in school, with computers. Part II asks for students' attitudes and opinions about computers, including whether or not they are interested in learning more about computers and how they feel about using computers. Part III is specific to the child's grade level. For example, a fourth-grade student would receive a different set of questions than a sixth-grade student. This section is designed to gather information related to the specific

Computer Curriculum for Grades 7 and 8

Goals

1. To install a computer literacy course into the fine arts curriculum as the fourth component in place of a study hall along with art, music, and living skills.
2. To introduce the microcomputer to every seventh grade student.
3. To continue computer literacy skills in eighth grade through the use of computer-assisted instruction. To develop an appreciation of the capabilities and limitations of a microcomputer.
4. To offer an opportunity to students to master the basic skills necessary to use the computer successfully.
5. To recognize the various computer languages including BASIC, FORTRAN, COBOL, Pascal, Applesoft, Apple Integer, and Logo.
6. To develop an ability to create elementary programs in BASIC and Logo.
7. To develop an appreciation for the computer as a tool to be used in school, in college, in a career, and in life.

Curriculum

The computer curriculum is composed of ten (10) subskills.

Subskills

1. History of computers
2. Introduction to the hardware
3. Data processing operation
4. Primary functions and limitations of a microcomputer
5. Introduction to software
6. Communication—introduction to languages
7. Introduction to keyboard and control commands
8. Programming in BASIC
9. Programming in Logo
10. Computer uses
    A. In education
    B. In a career

Key to Objective Competency Levels

I = Introduction
P = Practice
M = Mastery

Subskill 1—History of Computers

The student will:
—Sequence events of technological developments (I)
—Identify components of semiconductor technology—transistor, resistor, circuit, silicon chips, and microprocessor chips (I)
—Recognize the development of the minicomputer and the microcomputer (I)
—Discuss the potential technological advances regarding the microcomputer (I)

Subskill 2—Hardware

The student will:
—Identify the difference between RAM and ROM (I)
—Recognize the difference between microcomputers and microprocessors (I)
—Demonstrate the use of basic computer components—terminal, microprocessor, keyboard, disk drive, tape recorder, printer, modem, video display, speaker, and paddles (P)
—Distinguish between low-resolution graphics and high-resolution graphics (I)
—Identify the progress of semiconductor technology—transistor, resistor, integrated circuit, silicon chips, and microprocessor chips (I)
—Differentiate between the construction of a floppy disk, a hard disk, cassette tape, and firmware (I)

Subskill 3—Data Processing Operation

The student will:
—Follow a flowchart—input . . . processing . . . output (P)
—Appreciate the function of the storage unit (I)

Figure 7–15 A set of goals and subskills for a seventh- and eighth-grade computer curriculum.

—Examine the contents of memory (I)
—Compare uses of RAM and ROM (I)
—Create their own commands in Logo (P)

Subskill 4—Functions and Limitations of a Microcomputer

The student will:
—Identify categories of uses (e.g., have fun, make money, live more comfortably) (I)
—Assist with hobbies (I)
—Create music boards (I)
—Demonstrate graphic art abilities (I)
—Identify capabilities and limitations of the microcomputer (I)

Subskill 5—Software

The student will:
—Differentiate between the uses of a floppy disk, cassette tape, and firmware (I)
—Understand how software instructs the computer to work—the instructions (I)
—Identify software that may be purchased from publishing companies and computer companies (I)
—Explain how a program can be built and saved on software (I)

Subskill 6—Communication: Introduction to Languages

The student will:
—Compare communication language to morse code as a machine language (I)
—Understand the binary system of coding—"0" and "1" (I)
—Introduce various high-level computer languages, including BASIC, FORTRAN, COBOL, Pascal, Applesoft, Apple Integer, and Logo (I)
—Explain how humans communicate with computers (I)
—Begin to learn the BASIC and Logo languages (I)
—Learn the key words, control keys, and commands in BASIC and in Logo (P)
—Differentiate between commands and statements (P)

Subskill 7—Introduction to the Keyboard and Control Commands

The student will:
—Practice the keyboard lessons (P)
—Demonstrate the use of the control key, escape key, arrow keys, and other special function keys (P)
—Demonstrate the use of line numbers and key words (P)

Subskill 8—Programming in BASIC

The student will:
—Identify a problem for the computer to solve (P)
—Write a program to solve the problem (P)
—Run the program (P)
—Display the program on the monitor (P)
—Debug the program (P)
—Save the program on a disk (P)
—Print the program on a printer (P)

Subskill 9—Programming in Logo

The student will:
—Set up the Logo language program (P)
—Build a program using the print command (P)
—Meet the turtle (P)
—Teach the turtle to draw a square (P)
—Build a program in Logo
—Save and retrieve program (P)
—Edit programs (P)
—Create geometric figures (P)
—Recognize color commands for background and pen (P)

Figure 7–15 Continued

Subskill 10—Computer Uses

The student will in education and career:

—Be able to use the computer as a learning tool for extra help in various courses (I)
—Use the computer as a word processor and store reports and assignments on their own disk (I)
—Be required to have their own computer by many colleges (I)
—Complete course requirements on the computer (I)
—Do research on the computer (I)
—Store information in the computer (I)
—Find a computer to be a valuable tool in order to be more efficient and more productive (P)
—Discover that knowledge of the computer will be required for successful employment in many fields (P)
—Recognize that the ability to understand and use a computer will be an advantage in their career (P)
—List careers in which the use of a computer will play an important role (P)

(Waterford, 1983, pp. 6–10)

Figure 7–15 Continued

Third Grade

Computer Awareness

A3.1 What a Computer Is

Objective: The student can describe the computer as a machine possessing certain characteristics that can help solve problems (with words or numbers) or do a specific job quickly and easily.

Activities:

- Have students define (describe) what they think a computer is. Write down key words on the blackboard.
- Put an array of objects or pictures on a table and ask the students to identify each as a "computer" or "not a computer." Some objects that can be used are a typewriter, calculator, pencil sharpener, TV, hand-held electronic game, tape recorder, home video game system (e.g. Atari), an actual microcomputer, cash register, etc. Have students refer back to their definitions when categorizing the objects. They may want to refine their definitions.
- Look up the word "computer" in a dictionary or encyclopedia. Note key words and concepts. Discuss some of your objects as they relate to the definition.

Computer: A machine designed to accept information, store information, process information, and give out processed information

- Collect pictures of many types of computers and computer equipment. Discuss and make a bulletin board.
- Ask students if they have a computer at home. Ask how they use it.

A3.2 What a Computer Can Do

Objective: The student can describe realistically what a computer can and cannot do for humans.

Activities:

- Have each student design a fantasy machine which will perform some task for a human being. As students present their "inventions" to the class, discuss whether a computer could be part of the machine.
- Have students help compile on the blackboard two lists: "What a Computer Can Do" and "What a Human Brain Can Do." Compare the two, noting what does what better.

Computer Interaction

B3.1 Using the Keyboard

Objective: The student can locate and identify the letters, numerals, and special keys on a microcomputer keyboard.

Activities:

- Post a diagram of the keyboard on a bulletin board or use an overhead projector.
- Discuss why the keys aren't arranged in alphabetical order.
- Color special keys (such as RETURN, SHIFT, CONTROL, RESET) and discuss their function.
- Show students how to use the keyboard and how to correct typing mistakes.
- Have students type in their name (or a message) by entering

  PRINT "BILLY" ⟨RETURN⟩

Figure 7–16 Excerpts from a set of objectives and activities for a third-grade computer curriculum.

B3.2 Learning to Use a Computer

Objective: The student can load and run a pre-programmed program on the computer.

Activities:

- Demonstrate the steps involved with loading and running a program. Have students take turns operating the system. Use a simple program.
- Have students make up a chart with directions on how to use the computer *or* make a chart for the bulletin board.

Creativity

D3.1 Computer Art

Objective: The student can load and use a program that helps him create pictures.

Activities:

- Demonstrate a program that allows the student to create pictures (e.g., FACEMAKER or DELTA DRAW).
- Have each student use at least one of these programs.
- Have one or more students demonstrate the use of these creative programs to other adults such as the principal, teachers, or parents.

Computer Assisted Learning

E3.1 Learning Via a Computer

Objective: The student can use the computer to learn new concepts, practice subject material, and develop critical thinking.

Activities:

- Demonstrate to selected students how to use drill and practice software, a computer-assisted instruction package (CAI), or a game (e.g., Milliken Math, Arcade Math, MECC programs, Snooper Troops.)
- Have the students run the programs on their own and then explain to you what they think the purpose of the program is. Discuss.
- Have these students explain to other students how to use the programs.

(Regional District # 13, 1983, pp. 3–5)

Figure 7–16 Continued

computer education topics taught at the particular grade level of the individual student. The example for Part III given here is for the district's fifth-grade students and deals to a great extent with the Logo programming language, since that is the programming language taught during fifth grade in this curriculum. In addition, it contains test items related to hardware and software, as those topics are covered in fifth grade.

The results of such an evaluation would be used to improve the scope and sequence of the computer curriculum. Results might also be used by individual teachers to improve instruction at specific grade levels and as documentation when seeking funding for computer hardware and software.

Conclusion

Computer education for computer literacy, generally, aims at achieving computer literacy for students as defined earlier. Some districts have been pursuing this goal for some time, while many districts have only recently begun to teach with and about computers. The examples cited should provide a feeling for some of the types of curriculums being taught. Different districts may place

Regional School District 13
Computer Literacy and Awareness Assessment

Part I   Student Background Information

This part asks for information about yourself. Please mark your answers on the answer sheet.

1. I have used computers in school.
   A. Yes
   B. No
2. I have written computer programs.
   A. No
   B. Yes, 1 or 2 programs
   C. Yes, 3 to 10 programs
   D. Yes, more than 10 programs
3. I have played games on a computer.
   A. Yes
   B. No
4. I have used a computer to learn more about subjects like math, reading, or science.
   A. Yes
   B. No
5. My parents have encouraged me to learn about computers.
   A. Yes
   B. No
6. Where have you learned the most about computers?
   A. From movies and television
   B. From books, newspapers, and magazines
   C. From my friends
   D. From my parents
   E. From teachers and class activities
7. About how often do you presently use a computer in school?
   A. Every day or almost every day
   B. A few times a week
   C. A few times a month
   D. Once a month or less
   E. Never
8. Do either of your parents use a computer at work?
   A. Yes
   B. No
   C. I don't know.
9. Have you or has someone in your family thought about getting a computer for your home?
   A. Yes
   B. No

Part II   Student Attitudes and Opinions About Computers

This part asks for your opinion and attitudes about computers. Keep in mind that in this part the attitude questions (how you feel about computers) have no right answers or wrong answers. Just select the answer that best expresses how you feel. Please mark your answers on the answer sheet.

14. I would like to learn more about computers.
    A. Yes
    B. No
    C. Not sure
15. I would very much like to have my own computer.
    A. Yes
    B. No
    C. Not sure
16. I enjoy using computers in my classes.
    A. Yes
    B. No
    C. Sometimes

Figure 7–17 Examples excerpted from an instrument created in one district to perform a yearly evaluation of their computer education program.

17. I am able to work with computers as well as most other students my age.
    A. Yes
    B. No
    C. Not sure

18. Computers can be useful in learning at school.
    A. Yes
    B. No

19. Computers are hard to use.
    A. Yes
    B. No
    C. Depends on the program

27. Computers are able to think in every way just like people.
    A. Yes
    B. No
    C. Not sure

28. Almost all people are affected in some way by computers.
    A. Yes
    B. No
    C. Not sure

29. In order to use a computer, a person must know how to program.
    A. Yes
    B. No
    C. Not sure

30. Some computers have good and bad feelings like people.
    A. Yes
    B. No
    C. Not sure

GRADE 5

Part III   General Knowledge About Computers (at grade level)

This part is a test of your knowledge about computers. In this part there may be items you have not learned. Just answer as many as you can. Keep in mind that the right answer is the best choice for each question. Please mark your answers on the answer sheet.

31. Logo is the name of
    A. the computer we use
    B. a set of toy building blocks
    C. a computer language
    D. a turtle

32. People use Logo to
    A. do word-processing
    B. teach programming using turtle graphics
    C. do complicated math problems
    D. talk over telephone wires

42. What picture will this Logo program make?
    FD 20
    RT 90
    FD 20
    RT 90
    FD 20

A.   B.   C.   D.

Figure 7–17 Continued

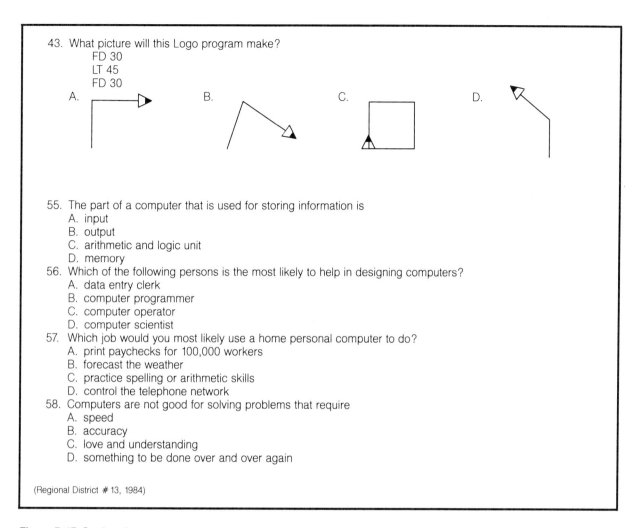

43. What picture will this Logo program make?
    FD 30
    LT 45
    FD 30

    A.   B.   C.   D.

55. The part of a computer that is used for storing information is
    A. input
    B. output
    C. arithmetic and logic unit
    D. memory
56. Which of the following persons is the most likely to help in designing computers?
    A. data entry clerk
    B. computer programmer
    C. computer operator
    D. computer scientist
57. Which job would you most likely use a home personal computer to do?
    A. print paychecks for 100,000 workers
    B. forecast the weather
    C. practice spelling or arithmetic skills
    D. control the telephone network
58. Computers are not good for solving problems that require
    A. speed
    B. accuracy
    C. love and understanding
    D. something to be done over and over again

(Regional District # 13, 1984)

Figure 7–17 Continued

an emphasis on different areas of computer education. Any curriculum developed for a district will certainly reflect the prevailing philosophies, instructional practices, and monetary resources of that district. Just as with any subject, the success of computer education depends on the excitement, energy, and creativity of the individual teacher. A well-trained teacher, supported by building and district administrators sensitive to this new role for teachers, can provide students with valuable skills and information that will help prepare them for life in the twenty-first century.

computer curriculum
computer education
computer literacy

Curriculum Alignment Service for
Educators (CASE)

Key Terms

Integrated Instructional Information   procedural thinking
    Resource (IIIR)   procedures

Questions

1. Why have educators and others become concerned about the question of computer literacy?

2. Interview three persons, one each from the following age-groups: 18 to 25, 35 to 45, 55 to 70. Ask them how they see computers affecting their lives today and how computers affected their lives when they were younger. Analyze and compare the responses and discuss your findings in class.

3. Is computer literacy the same for everyone? Why or why not?

4. How does the book define computer literacy for students? for teachers?

5. Write your own definition of computer literacy.

6. What are the components of a computer curriculum?

7. Locate an area school district that has implemented a computer curriculum. Choose a particular grade level that interests you, and discuss with a teacher of that grade what she does to implement the curriculum at her level. Try to find out how she feels about teaching with computers and teaching about computers.

8. Write a newspaper editorial in support of implementing a computer curriculum. Include an overview of what should be addressed in the curriculum and why.

9. Respond to the editorial you wrote for number 8 as a school board member opposed to teaching with and about computers. Include among your concerns the cost of such a program in terms of money and time.

10. Cite two specific examples of activities that might be included as part of a computer curriculum.

11. Analyze the components of the computer curriculum presented in Figure 7–11. Choose a grade level and a strand that interests you, one that you would like to teach. Why does it interest you? Do you think it would interest your students? Why or why not?

12. Choose one activity presented in Figure 7–16. Explain how you could use the activity you selected to teach about another content area in addition to the primary purpose of the activity, which is computer instruction.

References/Further Reading

Hunter, Beverly. *My Students Use Computers: Learning Activities for Computer Literacy.* Reston, Va.: Reston Publishing Co., 1983.

Judd, Wallace. "A Teacher's Place in the Computer Curriculum." *Phi Delta Kappan* 65, no. 2 (1983):120–122.

Mahopac Central School District. *Curriculum Guide: Educational Computing, K–12.* Mahopac, New York, 1985.

Radin, Stephen, and Fayvian Lee. *Computers in the Classroom: A Survival Guide for Teachers.* Chicago: Science Research Associates, 1984.

Regional District #13. *Computer Literacy Curriculum.* Middlefield, Conn., 1983.

———. *Computer Literacy and Awareness Assessment.* Middlefield, Conn., 1984.

Taylor, Robert P., ed. *The Computer in the School: Tutor, Tool, Tutee.* New York: Teachers College Press, 1980.

Trowbridge, David, and Robin Durnin. *Results from an Investigation of Groups Working at the Computer,* ERIC Report No. ED 238–724 (1984):12.

Waterford Public Schools. *Computer Education Program.* Waterford, Conn., 1983.

8

Logo: What and Why

TOPICS ADDRESSED

Why should teachers understand the theories on which educational methods and materials are based?

How are Logo, Jean Piaget, and Seymour Papert connected?

What topics from the work of Piaget are usually seen as important for educators?

What additional ideas from Piaget's work does Seymour Papert emphasize? How does Papert reinterpret Piaget?

How might Logo affect cognitive development in children?

How does Logo teach subject matter?

What aspects of Logo as a programming language reflect Papert's ideas about learning and cognitive development?

OUTLINE

Introduction
Theory and Practice
Piaget
Stages of Development
Sensorimotor Stage: Birth to Two Years
Preoperational Stage: Two to Seven
   Years
Concrete Operational Stage: Seven to
   Twelve Years
Formal Operational Stage: Twelve
   Years to Adult
Assimilation, Accommodation, and
   Schemas
More on Piaget

Piaget and Papert
Logo Characteristics
Logo Is Powerful
Logo Encourages Good Programming
Microworlds and Powerful Ideas
Logo Is Resonant with the Child's World
Logo, Students, and Teachers
Logo and Bugs
Conclusion
Key Terms
Questions
References/Further Reading

Introduction

This chapter presents some of the ideas behind the Logo programming language. The first topic to be considered is why it might be important for teachers to be concerned (and knowledgeable) about the theoretical assumptions behind the educational materials they use. Next, some ideas about learning and cognitive development from the Swiss researcher Jean Piaget are reviewed. Ideas from the work of Seymour Papert, the driving force behind the development of Logo, are presented and related to characteristics of Logo as a programming language. This material provides a meaningful background on which to build specific skills in using Logo, the topic of the next two chapters.

Theory and Practice

Educators, including teachers, administrators, and support personnel, are constantly asked to perform in an environment highly charged with emotion, energy, activity, and intellectual possibility. Everyone involved in education as it exists in schools today is part of this environment, an environment in which teachers are responsible for guiding students through the learning deemed appropriate by society. In preparation for this responsibility, teachers go through a process of education and training aimed at developing the attitudes, behaviors, and knowledge necessary to successfully fulfill their role. Some of this preparation is theoretical, some is practical. For example, a prospective teacher may study the theoretical basis for different types of questioning strategies. The same student may then engage in practicum experiences in an attempt to implement the strategies. The results of this practical application will often be discussed with others in the light of the theory previously studied. From this interaction of theory and practice, insight and appreciation evolve and necessary teacher skills begin to develop.

Understanding the relationship between theory and practice is necessary in education, as in other professions, as a basis for making competent decisions. In education this includes decisions about instructional materials, teaching strategies, curriculum choices, interpersonal relations, and classroom management practices. Developing this understanding as a basis for decision making is a process that begins with undergraduate education and continues through-

Reprinted by permission: Tribune Media Services

out a teacher's career. That is why teachers take graduate coursework and attend in-service professional development programs. The continual updating of skills is one of the hallmarks that distinguish any profession as a profession.

One danger, as educators faced with the vibrant, demanding world of the classroom, is to underestimate the need to connect theory with practice. The possibility exists that teachers, especially beginning teachers, may start to view their role as that of a technician, as someone responsible for finding materials to plug into the preexisting school curriculum. When such selections are made without careful thought about the theoretical assumptions on which curiculum materials are based, the teacher's role shifts from well-educated professional to minimally trained technician. If this happens, the teacher is capable of making superficial decisions about what is done in the classroom but loses the ability to control the spirit of the educational experience.

Teachers, as professionals, must know why they do what they do; they must have informed reasons for making the types of decisions outlined earlier. They must develop an educational philosophy based on the strategies and theories in which they believe, and they must put that philosophy into practice. For our purpose it is not important what that philosophy is. What is important is the development of a philosophy. An understanding of theory is a necessary part of that process.

For this reason this book examines Logo by first investigating the theory behind its creation. The intent is to provide meaningful information about how and why Logo came about so that teachers may decide if this particular educational tool has a place in the learning environments they create. Indeed,

Figure 8–1 Teachers must make informed choices about such things as educational strategies, instructional materials, and classroom management practices. They can thereby create the educational environment which reflects their philosophy of education.

one major theme of this text is that computers are tools that will probably be used by individual teachers in ways that reflect their own teaching style. Such choices must be made consciously, with an understanding of the tool chosen and used.

Piaget

Seymour Papert and his colleagues in the Logo Group at the Artificial Intelligence Laboratory at the Massachusetts Institute of Technology (MIT) created and refined the Logo programming language. Papert, in his book *Mindstorms: Children, Computers, and Powerful Ideas* (1980), explains the educational significance of Logo and offers a vision of the way computers may change education. An orientation to Papert's work is presented in this chapter. The ideas about children and learning that Papert holds are, partly, an outgrowth of the five years he spent in Switzerland working with Jean Piaget. In fact, it was soon after leaving Piaget that Papert went to MIT and began work there. Because the framework Piaget developed for understanding the world of the child is so much a part of the assumptions behind Logo, an overview of Piaget is presented below. For those familiar with Piaget's work, this material will serve as a review. For those unfamiliar with Piaget, it will provide necessary background information for understanding Papert's ideas about children and computers.

Stages of Development

Most teachers come to know of Piaget, at least initially, as a topic in a child development or educational psychology course. Some of his theories about cognitive development in children are usually presented and discussed. One topic that is invariably covered is Piaget's theory that all children pass through four stages of cognitive development. The precise age at which individual children go through the stages varies somewhat, but general age guidelines are given when identifying the stages. Piaget believed that regardless of cultural environment or geographical location, all children pass through these stages in order.

This passage takes place gradually and involves changes in the way the child perceives the world. What Piaget describes is a process of cognitive growth that is stimulated by the child's active involvement with the world. Each stage provides a way of looking at and interacting with the world and, most significant, with the experiences in the world that spur growth toward the next stage.

No stage exists in a pure form. Although a child will be firmly in one stage, elements of earlier and future stages will be, to some degree, present. Movement from one stage to another is not abrupt and precise. Rather, movement takes place over a period of time after much probing and experimenting.

Sensorimotor Stage: Birth to Two Years

During the sensorimotor stage, children explore and come to know the environment through the use of the senses and motion. Initially, children cannot differentiate themselves from the environment. This begins to change as they gain more experience in the world. As they progress through this period, children begin to develop some sense of cause and effect (I touch the rattle, it makes a noise). Another important occurrence is the development of visual pursuit. This is when children gain the ability to follow an object with their eyes. The development of object permanence, the ability to understand that when an object is taken from view it still exists, is also important and develops during this stage. Object permanence helps children to begin to define the world as separate from themselves. It also provides the beginnings of memory, of being able to picture things that are not there. This ability grows additionally toward the end of this period, when children start to plan to do things. They are able to recall actions and imitate them some time after they have originally observed the actions. By the end of this stage, children are aware of themselves as separate from the environment.

Preoperational Stage: Two to Seven Years

Several characteristics typify development during the preoperational stage. The term preoperational is derived from Piaget's notion of operations. An operation is a mental activity whereby information is combined or transformed. In the last two stages, concrete operations and formal operations, the ability to perform mental activity (operations) develops in particular ways. The groundwork for this development is laid during the preoperational stage.

During this stage children begin to use mental symbols and go through a profound period of language development. The average two-year-old has a

Figure 8–2 A child in the sensorimotor stage.

Figure 8–3 Children in the preoperational stage.

vocabulary of about 200 words and forms sentences of two words. By approximately age six, children have a vocabulary of around 2,000 words and can form grammatically correct sentences of eight to ten words.

By the beginning of this period, as mentioned previously, children are aware of themselves as separate from their environment. They are, however, egocentric; they see the world solely from their own perspective. This means that they cannot take another person's viewpoint. For example, during this period children have difficulty giving directions to another child. They simply cannot understand what the other child needs to know to accomplish a task. They cannot see the world from the other child's perspective.

Children rely heavily on intuition during this period, rather than on reason. When confronted with a quantity of water in a short, wide glass that is then poured into a tall, thin glass, children will state that there is more water in the tall, thin glass. They will see the tall, thin glass as bigger because it is taller and will, intuitively, assume that it contains more water. Piaget called the ability to understand that shape is not necessarily related to quantity, conservation. Hence, children in the preoperational stage are preconservationist. This also refers to conservation tasks related to other materials. For instance, a preoperational child who is first shown a number of beads grouped close together and then shown the same number of beads spread out will pronounce the beads that are spread out to be a greater quantity.

Imagination and intuition highlight this period. Children readily engage in fantasy and are capable of constructing their own imaginative world. It is an excellent time for providing children with experiences with language and encouraging verbal expression.

Figure 8–4 Each stage of development provides a way of looking at and interacting with the world.

During the stage of concrete operations children exhibit the ability to think abstractly with concrete objects. For example, during this period children presented with the conservation task of pouring water from a short, wide glass into a tall, thin glass will know that the quantity of water stays constant. Children have begun to understand the specific functional relationships of the situation. Indeed, a concern for specifics, in fact a literal-mindedness, tends to be prevalent during this stage. Children usually see one way to do things and do not readily consider or attempt alternatives.

Concrete Operational Stage: Seven to Twelve Years

Children at the concrete operational stage will be concerned with the facts of a given situation. Once their minds are made up, it will often be hard to change them. Opposing views may not be tolerated. Theorizing will be beyond their capability during this period. For example, if a group of youngsters at this stage were asked to suppose that they could fly and then comment on what the experience might be like, they would probably object strongly that they could not fly. They would be bound to the factual.

During this period children grow in their ability to perform mental operations, such as classifying. Children also grow in their ability to understand spatial and numeric relationships. Development of these operations depends on the child having concrete objects with which to work. Therefore, environments that emphasize activities such as counting, sorting, building, and manipulating will aid the child's cognitive growth.

The child in the concrete operational stage is able to reason about the world through the use of concrete objects. The child in the period of formal opera-

Formal Operational Stage: Twelve Years to Adult

Figure 8–5 Movement from one stage to another takes place over a period of time after much probing and experimenting.

Figure 8–6 Children in the concrete operational stage working at the computer.

Figure 8–7 In the period of formal operations, adolescents begin to think about their own thinking.

tions can, without the aid of concrete objects, use formal logic in reasoning about the world. For Piaget, formal logic does not mean a rigid form of logic, but rather the ability to use logical mental operations that are comprehensive and sophisticated.

In this stage children and adolescents are able to postulate and hypothesize about events and circumstances that are not physically, concretely represented to them. The ability to suggest and subsequently test an hypothesis is present. As the ability to compare and contrast sets of facts, theories, and opinions develops, adolescents experiment with various conclusions about the world and often form strong opinions. Students are capable of generalizing from examples and situations. Further, abstract thinking can be stimulated by providing activities in which symbolic materials may be manipulated. Such activities may include participation in drama, writing projects, and video productions.

During this period of formal operations adolescents begin to think about their own thinking. They begin to analyze how and why they arrive at certain conclusions based on various assumptions and facts. The adolescent starts to develop the formal operations that will be obvious at the adult level.

Piaget viewed cognitive development as taking place through the four stages cited above, according to the following process. As individuals interact with their environment and gain experience through activity, cognitive structures or

Assimilation, Accommodation, and Schemas

Figure 8–8 Abstract thinking can be stimulated by activities in which symbolic materials can be manipulated such as drama, writing projects, or video productions.

schemas are formed. These schemas dictate how we perceive and react to the world around us. For example, we may have a schema related to a favorite brother that will affect the way we perceive and interact with that brother. Schemas are not static; they change over time. The process of our schemas changing as we adapt to the world is the basis for the cognitive growth that eventually leads us through the different stages to the level of formal operations.

The way schemas change is through assimilation and accommodation. As we interact with our environment we are constantly exposed to information about the world. When we encounter information we first try to assimilate it into an existing schema. If a favorite brother gives us a thoughtful birthday gift, this information fits quite nicely into the schema we have for that brother. If, however, information from the environment does not readily fit into an existing schema, if the information is new, or unusual, then the schema must be changed in order to accommodate the new information. This is accommodation. In the case that the same favorite brother plays an unkind practical joke on us, the schema might change so that the favorite brother is now perceived of less favorably than before.

What is important to understand is that, in Piaget's view, we internalize and organize experience into schemas that assimilate information from the environment. When information cannot be assimilated into the existing schema, the schema changes to accommodate the new information. This dynamic process depends to a great extent on the individual's active participation with the environment. The process is stimulated by doing, by acting on the environment rather than passively letting the environment act on us.

This is especially true in the concrete operational period, when manipulation of concrete objects is necessary to engage in abstract thought, but it is also true in the other periods outlined. A major premise of Piaget's theory is that cognitive growth is facilitated by activity, not by passively listening and memorizing.

The brief discussion above is similar to the introductory material about Piaget that is presented to many prospective teachers. Papert points toward other concerns of Piaget that also deserve attention but that are not usually emphasized.

More on Piaget

The Piaget presented previously is one concerned with stages of cognitive development. This is true, as far as it goes. In fact, Piaget considered himself a genetic epistemologist. Epistemology refers to the theory of knowledge. Specifically, epistemology is concerned with investigating what conditions are necessary for knowledge to be valid. Piaget was concerned with the genesis or development of knowledge, both in the culture and in the individual. People working in genetic epistemology believe that to understand what is happening to an individual engaged in learning, you must also consider the structure and content of that which is being learned. What this means for teaching is that to teach, you must know how the condition of the learner and the structure of the subject matter interact to create learning.

This is not alien to the Piaget we have viewed so far. Rather, it is an added and important dimension of his work that is not usually considered by educators. The basis of this idea is that in order to understand how people know, think, and learn, you must understand how the structure of the subject being learned affects learning.

This is important for us because Logo can be seen as an environment that has been specifically structured to present subject matter in a particular way. What is to be known, the subject of learning, has been structured in a way that will have a particular effect on how the learner knows it.

Further, Piaget is noninterventionist. His work was that of a theorist, and he was responsible for giving the world a theory of cognitive development that has proved useful worldwide as a mechanism for investigating and explaining human behavior. He was not concerned with intervening in the child's world to accelerate cognitive growth. He was certainly not interested in curriculums designed to teach conservation or hurry children along in their cognitive development. Indeed, one major lesson for educators from Piaget's work is that a great deal of learning takes place without a teacher or a curriculum, as a by-product of a child's interaction with the environment. For example, almost all children learn how to talk without the benefit of schooling. Children also learn a host of social skills without any formal schooling. As Papert points out, this fact is often lost on teachers and curriculum designers who design curriculums based on Piaget's theories.

Piaget and Papert

Papert, then, emphasizes important areas of Piaget's work that educators often ignore. For Papert, Piaget is not a researcher concerned with identifying stages of cognitive development. Rather, Piaget is a researcher who investigated how knowing and knowledge come about, how the knower and the known interact to produce knowledge. For Papert, Piaget is the genetic epistemologist he described himself to be. This means that Papert is interested in structuring subject matter so that students will have to interact with it in special ways. Logo is such an attempt.

Papert emphasizes what he terms Piagetian learning: the notion that a great deal of high-quality learning (that is, successful, efficient learning) takes place without any formal schooling. He has dedicated himself to the search for ways to adjust the child's environment so that this type of learning may take place to a greater degree, and in different areas, than it currently does. Logo is an environment aimed at accomplishing this too.

Papert also reinterprets Piaget. We have seen that Piaget was noninterventionist in relation to the stages he identified. He did not promote trying to alter the way children go through the stages. Papert is very much an interventionist. He believes that the culture surrounding a child will determine the types of experiences the child will have. This will influence the activities the child performs, the materials she comes into contact with, and the actions she performs with those materials. He firmly believes that these activities will have a direct effect on how fast, and perhaps in what order, the child's development will progress. In short, if the culture changes in a profound way by presenting a substantially different set of activities available for exploration in the child's environment, there will be a corresponding change in the child's development. He is interested in creating environments that do just that.

As an example of the way materials in the child's environment promote learning, consider the following. In a culture without computers the child is provided with many opportunities to work with pairs (mother and father, knives and forks, shoes, etc.) and, eventually, provided with many opportunities to group objects. Using the objects and experiences available in the culture, what Papert calls Piagetian learning takes place. The child begins to discover (learn) about number and properties associated with number. The child learns to count, eventually learns that counting is separate from order, progresses to classification of objects based on more than one variable, and so on. Because of the types of experiences and objects presented in a pre-computer culture, Piagetian learning takes place in a particular way, in a particular order. Remember, for Papert, the materials provided by the culture are more important than for Piaget. Papert believes that if the materials and experiences available in a culture without computers are significantly changed, such as by providing specific types of experiences by way of computers, the stages of development will be affected.

This is where computers become important to Papert. He views the introduction of computers into a society as a sociological and anthropological phenomenon that could have far-reaching effects. He compares a culture that is computer-rich (has many computers available to people at all levels of society) with one that does not offer access to computers. He sees the computer-rich culture as providing a profoundly different set of circumstances for the child.

In a computer-rich culture it is possible to provide children with experiences in which they can explore their own thinking and be exposed to problem-solving strategies associated with learning to program a computer. Papert theorizes that the effect of working with computers in these ways will change the way children think. This change will be maintained not just when the child is at the computer, but also when she is away from it.

The key here is the way children interact with computers. Just using the computer for drill and practice or tutorial functions will not accomplish what Papert proposes. Logo is an environment specifically designed to encourage the type of growth in which Papert is interested. This is because Logo, as a computer language, encourages problems to be solved and programs to be written in a certain way. The specifics of how this is done will become clear as you work through the material in the next two chapters on programming in Logo. Other programming languages that have not been specially designed for learning will not accomplish the same thing. In this, Logo is unique, since its design was based on a combination of Piagetian theory and concepts from computer science in general and artificial intelligence in particular.

Papert believes that using the computer to develop children's problem-solving skills and explore their own thinking in a Piagetian learning environment will change the way children think. The basis for this belief is that the computer will allow children to make the formal, concrete; it will let children concretely represent ideas on the computer screen that were only available to them previously through abstract thinking (formal operations).

As an example, Papert offers a task associated with the stage of formal operations. Children in the concrete operational stage will have difficulty trying to think about how things may be. They can think about how things are but falter when asked to describe or imagine how things could be. The following task, cited by Papert (1980), would cause a problem for a child in the stage of concrete operations:

Input/Output

Roger Schank is a professor of computer science and psychology at Yale University, the chairman of Yale's computer science department, and director of the Yale Artificial Intelligence Laboratory. In his book The Cognitive Computer: On Language, Learning and Artificial Intelligence *he views Logo and artificial intelligence in the classroom in the following way:*

The watchwords of AI applications in the classroom have to be individuality, freedom, and above all, fun. A sweatshop approach is not our goal. We wouldn't strap all the kids in front of a terminal and make them hit keys for 40 minutes each day for each subject. The kids could go up to the knowledge system anytime and start a geometry game, then switch to a reading program, then play a logical reasoning game that also teaches beginning algebra. Children learn quickly when their interest is aroused. If the knowledge system became aware that little Billy hadn't done any math games for a long while, it could alert the teacher, who then could give him more personal attention. The system could even remind Billy by printing "What about the math game we were playing last week?"

The vision of such a computerized classroom may seem very radical. But we are just seeing the tip of the iceberg in AI's involvement in education. One example of AI is the programming language Logo, a valuable tool for teaching children how to program and how to think. Logo is a spin-off of AI research, developed specifically for children by Seymour Papert and his students at the AI laboratory at MIT. It is the first programming language to be developed for teaching programming and logical reasoning. Logo's value is that it teaches children to reason without overtly trying to do so. Logo challenges the children to draw a picture or solve a fun problem, and compels them to think carefully about what is going on. The kids get to do something they want to do in a logical way that ends up helping the child accomplish more than he had intended. The painful and tedious task of learning a new principle in the abstract is bypassed. The child has to form the principle himself to finish a game or get through a fun situation.

(Schank, 1984.)

A child is given a collection of beads of different colors, say green, red, blue, and black, and is asked to construct all the possible pairs of colors: green-blue, green-red, green-black, and then all the triplets and so on. Just as children do not acquire conservation until their seventh year, children around the world are unable to carry out such combinatorial tasks before their eleventh or twelfth year. (p. 174)

Learning to program in Logo provides the skills and experiences that may be used to solve this type of problem. Learning to program involves writing instructions, or algorithms, that the computer follows. It also involves observing what the computer does with the instructions. If the computer does something unexpected and the instructions do not accomplish what was intended, a bug has occurred in the program. The student then traces through the logic of the instructions and examines, concretely, the systematic thinking that the instructions represent. This allows an opportunity to find and fix the bug.

As an example, we will take a first look at Logo. **Figure 8–9** shows a computer screen with a small triangular figure, called the turtle, in the center. By giving the computer directions the turtle can be moved around the screen, leaving a line over whatever path it has taken. Commands are designed to be simple and obvious. FORWARD 50 would move the turtle forward fifty "turtle steps." RIGHT 90 would cause the turtle to rotate in place ninety degrees to the right. The turtle can be directed to draw pictures on the screen. Logo's ability to create pictures, or graphics, is called turtle graphics.

Figure 8–10 shows a set of instructions in Logo aimed at drawing a box, and the resulting picture. The turtle was instructed to move FORWARD 50, RIGHT 90, FORWARD 50, RIGHT 90, FORWARD 50, RIGHT 90. The figure drawn on the screen as a result of these instructions was not a box. At this point the child would analyze the program to find the bug. The bug in this program involves the lack of one more instruction to tell the turtle to move FORWARD 50 one more time. When this is done the box is drawn successfully (see **Figure 8–11**). The child was provided with the opportunity to see a representation of his own thinking, find the bug, correct it, and see the result.

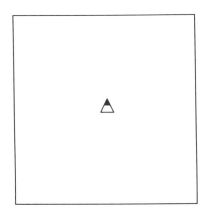
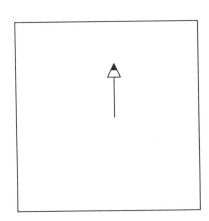
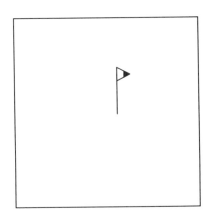

Figure 8–9 The screen at the left shows how the turtle appears in Logo. The center screen shows the effect of giving the turtle the command FORWARD 50. The screen to the right shows the effect of giving the turtle the command RIGHT 90.

```
FORWARD  50
RIGHT    90
FORWARD  50
RIGHT    90
FORWARD  50
RIGHT    90
```

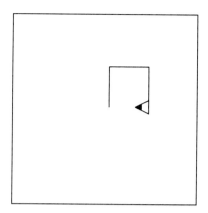

Figure 8–10 When the Logo commands on the left are given to the turtle, the figure on the right is the result. Since the intention was to draw a box on the screen, there is a bug in the instructions.

Papert (1980) proposes that concrete operational children provided with these types of activities will use their developing abilities to approach and solve the problem cited earlier. They will, thereby, have developed skills previously associated with the stage of formal operations. Because they have learned to write and debug systematic procedures, they will use a systematic procedure to solve the beads problem.

From a computational point of view, the most salient ingredients of the combinatorial task are related to the idea of procedure—systematicity and debugging. A successful procedure consists of some such procedure as:

1. Separate the beads into colors.

2. Choose a color as color 1.

3. Form all pairs that can be formed with color 1.

```
FORWARD  50
RIGHT    90
FORWARD  50
RIGHT    90
FORWARD  50
RIGHT    90
FORWARD  50
```

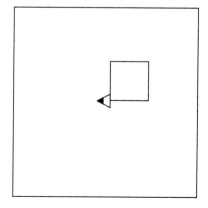

Figure 8–11 When the turtle is given the command FORWARD 50 one more time, the box is completed.

4. Choose color 2.

5. Form all the pairs that can be formed with color 2.

6. Do this for each color.

7. Go back and remove the duplicates.

So what is really involved is writing and executing a program, including the all-important debugging step. This observation suggests a reason for the fact that children acquire this ability so late: Contemporary culture provides relatively little opportunity ... with the elements of systematic procedures of this type.... In our culture number is richly represented, systematic procedure is poorly represented. (p. 175)

The reason this development has not taken place to date is because our culture does not present children with experiences in creating systematic procedures (such as learning to program). Because children have been presented with an environment rich in experiences with numbers (counting, pairing, grouping, etc.), the abilities associated with concrete operations, such as use of numbers, space, time, classification, and so on, begin to be seen quite readily at about age six or seven. Papert proposes that, given the right type of experiences, children may be able to accomplish tasks associated with formal operations before they can accomplish tasks associated with concrete operations. The way children think and develop may change. Computers provide the vehicle for presenting environments in which systematic procedures may be explored.

In Piagetian terms, he is saying that the materials a culture provides will affect the way schemas are developed by children. Experience within a culture, with the materials available in the environment, will determine what knowledge structures are built, how assimilation and accommodation take place. Our culture is changing in that a new, potentially powerful set of materials, computers, is becoming available to children, parents, and educators. These tools may be used to beneficially affect cognitive development as described by Piaget.

The role of educators in this changing culture will be to design and develop computer environments in which Piagetian learning may occur. The educator's role is not to design curriculums. Rather, educators must concern themselves with creating manipulable, explorable environments in which children may be in control of their own learning, worlds in which children may explore and examine their own thinking, alone and with others (including the teacher). Papert sees computer technology as providing powerful tools for developing such environments for children.

But the idea that coming into contact with computers in a certain way may affect a person's overall cognitive development is only part of Papert's concern. He is also interested in how specific content (knowledge) is presented to children. Logo, in addition to being an environment in which children may explore their own thinking, learn general problem-solving skills, and manipulate materials to explore procedural solutions to problems, is an environment for exploring a subject matter area—geometry. It is a purposeful restructuring of knowledge, of geometry, in a new form called turtle geometry, a computational form of geometry. It accomplishes this by presenting geometric concepts in an environment (turtle graphics) that the child controls. By using simple commands, the child can move the turtle around the screen and explore the various properties of figures. Children may create simple designs, such as a square, or more complex designs, such as those shown in **Figure 8–12**.

By writing programs to control the turtle, the child experiences the world of geometry in a meaningful way. This learning is emotionally and physically satisfying. Movements of the turtle on the screen can be investigated through corresponding bodily movements. By playing turtle, the child can act out what she expects the turtle to do, what shapes and structures the instructions programmed in Logo will yield.

Papert echoes Piaget as a genetic epistemologist by presenting geometry in a new form. Turtle geometry is not a toy, is not trivial. It is an intellectually honest presentation of the principles of geometry. The art of its structure is that it provides easy access to meaningful material. Because it is truly geometry, the principles it presents may be applied at various educational levels to varying degrees of complexity. In fact, turtle geometry is used not only with young children, but also to teach geometry at the secondary and college levels.

Papert believes that there should be a role in education for people who are experts in a particular subject area (English, sociology, physics, etc.) and whose job it is to radically restructure their subject matter in a way that is more meaningful to the learner. He does not mean designing a new set of worksheets to teach an old geometry or an old physics; rather, he means inventing a new geometry or a new physics. This restructuring must take into account the cognitive development of the learner. He further believes that this approach to teaching and learning can radically alter the way individuals in our culture view different subjects.

Logo is aimed at providing a compelling world that children can explore in ways that are meaningful to them, ways in which they can become positively emotionally involved. It is a world in which they can engage in Piagetian learning to both learn how to learn and gain expertise in subject matter (geometry). Logo is geometry (knowledge) redefined so as to be accessible to the child. It is also an environment to help children learn about learning and grow

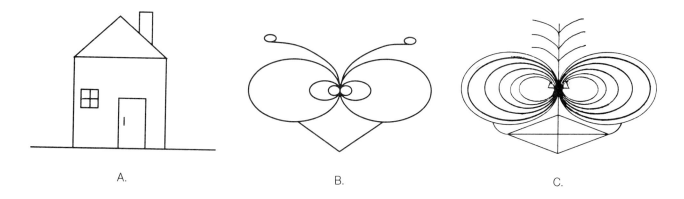

A.   B.   C.

Figure 8–12 Students may create Logo projects of varying degrees of complexity. Notice B and C above, which were done by the same student while experimenting with instructions to make arcs and ellipses.

Reactions and Research

Research on the use of Logo with children is far from conclusive regarding the possible cognitive outcomes educators can expect. Papert's interesting theoretical positions have, however, done exactly what theory is supposed to do—generated discussion and research related to the proposed theory. The following selections are from an article by Clements (1985) entitled "Research on Logo in Education: Is the Turtle Slow but Steady, or Not Even in the Race?" The selections offer some insight into what research has indicated about the use of Logo with children.

Of all the applications of computers to education, perhaps none has generated as much excitement, and as many claims as to potential benefits, as computer programming, especially Logo programming. Unfortunately, research results testing these claims are conflicting. Just as we can view a glass as half full or half empty, these results can be viewed in two distinct ways. Some have concluded that existing research is beginning to reveal significant social and cognitive benefits attributable to students' use of Logo; others, that the rather grand educational promises simply have not been substantiated....

SUMMARY AND CONCLUSIONS

Before summarizing research results, repetition of a few caveats is in order. Many of the studies reviewed are exploratory; sometimes case studies are suggestive and not conclusive. Some rely on teacher reports for data. While this is valuable information, it should be no slight to teachers' professionalism to admit that such evidence is amenable to bias or is confounded by other variables. Other studies are methodologically weak (e.g., no control group; lack of random assignment; no consideration of Hawthorne effect). Situational variables such as differing approaches to instruction, small training group sizes, the researcher-as-teacher, or, on the other hand, weak treatments, often limit generalizability. Finally, because many of the studies were presented at conferences, complete reports are still forthcoming. Still, the following summarization can be made:

1. Almost all children can learn to program in Logo at a functional level (e.g., Noss, 1984).

2. Young children learn at a slower pace, but there is no evidence that their understanding of programming concepts is inferior to that of older children (e.g., Clement, 1984a; Dytman & Wang, 1984; Noss, 1984).

3. Studies are beginning to provide descriptions of strategies used by children in Logo programming. Although the descriptions are necessarily incomplete, awareness of them can serve as a framework for observation and analysis of students' work....

7. More research is required before we will know what abilities are requisite for learning, and learning from, Logo. It appears that different abilities are required for different programming tasks, and that a multiplicity of variables, including certain mathematical, spatial, and problem-solving abilities, are involved.

8. Because different types of programming require different combinations of abilities, students with divergent profiles of strengths and weaknesses may be successful given appropriate guidance....

10. It appears that Logo can serve as a powerful tool in encouraging prosocial interaction, positive self-images, positive attitudes toward learning, and independent work habits.

11. Along these lines, teachers report that sense of control and *ownership* are essential components of an effective Logo environment (e.g., Kull et al., 1984; Noss, 1984). This does not imply that children discover everything by themselves, but that they experiment with, modify, and incorporate an idea or procedure enough to "make it their own."

12. Most researchers have found that programming in pairs is most advantageous.

13. Logo experience may facilitate achievement gains only in select areas in some children, within the context of Logo itself. Research results are conflicting, but even positive findings are not overly impressive. To maximize knowledge acquisition and its transfer, teachers should emphasize the mathematical content of Logo activities and the relationship between children's programming and other classroom tasks.

14. Programming appears to facilitate the development of specific problem-solving behaviors. It may be that children learn about the idea of theorems (Kull et al., 1984; Noss, 1984; Papert et al., 1979), thus fulfilling Logo's goal of teaching children to be mathematicians versus teaching children about mathematics (Papert, 1980)....

20. Transfer issues have not been settled. There are educators who argue that there will be no transfer, citing cognitive psychology research that demonstrates the difficulty of any transfer. Granting that transfer is not easily attained, it should also be noted that without transfer, the most significant goals of education cannot be attained. "Somewhere between the outmoded view of mental faculties and disciplines, and the

narrow psychological theory of transfer by identical elements, there is room for the hypothesis that transfer can occur by analogy among instructional learning tasks sharing only family resemblance'' (Snow, 1982, p. 30).

FINAL WORDS

There is a race to obtain the promised social-emotional and cognitive benefits of the educational applications of computers. Some have taken the pessimistic view that, because children's concepts of Logo—including such powerful ideas as variable, recursion, modularity, and so on—are limited, the turtle might need to be dropped from that race (e.g., Pea & Kurland, in press). The research reviewed here, in agreement with more optimistic reports (e.g., Blume, 1984) indicates that the turtle should continue, as Logo does appear to offer significant educational advantages. Realization of these advantages has not been fast in coming; however, slow and steady—that is, cautious and thoughtful—is probably the best way to attain the goal.

In this view, it is not that students cannot understand but that the ideas involved are sophisticated; and students therefore require time and teacher guidance to develop understanding. Piaget's discoveries concerning the difficulties children have developing concepts of number and logic led to our appreciation of the complexity of these notions and the usefulness of the clinical interview for exploring children's ideas. Likewise, students' difficulties in programming should not be construed as disproving the possible benefits of Logo. Rather, they should extend our appreciation of the sophistication of these processes and the usefulness of Logo as a medium that allows us to observe children's development of the processes while simultaneously aiding children in that development.

Criticism *is* essential. However, which view we adopt—pessimistic or optimistic—may affect how we use this tool and, therefore, its effects on students. Here it is concluded that positive research results are sufficiently suggestive to justify further study of the means to maximize these benefits. Logo does appear to hold potential to combine the abstract and mathematical with the concrete and aesthetic; the analytical with the intuitive; and culturally transmitted knowledge with personal introspection and self-discovery.

REFERENCES

Blume, G. W. (1984, April). *A review of research on the effects of computer programming on mathematical problem solving.* Paper presented at the annual meeting of the American Educational Research Association, New Orleans, LA.

Clement, C. (1984, April). *Assessment of the cognitive components of programming.* Paper presented at the annual meeting of the American Educational Research Association, New Orleans, LA.

Dytman, J. A., & Wang, M. C. (1984, April). *Elementary school children's accuracy and strategy use in problem solving.* Paper presented at the annual meeting of the American Educational Research Association, New Orleans, LA.

Kull, J. A., Cohen, B., Strong, J. S., Ferraro, L., & Bonanno, A. (1984). *Observations of first grade Logo learners.* Unpublished memos, Department of Education, University of New Hampshire, Durham, New Hampshire.

Noss, R. (1984). *Children learning Logo programming. Interim report No. 2 of the Chiltern Logo Project.* Hatfield, United Kingdom: Advisory Unit for Computer Based Education.

Papert, S. (1980). *Mindstorms: Children, computers, and powerful ideas.* New York: Basic Books.

Papert, S., Watt, D., diSessa, A., & Weir, S. (1979). *Final report of the Brookline Logo Project. Part II: Project summary and data analysis* (Logo Memo No. 53). Cambridge, MA: Massachusetts Institute of Technology, Artificial Intelligence Laboratory.

Pea, R. D., & Kurland, D. M. (in press.). *On the cognitive and educational benefits of teaching children programming: A critical look.* New Ideas in Psychology.

Snow, R. E. (1982). The training of intellectual aptitude. In D. K. Detterman & R. J. Sternberg (Eds.), *How and how much can intelligence be increased* (pp. 1–37). Norwood, NJ: Ablex.

(Clements, 1985)

---

cognitively in a general way that will perhaps transfer to other areas when they are away from the computer.

Some characteristics of Logo that help children accomplish the goals described are highlighted in this section.

Logo Characteristics

As a language, Logo is powerful (a great deal may be accomplished with it) and yet it is easy to use. It was designed to be easy to start using but at the same time capable of offering advanced functions associated with powerful computer-programming languages. In this sense it is similar to a native language, such

Logo Is Powerful

as English, which is accessible to children but in which literary masterpieces may also be created. In addition to turtle graphics, Logo offers advanced capabilities related to handling words, or lists, as well as other standard capabilities associated with a serious programming language.

Logo Encourages Good Programming

Logo is a relatively recent development and as such is designed to support current ideas about programming and learning. Structured programming, a term that will come up again in Chapter 11, on "Algorithms and the Teaching of Programming," refers to looking at a problem as a whole and then dividing it into smaller, more manageable pieces, called modules. Being able to work with modules makes the task of solving complex problems more understandable. The ability to modularize complex problems makes the very idea of complexity available to children. It also makes fixing anything that might go wrong in a program easier because it is less difficult to isolate problems when a program is divided into modules that do specific things. The way Logo emphasizes structured programming enhances its ability to give children access to systematic, procedural problem solving, which, as has been mentioned, is one of the main areas that Papert sees as positively affecting cognitive development.

If I want to draw a picture of a circle on top of a box (see **Figure 8–13**), I could divide the problem into three modules: (1) drawing a picture of a box, (2) moving the turtle to where the circle will be drawn, and (3) drawing a picture of a circle. I can then concentrate on each module separately. First, I would design and test the instructions to draw the box. When that was accomplished, the problem of moving the turtle to the correct location for drawing the circle would be analyzed and solved. Lastly, the module to draw the circle would be created and tested. By approaching the larger problem in this way, it has been reduced to three simpler, more manageable problems. When each of these three subproblems is solved, the solutions (modules) are combined to produce the solution to the larger problem. Also, if the complete picture is not drawn correctly once all the modules are combined, it is easy to locate the error and fix it. For instance, if the computer is told to draw the entire picture and the circle is not drawn correctly, the error must be in the module that draws the circle. Modularized problem solving may be of benefit both in learning to program and in learning general problem-solving skills.

Many programming languages are poor in their ability to allow modularization. BASIC, especially as it is generally available on microcomputers, is one such language. The pedagogical benefits claimed for Logo would not apply to a language like BASIC. A case can be made, however, that if BASIC is taught correctly, some benefit in regard to problem solving may occur. This is an especially important point for teachers, since BASIC is taught in many schools today. Proponents of Logo are quick to point out the real differences between Logo and BASIC. Logo was carefully developed to support and encourage the types of activities mentioned previously. It was made for learning and based on a particular theoretical orientation.

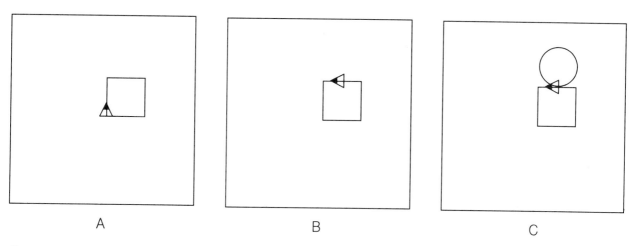

Figure 8–13 The problem of drawing a circle on top of a box can be divided into three tasks. First, draw a box (A, above). Next, move the turtle to the location where the circle will be drawn (B). Finally, draw the circle (C). Each set of instructions (module) to accomplish each task can be created and tested separately. All three modules can then be combined to produce the completed drawing.

Through the turtle, Logo provides what Papert calls a microworld for children to explore. A microworld is a self-contained environment that operates according to a specific set of consistent laws. Logo, as a programming language, is itself a microworld. The child knows the commands that will direct the turtle in the Logo microworld and may then explore within the boundaries of that world. Logo may also be used to create other microworlds for children. An example is a game called *Shoot*, described by Watt (1983). In *Shoot*, the player is shown a target and the turtle at different locations on the computer screen. He then estimates how many degrees the turtle must rotate in place to be aimed at the target. Next, he decides how many steps the turtle must take to arrive at the target. The turtle follows the instructions and the child observes the result. If the turtle misses the target, the player is given a chance to try again. *Shoot* is often used to give students practice in judging the movement of the turtle on the screen.

Further, microworlds, as environments, provide children with avenues of exploration through which they can discover and experiment with powerful ideas. In the Logo environment, powerful ideas are useful, generalizable principles. For example, if the turtle is moved around the perimeter of any closed regular figure (such as a circle, square, or star) so that it arrives at the exact place it started from, the number of degrees the turtle turns during the trip will be 360 or a multiple of 360 (see **Figure 8–14**). In Logo this is called the Total Turtle Trip Theorem and is an example of a powerful idea that, once discovered, will be used over and over again in solving and understanding other problems. Microworlds have been structured to teach a variety of other concepts, including ideas about Newtonian physics.

Microworlds and Powerful Ideas

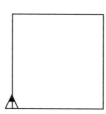 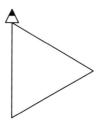

Figure 8–14 When the turtle completes a trip around the perimeter of any closed regular figure and arrives back at the exact place it started from, the number of degrees it will have turned will be 360 or a multiple of 360. To draw the square and return to the exact starting position, the turtle turned RIGHT 90 four times. To draw the triangle it turned RIGHT 120 three times.

Logo Is Resonant With the Child's World

As children experiment with Logo by attempting various projects, they become involved with their work both physically and emotionally. Physically, they use their bodies to play turtle, or act out the way the turtle is expected to move. Emotionally, they are engaged in meaningful projects to which they can relate. The fact that Logo relates quite closely to the child's world both physically and emotionally implies a type of involvement, an opportunity for learning, that should be powerful in its effect. It also implies the type of involvement necessary for Piagetian learning.

Logo, Students, and Teachers

In a school setting it is obvious that the teacher will have a role in the student's interaction with Logo. When Logo is used as intended, the teacher and student become collaborators, with the student having a vested interest in investigating a project she has created. The original idea for the project may have been suggested by the teacher or the student, or it may have grown out of other experiences with Logo. As the student and teacher interact, the teacher may suggest and show things to the student. The teacher's role is more that of an adviser than of a supervisor following a rigidly set, predetermined plan. This can be an exciting and stimulating experience for both student and teacher.

Logo and Bugs

As experimentation commences and continues during a programming project, invariably something will not work the way it was intended. In computer parlance, a bug will have been discovered. In a Logo environment a bug is seen as an opportunity to learn. A child's program is not right or wrong; rather, it is a meaningful piece of work that may need some polishing. By studying the bug new learning can occur, new insights may be gained. In addition to an immediate solution being found, new information may be discovered that will be of use at a later time. Such information may add a new technique to the child's knowledge of the specifics of Logo as a programming language, may provide insight into a new problem-solving strategy, or may suggest an idea for a new programming project.

Computers in the Classroom

Playing turtle refers to students acting out the directions that the turtle is given. By physically carrying out the instructions as if she were the turtle, a child can begin to know how the instructions relate to the movement of the turtle on the screen. This knowing is on the level of her muscles and can help in both building and debugging instructions. Playing turtle is an important technique in Logo.

Early introduction of activities in which children play turtle can help to instill the habit of using this technique when creating and fixing instructions in Logo. When beginning work with Logo, an area that represents the computer screen is designated on the classroom floor, or on the playground. One child is chosen to be the turtle. Another child, or small group of children, is chosen to give Logo commands (instructions) to the child who is the turtle. A task is set, such as making the turtle move to a certain point on the screen. Directions are given to the turtle, who must do only what the directions specify, such as move so many steps forward or rotate so far to the right or left. Other tasks may be set, such as drawing simple shapes. By considering the effects of different instructions, children begin to develop skills in Logo. Children take turns being the turtle and giving instruc-

tions. In later experiences with Logo children play turtle to explore solutions to problems and debug sets of Logo instructions. In an article in Byte, *E. Paul Goldenberg describes playing turtle:*

Playing turtle: pretending to be the turtle and walking through a turtle graphics procedure as the turtle might see it. This process can make fairly difficult geometric constructions transparent to young children with little or no formal training in geometry. Playing turtle, though, refers as much to the thinking through of a procedure before programming it as to walking through an existing procedure.

By way of example, some 10-year-olds were trying to figure out how to teach the turtle to make a circle. I suggested they play turtle. They concluded that if all they could tell the turtle was to go FORWARD and to turn, it would have to go just a little bit forward, turn a little, go a little bit forward again, turn a little again, and so on. After one kid had made it around the circle (one of the instructions was "keep doing that until you get back to the beginning"), they were convinced they had the right idea. To help them with the details, I reminded them of the Total Turtle Trip Theorem and again encouraged them to play turtle. They began to reason out the details of how much to turn, how many times to repeat the process, and how big they wanted to make each step.

(Goldenberg, 1982)

Conclusion

The ideas behind Logo are indeed revolutionary. Logo is currently used in many schools throughout the world. In some instances it is applied in exactly the manner Papert has intended, in settings where Piagetian learning is encouraged and supported. In other instances educators with different philosophies have incorporated Logo into more traditional settings, designing curriculums and structuring worksheets to specify what should be learned by students at particular times in their interaction with Logo. One thing is certain: Logo is well established in a variety of educational settings and will probably be around for some time. As you learn more about it, give careful consideration to the role you think it might have in the educational environments you create. Also, as you cover the material in the next two chapters and engage in hands-on experiences with Logo, observe your own learning style and your instructor's teaching style. How structured are your experiences? How do you react to your experiences? What does this suggest to you about how you might decide to use Logo?

Key Terms

accommodation
assimilation

concrete operational stage
conservation

egocentric

formal operational stage

genetic epistemology

microworld

modularized problem solving

module

object permanence

operations

Piagetian learning

playing turtle

preoperational stage

schema

sensorimotor

structured programming

systematic procedure

Total Turtle Trip Theorem

turtle geometry

turtle graphics

visual pursuit

Questions

1. Why, according to the material in this chapter, is it important for teachers to understand the theories behind the different educational methods and materials available for classroom use? What is your reaction to this position?

2. What are the four stages of development outlined by Piaget? Cite relevant characteristics for each stage identified.

3. What types of experiences are valuable for students in the concrete operational stage? The stage of formal operations? In each case explain why the types of experiences you mentioned would be valuable.

4. Explain the following terms: schema, assimilation, accommodation.

5. Which areas of Piaget's research does Papert emphasize that educators usually do not?

6. Compare and contrast a computer-rich and a computer-poor culture as viewed by Papert. In what ways might computers be used by children in a computer-rich culture, and how might this affect children?

7. According to Papert, will all applications of computers to education (for instance, drill and practice, tutorials, demonstrations) have the same effect as Logo on children? Why or why not?

8. What is a genetic epistemologist? Does Logo reflect any of the concerns of a genetic epistemologist?

9. List six characteristics of Logo as a programming language. Choose two of these characteristics and relate them to the theory behind the development of Logo.

10. What goals and philosophies do you see yourself bringing to the classroom as a teacher? From what you know of Logo so far, would it be of benefit in a classroom in which you were teaching? Why or why not?

References/Further Reading

Abelson, Harold, and Andrea diSessa. *Turtle Geometry*. Cambridge, Mass.: MIT Press, 1981.

Clements, Douglas H. "Research on Logo in Education: Is the Turtle Slow but Steady, or Not Even in the Race?" In *Logo in the Schools*, edited by Cleborne D. Maddus. New York: Haworth Press, 1985, 55, 66–69.

Goldenberg, E. Paul. "Logo—A Cultural Glossary." *Byte* 7, no. 8 (1982):210–228.

Kaplan, Paul S. *A Child's Odyssey: Child and Adolescent Development*. St. Paul: West Publishing Co., 1986.

Owen, Steven V., Robin D. Froman, and Henry Moscow. *Educational Psychology: An Introduction*. Boston: Little, Brown, 1981.

Papert, Seymour. *Mindstorms: Children, Computers and Powerful Ideas*. New York: Basic Books, 1980.

Piaget, J. *Science of Education and the Psychology of the Child*. New York: Viking Press, 1970.

Piaget, J., and B. Inhelder. *The Psychology of the Child*. New York: Basic Books, 1969.

Sarafino, Edward P., and James W. Armstrong. *Child and Adolescent Development*, 2d ed. St. Paul: West Publishing Co., 1986.

Schank, Roger C., with Peter G. Childers. *The Cognitive Computer: On Language, Learning and Artificial Intelligence*. Reading, Mass.: Addison-Wesley, 1984, 205–206.

Sprinthall, Richard C., and Norman A. Sprinthall. *Educational Psychology: A Developmental Approach*. Reading, Mass.: Addision-Wesley, 1974.

Watt, Daniel. "Logo in the Schools." *Byte* 7, no. 8 (1982):116–134.

———. *Learning with Logo*. New York: McGraw-Hill, 1983.

9

Logo: Starting Out

TOPICS ADDRESSED

How is learning to program like mastering a set of tools to learn a craft?

What is MIT Logo? Krell Logo? Terrapin Logo?

How is Krell Logo started up on an Apple II series microcomputer?

What is PRINT, and what are some ways editing can be done?

What is DRAW and NODRAW?

How may shapes be drawn in Logo using FORWARD, BACK, RIGHT, and LEFT?

What do the commands HOME, CLEARSCREEN, PENUP, PENDOWN, HIDETURTLE, and SHOWTURTLE accomplish?

How is the screen display affected by the commands SPLITSCREEN, FULLSCREEN, and TEXTSCREEN?

How can the REPEAT command be used?

OUTLINE

Introduction
MIT Logo
Starting Logo: PRINT, and Editing: A Brief Tutorial
DRAW and NODRAW
FORWARD, BACK, LEFT, and RIGHT
A First Shape
HOME and CLEARSCREEN
  Exercises
PENDOWN and PENUP

HIDETURTLE and SHOWTURTLE
SPLITSCREEN, FULLSCREEN, and TEXTSCREEN
  Exercises
REPEAT
  Exercises
Conclusion
Key Terms
References/Further Reading

Introduction

The point has been made that to learn about a programming language, a person must program on a computer in that language. There is no substitute for hands-on experience. This chapter and the one that follows are an introduction to the Logo programming language. The material is intended to provide a starting point for programming in Logo as a basis for working with Logo and children. In order to accomplish this it is necessary to learn some of the commands available in Logo and try them out on a computer. Exercises are built into the chapters at appropriate places. Your instructor will make sure you have access to Logo and a computer on which to run it.

In learning any programming language it is important to remember one major fact of life in computer programming: do not be concerned or overwhelmed by all that you do not know about the programming language you are learning. Rather, concern yourself with what you do know and are currently learning as it relates to the program you are trying to write. Consider the following analogy. There are hundreds, perhaps thousands, of tools available for working with wood. Yet a person with a basic knowledge and skill set related to several tools, such as a hammer, saw, pliers, screwdriver, drill, and file, will be able to make competent, perhaps even elaborate, projects in wood. Also, when this basic understanding is coupled with the ability to locate and learn about a new, appropriate tool for some specific job, the same person's skill as a carpenter has the potential to expand dramatically. It is the same with learning about programming. By mastering a few simple commands and exploring their possibilities, students quickly gain some facility with a new programming language. Once this beginning is made, it is a simple and enjoyable matter to explore more commands and apply problem-solving techniques to more complex problems, many of which are generated by the students themselves. Indeed, the learning of new commands in a programming language often occurs because students see things they would like to do in their programs and want to know if the programming language provides a way to do them. As you work with Logo concentrate on what you need and want to know as it applies to the problem on which you are working. Do not worry about all the things about computers and programming that you do not know.

As you gain experience with Logo ponder how a child at a grade level in which you are interested might respond to some of your experiences. How would you, as a teacher, respond to the child?

MIT Logo

This book introduces MIT Logo. Two companies, Krell and Terrapin, offer versions of MIT Logo which have become quite popular. Both versions are essentially the same. The examples in this book were written and tested on an Apple IIc microcomputer using Krell Logo. Other popular versions of Logo are available for microcomputers. Although all may be said to be Logo, there may be significant differences between them. These differences may involve the type and number of Logo commands offered and may include special features introduced by the particular publisher. A basic understanding of one version of Logo will readily transfer to another version, since there should always be more similarities than differences between versions.

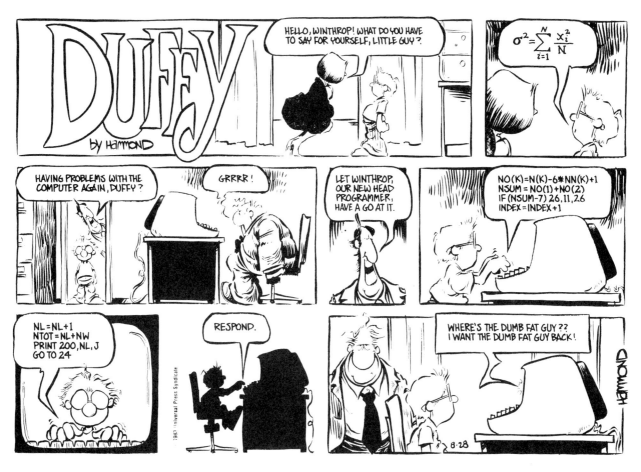

If you are using an Apple IIe or Apple IIc, be sure the Caps Lock key is pressed down before you start working with Logo. To start, take the Logo language disk from its protective envelope. Hold the disk by its cover (do not touch the exposed parts). With the label side up and toward you, slide the disk into the disk drive and close the disk drive door. Turn on the monitor and then turn on the computer. The light on the disk drive will come on for a few seconds while the computer loads a copy of the Logo language into the computer's memory. When the language is loaded and ready for use, the following information will appear on the computer screen:

Starting Logo: PRINT and Editing—A Brief Tutorial

```
PROGRAMMED AT MIT UNDER THE SUPERVISION OF H. ABELSON
COPYRIGHT (C) 1981 MIT
VERSION A. BY MARK FRIEDLAND
INSTANT LOGO TUTOR
COPYRIGHT (C) 1982 KRELL SOFTWARE

WELCOME TO LOGO
?▮
```

Next to the question mark that appears on the screen is a blinking rectangle called a cursor. Whenever Logo presents you with a question mark followed by the cursor, it is waiting for you to do something; it is waiting for the person sitting at the computer to type in something. Suppose you typed in a name.

MARY

After typing the name, press the key labeled RETURN. To enter information into the computer the RETURN key must be pressed. The computer responds by printing

THERE IS NO PROCEDURE NAMED MARY

This is because there is no Logo command named MARY. The computer is saying that it does not understand what you want it to do because the Logo language does not contain a command named MARY. Next, type in the following:

PRINT [MARY]

and press the RETURN key. The computer prints out

MARY

The computer was given the Logo command PRINT and responded to it by printing the name specified within the brackets. The format of the PRINT command in Logo is

PRINT [   ]

Whatever is to be printed must be enclosed in brackets. (If you are using an Apple II series computer and there are no brackets on the keyboard, you can get a left bracket ([ ) by holding down the Shift key and then pressing the key labeled N (Shift-N); for a right bracket ( ]), press Shift-M.)

Sometimes, in giving the computer an instruction, a typing error is made. If you wanted Logo to print out the name ROSELLEN but typed the instruction incorrectly, for instance,

PRUNT [ROSELLEN]

you would need to go back and edit (change) the line before pressing the RETURN key. If you did not edit the line so that the correct command, PRINT, was given, the computer would not know what to do, since there is no instruction PRUNT in Logo.

One way to edit the line is to move the cursor to the letter just after the letter you wish to delete and then press the ESC key. ESC stands for escape. When the ESC key is pressed, it deletes the letter immediately to the left of the cursor. You could then type the correct letter, which would be inserted at the location of the cursor.

Another way to edit the line is to place the cursor directly on the letter to be deleted, hold down the key labeled Control, and then press the key labeled D. This is written as CTRL-D and deletes the letter under the cursor. Again, you could then type the correct letter, which would be inserted at the cursor location. In either case the line would now look like this:

PRINT [ROSELLEN]

As mentioned earlier, letters and numerals (and special symbols such as punctuation marks and dollar signs) that are typed on the screen or printed on a printer are called characters. ESC and CTRL-D each edit one character at a time.

Another way to edit the line is to press CTRL-K (hold down the Control key and simultaneously press the K key). This command deletes the rest of the line from the current cursor position on. For instance, if the following appears on the screen

PRUNT [HELEN]

and the cursor is positioned over the U in PRUNT, pressing CTRL-K would cause the entire line from the U on to be deleted and the screen would appear as follows:

PR

The rest of the line could then be typed in correctly:

PRINT [HELEN]

Now the RETURN key would be pressed to send the command to the computer. The computer would then print out

HELEN

These three commands in Logo provide a way to edit lines on the screen. If you have already pressed RETURN and see that there is something you wish to change in a line you have typed previously, simply retype the line.

DRAW and NODRAW

Two modes possible in Logo are DRAW and NODRAW. When the Logo language boots, or first starts up, the NODRAW mode is automatically selected. To enter the DRAW mode, simply type DRAW and press RETURN. (From this point on you may assume that RETURN must be pressed after a command is typed on the screen, unless told otherwise. Pressing RETURN is what causes the computer to execute the command that has been typed on the screen.) After the DRAW command is entered, the screen clears and a triangle with one point shaded appears near the center of the screen, while a question mark and the cursor appear toward the lower left on the screen (see **Figure 9–1**). The triangular object is referred to as the turtle. In the DRAW mode it is possible to make use of the turtle graphics aspect of Logo. As mentioned in Chapter 8, by using Logo commands to give the turtle instructions, the turtle may be moved around the screen, leaving a line over the path it has taken. In this way different shapes may be drawn on the screen.

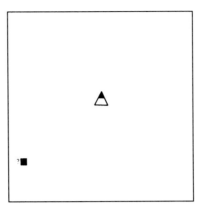

Figure 9–1 The screen after the DRAW command is entered. The turtle is near the center of the screen and the bottom four lines on the screen are reserved for text.

In Logo, drawing shapes is a much simpler process than in other programming languages, where shapes must be plotted as a series of points in reference to Cartesian coordinates. Logo, therefore, makes powerful graphics capabilities available simply and understandably to students of all ages.

Notice that while in the DRAW mode, the bottom four lines on the screen are reserved for displaying text, for displaying the commands typed into the computer. The upper portion of the screen, as it now appears, is where shapes will be drawn. To leave DRAW mode, use the command NODRAW.

FORWARD, BACK, LEFT, and RIGHT

Once in the DRAW mode, or turtle graphics environment, the turtle can be given commands that it will immediately carry out. As shown in Chapter 8, if the command FORWARD 50 is entered, the turtle moves forward fifty units, called turtle steps, leaving a line (see **Figure 9–2**).

The command LEFT causes the turtle to rotate in place toward the left whatever number of units (degrees) are specified. For instance, the command LEFT 90 would cause the turtle in Figure 9–2 to rotate ninety degrees to the left. It would then appear on the screen as shown **Figure 9–3**.

BACK causes the turtle to move backwards from its current position whatever number of turtle steps are specified. The command BACK 50 would make the turtle move back fifty turtle steps, leaving a line. The result may be seen in **Figure 9–4**.

The RIGHT command causes the turtle to rotate in place to the right whatever number of turtle steps are specified. For example, RIGHT 90 makes the turtle rotate in place ninety degrees to the right. Given the command RIGHT 90, the turtle in Figure 9–4 would rotate ninety degrees to the right and end up as shown in **Figure 9–5**.

Each of the commands covered so far (and many other Logo commands) have short forms. Listed below are the commands given above and their corresponding short forms. Note that a space precedes the number specified for each command. Any command in Logo must be entered exactly as Logo expects it; otherwise, the computer will not understand what instruction is to be

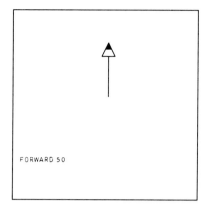

Figure 9–2 The way the screen appears after the command FORWARD 50 is entered.

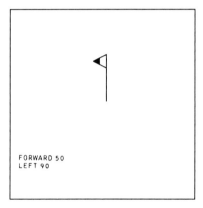

Figure 9–3 After moving FORWARD 50 the turtle is instructed to rotate LEFT 90.

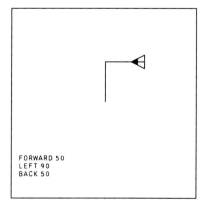

Figure 9–4 After moving FORWARD 50 and LEFT 90, the turtle is instructed to move BACK 50.

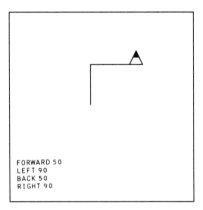

```
FORWARD 50
LEFT 90
BACK 50
RIGHT 90
```

Figure 9–5 The turtle has been given the commands FORWARD 50 LEFT 90 BACK 50 RIGHT 90 with the result shown above.

carried out. If Logo expects a space (as it does below), the command must be entered that way.

FORWARD 50   FD 50

LEFT 90   LT 90

BACK 50   BK 50

RIGHT 90   RT 90

Observe that each command needs a number to specify either how many turtle steps the turtle must move or how many degrees the turtle must rotate. The number needed for each command is called an input. Each of the four commands above needs an input. If any of the commands were entered without an input, such as

FORWARD

Logo would not be able to process the command and would write a message on the screen stating that FORWARD needed an input. Some commands in Logo require inputs, others do not. (When entering a number in Logo, do not use commas. For example, enter 1000 rather than 1,000.)

A First Shape

Before reading further, imagine that you want to use the two commands FORWARD and RIGHT to draw a triangle on the screen. Stand up, put the book down, and pretend that you are the turtle. By giving yourself the appropriate commands and following them (you can estimate degrees and size of turtle steps), trace the path that would draw a triangle on the floor. Or if a friend is available, you might have him be the turtle while you give the commands.

The following set of commands will cause the turtle to draw a triangle on the screen (see **Figure 9–6**).

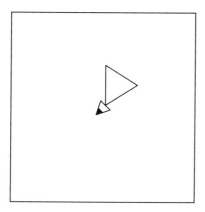

Figure 9–6 The triangle above is drawn by ebtering the following commands: FD 50 RT 120 FD 50 RT 120 FD 50.

```
FD  50
RT  120
FD  50
RT  120
FD  50
```

As each command is entered the turtle responds immediately by carrying out the instruction it is given. This immediate execution mode is valuable for becoming acquainted with what Logo commands can do and for experimenting and planning Logo projects.

HOME, CLEARSCREEN

When the draw mode is entered, the turtle first appears in the center of the screen. This is called the home position. The command HOME will move the turtle from any position on the screen back to the home position. Suppose the commands FD 50 RT 90 FD 50 had been given to the turtle to produce the shape shown in screen 1 of **Figure 9–7**. If the next command entered was HOME, the turtle would move to the center of the screen, to the position it originally was in when DRAW mode was entered. Notice in screen 2 of Figure 9–7 that this is the case. Also notice that the turtle left a line along the path it took to get to the home position.

If the next command entered is CLEARSCREEN (or CS, the short form), all the lines on the screen will be cleared and the turtle will remain in its current position (which, in this case, happens to be the home position). The result of typing CLEARSCREEN may be seen in **Figure 9–8**. The screen has been cleared of all lines.

So, if at any time you want to erase everything on the screen and leave the turtle where it is, use CLEARSCREEN. If you want to move the turtle to the home position, use HOME. If, while in the DRAW mode, you want to simultaneously erase the screen and move the turtle to the home position, use the DRAW command and it will have that effect.

Input/Output

One of the most thoughtful critics of computer education in the schools (including Logo) is Joseph Weizenbaum, a computer scientist at Massachusetts Institute of Technology. In the mid-sixties Weizenbaum created the computer program Eliza, *which mimics responses a psychologist might offer in a session with a client. Although the program was intended to demonstrate how a computer could process information, some psychiatrists chose to see it as a serious tool for psychotherapy, a use for which it was definitely not designed or intended. The following excerpt is from an interview with Weizenbaum by Brady (1985) that appeared in the magazine* Classroom Computer Learning.

"This reaction to Eliza," Weizenbaum comments, "showed me more vividly than anything I had seen hitherto the enormously exaggerated attributions an even well-educated audience is capable of making, even strives to make, to a technology it does not understand." It is a reaction, Weizenbaum believes, that's not at all uncommon among the general public and that currently may play a part in the uncritical way that computers are being incorporated into our nation's curriculum....

In his years at MIT, Weizenbaum has surely taught some of the best and brightest young programmers in the country. Yet he sees very little merit in teaching programming in either elementary or high school for the reasons currently given.

"There may be some justification for teaching programming as a vocational skill above the tenth grade. And I have no objection to having a computer club in school so that students who want to fiddle with computers—sort of naturally and extra-curricularly—have a chance to do so. But I oppose the idea of teaching programming as a form of 'computer literacy'—something children are supposed to need for a future world pervaded by computers. Oh, there's no doubt that our world will be pervaded by computers. But they will be essentially invisible in the same way that electric motors are invisible: we use electric motors all the time, but we don't have to be trained as electrical engineers to do so."

Teaching programming as part of a computer literacy course doesn't interest computer booster Seymour Papert any more than it does Weizenbaum. Papert's main motive for promoting the programming language Logo in the schools—especially in elementary school—has been to help children develop at an early age solid problem-solving skills that become the basis for logical, scientific thought processes. And here is where he and Weizenbaum differ most vehemently.

"I think," Weizenbaum explains, "that our world is much too bound by scientific standards of thinking. We have fostered the attitude in our schools that everything can be 'figured out.' Even if we can use computers to teach young children the 'logical' way of thinking, I'm not at all convinced that we should.

"Let me explain further: I think that children have a power to imagine that is almost magical when compared to the adult imagination, and there is something irrecoverable that a child loses when he or she becomes bound by logic. We adults continue to have our children's power of imagination only in our dreams. When in a dream, you see a little man selling ice cream and in the very next moment he becomes your mother who died twenty years before, you're not surprised at all. And so it is with children—even when they're awake. Of course, it's awfully necessary that children not run their entire lives on the basis of such thinking; they need to learn how to think logically. But the world will soon teach that to them. And in overabundance! I think we should do everything we can to make it possible for children to hang on to the power to imagine in the almost magical sense for as long as possible.

"Now, I am not unaware of the fact that American students today generally do not test as well in math and the sciences as their counterparts in Japan and other countries. But I don't believe that inadequate science instruction is the primary reason. I suggest that a more significant reason is that students have no language in which to express themselves, externally or internally, in these subject areas. A computer enthusiast might jump in here and suggest that Logo, and all that goes with it, is in a broad sense the required language. But in my opinion what many children lack is mastery of their own language—of English. If you don't have mastery of your mother tongue, you lack the most basic foundation of scientific or any other kind of thinking."

(Brady, 1985)

A summary of the commands covered so far appears in **Table 9–1.** Each command is given, including the applicable short form, followed by a brief description and then an example of the command.

EXERCISES

The following exercises provide you with opportunities to become familiar with Logo. By spending some time at the computer and experimenting with the commands presented so

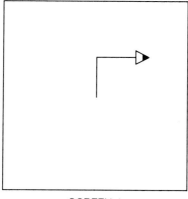

SCREEN 1

Given the commands: F D 5 0 R T 9 0
F D 5 0 the turtle draws the shape
above.

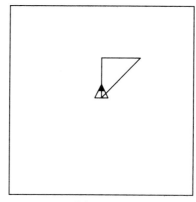

SCREEN 2

The command HOME causes the turtle to move from its current position to
the home position, leaving a line on
the screen.

Figure 9–7

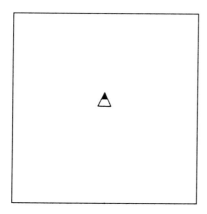

Figure 9–8 Entering the CLEARSCREEN command clears all lines from the screen and leaves the turtle in
its current position (which here happened to be the home position).

far, you will gain a better idea of how the individual commands work. You will also begin to
experience problem solving as it relates to computer programming in general and Logo in
particular.

1. Boot Logo and get into DRAW mode.

2. Explore the commands FORWARD, BACK, LEFT, RIGHT, HOME, and CLEARSCREEN by
   trying the following:

   ▪ Use the FORWARD command with various size numbers.

   ▪ Do the same for BACK.

   ▪ Clear the screen with CLEARSCREEN.

   ▪ Move the turtle FORWARD 30, then RIGHT 45, and then FORWARD 30 again.

   ▪ Repeat this sequence with different size inputs.

   ▪ Move the turtle BACK 50, then LEFT 90, and then BACK 80.

Command	*Description*	*Example*
PRINT PR	Causes whatever is within the brackets to be printed.	PRINT [ADELE] PR [ADELE]
ESC	Deletes the character to the left of the cursor.	ESC
CTRL-D	Deletes the character under the cursor.	CTRL-D
CTRL-K	Deletes the rest of the line from the cursor position on.	CTRL-K
DRAW	Used to enter DRAW mode.	DRAW
NODRAW	Used to exit DRAW mode.	NODRAW
FORWARD FD	Moves turtle forward the specified number of turtle steps.	FORWARD 45 FD 45
BACK BK	Moves turtle back the specified number of turtle steps.	BACK 70 BK 70
RIGHT RT	Rotates turtle in place the specified number of degrees to the right.	RIGHT 50 RT 50
LEFT LT	Rotates turtle in place the specified number of degrees to the left.	LEFT 65 LT 65
HOME	Moves the turtle to the home position.	HOME
CLEARSCREEN CS	Erases the screen, leaves the turtle in its current position.	CLEARSCREEN CS

Table 9–1

- Repeat this sequence with different size inputs.
- Move the turtle around the screen.
- Try to make the turtle go to each of the corners of the screen.
- What is the smallest amount that you can make the turtle move? What is the smallest amount that you can make the turtle move and see a line left on the screen?
- How far can you make the turtle move with one command?
- Make the turtle draw a diagonal line on the screen. Is the line smooth?
- Place the turtle in the home position and erase the screen.

3. Look around the room you are in. Select three shapes from all of those surrounding you. One at a time, try to draw each shape on the screen. After you complete one shape, return the turtle to the home position, clear the screen, and try the next one.

4. Ask a friend in class to show you the shapes she chose. Select one of her shapes and try to draw it on the screen.

PENDOWN and PENUP

When the turtle first appears on the screen after typing DRAW, it will draw a line on the screen when given a command such as FORWARD 70 or BACK 23. If the command PENUP is entered and then the turtle is given a command that causes it to move, such as FORWARD 70 or BACK 23, the turtle will move exactly as before but it will not leave a line on the screen. Imagine that a pen is attached to the turtle and that when the pen is down the turtle draws a line as it moves. The imaginary pen is retracted by the command PENUP so that no line is drawn when the turtle moves. To once again have the turtle leave a line on the screen, the command PENDOWN is used.

PENUP and PENDOWN are useful when making drawings that require the turtle to draw a shape and then be repositioned somewhere else on the screen before beginning to draw another shape.

Another way to describe the fact that when the DRAW mode is first entered the turtle's pen is down is to say that the state of the turtle when DRAW mode is entered is that the pen is down. To change the state of the turtle so that the pen is retracted, the PENUP command would be entered. To change the state of the turtle back so that the pen is down again, the PENDOWN command would be entered. The term state refers to the attributes associated with the turtle at a particular moment. Such attributes can include, among others, whether the pen is up or down, the direction in which the turtle is pointing, or the location of the turtle on the screen.

Figure 9–9 shows the use of PENUP and PENDOWN to draw parallel lines on the screen. **Figure 9–10** shows the use of PENUP and PENDOWN to draw two boxes at different locations on the screen.

To have the turtle disappear from the screen, the command HIDETURTLE is entered. Even though the turtle does not show on the screen, it will still do whatever it is commanded to do. **Figure 9–11** shows the effect of the HIDETURTLE command. The commands given to draw the shape in Figure 9–11 were exactly the same as those given in Figure 9–10, except that the HIDETURTLE command was issued before drawing began.

The SHOWTURTLE command causes the turtle to be displayed on the screen again. When the SHOWTURTLE command is entered, the turtle appears on the screen at its current location.

HIDETURTLE and SHOWTURTLE

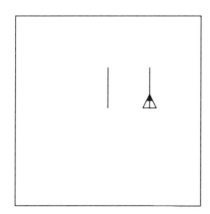

Figure 9–9 The turtle started in the home position. The command FD 50 was entered, which drew the line in the center of the screen. The command PENUP was entered and the turtle was moved RT 90 FD 50 LT 90. The command PENDOWN was entered followed by BK 50, which drew the second line. The commands are as follows: FD 50 PENUP RT 90 FD 50 LT 90 PENDOWN BK 50.

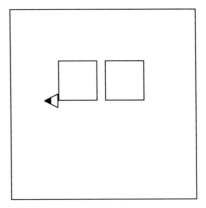

Figure 9–10 With the turtle starting in the home position, the box on the right is drawn with the following commands: FD 50 RT 90 FD 50 RT 90 FD 50 RT 90 FD 50. Next, the command PENUP is entered and then the turtle is given the commands: FD 60 RT 90. To position it where desired before drawing the second box. The command PENDOWN is entered and the following commands are given to draw the second box: FD 50 RT 90 FD 50 RT 90 FD 50 RT 90 FD 50.

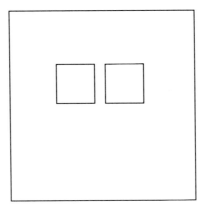

Figure 9–11 The HIDETURTLE command causes the turtle to disappear from the screen, although it will still execute whatever commands it is given. The SHOWTURTLE command would cause the turtle to appear on the screen again at its current location.

When the turtle is hidden, Logo is able to draw pictures somewhat faster than when the turtle is shown. This is because when the turtle is shown on the screen and appears to move, the computer is really erasing the turtle and then drawing it again slightly ahead of its current location, erasing it, redrawing it a little further on, erasing it, redrawing it again, and so on. This happens quickly so that the effect of motion is achieved. When the computer does not have to animate the movement of the turtle in this way, the line is drawn more quickly. Usually, when planning and working out Logo projects, the turtle needs to be seen on the screen to help understand how the commands are affecting it. Hiding the turtle to speed up drawing is sometimes valuable as a last step in a finished Logo project.

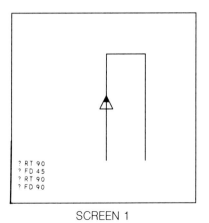
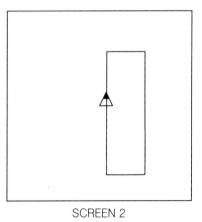
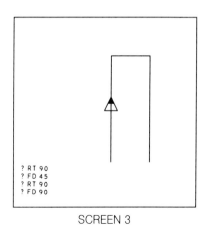

SCREEN 1   SCREEN 2   SCREEN 3

Figure 9–12 Screen 1 shows the shape displayed when, in SPLITSCREEN, the following commands are entered: FD 90 RT 90 FD 45 RT 90 FD 180 RT 90 FD 45 RT 90 FD 90 . In screen 2, the entire shape is displayed after the FULLSCREEN (CTRL–F) command has been entered. Screen 3 shows the resulting display after the SPLITSCREEN (CTRL–S) command has been entered.

SPLITSCREEN, FULLSCREEN, and TEXTSCREEN

For all of the examples presented so far while in DRAW mode, the screen has been split between a text display (the bottom four lines of the screen) and a graphics display (the upper portion of the screen). When commands are entered in DRAW mode, the text on the screen scrolls, or moves, upward and seems to disappear behind the graphics portion of the screen. Also, the turtle, when directed to move far enough toward the extreme bottom of the screen, seems to disappear behind the text portion of the screen.

The command FULLSCREEN (which may also be entered by pressing the Control key and then the F key, written as CTRL-F) will cause the computer to display the entire screen as a graphics screen. This will reveal that even when the turtle seems to disappear behind the text at the bottom of the screen, it is in reality still executing whatever command it has been given. **Figure 9–12** shows a series of commands to draw a rectangle on the screen and the result when the screen is split between text and graphics. It then shows what the screen will look like after the command FULLSCREEN has been entered. Notice that the entire object can now be viewed. In FULLSCREEN it is possible to give the turtle commands, but the text typed on the keyboard will not appear on the screen. The last display in Figure 9–12 shows the screen restored to a split screen. This is done by entering the command SPLITSCREEN.

The command TEXTSCREEN (or CTRL-T) causes the display to change to all text. The commands that have been entered and have scrolled upward are made available for viewing by entering the command TEXTSCREEN. **Figure 9–13** shows a screen display before entering the TEXTSCREEN command and then after the command has been entered. To restore the screen to the way it was originally in Figure 9–13, the command SPLITSCREEN (or CTRL-S) would be entered.

The TEXTSCREEN command is valuable if you need to review the series of commands you have entered. It allows you to look back and see the previous twenty lines of text entered. The ability to review in this way is sometimes

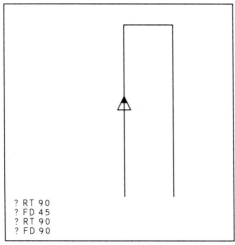

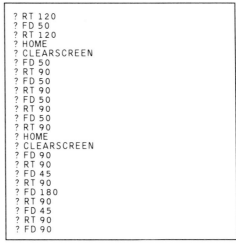

SCREEN 1   SCREEN 2

Figure 9–13 When the command TEXTSCREEN (CTRL–T) is entered, screen 1 changes to screen 2, a full screen of 24 lines of text. To change the display back to screen 1, the command SPLITSCREEN (CTRL–S) would be entered.

valuable in discovering how the turtle was made to accomplish a task. (Lines entered prior to the last twenty lines have scrolled off the top of the screen and are not available for viewing.) The FULLSCREEN command allows the use of the entire screen for the development of Logo projects, as needed. It provides an expanded area in which to develop and subsequently display Logo drawings. Working in SPLITSCREEN is the main way experimentation and planning are achieved in Logo, especially in the early stages of planning a project. Each display has a use and each is a valuable tool in Logo.

Command	Description	Example
PENDOWN PD	Causes the turtle to draw a line as it moves.	PENDOWN PD
PENUP PU	Retracts the pen. The turtle will not draw a line while moving when the pen is up.	PENUP PU
HIDETURTLE HT	Erases the turtle from the screen.	HIDETURTLE HT
SHOWTURTLE ST	Causes the turtle to reappear on the screen.	SHOWTURTLE ST
FULLSCREEN CTRL-F	Displays the entire screen for drawing, for graphics.	FULLSCREEN CTRL-F
TEXTSCREEN CTRL-T	Displays the entire screen for text.	TEXTSCREEN CTRL-T
SPLITSCREEN CTRL-S	Displays the bottom four screen lines as text and the rest of the screen as graphics (for drawing).	SPLITSCREEN CTRL-S

Table 9–2

EXERCISES

1. Draw a rectangle. Move the turtle to another part of the screen (without leaving a line) and draw the same rectangle again.

2. Clear the screen. Draw a square on the screen. Draw another square, half the size of the first one you drew, at another location on the screen.

3. Clear the screen. Draw a triangle that does not have three sides of equal length.

4. Draw several triangles of different sizes at different locations on the screen.

5. Clear the screen. Choose three letters and draw them.

6. Choose three numbers and draw them.

7. Draw a triangle within a triangle (see below).

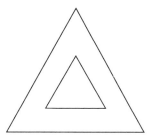

8. Draw one or more of the following shapes on the screen:

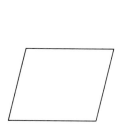  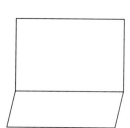 

9. What are the last twelve commands you have entered?

10. Draw the largest triangle you can on the screen.

The REPEAT command is used to cause one or more Logo commands to repeat a specified number of times. For example, if the turtle starts in the home position and the following commands are entered

REPEAT

```
FD  70
RT  90
FD  35
RT  90
```

the result will be the drawing in **Figure 9–14**.

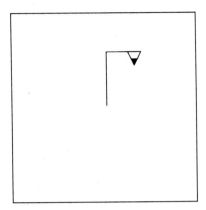

Figure 9–14 The above shape is drawn after entering the following commands: F D 7 0 R T 9 0 F D 3 5 R T 9 0 .

Using the REPEAT command, this, or any, series of commands can be repeated whatever number of times is desired. For instance,

REPEAT 2 [FD 70 RT 90 FD 35 RT 90]

will make the series of commands contained within the brackets repeat whatever number of times is specified. In this case, 2 is specified so Logo will execute each instruction within the brackets once, in order, and then go back to the beginning of the instructions in the brackets and execute each instruction, in order, again. The effect of the REPEAT command, when the turtle starts from the home position, can be seen in **Figure 9–15**. The same effect could have been achieved by typing in each command, one at a time, in the following manner:

```
FD 70
RT 90
FD 35
RT 90
FD 70
RT 90
FD 35
RT 90
```

The REPEAT command is a powerful way to draw figures in Logo, saving the need to individually code long series of repetitive commands. The benefits of the REPEAT command will become apparent as you work with it in designing various drawings.

Command	*Description*	*Example*
REPEAT	Repeats the series of commands within the brackets whatever number of times is specified.	REPEAT 4 [FD 50 RT 90]

Table 9–3

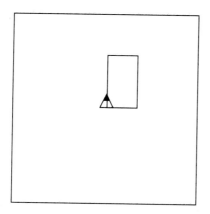

Figure 9–15 The above shape is drawn as a result of entering the command REPEAT 2 [FD 70 RT 90 FD 35 RT 90].

![Computer icon] ## Computers in the Classroom

Once students have learned a few Logo commands and can draw simple shapes such as a box, triangle, or circle, they can use these (and other) figures to create more involved drawings. Suppose a figure is drawn so that the turtle ends up in the same location as when it started. For example, the following instructions are used to draw a square:

```
FD 50
RT 90
FD 50
RT 90
FD 50
RT 90
FD 50
RT 90
```

The last command, RT 90, is not absolutely necessary to complete the figure, but it serves the purpose of returning the turtle to the exact location it was in when it started to draw the square. Using the REPEAT command in the following way will have the same effect.

```
REPEAT 4 [FD 50 RT 90]
```

Once the figure is drawn, if the turtle is rotated to the right (or left) some amount and the figure is drawn again, an interesting design begins to form. This process of drawing a figure, rotating the turtle right (or left), and drawing the figure again can be repeated a number of times. One way to do this is shown below. Entering the following commands will produce the figure shown:

```
REPEAT 4 [FD 50 RT 90]
RT 60
REPEAT 4 [FD 50 RT 90]
RT 60
REPEAT 4 [FD 50 RT 90]
RT 60
REPEAT 4 [FD 50 RT 90]
RT 60
REPEAT 4 [FD 50 RT 90]
RT 60
REPEAT 4 [FD 50 RT 90]
RT 60
```

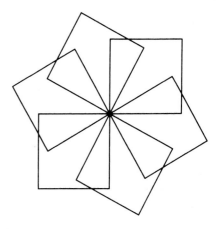

A shorter way to do this would be to nest one REPEAT command within another. The effect of the following instruction will be the same as the instruction above.

A square will be drawn and then the turtle will be rotated sixty degrees to the right; this will be repeated six times.

REPEAT 6 [REPEAT 4 [FD 50 RT 90] RT 60]

Of course, this type of drawing can be created from any figure, not just a square. Try the instructions above and then experiment with other figures.

Once students have created designs (any designs), their creations can be used as vehicles for practice in expressing themselves. Have students write a description of their favorite design. If a printer is available, a copy of the design can be printed and posted on a bulletin board along with the written description. Another option is to set up an activity center by the computer. A set of descriptions of designs, without accompanying pictures, can be posted. The students, who have never seen the original pictures, are challenged to choose a description and write the Logo instructions that will produce the design described. After they have completed the project, their picture can be compared with the original.

EXERCISES

1. Enter the following REPEAT command:

    REPEAT 4 [FD 80 RT 90 FD 40 RT 90]

    What shape is drawn? Change the number specified to eight. What happens?

2. Clear the screen. Enter the command given in number 1, then move the turtle forward some number of turtle steps (you decide how many), and then enter the command given above again. What happens?

3. Using the REPEAT command, draw any size circle.

4. Using REPEAT, and other commands as necessary, draw the figures below. Hint: As you first look at a figure you are going to draw, try to find a figure within it that may be drawn using the REPEAT command (such as a rectangle in the first figure). Next, determine how to write a REPEAT command to draw the smaller figure of which the total figure is comprised. Once you have done this you can draw the entire figure by using the REPEAT command you wrote, moving (or rotating) the turtle to the position on the screen where you want to draw the figure next, again using the REPEAT command you discovered, moving (or rotating) the turtle again, and so on until the entire figure is drawn.

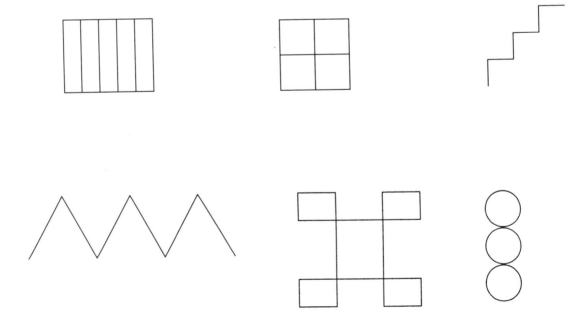

Reactions and Research

As noted in the Reactions and Research section of Chapter 8, the research on Logo is not conclusive. Some take a pessimistic view of the indications from the research, while others adopt a more optimistic view. Presented here are excerpts from two articles. The first, by Ginther and Williamson (1985), offers a highly critical view of both the methodology used in some of the research on Logo and the findings as they relate to Papert's theory. The second, by Vaidya and McKeeby (1985) is more optimistic. The fact that these two selections seem to contradict each other is an indication of the somewhat contradictory state of hard empirical evidence on Logo as it affects children. As research on any theory progresses, it is usual that researchers discuss and debate their different findings and interpretations of findings in their search for the reality of the situation.

Based on the review of these existing data-based studies, what can be concluded regarding the current state of knowledge regarding the possible outcomes of learning Logo? First, after nearly 20 years since the development of Logo, there is little empirical evidence concerning the effects, positive or otherwise, of teaching Logo to children. If Logo continues to be introduced into classrooms across the United States, it will not be a result of the large body of "hard" evidence which supports the benefits of teaching Logo. Secondly, several of the existing data-based studies have selected as dependent measures tasks that have but the thinnest of rationale for their selection. For example, Statz (1973) selected four problem-solving tasks (word puzzle, permutation, Tower of Hanoi, and horserace); while Gorman and Bourne (1983) preferred a fourfold rule learning task. It appears as if these researchers randomly selected tasks generally regarded as requiring problem-solving abilities but which have no direct connection to the activities involved in learning Logo. This lack of logical clarity in the selection of dependent measures can be directly traced to Papert's rather broad and vague assertions regarding the benefits of teaching Logo to children. In contrast to Papert's claims, decades of research on problem solving, with both animal and human subjects, has shown that transfer of general problem-solving skills is difficult to achieve. There is no reason to believe that Logo offers a magical exception to this well-supported generalization.

Current research concerning Logo should be more directly tied to outcomes that are related to learning a structured computer language, such as the child's use and understanding of variables, conditional statements, procedures, iteration, and recursion (see Pea & Kurland, 1983a). The authors are currently conducting research employing such dependent measures. Children's understandings of these fundamental concepts form the basis for the execution of more advanced problem-solving skills in Logo. If these basic cognitive outcomes cannot be documented, attention to more complex problem-solving outcomes ap-

pears superfluous. Finally, it might be suggested that the most significant outcomes of learning Logo are not along the logical-analytical dimension, but rather exist in the personal-social sphere. Persistence in response to frustration, articulate communication, recognition of the need for assistance balanced with appropriate independence, cooperation and sharing of resources with peers, attention to detail, and following directions are outcomes along the personal-social dimension that are suggested by observation of children involved in learning Logo. Once again, however, there is little research to support this speculation. Research concerning the outcomes of learning Logo will require investigators that understand both developmental, cognitive, and social psychology as well as the essential elements of computer science.

REFERENCES

Bandelier, N. (1982). TI Logo and first graders—A winning combination. *The Computing Teacher, 10*(3), 38–39.

Gorman, H., & Bourne, L. E. (1983). Learning to think by learning Logo: Rule learning in third-grade computer programmers. *Bulletin of Psychonomic Society, 21*, 165–167.

Harvey, B. (1982). Why Logo? *Byte, 7*(8), 163–195.

Lawler, R. W. (1982). Designing computer based microworlds. *Byte, 7*(8), 138–160.

Papert, S. (1980). *Mindstorms: Children, computers and powerful ideas.* New York: Basic Books.

Piaget, J. (1971). *The science of education and the psychology of the child.* New York: Viking Press.

Pea, R. D. (1983). *Logo programming and problem solving* (Technical Report No. 12). New York: Bank Street College of Education, Center for Children and Technology.

Pea, R. D., & Kurland, D. M. (1983a). *On the cognitive effects of learning computer programming* (Technical Report No. 9). New York: Bank Street College of Education, Center for Children and Technology.

Pea, R. D., & Kurland, D. M. (1983b). *Children's mental models of recursive Logo programming* (Technical Report No. 10). New York: Bank Street College of Education, Center for Children and Technology.

Pea, R. D., & Kurland, D. M. (1983c). *On the cognitive prerequisites of learning computer programming* (Technical Report No. 18). New York: Bank Street College of Education, Center for Children and Technology.

Pea, R. D., & Kurland, D. M. (1984). *Logo programming and the development of planning skills* (Technical Report No. 16). New York: Bank Street College of Education, Center for Children and Technology.

Ross, P., & Howe, J. (1981). Teaching mathematics through programming: Ten years on. In R. Lewis & D. Tagg (Eds.), *Computers in education.* Amsterdam, Holland: North Holland-Amsterdam.

Solomon, C. (1982). Introducing Logo to children. *Byte, 7*(8), 196–208.

Statz, J. A. (1973). *The development of computer programming concepts and problem solving abilities among ten-year-olds*

Learning Logo. Unpublished doctoral dissertation, Syracuse University, Syracuse, NY.

Watt, D. (1982). Logo in the schools: Putting Logo in the classroom has led to some interesting results. *Byte, 7*(8), 116–134.

Weir, S., Russel, S., & Valente, J. A. (1982). Logo: An approach to educating disabled children. *Byte, 7*(9), 346–360.

Wierzbicki, B. (1984, January 23). The success of Logo hinges on teacher training. *InfoWorld*, pp. 50–51.

(Ginther and Williamson, 1985)

The second selection offers an appreciably different view.

Our work with Logo (Vaidya, 1983; Vaidya & McKeeby, 1984) and that of others has demonstrated that by using a developmentally appropriate language such as Logo, children can actually design computer programs to solve real problems and acquire knowledge that is transferable to other areas such as reading, communication, mathematics, and reading skills. Furthermore, we have shown that the knowledge and concepts the children encounter during their interactions with the computer are transferable to their everyday experiences (Vaidya & McKeeby, 1984). In addition to the computer's potential to enable children to understand the world by giving them power to control and manipulate important features of a microworld, we have shown how the computer can be used to encourage and promote effective communication and collaborative strategies among individual kindergarten children (McKeeby, 1984). These studies demonstrate that Logo can be a powerful medium for preschool children to use in developing knowledge and building models about the world.

At the present, we are conducting a longitudinal study investigating the long-term effects of learning Logo. Preliminary findings of this study show that the children demonstrate a continuity in the development of concepts over time and are able to learn simple programming skills.

However, we need more data and are awaiting results of the study to determine the systematic conceptual effects of Logo learning on thought development. Furthermore, other questions arise from our investigations: What are the mind-altering effects of programming skills for young children? How will these experiences affect other learning? Or, do the children merely see the computer as providing fun and enjoyable activities that need not transfer to other areas of learning? Many of these questions may be answered by further research.

REFERENCES

Cooper, C. (1980). Development of collaborative problem solving among preschool children. *Developmental Psychology, 16*(1), 96–100.

Garvey, C., & Hogan, R. (1983). Social speech and social interaction: Egocentrism revisited. *Child Development, 44*(2), 562–568.

Maddus, C. D. (1984). Educational microcomputing: The need for research. *Computers in the Schools, 1*(1), 35–41.

McKeeby, J. (1984). *The communication styles of preschool children engaged in collaborative problem solving using Logo.* Unpublished master's thesis, Drexel University, Philadelphia, PA.

Rubens, T. M., Poole, J., & Hoot, J. L. (1984, Spring). Introducing microcomputers to microlearners through play. *Daycare and Early Education*, pp. 29–31.

Steg, D., Vaidya, S., & Hamdan, P. (1982). A longitudinal analysis of early intervention through technology. *Journal of Educational Technology Systems, 11*(3), 203–214.

Vaidya, S. (1983). Using Logo to stimulate children's fantasy. *Educational Technology, 23*(12), 25–26.

Vaidya, S., & McKeeby, J. (1984). Conceptual problems encountered by children while learning Logo. *Journal of Educational Technology Systems, 13*(1), 33–39.

Watt, D. (1983). *Learning with Logo.* New York: McGraw-Hill.

(Vaidya and McKeeby, 1985)

Conclusion

This chapter has introduced a series of Logo commands as a beginning in working with the language. Chapter 10 offers additional commands, concepts, and exercises designed to increase your understanding of Logo.

Key Terms

cursor
MIT Logo
turtle steps

Logo commands
BACK (BK)
CLEARSCREEN (CS)

DRAW		RIGHT	(RT)
FORWARD	(FD)	SHOWTURTLE	(ST)
FULLSCREEN	(CTRL-F)	SPLITSCREEN	(CTRL-S)
HIDETURTLE	(HT)	TEXTSCREEN	(CTRL-T)
HOME			
LEFT	(LT)	To Edit	
NODRAW		CTRL-D	
PENDOWN	(PD)	CTRL-K	
PENUP	(PU)	ESC	
PRINT			
REPEAT			

References/Further Reading

Abelson, Harold. *Apple Logo.* New York: McGraw-Hill, 1982.

———. *Logo for the Apple II.* New York: McGraw-Hill, 1982.

Beardon, Donna, et al. *The Turtle Sourcebook.* Reston, Va.: Reston Publishing Co., 1983.

Billstein, Rick, Shlomo Libeskind, and Johnny Lott. *Logo: MIT Logo for the Apple.* Menlo Park, Calif.: Benjamin/Cummings, 1985.

Bitter, Gary, and Nancy Watson. *Apple Logo Primer.* Reston, Va.: Reston Publishing Co., 1983.

———. *Commodore 64 Logo Primer.* Reston, Va.: Reston Publishing Co., 1983.

Brady, Holly. "Hang On to the Power to Imagine: An Interview with Joseph Weizenbaum." *Classroom Computer Learning* 6, no. 3 (1985):24–27.

Burnett, Dale. *Logo: An Introduction for Teachers.* Morris Plains, N.J.: Creative Computing Press, 1982.

Ginther, Dean W., and James D. Williamson. "Learning Logo: What Is Really Learned?" In *Logo in the Schools*, edited by Cleborne D. Maddus. New York: Haworth Press, 1985, 76–78.

Ross, Peter. *Introducing Logo.* Menlo Park, Calif.: Addison-Wesley, 1983.

Vaidya, Sheila, and John McKeeby. "Developing a Logo Environment in the Preschool." In *Logo in the Schools*, edited by Cleborne D. Maddus. New York: Haworth Press, 1985, 88–89.

Watt, Daniel. *Learning with Logo.* New York: McGraw-Hill, 1983.

———. *Learning with Apple Logo.* New York: McGraw-Hill, 1983.

———. *Learning with Commodore Logo.* New York: McGraw-Hill, 1984.

10

Logo: Expanding the Possibilities

TOPICS ADDRESSED

How are procedures created in Logo? What is the editor, and how does it work?

What is working memory, or workspace? How is working memory used? What commands are used to see what is in working memory and to erase procedures?

How may the procedures in working memory be saved to disk? How may files be read from disk? How may files be erased from disk?

What are subprocedures?

What is recursion? How are recursive procedures written?

How can a printer be used with Logo?

What might be one beneficial way to plan a Logo project? Should this type of approach always be followed?

What types of learning styles might students exhibit when working with Logo? What can the teacher do to help children work successfully with Logo?

What are some attributes of Logo not covered in this introduction?

OUTLINE

Introduction
Procedures
    What Is a Procedure?
    Creating Procedures
    Edit Commands
    More on Procedures
    Exercises
Managing Logo
    Working Memory
    Saving Procedures

    Reading Files
    Exercises
Subprocedures
    Exercises
Recursion
    Exercises
Teaching Logo
Conclusion
Key Terms
References/Further Reading

The information in this chapter builds on the material presented in Chapters 8 and 9, to expand your knowledge of Logo. Several new commands and concepts are introduced. As with any programming language, the more commands and programming concepts a user understands, the more power the user will have within the language.

Procedures

What Is a Procedure?

In the work on Logo covered so far, entering a Logo command has caused the computer to do, immediately, whatever the Logo command instructed. For instance, if the turtle started in the home position on a clear screen and the instruction

```
FD 30
```

was entered, the turtle would go forward thirty turtle steps and leave a line on the screen (see **Figure 10–1**). If next the turtle was given the command

```
RT 90
```

the turtle would immediately rotate in place ninety degrees to the right.

Assume once again that the turtle starts in the home position on a clear screen. If the following instructions were entered one after another, a rectangle would be drawn on the screen (see **Figure 10–2**).

```
FD 30
RT 90
FD 50
RT 90
FD 30
RT 90
FD 50
RT 90
```

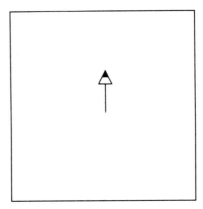

Figure 10–1 In the immediate execution mode, the turtle immediately carries out any instruction it is given.

*"Oh, we finished the basic subtraction. Now we're designing
a series of inter-related transformational geometric
comparisons!"*

It is not necessary to type in all the commands shown above every time a
rectangle needs to be drawn. In Logo it is possible to create procedures.
Procedures are named groups of commands. The programmer specifies a set of
commands and a name by which the commands will be known to Logo. For
instance, the series of Logo commands needed to draw a rectangle could be
given a name, perhaps REC. Anytime REC was typed in, all of the commands
associated with it would be executed. The effect, in this case, would be to

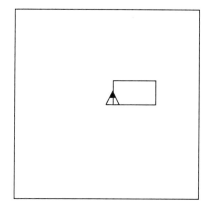

Figure 10–2 If the commands to draw a rectangle, FD 30 RT 90 FD 50 RT 90 FD 30 RT 90 FD 50 RT
90, are entered a rectangle will be drawn.

draw a rectangle on the computer screen. An example of how procedures are defined in Logo will best illustrate.

Creating Procedures

Once the name of the procedure and the set of commands that Logo will associate with that name are known, type TO, followed by the name to be used for the procedure. For example, to create the procedure REC, first type

```
TO REC
```

This will cause Logo to place you in the EDIT mode. It is in the EDIT mode, or editor, that the commands associated with the procedure will be entered. **Figure 10–3** shows the command TO REC entered and the result. At the top of the screen appears TO and the name of the procedure. At the bottom of the screen is a line stating that Logo is in EDIT and giving two ways that EDIT may be exited (CTRL-C and CTRL-G). (More will be said about these two commands shortly.) The central portion of the screen is blank. In this area the commands that will define the procedure REC will be entered. Commands entered while in EDIT will not be executed immediately. Their execution is deferred until after the procedure has been created. Once the procedure is created, the commands associated with the procedure may be executed by typing the name of the procedure. As this example continues we will first enter the commands for the procedure REC and then define the procedure to Logo. Lastly, we will execute the procedure.

Notice in Figure 10–3 that, once in EDIT, the cursor is on the first blank line on the screen. It is at this point that commands may be typed. **Figure 10–4** shows the result of typing the first command, FD 30, and pressing RETURN. The RETURN key must be pressed after a command has been typed. This causes the cursor to proceed to the next line so that the next command may be typed. In this way all the remaining lines may be entered: type a command,

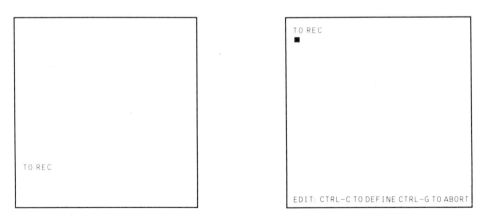

Figure 10–3 On the left, the command TO REC is entered. The result, on the right, is EDIT mode. The name of the procedure appears at top. At bottom is a prompt to remind the user that pressing CTRL–C will define the procedure, pressing CTRL–G will abort the edit.

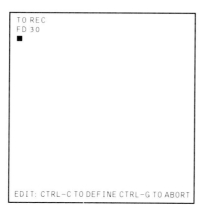

Figure 10–4 The screen after entering the first command, FD 30, for the procedure REC.

press RETURN, type another command, press RETURN, and so on. After all the commands that will define the procedure REC have been entered, the command END is entered as the last line of the procedure. When the procedure executes, Logo will execute each line within the procedure. When Logo encounters the command END, it will serve as a signal that all the lines in the procedure have been executed and the procedure is finished.

Now that the procedure is typed in, the next step is to define the procedure to Logo. By pressing CTRL-C (pressing the CTRL key, holding it down, and then simultaneously pressing the C key), the procedure will be defined to Logo and the editor will be exited. A short message will appear on the screen, noting that the procedure has been defined. **Figure 10–5** shows how the screen will appear after pressing CTRL-C. From this point on all the commands associated with the procedure REC can be executed by typing in the procedure name REC. **Figure 10–6** shows what happens when REC is entered.

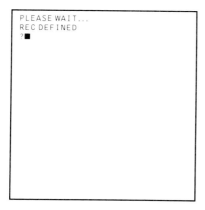

Figure 10–5 The screen as it appears after pressing CTRL–C from the editor to define the procedure REC.

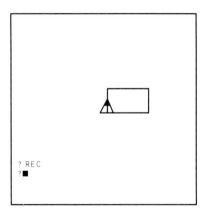

Figure 10–6 Entering REC, causes the instructions defined in the procedure REC to be executed.

If, while still in the editor, it is desirable to exit the editor without defining the procedure to Logo, this can be accomplished by pressing CTRL-G.

Edit Commands

When entering commands in the editor, sometimes it is necessary to delete and retype text. It may also be necessary to insert new lines. Logo provides a number of editing commands to help accomplish this. Three of these commands were introduced in Chapter 9: ESC, CTRL-K, and CTRL-D. These work the same way in the editor as they do outside the editor.

Three additional commands are of value in moving the cursor while in the editor. CTRL-P will cause the cursor to move up one line. CTRL-N will cause the cursor to move down one line. CTRL-O causes a new blank line to be inserted at the cursor location.

More on Procedures

The ability to create procedures in Logo is one of the things that makes Logo a powerful programming language. By creating procedures, a programmer is essentially creating new Logo commands. Logo comes with a certain number of commands already defined (FD, RT, LT, etc.). These are called Logo primitives. Creating new procedures extends the number of commands available in Logo and allows individuals to tailor the language to their needs. Procedures also encourage students to modularize their problem solving.

To create a procedure, it is often helpful to first work out the Logo commands that will make up the procedure. If the object was to create a procedure that drew a square, it would be beneficial to first experiment in the DRAW mode and find the series of commands that drew the desired square. Next, decide on the name for the procedure. If possible, it is good to make the name of the procedure descriptive of what the procedure does (i.e., SQUARE for a procedure that draws a square, HOUSE for a procedure that draws a house). At this point the procedure should be typed in and defined to Logo. Lastly, the procedure should be tested to see if it works as expected. If it is necessary to change

```
TO LEAF
HT
FD 10
LT 45
REPEAT 30 [FD 1 RT 3]
RT 90
REPEAT 30 [FD 1 RT 3]
RT 135
BK 10
END
```

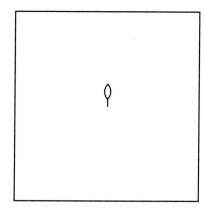

Figure 10-7 The commands above define the procedure LEAF, which will draw the figure shown.

the procedure, simply type TO, followed by a space and then the name of the procedure. This will present the procedure as it currently exists and place Logo in the edit mode. The procedure could then be changed as desired, defined to Logo in its new form by pressing CTRL-C, and tested again.

Figure 10–7 is an example of another procedure. This one is named LEAF. The commands that constitute the procedure are shown on the left, and the result of executing the procedure is shown on the right.

EXERCISES

1. Create a procedure to draw a long, thin rectangle.

2. Create a procedure to draw a triangle.

3. Create a procedure to draw any shape of your choice.

4. Look at the procedure given in Figure 10–7 to draw a leaf. Modify that procedure to draw a larger leaf. Modify it again to draw a smaller leaf.

Command	Description	Example
TO	Places Logo in the EDIT mode for the procedure name specified. Allows creation of the procedure specified by typing CTRL-C.	TO REC
ESC	Erases the first letter to the left of the cursor.	ESC
CTRL-D	Erases the letter under the cursor.	CTRL-D
CTRL-K	Erases the rest of the line from the current position of the cursor on.	CTRL-K
CTRL-P	In the editor, moves the cursor to the previous line.	CTRL-P
CTRL-N	In the editor, moves the cursor to the next line.	CTRL-N
CTRL-O	In the editor, opens a new line.	CTRL-O

Table 10–1

5. Create a procedure to draw a small circle. Modify it to draw a large circle.

6. Create one procedure for each of the figures below.

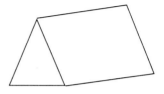

Managing Logo

Working Memory

When working in Logo the computer reserves an area in its memory where all of the procedures created are kept under their respective names. Think of this as a workspace or working memory in which the computer keeps procedures. To see a list of the titles of all procedures that are in the working memory at a given time, use the command POTS (this stands for print out titles). This command is effective in either the DRAW or the NODRAW mode. If entered while in DRAW, the titles may scroll up under the graphics portion of the screen. If this happens, just use CTRL-T to go to the textscreen, view the titles, and then use CTRL-S to return to the splitscreen, as covered in Chapter 9.

It is also possible to print out on the screen the commands that define a given procedure currently in working memory. By entering the command PO, followed by the name of the procedure desired, the commands that define the specified procedure will be printed on the screen. For example, to print out the procedure REC, the following command would be entered

```
PO REC
```

After this command was entered, the procedure would be printed on the screen as follows:

```
TO REC
FD 30
RT 90
FD 50
RT 90
FD 30
RT 90
FD 50
RT 90
END
```

To print out all the titles and associated commands for every procedure currently in working memory, the command PO ALL is used.

Sometimes it is of value to erase a procedure from working memory. An individual procedure may be erased from working memory by entering the ERASE command, followed by the name of the procedure to be erased. The command

```
ERASE HOUSE
```

would cause the procedure named HOUSE to be erased from working memory.

The command ERASE ALL would cause all of the procedures in working memory to be erased. The command GOODBYE will erase all procedures and restart Logo.

In virtually all microcomputers currently available, computer memory where work is stored is volatile, meaning that when the computer is turned off, the work stored in the computer's memory is lost. It would not be practical to have to type in Logo procedures every time they needed to be used. For this reason, procedures may be saved to disk for use at a later time. A basic discussion of disk drives is given in Chapter 2. To be able to save Logo procedures to disk, an initialized (formatted) disk is needed. The procedures given in Appendix C may be used to format a disk for use with Krell Logo on Apple II series microcomputers.

To save the procedures in working memory to disk, be sure to first have an initialized disk in the disk drive. The command

> Saving Procedures

```
SAVE "filename
```

will save a copy of all the procedures in working memory to the disk under the filename specified. The filename is chosen by the programmer. (The quote mark is part of the command.) Note that all of the procedures in working memory at the time the SAVE command is issued are saved under the name specified. For example, if there were four procedures in working memory—SQUARE, TRI, REC, and HOUSE—and the command

```
SAVE "MYPROCS
```

was entered, a copy of all four procedures would be saved to the disk under the filename MYPROCS. The file created, MYPROCS, is analogous to having a paper file folder labeled MYPROCS that contains four pieces of paper. On each piece of paper would be one of the four procedures. **Figure 10–8** shows this concept.

To see the names of the files stored on the disk, use the command CATA-LOG. This will cause a list of the filenames currently stored on the disk to be printed on the screen. The list might look like this:

```
A 002 HELLO
B 002 MYPROCS.LOGO
B 002 IGLOO.LOGO
B 003 CLOWN.LOGO
```

The first column identifies the file type, the second column shows how much space the file takes up, and the third column gives the name of the file. The first file in the list was created when the disk was initialized. The A denotes that it is an Applesoft Basic file. The 002 refers to the fact that the file takes up two sectors worth of space (a sector is an amount of space that the computer divides the disk into when the disk is initialized). The name of the file is HELLO.

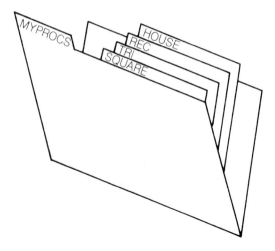

Figure 10–8 The file MYPROCS contains the procedures HOUSE, REC, TRI, and SQUARE.

All of the other files on this disk are Logo files. The B means that the files are binary files. The numbers tell how much space each file takes up, in sectors. Notice that the computer has automatically added .LOGO to each Logo file name to denote that it is a Logo file.

Reading Files

Once a file is stored on disk, a copy of it may be read back into the computer's memory by using the READ command. The format of the READ command is

READ "filename

The programmer specifies the name of the file to be read into memory. For example, to read the file MYPROCS into memory, the following command would be entered:

READ "MYPROCS

Once the file is in the computer's memory, the procedures that are contained in the file may be worked with, edited, or executed, as the programmer wishes.

It is also possible to erase files from the disk. The command

ERASEFILE "filename

will erase the filename specified from the disk. To erase a file named TEDDY from the disk, the command ERASEFILE "TEDDY would be entered.

Being able to save, read, and erase files from disk is of great value when working in Logo. It is of obvious benefit to be able to save completed procedures for future use and for sharing with others. It is also beneficial, when working on longer Logo projects, to be able to save work completed to date, turn off the computer, and then return later to continue work.

Input/Output

In her book The Second Self: Computers and the Human Spirit, *Sherry Turkle examines the new computer culture, at all levels, from the perspective of a humanist. Here she relates an interesting observation of second graders interacting with Logo. The school, which she calls Austen, was involved in a research project dealing with computer education. The sprites referred to are available in some versions of Logo.*

When children learn to program, one of their favorite areas of work is computer graphics—programming the machine to place displays on the screen. The Logo graphics system available at Austen was relatively powerful. It provided thirty-two computational objects called sprites that appear on the screen when commanded to do so. Each sprite has a number. When called by its number and given a color and shape, it comes onto the screen with that shape and color: a red truck, a blue ball, a green airplane. Children can manipulate one sprite at a time, several of them, or all of them at once, depending on the effect they want to achieve. The sprites can take predefined shapes, such as trucks and airplanes, or they can be given new shapes designed on a special grid, a sprite "scratchpad." They can be given a speed and a direction and be set in motion. The direction is usually specified in terms of a heading from 0 to 360, where 0 would point the sprite due north, 90 would point it due east, 180 south, 270 west, and 360 north again.

At the time the system was introduced, the teachers thought the manipulation of headings would be too complex for second graders because it involves the concept of angles, so these children were introduced to the commands for making sprites appear, giving them shapes and colors, and placing them on the screen, but not for setting them in motion. Motion would be saved for later grades.

The curriculum held for two weeks. That is, it held until one second grader, Gary, caught on to the fact that something exciting was happening on the older children's screens, and knew enough to pick up the trick from a proud and talkative third grader. In one sense, the teachers were right: Gary didn't understand that what he was dealing with were "angles." He didn't have to. He wanted to make the computer do something, and he found a way to assimilate the concept of angle to something he already knew—secret

codes. "The sprites have secret codes, like 10, 100, 55. And if you give them their codes they go in different directions. I've taught the code to fourteen second graders," he confided to a visitor. "We're sort of keeping it a secret. The teachers don't know. We haven't figured out all the codes yet, but we're working on it." Two weeks later, Gary and his friends were still cracking the code. "We're still not sure about the big numbers" (sprites interpret 361 as 1, one full revolution plus 1), but they were feeling very pleased with themselves.

Gary's discovery, not the only one of its kind, contributed to creating a general pattern at Austen. Students felt that computer knowledge belonged to them and not only to the teachers. Once knowledge had become forbidden fruit, once appropriation of it had become a personal challenge, teachers could no longer maintain their position as the rationers of "curricular materials." In a setting like Austen, ideas about programming travel the way ideas travel in active, dynamic cultures. They sweep through, carried by children who discover something, often by chance, through playful exploration of the machine.

Gary and his fellow decoders finally presented their discoveries to the authorities with pride of authorship. At Austen programming tricks and completed programs are valued—they are traded and they become gifts. In traditional school settings, finished book reports are presented to teachers who try to instill a sense of the class as community by asking the children to read them aloud to the group. In the context of children and programming projects, the sharing usually happens naturally. Children can't do much with each other's book reports, but they can do a great deal with each other's programs. Another child's program can be changed, new features can be added, it can be personalized. (One child can figure out how to get the computer to engage in a "dialogue," but a second child can change the script; one child can figure out how to write a program that will display an animated drawing of a rocket going to the moon, but a second child can build on it and have the rocket orbit once it gets there.) Most objects can't be given away and kept at the same time. But computer programs are easily shared, copied from one child's personal storage disk or cassette to that of another. As the child experiences it, the originator of the program gets to be famous. And other people get to build on his or her ideas.

(Turkle, 1984)

EXERCISES

1. Create any three procedures of your choice, either procedures you have worked with before or new procedures of your own design. After your procedures are tested (and without turning the machine off), go through the following in order. You will need an initialized disk, which should be in the disk drive as you work through the list below.

   ■ Print out the titles of your procedures.

   ■ Choose one procedure and print it out on the screen.

Command	Description	Example
POTS	Causes the titles of all the procedures in working memory to be printed on the screen	POTS
PO	Prints on the screen the procedure specified or all the procedures in working memory if ALL is specified	PO REC PO ALL
ERASE	Erases the procedure specified from working memory	ERASE BUNNY
GOODBYE	Clears working memory of all procedures and restarts Logo	GOODBYE
SAVE "filename	Saves all procedures in working memory to disk under the filename specified	SAVE "AUTO
CATALOG	Displays a listing of all files on disk	CATALOG
READ "filename	Reads the file specified by filename into working memory	READ "AUTO
ERASEFILE "filename	Erases the file specified by filename from disk	ERASEFILE "AUTO

Table 10–2

- Print out all the procedures in working memory.

- Save your procedures to disk under a name of your choice.

- Check to see the names of the files stored on your disk.

- Choose one procedure and erase it from working memory.

- Print out the titles of all procedures in working memory. Is the procedure you erased gone?

- Clear the working memory and restart Logo using only one command.

- Try to print out, on the screen, the titles of any procedures in working memory. What happens?

- Read into working memory the file you saved on disk.

- Go into DRAW mode and test your procedures.

- Erase the file that you created on the disk. Check to see that it was really erased. (You may want to save the file again before turning the machine off.)

Subprocedures

A procedure may contain within it, as a Logo command, another procedure. When a procedure is used as a command within a procedure, it is called a subprocedure. Suppose there is a procedure called BOX that draws a box on the screen. The procedure consists of the following:

```
TO BOX
REPEAT 4 [FD 30 RT 90]
END
```

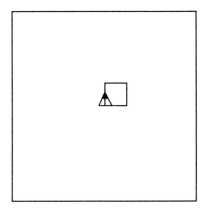

```
TO BOX
REPEAT 4 [FD 30 RT 90]
END
```

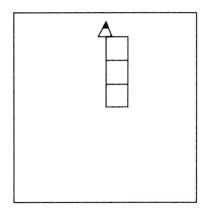

```
TO STACK
REPEAT 3 [BOX FD 30]
END
```

Figure 10–9 The procedure BOX is shown on the left. The procedure STACK, shown on the right, uses BOX as a subprocedure.

This procedure can be used within another procedure, as a subprocedure. To create the procedure STACK, which would draw a stack of three boxes on the screen, the procedure BOX might be used as a subprocedure, as shown below.

```
TO STACK
REPEAT 3 [BOX FD 30]
END
```

Figure 10–9 shows the results of the procedure BOX and the procedure STACK, where BOX is used as a subprocedure. Notice that in the procedure BOX, the turtle is left, at the completion of drawing a box, in the same position in which it started. Knowing where the turtle will be left each time a procedure is executed helps in planning how to use that procedure as a subprocedure. Because it is known where the turtle will be after BOX is executed, it is a simple matter to plan to move the turtle forward thirty turtle steps (the length of one side of the box) to position the turtle where it needs to be before drawing the next box in the STACK procedure.

Figure 10–10 is another example of a subprocedure. The procedure TRI is used to create a triangle. By using TRI as a subprocedure in the procedure PINWHEEL, a pinwheel can be easily constructed.

Figure 10–11 is another example. The procedure LEAF (which was presented in Figure 10–7) is used as a subprocedure in the procedure IVY, while the procedure IVY is used as a subprocedure in the procedure MANYIVY. Building multiple levels of subprocedures in this way is often beneficial when working on Logo projects.

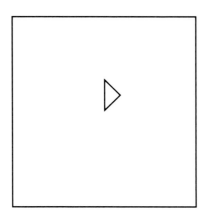

```
TO TRI          TO PINWHEEL
HT              REPEAT 4 [TRI RT 90]
FD 70           END
RT 135
FD 50
RT 90
FD 50
RT 135
END
```

Figure 10–10 The procedure TRI, on the left, is used as a subprocedure to create the procedure PINWHEEL on the right.

```
TO IVY                  TO MANYIVY      LT 90
REPEAT 6 [LEAF RT 60]   PU              PD
END                     LT 90           IVY
                        FD 95           PU
                        RT 90           RT 90
                        PD              FD 95
                        IVY             LT 90
                        PU              PD
                        RT 90           IVY
                        FD 95           END
```

Figure 10–11 The procedure LEAF (which was introduced in Figure 10–7) is used as a subprocedure to create the procedure IVY on the left. The procedure IVY is used as a subprocedure to create the procedure MANYIVY shown on the right.

EXERCISES

1. Create a procedure BOX and a procedure CIRCLE. Use these two procedures as sub-procedures in a procedure you create that will draw the following:

2. Create a procedure TRI to draw a triangle. Using the procedure TRI and the procedure BOX (from number 1) as subprocedures, create the drawing below.

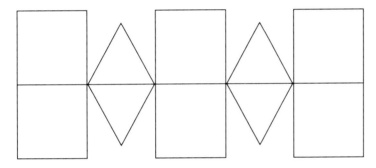

3. Use the procedures BOX and TRI as subprocedures to create a procedure to draw the following shape:

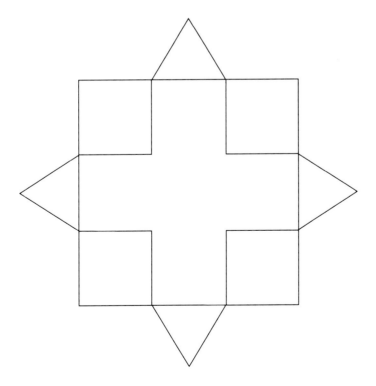

4. For each of the drawings below do the following:

- Select the basic shape of which the drawing is made up (the shape that is repeated a number of times).
- Write a procedure to draw that shape.
- Use the procedure you created as a subprocedure in the new procedure you create to reproduce the entire drawing.

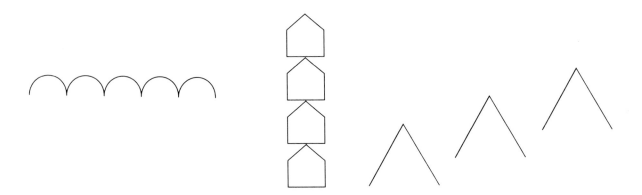

5. Use procedures and subprocedures to create the procedure HOUSES, which will produce the following drawing:

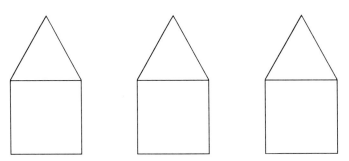

Recursion

One way to have one or more commands repeat is to use the REPEAT command. Another way to cause commands to repeat is through the use of recursion. When a procedure calls itself, uses itself as a subprocedure, it is said to be a recursive procedure. Recursion is one of the most powerful attributes Logo offers as a programming language. Although a full discussion of recursion is beyond the scope of these introductory chapters, a few examples will serve to introduce the concept as the basis for some experiments with recursion.

Suppose the procedure given in **Figure 10–12** is used to draw a tilted box on the screen, as shown. If the command TILTBOX is added at the end of the procedure, if TILTBOX is used as a subprocedure of itself, the effect of the now recursive procedure is very different, as shown in **Figure 10–13**. What happens in the recursive procedure is that each command is executed and the first tilted box is drawn on the screen. When Logo encounters the TILTBOX command at

```
TO TILTBOX
HT
RT 30
REPEAT 4 [FD 30 RT 90]
END
```

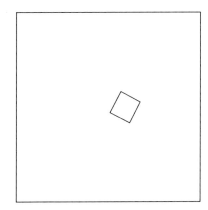

Figure 10–12 The procedure TILTBOX.

```
TO TILTBOX
HT
RT 30
REPEAT 4 [FD 30 RT 90]
TILTBOX
END
```

Figure 10–13 The recursive procedure TILTBOX.

the end of the series of commands, the entire procedure begins to execute again. The first command in the procedure is executed, then the next, and so on. This causes a second tilted box to be drawn on the screen in a new location. Again the command TILTBOX is encountered and again the entire procedure repeats, causing a third box to be drawn on the screen in yet a new location. This process continues indefinitely, theoretically infinitely, since there is no mechanism in this recursive procedure to stop the repetition. In fact, once the entire figure has been drawn on the screen, the turtle will just continue to retrace all the boxes again and again unless CTRL-G is pressed. This will cause Logo to break out of the recursive procedure. (It is possible to control the number of repetitions of a recursive procedure with commands within the procedure, although that won't be covered here. What is important for now is that a feeling for the power and the possible effects of recursion be gained.)

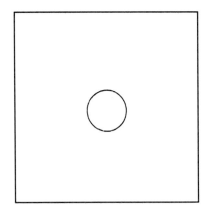

```
TO MYCIRCLE
HT
RT 45
REPEAT 90 [FD 1 RT 4]
END
```

```
TO MYCIRCLE
HT
RT 45
REPEAT 90 [FD 1 RT 4]
MYCIRCLE
END
```

Figure 10–14 On the left, the procedure MYCIRCLE is presented. On the right, MYCIRCLE has been made into a recursive procedure.

Figure 10–14 shows another example of recursion. The procedure MYCIRCLE and its result are shown at left. On the right, MYCIRCLE has been made into a recursive procedure and the result shown. Notice, in the original MYCIRCLE procedure, that the turtle is rotated to the right before the circle is drawn. If this was not done, when MYCIRCLE was made into a recursive procedure it would just continue to draw the same circle over and over again.

EXERCISES

1. For each of the shapes below, write a recursive procedure that will draw the shape. (Hint: Start by identifying the shape that will be repeated a number of times and write a procedure to draw it. Then, make the procedure you've created into a recursive procedure that will draw the complete shape.)

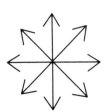

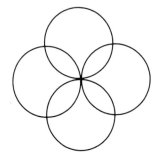

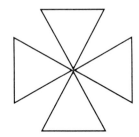

2. For each shape below, write a recursive procedure that will draw the shape.

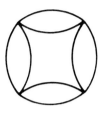 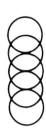 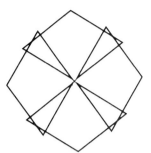

3. Write a recursive procedure to draw the shape below.

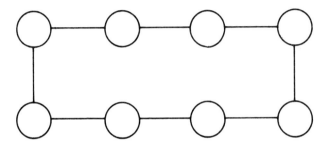

In working with Logo projects it is often desirable to encourage students to analyze the component parts of the desired finished product. If the goal of a Logo project is to draw a picture of some balloons, a starting point might be a sketch of what the finished product should look like (see **Figure 10–15**). The component parts of the sketch can be analyzed. One part is a circle (balloon).

Teaching Logo

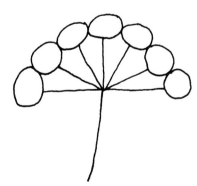

Figure 10–15 The starting point of a Logo project is often a sketch of the desired outcome.

Computers in the Classroom

The following Logo activities appeared in the Byte-size Ideas section of the magazine Classroom Computer Learning *(September 1985). In Byte-size Ideas, short suggestions for computer activities adaptable to all grade levels appear in each issue of* Classroom Computer Learning. *Ideas deal with all aspects of computers in the schools, including programming and computer literacy.*

SKETCH AND CHECK

Children delight in being asked to predict what will happen—it's the element of surprise that they enjoy. Capitalize on this enthusiasm by having kids predict where the turtle trails for Logo commands will be.

Give students the following set of Logo commands and have them draw the turtle's trail, being sure to mark the ending point.

```
FD 40
BK 20
RT 90
FD 10
LT 90
FD 20
BK 40
```

Rather than drawing the letter freehand, students who have difficulty estimating distances and angles can use graph paper to measure the line segments and 90-degree turns. Each square on the graph paper could equal ten turtle steps, for example.

To check their sketches, students type in the commands and compare the screen image with their drawings. Are the line segments proportional? Does the turtle trail turn in the right direction? Is the angle of the turn correct? If there are discrepancies, students can retrace the steps in the commands one at a time to isolate the problem.

After children have corrected any errors, challenge them to sketch their prediction of what this four-letter message says:

```
FD 40    LT 90    LT 90    FD 40
BK 20    FD 10    FD 10    RT 90
RT 90    RT 90    RT 90    FD 10
FD 10    FD 20    FD 40    RT 90
LT 90    RT 90             FD 20
FD 20    FD 10             RT 90
BK 40    BK 10             FD 10
         LT 90
         FD 20
         RT 90
         FD 10
```

Before students check their sketches on the computer, warn them to clear the screen after typing in the commands for each letter. Otherwise the computer will begin drawing one letter where it left off drawing the last one.

Idea by: Phyllis Kalowski, Newton, Mass.

THE KEY TO ADVENTURE

Encourage your students to be pirates? Sure—if they're pirates burying treasure for classmates to find. Have each student imagine a scene for a treasure hunt—an exotic island in the Pacific or a space station on Mars, for example—and then draw a treasure map and write a suspense thriller to go with it.

To begin, students decide what objects—houses, trees, roads, mountains, lakes—they would like to place on their maps. For each object, students create a simple picture symbol and write a Logo procedure that draws it. Here's a procedure for a tree:

```
TO TREE
FD 5 LT 90 FD 5
REPEAT 3 [RT 120 FD 10]
HT
END
```

A printout of all the symbols could then be used as a map key:

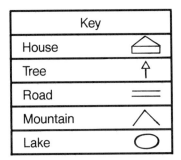

The next step is to program the computer to draw the outline of the island, space station or other location and to place the objects on the map where desired.

Students should refer to printouts of their maps while they plan and write their stories, which guide the reader through the map environment in search of a treasure. When completed, the stories should be typed and edited on the word processor. Then hard copies of both the story and the map can be made.

As an alternative to fantasy maps, you could have students research real places, draw maps showing the locations of significant sites and write on-the-scene tour guides.

Idea by: Phyllis Kalowski, Newton, Mass.

(Kalowski, 1985.)

Another part is the string that is attached to each balloon. The drawing can be seen as being made up of seven balloons, with strings attached, and one other string attached to all the strings from the individual balloons.

The next step is to create a procedure for each of the component parts. **Figure 10–16** shows the procedures created to complete the project. A procedure CIRCLE is created and tested. Next, the procedure ABALLOON is written and tested. This procedure makes use of the previously created procedure CIRCLE. Lastly, the procedure BALLOONS is written and tested. This procedure uses the procedure ABALLOON to create the finished product. This process, by which a problem is analyzed and divided into parts, each part created and tested, and the parts put together to create the finished product, is an example of a classic programming style.

Solomon (1982) presents a model of student learning styles that may be observed as children come into contact with Logo. The classic programming style outlined above is not necessarily the style shown by students working with Logo. Different students will have different ways of approaching Logo. Indeed, although this classic approach is worth developing, work with Logo, especially if pursued in a Piagetian-like atmosphere of exploration, will offer opportunities for the teacher to be sensitive to students' individual learning styles. Within the framework of the student's individual style the teacher's job is to encourage growth by guiding the child toward developing his own intellectual capacities. The teacher can use the child's prevalent style to work toward experimentation with other styles and, ultimately, toward experimentation with a classic approach.

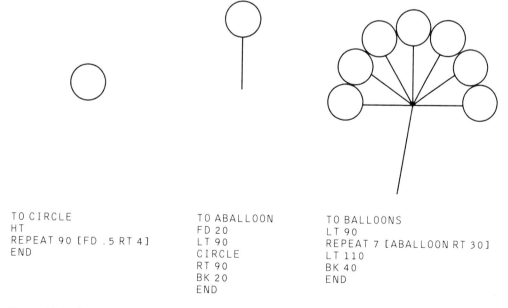

```
TO CIRCLE
HT
REPEAT 90 [FD .5 RT 4]
END
```

```
TO ABALLOON
FD 20
LT 90
CIRCLE
RT 90
BK 20
END
```

```
TO BALLOONS
LT 90
REPEAT 7 [ABALLOON RT 30]
LT 110
BK 40
END
```

Figure 10–16 To create the desired drawing, first the procedure CIRCLE is created. This is used as a subprocedure to create the procedure ABALLOON. The final procedure, BALLOONS, uses ABALLOON as a subprocedure.

Solomon identifies three learning styles that children exhibit in working with Logo. Students may build Logo programs in a structured manner, may exhibit a classic programming style. Solomon calls these students, planners. They begin with a coherent plan for the project they will undertake and proceed, somewhat methodically, to achieve the finished product.

Another learning style is that of the macro-explorer. This student, rather than starting out with a specific goal in mind, tends to enjoy experimenting with subprocedures or building blocks and exploring the results of that experimentation. This type of exploration is open-ended, is commenced without a specific goal in mind. The product may be as much of a surprise to the student as to anyone else.

Other children are identified as micro-explorers. These students explore the Logo environment in a gradual, careful manner. Such a student might instruct the turtle to move RT 30, RT 30, RT 30 and check the position of the turtle to be sure the turtle has acted in the same way as when the instruction RT 90 is given. Whereas macro-explorers engage in experimentation on a larger scale, micro-explorers tend to experiment with smaller pieces of the Logo environment to gain assurance as to how the environment operates.

All three styles may be present in any student's Logo activity, to varying degrees. What is important is to be sensitive to how the student is approaching experimentation in Logo. Once the teacher is sensitive to learning styles, the student may be guided toward further discovery. Students who are micro-explorers may be encouraged to explore commands without any specific goal in mind, just to see the effect on the turtle. Later, the teacher may begin to suggest some specific, although simple, easily accomplished goal that the micro-explorer can accomplish in the style most comfortable for her. Perhaps the student may be led toward choosing a goal herself.

Children may also be led toward a macro-explorer style. Students generally discover something in Logo that excites or interests them. Teachers can use this opportunity to encourage a macro-explorer style by guiding the child toward making a procedure of the drawing that interests him. Further experimentation with the procedure, perhaps using the procedure as a subprocedure, yields experiences as a macro-explorer.

Providing children with a series of interesting designs to choose from, or asking them to design drawings of their own, will lead them to experiences as a planner. The process of developing a Logo project as a planner will often cause children to operate in all three learning styles; procedures are identified, developed, and tested and Logo commands, both new and old, are experimented with in different ways. An interesting sidetrack may be pursued and may yield new insight into Logo programming techniques or some mathematical concept. Such diversions from the plan may suggest new projects or ways to alter the current project. Allowing flexibility in the direction Logo projects take, as well as an awareness of individual learning styles, can help to make Logo a success in the classroom.

As you think back on your experiences with Logo so far, and as you engage in future experiences, notice what learning style you exhibit as you program in Logo. Are you primarily a planner? A micro-explorer? A macro-explorer? Are you all three, and if so, under what circumstances do you exhibit different learning styles? How does your instructor relate to individual learning styles? Such careful observation can help in subsequent work with children and Logo.

Reactions and Research

The following article by Seymour Papert, which appeared in the April 1986 issue of Classroom Computer Learning, *introduces an extension of Logo called LogoWriter.*

In *Mindstorms: Children, Computers and Powerful Ideas* I discuss the pattern by which many new technologies seem to make their way into general use. When a new technology appears, people first seem to use it to do better what they have been doing all along. For example, when motion picture cameras first appeared, they were used not to create the new art form that we now know as films, but only to record the performance of plays.

Similarly, computers were first used in education as instruments to improve the delivery of an otherwise unchanged curriculum. The prototypical example of this "first tier" use of computers in education is, of course, drill in basal skills. The same pre-computer material that had been emphasized in schools for years appeared via a new, improved delivery system.

Another example of first tier use is the word processor, when it is employed as a high-powered electric typewriter. Please understand that I am not condemning this particular use of the word processor. I was one of the first to recommend word processing as a learning tool, and I am delighted when I see how much better children write and how much more they gain from the experience of writing when they use this tool. Nonetheless, to use the word processor in this way is to go no further than a first tier use.

A NEW BREED OF TEACHING TOOLS

And what are second tier uses? Logo, in the form that is now used in more than half of all computationally conscious American schools, is one. Another is a new form of Logo, called LogoWriter, conceived by myself, Brian Silverman and the development team at Logo Computer Systems, Inc. I'd like to explain both examples in some detail.

A guiding metaphor in the development of Logo was the idea of Mathland, a place where you learn math as easily as a child growing up in France learns French. Math seems to be difficult for many people. They think they don't have an aptitude for it, just as some think they can't learn French. Yet it is absurd to conclude that people don't have an aptitude for French: They would have learned French easily had they been born in France. If they lack any aptitude, it is the aptitude for learning French *in the classroom*, a horse of a different color altogether! When people think they "don't have a head for math," I say that what they don't have a head for is learning math as a dead language in the classroom; they would learn it perfectly well, and love it, if they lived in Mathland and could learn it as a living language.

The Logo turtle was the basis of the most successful of several attempts to make an artificial Mathland. The turtle is a cybernetic creature that lives in a microworld on the computer screen. It obeys commands expressed in a mathematical language, drawing a simple square when a novice gives it the instruction REPEAT 4 [FORWARD 50 RIGHT 90] and a complex mathematical object when a more experienced user gives it the instruction REPEAT 360 [SETX (XCOR + 1) SETY (20 × SIN XCOR)]. In practice, children using Logo don't bother much with either squares or sine curves. Rather, they use Logo as a programming language to make the computer do what they want it to do. Two factors conspire to make this a good learning experience. First, learning is facilitated by being rooted in informal, intuitive knowledge that all children possess: You start to think about how to get the turtle to do something by thinking about how you would do it yourself. Second, learning is fueled by being rooted in desire: You learn what you have to learn through doing what you want to do (just as the baby learns what it has to learn about the rules of its native language by attempting to say what it wants to say). The microworld of the turtle thus becomes a place where a child can learn some specific mathematical ideas, some important programming ideas, some "thinking skills" and a lot of self-confidence.

As I watched many schools in which these things happened with varying degrees of success, I gradually formulated a research agenda with three items: to enrich the microworld so that more can be learned, to get rid of some features of Logo that have proven to be sources of frustration for children and to find ways to nurture the development of a "Logo culture" among teachers. And here is where LogoWriter comes in.

A SUCCESSOR TO LOGO

Let me focus on just one of LogoWriter's features—the one that gives it its name and the one that qualifies it as a second tier successor to the concept of word processing. Just as Logo provides children with the power to manipulate *graphics* in an easy-to-learn, natural fashion, LogoWriter gives them the power to manipulate *text* in a way that's easy, natural and learnable. Readers who know Logo well will be aware that it has always had the capacity to manipulate text through programming methods known as "list processing," developed largely in the artificial intelligence world. LogoWriter offers similar capabilities, adding to them a radically new and much more accessible way to handle text, which we call "programmable word processing." In short, Logo has appropriated the word processor.

What does this mean? At the very least, it means that whatever you can do with a word processor you can now do with Logo. When you turn on LogoWriter, you see a screen with the turtle familiar to all Logo users and you see the cursor familiar to all users of word processors. If you like, you can instruct the turtle to vanish, leaving you with a pure word processor that allows you to write and edit a story, file it on disk and/or print it out.

But there is a striking difference between LogoWriter and any word processor you will find in a school: You can change LogoWriter simply by writing short Logo programs. Even elementary school students can customize LogoWriter to suit their needs and tastes. By changing their word processor, they gain the sense of control over the computer that lies at the heart of the Logo philosophy. (It is profoundly anti-educational to give children software tools as "black boxes" they cannot understand or change!) And they find a new microworld in which to exercise mathematical and programming skills.

An even more striking difference between LogoWriter and the average word processor becomes apparent when you instruct the turtle to reappear. Now you can mix text with graphics (and music, as well) to make thoroughly integrated multimedia events. Such events are more than just "flashy." In the same way that the turtle makes an educationally significant transition between intuitive and formal math, LogoWriter allows the user to exercise writing skills in a context that is more akin to spoken language.

Let me explain this last statement a bit further. The hardest skills in writing are not the "low-order" skills of spelling and grammar, but "high-order" skills, including control over the flow of a piece, a sense of drama, the building and resolution of tension, expectation and surprise. Think of a child who writes in a plodding, one-word-after-the-other style, but who can tell a story or conduct a rap performance with all the elements of dramatic flow you could ever want. The question becomes: How can we help this child bring the same sense of dramatic flow to working with text; how can we help him to mobilize the skills of performance, drama and communication for the written medium?

One way is by offering the student a new kind of medium to work with, something between text and speech. This something is a LogoWriter program, which presents text on the screen where you wish and at the tempo you wish—pausing for dramatic effect, moving slower and then faster. And not only text: It can present graphics—even animated graphics—as well. The flow of a story can be captured, and the techniques seen in TV commercials and movie titles can be imitated. LogoWriter offers all this, along with more flexibility to edit and change and cut-and-paste than most word processors have.

I am sure you can imagine such a performance better than I can describe it, though probably not nearly as well as many students who seem to be dull writers could show you. So I leave the rest to your imagination and conclude with two remarks. The first recalls my hope that this extension of Logo will contribute to the growth of the Logo culture among teachers. Many teachers who feel more comfortable dealing with domains that focus on verbal or dramatic content rather than on mathematical concepts will now have access to the Logo culture. My second remark anticipates the inevitable question: "But will this skill of making LogoWriter presentations transfer to increased writing skills in general?" My answer is simple. If you see transfer as an automatic process that needs no encouragement from you, it may or may not. But I am convinced that your imagination as a teacher will show you how to use LogoWriter programming as a transition to pure writing.

(Papert, 1986)

Conclusion

Owing to Logo's popularity, some software companies offer products that are Logo-like. *Delta Drawing*, published by Spinnaker, offers abbreviated commands that allow drawing on the screen to be accomplished in a simplified manner. For example, by pressing the F key the turtle moves forward a predetermined number of steps. Pressing R turns the turtle to the right a predetermined number of degrees. These types of programs can be valuable in introducing young children to the concept of turtle graphics, primarily because of the ease of pressing only one key to have a result appear on the screen. As such, they have the possibility of real educational value. The ability of this type of software to allow full exploration of all aspects of Logo as it was developed is, obviously, limited. As an introduction, programs like *Delta Drawing* can be valuable. However, such programs cannot substitute for a full implementation of Logo.

In the last three chapters we have touched on some theory related to the development of Logo and presented an introduction to the language. Some of the points that Seymour Papert makes are indeed challenging and exciting to both educators and parents. Logo as a language provides a wide range of opportunities for growth and exploration to teachers, parents, and children. Logo finds its way into many classrooms throughout the world and is probably adapted to a given teacher's situation more often than it is implemented in a purely Piagetian learning type of atmosphere. The long-term effects of Logo in the schools remain to be seen, as do the effects of Logo (and of computers) on our culture and other cultures. If you use Logo with students, an understanding of how, why, and in what way it is used in your classroom is essential. It appears to be a powerful tool for accomplishing a variety of objectives.

The turtle graphics environment in Logo provides many other capabilities beyond what has been covered in this introduction. For example, drawings may be done in different colors. Also, on some computers, objects called sprites (mentioned in the Input/Output section of this chapter) may be designed as to shape, size, and color and then animated on the computer screen. Layers of sprites may be built so that if a sprite designed as a man walks across a screen showing a sprite designed as a tree, the illusion of three dimensions can be achieved. It would seem that the man was in front of the tree. A sprite designed as a dog could be introduced into the scene, and it could be made to seem that the man was in front of the tree and behind the dog. Logo allows this to be accomplished very easily. The programmer simply designs the sprites and tells them how to move across the screen.

Although the major emphasis in education has been on the turtle graphics aspect of Logo, it should be emphasized that Logo is a full-fledged programming language with other attributes besides turtle graphics. One other major strength of Logo is the way it processes words and sentences. More experience can be gained with Logo by either taking a full course in it or attending advanced workshops. Several of the references at the end of this chapter offer excellent opportunities for independent study. Appendix B includes organizations dedicated to teaching and learning Logo.

Key Terms

editor
file
Logo primitive
macro-explorer
micro-explorer
planner
procedure
recursion
sprite
subprocedure
working memory
workspace
Logo commands
  ERASE
  ERASEFILE

GOODBYE
PO
POTS
SAVE
TO
READ
To Edit
  CTRL-D
  CTRL-K
  CTRL-N
  CTRL-O
  CTRL-P
  ESC

References/Further Reading

Abelson, Harold. *Apple Logo.* New York: McGraw-Hill, 1982.

————. *Logo for the Apple II.* New York: McGraw-Hill, 1982.

Beardon, Donna, et al. *The Turtle Sourcebook.* Reston, Va.: Reston Publishing Co., 1983.

Billstein, Rick, Shlomo Libeskind, and Johnny Lott. *Logo: MIT Logo for the Apple.* Menlo Park, Calif.: Benjamin/Cummings, 1985.

Bitter, Gary, and Nancy Watson. *Apple Logo Primer.* Reston, Va.: Reston Publishing Co., 1983.

————. *Commodore 64 Logo Primer.* Reston, Va.: Reston Publishing Co., 1983.

Brady, Holly. "Hang On to the Power to Imagine: An Interview with Joseph Weizenbaum." *Classroom Computer Learning* 6, no. 3 (1985):24–27.

Burnett, Dale. *Logo: An Introduction for Teachers.* Morris Plains, N.J.: Creative Computing Press, 1982.

Kalowski, Phyllis. "Byte-size Ideas." *Classroom Computer Learning* 6, no. 1 (1985):70–73.

Papert, Seymour. "The Next Step: LogoWriter." *Classroom Computer Learning* 6, no. 7 (1986):38–40.

Ross, Peter. *Introducing Logo.* Menlo Park, Calif.: Addison-Wesley, 1983.

Solomon, Cynthia. "Introducing Logo to Children." *Byte* 7, no. 8 (1982):196–208.

Turkle, Sherry. *The Second Self: Computers and the Human Spirit.* New York: Simon & Schuster, 1984, 98–100.

Watt, Daniel. *Learning with Logo.* New York: McGraw-Hill, 1983.

————. *Learning with Apple Logo.* New York: McGraw-Hill, 1983.

————. *Learning with Commodore Logo.* New York: McGraw-Hill, 1984.

11

Algorithms and the Teaching of Programming

TOPICS ADDRESSED

What responsibility do teachers have in relation to good programming practices?

What are syntax and logic as they relate to the development of computer programs? What is the importance of each?

What general steps can be outlined to aid in problem solving, and how are they applied to a problem?

What is an algorithm? What specific characteristics must an algorithm have? What is pseudocode?

What are flowcharts, and how are they used?

What is structured programming, and why is it important? What are the structured programming constructs?

Why is structured design important? What are structure charts, and what is the purpose of using them?

OUTLINE

Introduction
Syntax and Logic
Problem Solving
   Example 11–1
Algorithms
   Example 11–2
   Example 11–3

Flowcharts
Structured Programming
Structured Design
Conclusion
Key Terms
Questions
References/Further Reading

Programming is taught in schools, for various reasons, from the early years in elementary school through the high school and college years. At the college level, programming is often taught as a skill that will directly translate into employment possibilities as a scientific or business programmer. It is also taught as a skill that may be applied within other disciplines, such as scientific research, music, or mathematics. At the high school level, programming may be taught as preparation for entering college or as a vocational subject. On the elementary and middle school levels, familiarity with a programming language may be seen as valuable in achieving an understanding of computers and their place in the world. Many school systems have a coordinated computer curriculum that provides students with early experiences with computers and programming and builds toward the opportunity of gaining more programming expertise in the upper grade levels.

Computer programming is much like any other subject in which the mastery of some skill is required; it is possible to learn to program incorrectly, and thus acquire bad habits that must eventually be unlearned before correct techniques are learned. Even in the elementary school, where the BASIC and Logo computer languages are often introduced, some care should be taken to introduce programming concepts in the light of correct programming practices. Naturally, this can be done only by teachers who understand the rudiments of such practices. The concepts related to good programming are not difficult, and a reasonable understanding of them can be attained by any teacher who is willing to invest a little time. Indeed, many of the techniques used to write understandable, quality computer programs may be of use in other problem solving activities that require the careful application of logic to arrive at a solution.

The notion that teachers, if they are to introduce programming concepts, have a responsibility to become familiar with how computer programs should be developed is not the same as requiring teachers to become computer programmers. To fully master a programming language and be able to work professionally as a programmer would require more time and effort than most teachers would, or should, be willing to expend. Rather, what is intended is that teachers and prospective teachers gain a conceptual understanding of such techniques as well as some hands-on experiences with computers, using one or two programming languages that are popular in the schools.

As the teaching of computer concepts and computer programming has made its way into the school curriculum, it has sometimes been assumed that programming and mathematics are the same subject. This is not true. Computer programming is an outgrowth of computer science. The techniques for writing computer programs and solving complex problems have been applied extensively in various settings, including the world of business. It is true that mathematicians program and use computers for mathematical applications, but a host of people in other areas also program and use computers. To be able to program a computer in a high-level language does not require a great degree of mathematical skill. What is necessary is an ability to work with logic, as well as the patience to accomplish detailed tasks.

In this chapter we will trace through some of the techniques used to solve problems and prepare to write a computer program. In Chapter 12 the BASIC programming language is introduced as a high-level language available extensively in the schools. (The acronym BASIC stands for *B*eginners' *A*ll-Purpose

*S*ymbolic *I*nstructional *C*ode.) Some weaknesses in the teaching of programming as it often exists in the schools are identified, and a background is provided for understanding why those weaknesses exist and what may be done about them.

Syntax and Logic

A high-level computer programming language consists of a set of instructions that a computer is able to understand. The word understand in this context does not mean understand as a human being is capable of understanding. Instead, it means the computer can do what the instructions require it to do because the instructions are in a form the computer has been set up to recognize. For example, BASIC is made up of a number of instructions that, when expressed exactly as is required, the computer will understand. One such instruction is PRINT. If I express this instruction correctly, the computer will understand what action I want it to take and will print what is desired. The term syntax refers to the expression, or coding, of instructions in the exact format required by the programming language in order to have the computer understand the language. If I write PRINT "HELLO", the computer will understand what I want it to do and will print HELLO because I have expressed my desire in the correct BASIC syntax. If I write PRNT "HELLO", the computer will not do what I want it to, since the statement contains a syntax error (PRINT is not spelled correctly).

The necessity of communicating with the computer in exactly the form required by the programming language leads to a need to keep careful track of details when writing computer programs. A misplaced letter or other symbol, which would not bother a human, who could infer the correct meaning, will cause a computer to have a problem in understanding its instructions. The need to be precise in writing a computer program to accomplish a task on the computer cannot be overemphasized.

Before writing a program in the correct syntax of a programming language, the logical solution to the problem under consideration must be prepared and presented. The process is such that a problem is posed for which a computer program will be written. Perhaps a teacher wants to keep track of her students' grades on the computer and have the grades calculated by the computer at the end of the semester or grading period. Before a computer program is coded, the logic of the solution to the problem must be decided upon. Remember that the finished program will be a set of instructions. In order to write the instructions, the programmer must first decide what the instructions must do and how (in what order) the instructions must be expressed so that by following them, a solution to the problem will be accomplished. After the logic for the program has been carefully worked out and tested, the programmer then translates that logic into the syntax of the chosen computer language (i.e., BASIC). The actual coding of the program does not happen until the problem has been solved logically and the solution recorded as a series of steps. Once the program is coded, the programmer then debugs it. Debugging consists of correcting any syntax errors and testing the program to see that it functions as it should when processing data similar to what it will be expected to process. In our example, student grades would be used as test data, since that is the type of data the program will be expected to handle. This process of first carefully determining the logical solution to the problem and then translating that solution into the syntax of a programming language helps to ensure the creation of a clear, understandable computer program.

The ability to code syntax correctly in a programming language is the least important aspect of both developing a computer program and learning how to program. The ability to design the logic of a solution to a problem, before coding the solution in a programming language, is, by far, more important. In fact, people who thoroughly master a programming language will become fluent in it to the point that they seldom think about syntax when coding a program. They automatically express their instructions in the programming language in which they are fluent. This is similar to fluency in reading or writing a human language.

In some cases, programming is taught with little regard for the techniques and concepts necessary to produce good computer programs. Sometimes it is introduced as syntax only, by presenting a programming language as if the different instructions in the language were vocabulary words. Students are then turned loose to write programs with little regard for the program's logical design. This eventually leads to programs filled with logic that is hard to follow and difficult to work with. Such instruction is especially inappropriate with BASIC, which has gained popularity in the schools. It is difficult to write good computer code in BASIC and many people think that it should not be taught in the schools. (The Input/Output section of this chapter presents this viewpoint.) Other languages, such as Logo and Pascal, are designed to enforce good programming habits. The fact is that most microcomputers come with BASIC built in and many schools do teach BASIC to students. Further, BASIC was originally designed to allow the presentation of computer programming in a way that was easily understandable by beginners. Also, many teachers and students have invested time and effort in learning and using BASIC, so it is not likely to disappear anytime soon. It can be an effective tool in working with computers, especially when care is taken to introduce it in the light of modern programming techniques. On the elementary school level, this may involve teaching some concepts about problem solving. At higher levels, it might mean teaching and enforcing specific techniques to allow the writing of clear, understandable code.

When introducing any programming language, especially at the elementary school level, students' initial experiences will be simple examples and problems. At this stage, as at any stage, experimentation and discovery are valuable. The intention is not to suggest that student interest and experimentation be stifled by enforcing a rigid, convergent approach to producing computer programs. Rather, appropriate problem-solving and program design concepts and techniques should be introduced gradually. Then, as students gain more facility with the programming language and the programs written become more complex, they may apply those tools in arriving at their own unique computer programs.

Problem Solving

The importance of first arriving at the logical solution to a problem is evident in the many tools and techniques available that have been designed to aid in the expression and clear communication of such solutions. A good understanding of some of these techniques is beneficial in working with students and computers at any level.

The process of arriving at a solution is made up of the following steps (for a full discussion of these steps, see the classic work *How to Solve It*, by G. Polya):

1. Understand what the problem asks.

2. Devise a solution.

3. Apply the solution.

4. Analyze the results.

The most important of these steps is the first. A good understanding of what the problem requires will set the direction that the remaining three steps will take. If the problem is misunderstood, a false direction will be taken and the results of the remaining steps will be of little value. It does no good to successfully solve the wrong problem.

Consider the following example. If asked to find the class average on a quiz, we would first realize that we had been asked to present a single number to describe class performance. Next we would devise a solution, perhaps the series of steps outlined below.

Example 11–1

- Gather all the quiz scores.
- Sum the quiz scores.
- Count the number of quiz scores.
- Divide the sum of the quiz scores by the number of quiz scores.
- Present the result.

By arriving at this solution we have fulfilled the first two steps in problem solving; we understand the problem (step 1) and have arrived at a way to solve it (step 2). Next, we apply the solution (step 3) by gathering some actual quiz scores and using them as data to which the series of steps can be applied. This

Input/Output

In the following selection, Alfred Bork makes a case against teaching BASIC. A considerable number of people agree with the position he presents. There are also, however, many people who think that BASIC offers a good first experience in computer programming. The debate is likely to continue for some time.

Why Shouldn't We Teach BASIC? When languages such as BASIC and FORTRAN were developed, there was little experience with programming, particularly for large, complex activities. However, this is no longer the case. Today we have much experience with writing elaborate programs. Our experience has led to a series of strategies which make it easier to write such programs with fewer errors, and easier to revise these programs. While not everyone is going to write complex programs, many people in the future will be involved in this activity. Indeed, all projections indicate that we will not have enough programmers, given our current ways of producing programmers, to meet this need.

The set of ideas that has evolved for good programming practice sometimes goes under the name of "structured programming." A variety of factors are involved, which I will not attempt to review. Components of software engineering also play a very important role.

BASIC, because it does not lead easily to structured programming, tends to develop poor programming habits, particularly as it is almost universally taught. These programming habits are very difficult for students to overcome later. We have not done students a service if we teach them fundamental ideas and ingrained ways of working which they later must destroy, particularly if these are the *first* ideas that they encounter in the area. It is difficult to correct such early habits. So BASIC hurts students in the long run, in spite of any short-run advantages (and, as will be seen, I claim that there are not really any short-range advantages either!).

We have seen many students at Irvine who have learned BASIC in high school or on their own who have considerable difficulty in the beginning programming courses. Our situation is not unique. For example, I have heard of very similar cases at the Air Force Academy in Colorado Springs. It is not easy to overcome some ingrained habits, particularly if they have been ingrained for a long time.

Another factor to be considered is the lack of standardization in existing BASICs. Although there is a BASIC standard underway, I do not see any widespread move of existing BASICs, or even newly developed BASICs, to conform to that standard. In fact, it seems extremely unusual that a standard for an existing language should depart so much from the current implementations of the language.

Finally, and perhaps the most critical point, *there are better languages for the student to begin with*. The languages in the ALGOL family, such as Pascal, do allow a natural approach to structured programming. They too are not always taught in this fashion, unfortunately, because often the textbooks are written by people with the same bad habits I referred to above! But the percentage is certainly much better; that is, more people learn to program in a satisfactory fashion with Pascal, for example, than with a language such as BASIC.

The coming likely importance of Ada is also an important factor to consider. If Ada becomes as widely used as seems likely, given the strong interest of the Department of Defense, it is likely to require a whole new generation of programmers to work on it. It is very hard to imagine that students brought up on BASIC are likely to become good Ada programmers....

The first argument that is often made for BASIC is that it is common, particularly on small microcomputers. This is true. Most microcomputers have some version or other of BASIC. But these versions differ widely. As already indicated, BASIC is one of the least standardized languages around, with widely varying dialects. This is particularly true when one gets beyond the most elementary level.

But I do not feel that this is a good argument. If we always stuck with what was common in a particular time, a new and better idea would never be used. That is, we would never make any progress. Certainly, at one time FORTRAN was extremely common, when BASIC was first being introduced. The same argument could have been used at one time by FORTRAN users to persuade people not to study BASIC. Other languages, including Pascal, are increasingly available.

The second reason one often hears for teaching BASIC as a first language is the belief that BASIC is easy to teach. I believe that this is an old wive's tale, a position not supported by empirical evidence. As a teacher who has taught many different programming languages, it seems to me that for almost any language a reasonable subset is relatively easy to teach to beginners. The ease depends not so much on the language but on two quite different factors. One of these is the implementation....

The second important factor in how rapidly beginners become acquainted with the language is the *method* in which the language is taught. Users can become familiar with the language in widely different amounts of time, depending on just how the language is introduced. Many methods of teaching languages, particularly those based on grammatical approaches, waste large amounts of student time, independent of the language being used. But this is a separate topic that cannot be adequately addressed within the present column.

Perhaps the most important objection is the one I have left for last. It is often argued, correctly, that one *can* teach BASIC in a structured fashion. This can certainly be done to some extent. But the truth is that it is *almost never* done! One can find very few examples of teaching BASIC in this way. Certainly, in the commonly available books which students usually use in learning BASIC, one sees almost no teaching of BASIC in a structured fashion. There are some exceptions to this, but very few.

(Bork, 1986)

yields a result that can be analyzed (step 4) by checking to see if the result is reasonable and accurate.

Algorithms

Computers operate on instructions that are precisely presented in a sequential manner. It is unlikely that a human being presented with the problem of averaging quiz scores would need to consciously outline and follow the steps given in Example 11–1. A teacher would know what was meant when asked to present a class average and, based on previous experience, would just go ahead and do it, probably in an automatic way. Computers cannot make that type of leap. They require instructions that are clear, complete, and sequential; nothing can be left to chance. Therefore, a solution that will later be coded into a computer program must be in a form that has the characteristics required by the computer. The form the solution takes is called an algorithm. The series of steps to average quiz scores in Example 11–1 is an algorithm. Put simply, an algorithm is a series of instructions that will carry out a specific task. When writing a program, the programmer must first arrive at an algorithm that solves the problem. The algorithm, when translated into a computer language, becomes a computer program.

The four steps for solving a problem can now be amended by changing step 2 and step 3.

1. Understand what the problem asks.

2. Devise an algorithm to solve the problem.

3. Apply the algorithm.

4. Analyze the result.

Algorithms are also used to accomplish many things that are not computer-related. A common example is a recipe. Example 11–2 presents a recipe for sugar cookies.

Grandma's Homemade Sugar Cookies   Example 11–2

Gather the following ingredients:

1 cup light brown sugar	4 teaspoons baking powder
1 cup granulated sugar	1 teaspoon baking soda
1 cup shortening	$\frac{1}{4}$ teaspoon nutmeg
3 eggs	$\frac{1}{2}$ teaspoon salt
1 teaspoon vanilla	1 cup milk
$4\frac{1}{2}$ cups flour	

Mix together shortening and sugars, until creamy.
Beat the eggs while adding vanilla to the eggs.
Mix the eggs and vanilla with the creamed sugar and shortening.
Sift together the flour, baking powder, baking soda, nutmeg and salt.
Add dry ingredients alternately with milk to creamed mixture.

Roll dough to ¼ inch thick and cut with cookie cutter. Place on well-greased cookie sheet.

Bake for 12 minutes at 350 degrees.

There are four characteristics that any algorithm must have.

1. *An algorithm must be effective.* The algorithm must achieve the desired result. If the algorithm to average quiz scores produced an incorrect average, it would be ineffective. If the recipe for sugar cookies produced cookies that were not pleasant-tasting, it would not be effective.

2. *An algorithm must be precise.* The algorithm, as a whole, must specify exactly what is to be done. Each step within the algorithm must explicitly describe the action to be taken. Vagueness is unacceptable. If the temperature or baking time for the cookie recipe were not exact, the algorithm would not produce a correct outcome.

3. *An algorithm must be complete.* The algorithm must contain all the information needed to arrive at a successful result. Each step within the algorithm must contain all the information necessary to successfully perform the instructions for that step, as is the case in examples 11–1 and 11–2.

4. *An algorithm must be finite.* The algorithm must come to an end. It must contain a fixed, finite number of instructions, and the process the instructions describe must terminate. Both examples presented have a finite number of instructions and both sets of instructions describe a process that comes to an end. An example of an algorithm that did not terminate would be one in which one or more instructions were executed repeatedly, without ever stopping. If, at the end of the cookie recipe, we added the instruction "Go to the beginning and do everything again," theoretically, once the steps in the recipe were started, the process would never end. The steps would be gone through once and then would repeat, without stopping. The process would not be finite.

In understanding a problem statement and then devising an algorithm to solve the problem, it is often helpful to analyze the problem in terms of input, process, and output. Identifying the input and output makes it easier to arrive at the process necessary to turn the input into the desired output, especially with complex problems. **Figure 11–1** shows Example 11–1 presented in this way. The input consists of student scores, the desired output is one number (the numerical average), and the process consists of the instructions that manipulate the input to arrive at the output. In **Figure 11–2** the sugar cookie

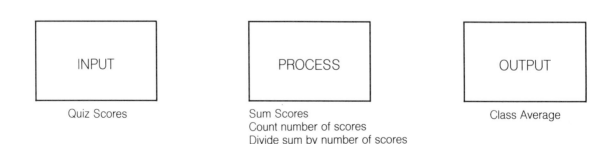

INPUT

Quiz Scores

PROCESS

Sum Scores
Count number of scores
Divide sum by number of scores

OUTPUT

Class Average

Figure 11–1 This figure shows Example 11–1 divided into input, process, and output.

recipe from Example 11–2 is presented as input, process, and output. The input is the list of ingredients, the output is a batch of sugar cookies, and the process consists of the list of instructions to be applied to the ingredients to produce the cookies.

Suppose a teacher has a list of grades for each student in her class and wants to obtain each student's average. She then wants to print out the student's name and "Passed" if the student's average is greater than or equal to 70. If the student's average is less than 70, she wants to print out the student's name and "Not Passed." The output, in this case, is the list of student names and the appropriate "Passed" or "Nor Passed" message and the input is the list of student grades. Example 11–3 presents an algorithm to accomplish this task.

Example 11–3

```
1. Get the name and grades for a student.
2. Compute the average for the student.
3. If the average is greater than or
      equal to 70
      print the student's name and "Passed"
   Else
      print the student's name and
      "Not Passed".
4. If there are more students to process
      go to step 1.
5. End.
```

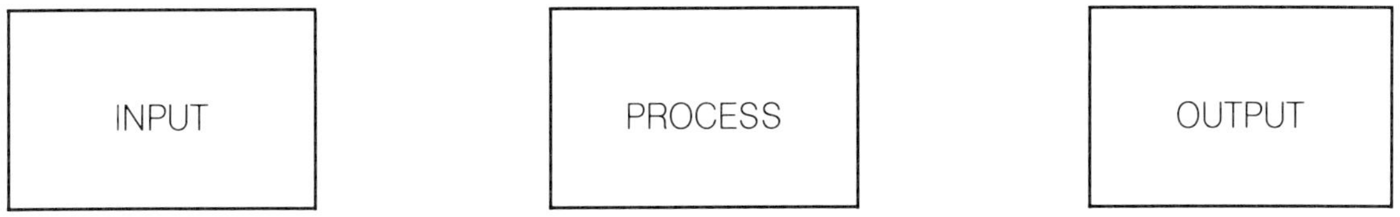

INPUT	PROCESS	OUTPUT
1 cup light brown sugar 1 cup granulated sugar 1 cup shortening 3 eggs 1 teaspoon vanilla 4½ cups flour 4 teaspoons baking powder 1 teaspoon baking soda ¼ teaspoon nutmeg ½ teaspoon salt 1 cup milk	Mix shortening and sugars until creamy. Beat eggs and add vanilla. Mix eggs and vanilla with sugar and shortening. Sift together flour, baking powder, baking soda, nutmeg, and salt. Add dry ingredients alternately with milk to creamed mixture. Roll dough to ¼ inch thick, cut with cookie cutter and place on well-greased cookie sheet. Bake for 12 minutes at 350 degrees.	Batch of sugar cookies.

Figure 11–2 This figure shows Example 11–2 divided into input, process, and output.

This algorithm will accomplish the job for which it was intended for whatever number of students the teacher might need to process. It also fulfills the requirements for an algorithm; it is effective, precise, complete, and finite.

Algorithms may be expressed in a number of ways. One popular method is to use an English-language narrative description of the algorithm as a series of steps, such as in Example 11–3. This is called pseudocode when it is presented a bit more formally than in our example. (An example of pseudocode is given in chapter 1.) A more thorough presentation of the concept of pseudocode is beyond the scope of this text. For now it will do no harm to view Example 11–3 as an example of pseudocode.

Flowcharts

Another way of describing algorithms is through the use of flowcharts. A flowchart is a pictorial representation of an algorithm. A particular set of symbols is used to draw a flowchart. Several of the most frequently used symbols, shown in **Figure 11–3**, are as follows:

- *Terminal symbol*: Signifies the beginning or ending point of the flowchart. Will have either Begin or End written within it.

- *Process symbol*: Denotes some operation to be done such as an arithmetic operation; contains within it a description of the process to be carried out.

- *Input/Output symbol*: Represents data to be input to or output from the algorithm; represents output that will appear on a cathode ray tube (softcopy), may represent output that will be printed on a printer (hardcopy).

- *Document symbol*: Indicates only output that will print on a printer (hardcopy).

- *Decision symbol*: Represents a choice to be made within the algorithm. The condition for the choice will be stated within the symbol as a question. If the question evaluates as true, the logic flow of the algorithm follows the exit point of the symbol marked T (for true). If the question evaluates as false, the logic flow follows the exit point of the symbol marked F (for false).

- *Processing flow symbol*: Shows the direction of the logic flow. Specifies in what order instructions may be carried out.

- *Connector symbol*: Denotes movement from one place in a flowchart to another.

Figure 11–4 is a flowchart of the algorithm presented in Example 11–3, the algorithm to average student grades and print out the student's name and "Passed" or "Not Passed."

Flowcharts are read from the top down unless a processing flow symbol or the result of a condition in a decision symbol directs the flow in another direction. Starting at the top in Figure 11–4, the first symbol is the terminal symbol labeled Begin. The next symbol is an input symbol. This indicates, as written within the symbol, that this is where the input (grades and name) is entered for one student. Next, as noted, the grades are processed (hence the process symbol) by computing the student's average. At this point it is necessary to make a decision about the student's average. The decision symbol

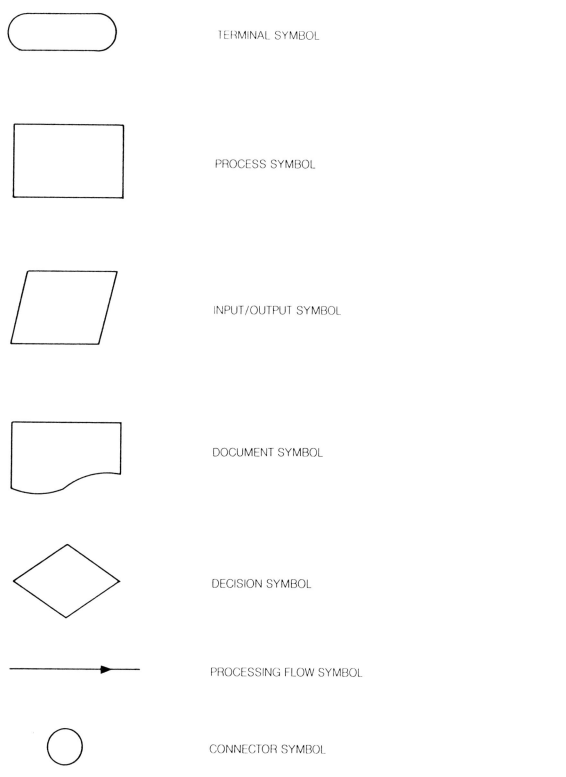

TERMINAL SYMBOL

PROCESS SYMBOL

INPUT/OUTPUT SYMBOL

DOCUMENT SYMBOL

DECISION SYMBOL

PROCESSING FLOW SYMBOL

CONNECTOR SYMBOL

Figure 11-3 Flowchart symbols.

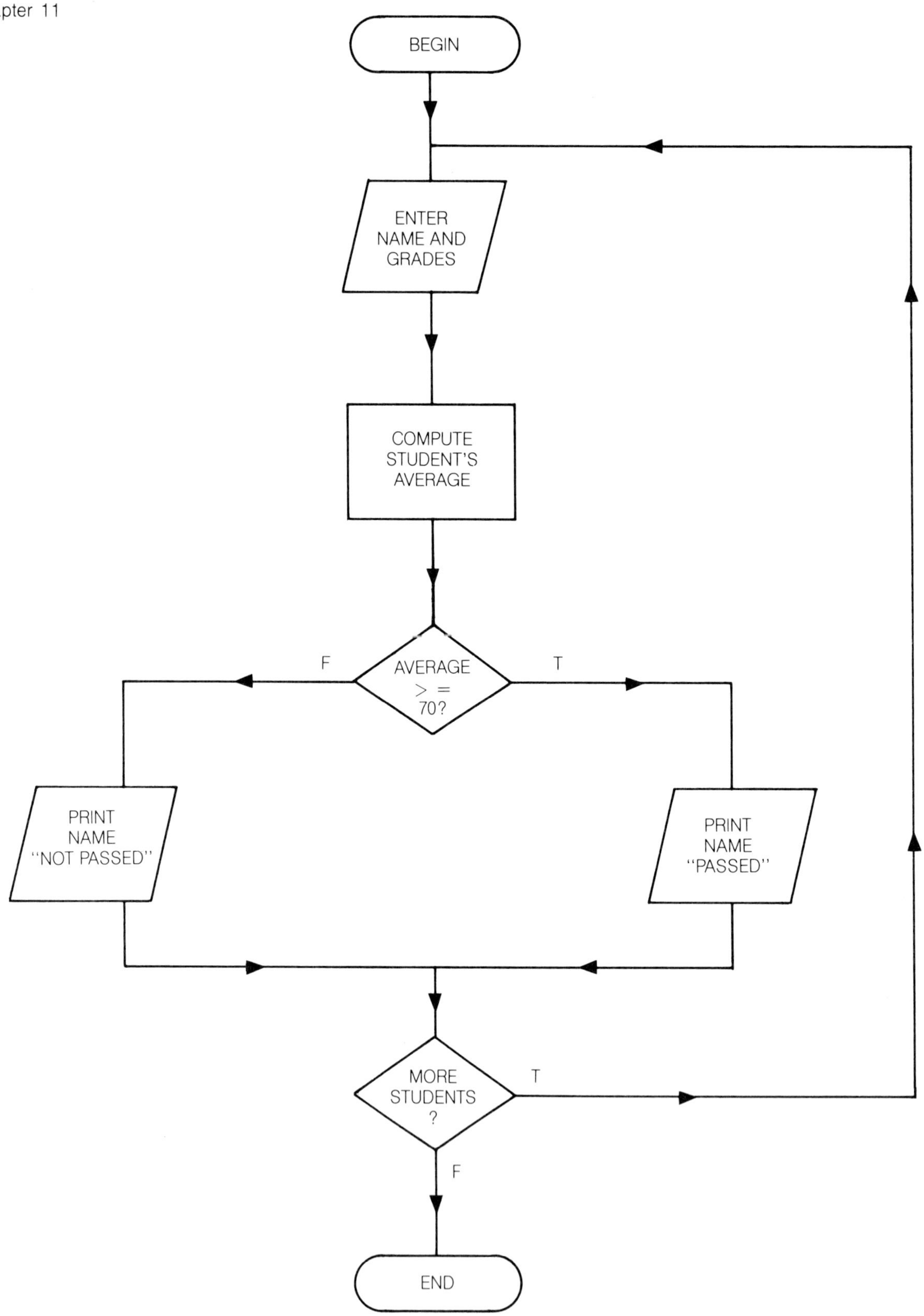

Figure 11–4 A flowchart of Example 11–3.

contains the question "Average $>$ = 70?" The exit point at the right side of the decision symbol is labeled T. If the question is answered true, if the average is greater than or equal to 70, the processing flow will exit the decision symbol at the right side. It will then encounter an input/output symbol containing instructions to print the student's name and "Passed." If the question is evaluated as false, if the grade is not greater than or equal to 70 (if the grade is less than 70), the processing flow will exit at the left side of the decision symbol. It will then encounter an input/output symbol with directions to print the student's name and "Not Passed." Whichever path the flow takes it will next arrive at another decision symbol that contains the question "More students?" If there are more students to process, the flow follows the arrow exiting the right side of the decision symbol and leading back to just before the input symbol. Another way to say this is that the processing flow loops back to the input symbol. The instructions in the flowchart will then be executed (performed) again. This repetition will continue until the condition in the decision symbol labeled "More students" evaluates as false (F). If there are no more students to process, the flow exits the decision symbol at the point labeled F and the flowchart ends at the terminal symbol labeled End.

Usually, flowcharts contain more detailed information about how the different steps of an algorithm will be accomplished than is present in an algorithm written as a series of steps in pseudocode. For example, in the process symbol labeled "Compute average" in Figure 11–4, instead of the general statement of "Compute average," which tells what will be done, a more specific statement would be offered to show how the average will be computed. If we knew that each student had five grades to be averaged, we could represent each grade with a variable name, such as G1, G2, G3, G4, and G5. We could then give a variable name—AVG—to the average. Now the process box could contain the specific instruction "Let AVG = (G1 + G2 + G3 + G4 + G5)/5," which specifically shows how the average will be arrived at (by adding together the values stored in the variables G1, G2, G3, G4, and G5 and dividing the sum by 5). The point is that when flowcharts are used to present algorithms, they are usually specific and show how to do the steps in the algorithm. A pseudocode description of the steps is more general. When analyzing a problem the intent is to come up with a generalized idea for the algorithm by using an appropriate technique, such as a narrative description (pseudocode). The algorithm can then be refined, made more specific, by using a technique like flowcharting. This process aids in solving complex problems.

Although flowcharts are still used extensively in the teaching and practice of programming, many consider them undesirable. One criticism is that by the time a correct flowchart is drawn for an algorithm, it can be so detailed that the programmer may as well have directly written the code in the chosen programming language. Another, more important criticism is that flowcharts do not promote the writing of structured programs, programs whose design reflects modern programming practices that produce reliable, understandable code. Many believe that more modern techniques, such as pseudocode and structure charts (covered later in this chapter), when used in conjunction with the concepts and techniques of structured programming and structured design (discussed below), make flowcharts obsolete. Whether or not this is true, the reality is that flowcharting is not going to disappear overnight. Also,

Computers in the Classroom

Children often enjoy seeing what happens when directions are followed literally. This interest can be the basis for teaching students that the computer can only follow literal instructions. It can also be the basis for teaching about algorithms.

One time-honored exercise for teaching about literal instructions and algorithms is the peanut butter-and-jelly-sandwich activity. Gather together bread, a jar of peanut butter, a jar of jelly, a knife, and some napkins. Arrange these things on a table and invite children to tell you, giving one instruction at a time, how to make a peanut butter and jelly sandwich. Explain that the end product of the activity will be a set of instructions for making a peanut butter and jelly sandwich (and the sandwich itself!). As each instruction is offered, carry it out. Be careful to follow all instructions literally, taking nothing for granted. Initially, when suggesting instructions, students tend to overlook simple necessities. For example, students will often tell the teacher to put jelly on the bread before they have instructed her to remove a piece of bread from the wrapper. (In which case the teacher would automatically put jelly on the loaf of bread enclosed in the wrapper.) By finding and fixing the bugs in faulty instructions, children soon arrive at a successful set of instructions. At the end of the exercise, point out how the original instructions were debugged until a successful set was generated. The final instructions can be identified as an algorithm and used to point out the characteristics of an algorithm identified in this chapter. At the end of the exercise, it's peanut butter and jelly sandwiches for everyone!

Writing a set of instructions to accomplish other common activities, such as tying shoes, washing hands, or cleaning the chalkboard, can also be of value. Children may have their own ideas about tasks for which it would be fun to write algorithms. The writing of algorithms can be accomplished as a group activity or can be done individually by students. For children who are learning flowcharting techniques, an algorithm for a task can be written first and then a flowchart can be created from the algorithm.

even when structured programming concepts are adhered to, flowcharts, when used appropriately, can be of value in working out the logic of complex solutions. Just as with the BASIC programming language, many people learned programming through the use of flowcharts, and therefore flowcharting is embedded in the computer culture.

Structured Programming

Structured programming refers to the type of control structures that appear in both a computer program and the algorithm from which it is coded. It should be evident by now that an algorithm, whether expressed in pseudocode or in a flowchart, describes a process of logic that, when followed, will yield a solution to a problem. The logical structures that control the flow of that logic can be identified and described. In fact, any algorithm, and therefore any program, can be written by using only three control structures. When algorithms are designed and programs written with the aim of using only these three control structures, called structured programming constructs, the result will be a structured algorithm and, subsequently, a structured program. The benefit of structured programming is that the end product, the program, is more reliable and easier to understand than an unstructured program. This is important for teaching purposes because it can provide a clearer understanding of complex problems and their resolution. As algorithms and programs are arrived at and explained, they are in a more readily understandable form than if structured programming techniques had not been used. This also aids the student during debugging by making it easier to locate problem areas within the program. For professional programmers, structured programming often reduces the time it takes to produce reliable programs or successfully change existing programs to perform new functions, resulting in a savings for the employer.

The three structured programming constructs are as follows:

- *Sequence*: Whenever two or more instructions are performed in order, they are accomplished in sequence.

- *Selection*: When there is a choice to be made between which logic path to follow based on some condition, a selection takes place.

- *Repetition*: When one or more instructions may be repeated, the possibility of repetition exists.

Figure 11–5 shows a flowcharted general representation and specific example of each construct. The sequence construct denotes that first instruction 1 will be processed, then instruction 2, and then instruction 3. In the specific example, first $X = X + 1$ would be evaluated, then $A = X/5$, and then PRINT A. Unless a specific instruction directs the computer to do otherwise, the computer processes instructions in sequence.

The selection construct shows that, based on the evaluation of the condition in the decision symbol as true (T) or false (F), one of two logic paths will be followed. In the first instance if the condition evaluates as true, instruction 1 will be performed. If the condition evaluates as false, instruction 2 will be performed. In the specific example, if the condition $C > 30$ is true, PRINT TOTAL will be done. If the condition evaluates as false, LET $C = C + 1$ will be done.

The second example of the selection construct shows that a decision to do nothing may be made. In the case where the condition evaluates as true, instruction 1 will be executed. In the case where the condition evaluates as false, nothing is done and the flow of logic will just pass on to whatever comes next. In the specific example if $A > 3.5$ is true, PRINT "DEANS LIST" is done. If $A > 3.5$ is false, nothing is done before the logic flow continues on to whatever instruction comes next.

The repetition construct indicates that if a condition evaluates as true, instruction 1 will be carried out. The logic flow then loops back to the condition to test it again. As long as the condition continues to be evaluated as true, instruction 1 will continue to be carried out. When the condition evaluates as false the repetition will cease. In the specific example as long as $G < 5$ evaluates as true, the instruction "LET $G = G + 1$" will be executed. When $G < 5$ is no longer true the repetition will stop.

In the examples for the selection and repetition constructs it is possible to specify more than one instruction to be carried out based on the results of a decision. In other words, wherever instruction 1 or instruction 2 is specified in the general presentation of the selection and repetition constructs in Figure 11–5, a series of instructions could be specified.

Structured Design

When dealing with a complex problem it is often helpful to divide the problem into a series of smaller problems, or modules, in order to understand it and arrive at a solution. Structured design refers to analyzing a problem in this way and then presenting a generalized solution—more generalized even than a

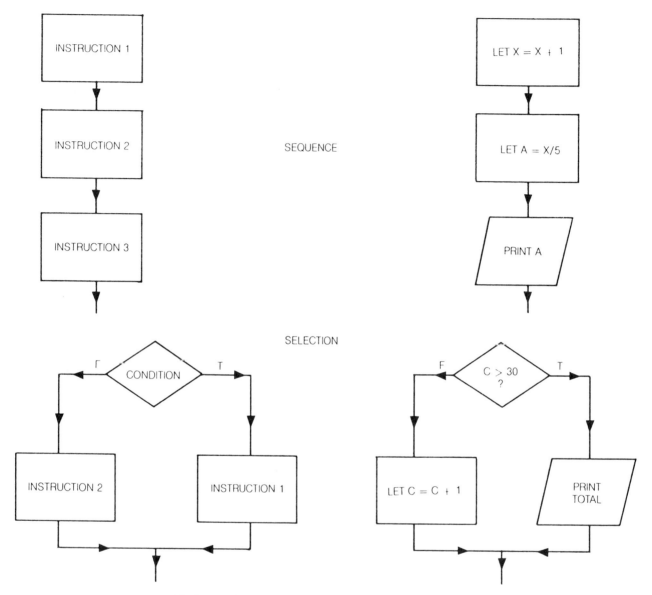

Figure 11–5 Structured programming constructs.

pseudocode representation. From there this first solution is refined into more detail. Structured design and structured programming go hand in hand. The techniques used in structured design provide a solid framework on which structured programs may be built. One technique in structured design (sometimes called top-down design) is the structure chart, which consists of a series of boxes arranged in a hierarchical fashion. Structure charts are read from top to bottom and left to right. **Figure 11–6** shows a structure chart that depicts the tasks necessary in planning a dinner party. Each box, or module, describes in general terms a task to be performed.

The topmost box describes the overall procedure, in this case Plan Dinner Party. Because there are no more boxes on this level we go down one level and

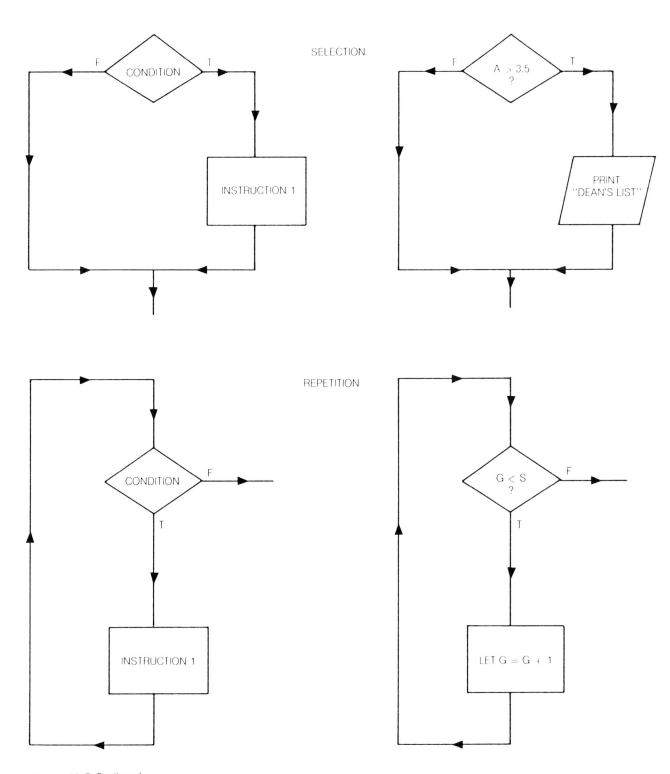

Figure 11-5 Continued

as far to the left as possible, where we encounter the module labeled Invite Guests. Each module denotes a task to be performed, but only in general terms. The next module is labeled Plan Menu, followed by Clean House. The latter

Reactions and Research

In this selection from an article by Ben Shneiderman, "When Children Learn Programming: Antecedents, Concepts and Outcomes," the author suggests what knowledge children might need before studying computer programming.

ANTECEDENT KNOWLEDGE

Programming is a complex and creative activity which requires the smooth integration of multiple skills. Children who don't recognize that 20 precedes 30 will have a hard time understanding line-number sequencing in a program. Children who can't repeat a sentence three times will have difficulty planning to use a loop. I don't profess to have a complete list, but I found even this introspectively created list useful in predicting success in learning programming concepts. Of course, a child who has the antecedent knowledge is not guaranteed success in learning the related programming concept, but without this knowledge, learning is very difficult.

In many ways the antecedent knowledge for programming is similar to the skills required for reading readiness:

- **Sequencing:** Spatial: Horizontal (left, right) and vertical (up, down). Numeric ordering of integers: ascending, descending, greater than, less than, equality. Temporal: order of events (before, after, from now on).

- **Same or different:** Similarity, grouping by attributes (shape, color, size, etc.).

- **Character recognition:** Numbers, letters, special characters and blanks.

- **Part/Whole relationships:** Letters make up words, words make up sentences, commands make up programs, etc.

- **Beginning/Middle/End:** Start/work/stop; first/middle/last; etc.

- **Conditional forms:** This or that, yes or no, present or absent, etc.

- **Example of a concept:** "Red" is an example of a color; "A" is an example of a letter; "3" is an example of a number, etc.

- **Difference between an object and the name of an object:** Book vs. title, person vs. name, etc.

- **Repetition:** Knock three times, jump six times, write four letters, keep on dancing, pick up all the cards, etc.

- **Incrementation:** Do it one more time, add another block, say it again, etc.

- **Arithmetic:** Addition, subtraction, multiplication, division.

Precise tests for these and other antecedent knowledge items would be a valuable contribution, as would more precise linkage between them and specific programming concepts. Elementary school teachers can look for imaginative ways to convey this knowledge and expand this list with their own items. When antecedent knowledge is acquired, students can do more than just copy programs—they can create their own programs.

(Shneiderman, 1985)

---

module is subdivided into four lower-level modules—Get Spouse's Help, Dust and Vacuum, Wash Windows, and Wax Floors—which are the tasks to be performed in order to accomplish the overall task of Clean House. Because there are no more modules under Clean House, the next module after it, Shop, is executed. This module is subdivided into Stop at Bank, Go to Supermarket, and Go to Butcher Shop, which, when all are performed, will accomplish the higher-level module Shop. The last two modules are Prepare Meal and Serve Guests.

Structure charts aid in breaking down problems into their component tasks, ordering the sequence in which tasks should be done, and noting the relationships between different tasks. When used to portray complex programming problems in business and industry, they can become quite involved, consisting of forty to fifty pages—and sometimes more.

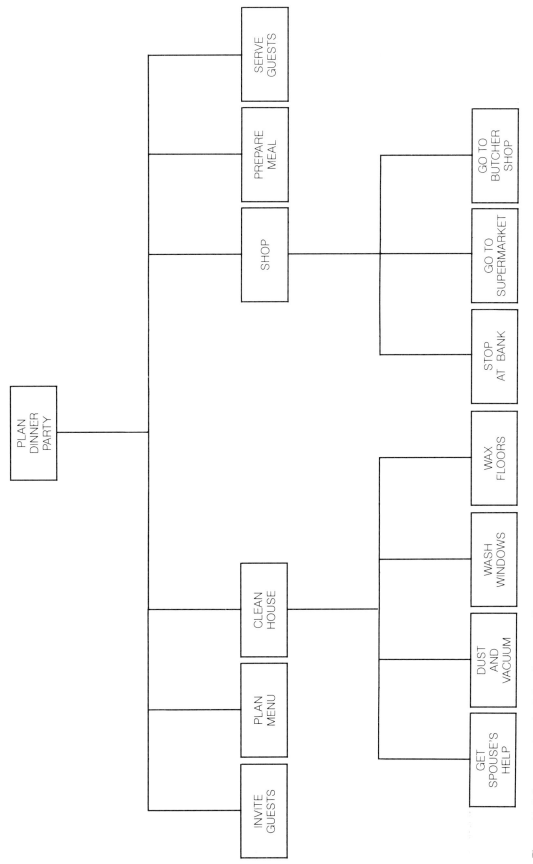

Figure 11–6 Structure chart for "plan dinner party."

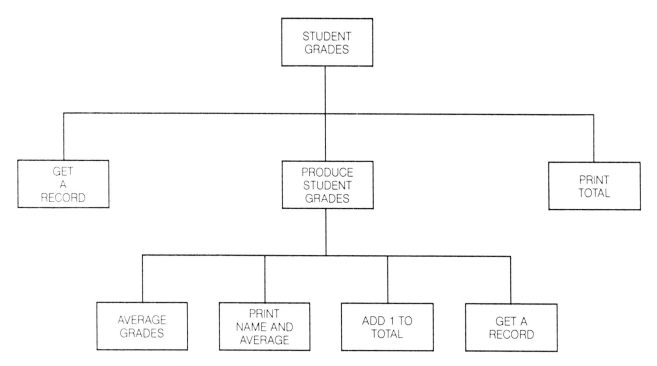

Figure 11-7 Structure chart for "Student Grades."

Figure 11–7 shows a structure chart for a program to produce a list of student grades and then print out the total number of grades calculated. The name of the program appears in the topmost box, Student Grades. The first module is labeled Get a Record and indicates that a student record, with student name and the student's grades, must be retrieved. The next module is labeled Produce Student Grades and is accomplished by performing the lower-level modules Average Grades, Print Name and Average, Add 1 to Total, and Get a Record. These four modules will be repeated until there are no more student records. Control will next flow to the last module, Print Total, where the total number of students processed will be printed.

This structure chart provides a conceptual basis for the solution to the problem of averaging the students' grades. The next step in the process would be to write out a more detailed series of steps, in pseudocode, that would follow the logical organization of the structure chart but would be more specific. Then a flowchart could be drawn using the pseudocode as a guide. The flowchart would add yet another level of detail. Lastly, the flowchart would be used to code the computer program. The process of starting at the most general level by breaking the problem down into a series of modules and then progressively adding more detail to the algorithm, by using such techniques as pseudocode and flowcharting, is a process through which solutions can be arrived at that may then be translated into a programming language. By using only the structured programming constructs and following these steps, well-designed structured programs can be achieved.

Computer programming is taught at different levels for various purposes. If computer programming is in the curriculum, some attention must be given, even in the earliest grades, to the procedures followed to achieve well-written programs. Instruction in the steps of problem solving and in problem-solving techniques can be presented in a simplified form in the primary grades. These topics can be built on and expanded as children grow in ability and are offered more opportunity to interact with computers and programming languages.

The choice of a modern programming language like Logo that encourages good programming habits is something to carefully consider when making curriculum decisions for the elementary grades. However, care in introducing and teaching BASIC can lead to a successful introduction to programming concepts. In the upper grades, Pascal, a modern, powerful programming language designed to encourage good programming, will usually be the language of choice.

Conclusion

Key Terms

algorithm
connector symbol
decision symbol
document symbol
flowchart
hardcopy
input/output symbol
logic
process symbol
processing flow symbol
pseudocode

repetition
selection
sequence
softcopy
structure chart
structured design
structured programming
structured programming construct
syntax
terminal symbol

Questions

1. Should care be taken to introduce computer programming, at whatever level it is covered in the curriculum, in the light of good programming practices? Why, or why not?

2. Discuss the difference between syntax and logic in a computer program. Is attention to detail important in computer programming? What must be done before a computer program can be coded?

3. What steps can be followed to solve a problem?

4. What is an algorithm? What characteristics must an algorithm have?

5. With the characteristics mentioned in your response to question 4 in mind, choose one of the following and write an algorithm as a series of English-language steps (pseudocode) to accomplish the task.

   ▪ You are sitting at home in your living room. Write an algorithm to drive to the store, purchase a loaf of bread, and return home.

   ▪ Write an algorithm to make a strawberry ice cream soda.

■ A teacher has calculated her students' numerical grades for the term. She now must fill out the report cards that are currently in the school office. Report card grades must be expressed as A, B, C, D, or F and must contain at least one remark per subject per child. The teacher teaches five subjects. Write an algorithm to produce and distribute the finished report cards.

6. What are flowcharts, and how do they relate to pseudocode? What are two criticisms of flowcharts?

7. Draw a flowchart representation of the algorithm you created in question 5.

8. Obtain an algorithm that someone else created for a different task from the one you did for question 5. Draw a flowchart of that algorithm. Is it harder to draw a flowchart from someone else's algorithm or from your own?

9. Why is structured programming important? What are the structured programming constructs?

10. Identify the structured programming constructs in the flowchart presented in Figure 11–4.

11. Find the structured programming constructs present in the flowchart you drew for question 7. Do the same for the flowchart you drew for question 8.

12. What is structured design, and how does it relate to structured programming? What is a structure chart?

13. Describe the process a person might go through in creating a structured program. Identify and explain the proper use of each of the following: structure chart, pseudocode, flowchart.

14. A teacher is planning a bake sale. Draw a structure chart for planning and holding a bake sale.

15. Choose one module from the structure chart you drew for question 14 and write the pseudocode to accomplish that task. Draw a flowchart from your pseudocode.

References/Further Reading

Bent, Robert J., and George C. Sethares. *BASIC: An Introduction to Computer Programming with the Apple*. Monterey, Calif.: Brooks/Cole Publishing, 1983.

Bohm, Corrado, and Guiseppe Jacopini. "Flow Diagrams, Turing Machines and Languages with only Two Formation Rules." *Communications of the ACM* 9 (May 1966):366–371.

Bork, Alfred. "Don't Teach BASIC." In *RUN: Computer Education*, edited by Dennis O. Harper and James H. Stewart, 2d ed. Monterey, Calif.: Brooks/Cole Publishing, 1986, 171–173.

Graham, Neill. *Introduction to Computer Science*. St. Paul: West Publishing Co., 1985.

Hartling, J., L. Druffel, and F. Hilbing. *Introduction to Computer Programming: A Problem Solving Approach*. Bedford, Mass.: Digital Press, 1983.

Polya, G. *How to Solve It*. Princeton, N.J.: Princeton University Press, 1945.

Shneiderman, Ben. "When Children Learn Programming: Antecedents, Concepts and Outcomes." *The Computing Teacher* 13, no. 6 (1985):14-17.

12

BASIC: A Beginning

TOPICS ADDRESSED

What are different dialects, or implementations, of BASIC?

What are numerical variables and numerical constants in BASIC?

What are string constants and string variables in BASIC?

How are arithmetic operations performed in BASIC?

How are the following BASIC statements used: PRINT, REM, END, HOME, LET, INPUT?

What are the commands RUN, LIST, SAVE, LOAD, and CATALOG used for?

How does the development of an algorithm relate to the writing of a BASIC program?

OUTLINE

Introduction
Beginning BASIC
Getting to Applesoft BASIC
Variables and Constants
  Numerical Constants and Variables
  String Constants and Variables
  Exercises
Reserved Words, Commands and
  Statements
PRINT, END, REM, and HOME
  PRINT
  END
  REM
  HOME

  Example
  Exercises
Arithmetic Operations
LET
  Example
  Exercises
PRINT—One More Time
INPUT
  Example
  Exercises
Conclusion
Key Terms
References/Further Reading

Introduction

In Chapter 11 the difference between logic and syntax was emphasized. The importance of logically solving a programming problem before writing a computer program was noted. With that in mind this chapter presents some of the syntax of the BASIC language. At the outset, because of the simplicity of the initial problems and examples, the tools presented in the previous chapter will not be used extensively. As additional features of BASIC are introduced and problems become more involved (and interesting!), these techniques will be used to a greater extent.

Beginning BASIC

Although the BASIC language, as implemented on microcomputers, is fairly standard, there are differences in BASIC as implemented on different types of microcomputers. What this means is that BASIC on one brand of computer may not work exactly the same as on another brand of computer. For example, BASIC on the Apple IIe is not exactly the same as BASIC on the IBM PC. The key word here is *exactly*, since there are more similarities than differences. This is analogous to dialects in spoken American English. Although we all may speak American English, dialects are different from region to region. Even though we may not know the dialect of a different region, our general command of the language allows us to communicate with people living there. The same is true of a programming language. If we understand the types of commands available and the correct syntax of BASIC for one brand of computer, the minor variations among BASIC as implemented on other brands will be no more than a slight inconvenience.

This introduction to BASIC will present Applesoft BASIC, the version of the language available on Apple II series microcomputers. The choice was made primarily because, as of this writing, Apple is the most prevalent type of computer in the schools.

"Gee, Dad, how can I tell you what's bothering me if you don't speak Basic, Cobol, Fortran, or Pascal?"

If you are using an Apple II series computer, Appendix C explains how to initialize a disk, use the RETURN key, save and load programs, catalog a disk, run, and edit your programs. Some of this information is included in Table 12–1 for review purposes. If you are using another type of computer, your instructor will provide you with this information. The following assumes that the computer is in the Applesoft environment (which means that the Applesoft BASIC language is available for use). The Applesoft prompt ( ]) should show on the screen with a blinking rectangle, called the cursor, next to it.

Getting to Applesoft BASIC

Before introducing any BASIC commands, it is necessary to understand a few points about how computers handle variables and constants. Computers manipulate and store data. Such data, for our purposes, can be said to be any of four types: numerical constants, numerical variables, string constants, and string variables.

Variables and Constants

A variable is a storage location for some value. A constant is a specific value. For instance, the number 12 is a constant. Its value is unchanging. Because 12 represents the number 12, it is called a numerical constant. Any numeral can represent a numerical constant. When entering numerical constants do not use commas, i.e., 1000 is correct, 1,000 is not.

A numerical variable is a storage location where a numerical constant may be stored. For instance, the letter A my be used as a numerical variable. If a value of 12 is assigned to A,

Numerical Constants and Variables

$$A = 12$$

the numerical constant 12 will be stored in the storage location named A. From then on, until a different value is assigned to A, it is always treated as having the value of 12. A numerical variable may be used just as if it were a numerical constant. If the numerical constant 12 was stored in A, the expression,

$$B = A + A$$

would store the sum of A + A (12 + 12) in B, giving B a value of 24.

In BASIC, numerical variables may be named by using any letter of the alphabet (A through Z) and any digit (0 through 9) as long as the name begins with a letter and is not, or does not contain, a word already used by Applesoft BASIC, called a reserved word. Examples of reserved words are REM, PRINT, and END. (A complete list of reserved words is given at the end of Appendix C.) Therefore, a numerical variable name might be A1, B, C7, or AVG, but not SAT (contains the reserved word AT), 12b (does not begin with a letter), or STU–15 (is not made up of only letters and digits).

One other important point is that Applesoft BASIC distinguishes between variable names based only on the first two positions in the name. Two variables name G12 and G15 would describe the same variable, the storage location G1. The variables V5 and V6 would describe two variables, two storage locations—V5 and V6.

String Constants and Variables

When a sequence of BASIC characters is enclosed in quotation marks, it is referred to as a string constant, or string. The following are all string constants:

```
"JOANNE"
"HALL MEMORIAL SCHOOL"
"2479"
"STRATFORD, CT 06497"
"+++++++++"
"THE AVERAGE = "
```

The characters contained within the quotation marks constitute the string. The value of the first string is JOANNE, the value of the last string is THE AVERAGE IS = . Note in the last string that the blanks before and after the equal sign count as part of the value of the string.

A string variable is a storage location where the value of a string may be stored. String variables are named according to the same rules as numerical variables except that they must end with a $. This is what makes them string variable names. The following are valid string variable names:

```
NAME$
A$
Z12$
STUDENT$
ADDRESS$
```

The $ in a string variable is read as the word string. For instance, the first variable would be read as Name string. The second would be read as A string. String variables have many uses, some of which will be illustrated later in the chapter.

EXERCISES

1. Identify each of the following as valid or invalid variable names.

a.	CHR$	g.	SUM7$
b.	BILL$	h.	12TEST
c.	-123	i.	ADDRESS.$
d.	B24	j.	INTEREST
e.	SUM	k.	X
f.	FORM$	l.	XYZ?

2. Create a variable name for each of the following:

```
a. a student's name
b. the class average on a test
c. the title of a book
d. a teacher's salary
e. today's date
```

Reserved Words, Commands, and Statements

BASIC consists of a set of reserved words that are used to give instructions to the computer. These reserved words may also be called BASIC commands, or simply commands. Each line in a BASIC program starts with a line number, as covered in Appendix C. A BASIC command, or a BASIC command with a line number, may also be referred to as a statement (as in the material below). Commands that are used to direct the operation of the computer system (such as SAVE, LOAD, RUN, etc., as covered in Appendix C) are sometimes referred to as system commands.

PRINT, END, REM, and HOME

The PRINT statement causes output to be displayed on the screen or printer. The PRINT statement may be used with variables or constants. The program line

PRINT

```
10 PRINT "JOHN"
```

would cause the string

```
JOHN
```

to appear on the screen when the program was run, whereas the program line

```
10 PRINT 576
```

would cause the numerical constant

```
576
```

to appear on the screen.

If a value of 45 was stored in the numerical variable Z, the program line

```
10 PRINT Z
```

would cause the value stored in the variable, in this case 45, to be printed on the screen. If the string value BERT was stored in the string variable STUDENT$,

```
10 PRINT STUDENT$
```

would cause the value stored in the variable, in this instance BERT, to be printed.

The general format for any BASIC statement can be given by specifying, in general terms, the syntax that the statement requires. "Line number" in the general format given below for the PRINT statement refers to any line number in a program.

```
line number PRINT any numerical or string expression
```

The END statement is always used as the last program line in a BASIC program. It instructs the computer to stop running (sometimes called executing) the program; it signals that the program is finished. The general format for the END statement is

END

Input/Output

The following excerpt is from an article about the creators of BASIC—John Kemeny and Tom Kurtz. Kemeny and Kurtz speak about some of the features available in modern BASIC and present a positive view of BASIC, in its most recent form, as an up-to-date, desirable computer programming language.

A revolution was the last thing John Kemeny and Tom Kurtz expected when they invented BASIC in 1964.

"As a matter of fact," says Kemeny, "Tom was worried that Dartmouth students might be stuck with a language they wouldn't be able to use anywhere else."

Conceived as a tool to help fulfill their dream of teaching every liberal arts student how to program, BASIC quickly spread to other universities. With the advent of microcomputers in the early 1970s, BASIC became the ticket for millions to enter the once mysterious and arcane world of computer code.

Today, aware that the very simplicity that made BASIC so accessible leads many programmers to abandon it when their skills demand tools more powerful and advanced, Kemeny and Kurtz are fighting to show the world that their baby has grown up, too.

"People who know the language only through microcomputers are totally unaware of the power of modern BASIC," insists Kemeny. . . .

"There have been enormous changes in BASIC, as in all languages, in the past decade," says Kemeny. The public perception of BASIC, however, has remained static.

"I think the BASIC that Microsoft squeezed into 4K bytes, or whatever it was, is ingenious," observes Kurtz, "but because they did not keep it up-to-date as the hardware for personal computers advanced, millions of people out there think it is the only kind of BASIC there is."

BASIC continued to evolve in the mainframe environment, they explain, paralleling the general evolution of computer languages into powerful coding and development tools. While this evolution is well-known in such currently popular languages as C and Pascal, Kemeny and Kurtz believe most programmers are unaware that BASIC has incorporated many of the advancements that account for their popularity.

Kemeny feels the single most important idea to gain wide currency is designing a program so it can be written in pieces and writing each piece separately. "BASIC is now just such a fully structured language," he says.

Closely related to this is a second major development. "You find you tend to write the same pieces over and over again," continues Kemeny. "A library of subroutines allows you to write a piece just once, stick it in the library, and call it up when you need it in a program." Modern BASIC allows for the creation of such separately compiled subroutine libraries. . . .

Kurtz notes that modern BASIC also employs the full-screen editing capability of the microcomputer which, along with the incorporation of structures previously lacking, has eliminated the need for line numbers.

"We've been using BASIC without line numbers at Dartmouth for five or six years now," observes Kurtz. "It's ancient." . . .

In a further sign that BASIC is maturing as a language, from 1974 to 1984 Kurtz chaired the American National Standards Institute (ANSI) committee responsible for developing a standard for BASIC. The standard they came up with is now undergoing review in the final phase before formal approval.

True BASIC is Kemeny and Kurtz's microcomputer implementation of this ANSI standard, and it is the first product they've developed at True BASIC. Incorporating the advanced features they've used for years in Dartmouth mainframe BASIC, True BASIC exemplifies the reasons why they believe programmers should consider BASIC a serious contender with the languages currently in vogue.

(Millison, 1985)

line number END

The following is a BASIC program to print out a student's name, grade level, and test score using the PRINT and END statements as well as numerical and string constants.

```
10 PRINT "JENNIFER JONES"
20 PRINT "GRADE 6"
30 PRINT 91
40 END
```

This program, when run, will produce the following output:

```
JENNIFER JONES
GRADE 6
91
```

The REM statement tells the computer to ignore whatever follows in that program line. It is used to place remarks in a program that may be of help to the person writing the program. This is sometimes called documenting the program. It is always beneficial to use REM at the beginning of a program to document the purpose of the program. REM statements may be added to the program given earlier to clarify its purpose.

REM

```
10  REM PROGRAM TO REPORT
20  REM STUDENTS TEST SCORE
30  PRINT "JENNIFER JONES"
40  PRINT "GRADE 6"
50  PRINT 91
60  END
```

When this program executes, it will produce exactly the same output as shown earlier. The REM statements will be ignored by the computer. However, when the program is listed, the REM statements will appear in the listing. The value of documenting programs with REM statements is evident when programs are complex. People frequently work on computer programs over a period of time. Documentation helps to remind them of what the program does and how it does it.

The HOME statement clears the screen and places the cursor at the top left-hand corner of the screen. The general format for HOME is

HOME

```
line number HOME
```

Adding the HOME statement to the program would cause anything displayed on the screen before the program runs to be erased when the program encounters and executes the HOME statement. The output of the program would then display beginning at the top left-hand corner of the screen. The program would now look like this:

```
10  REM PROGRAM TO REPORT
20  REM STUDENTS TEST SCORE
30  HOME
40  PRINT "JENNIFER JONES"
50  PRINT "GRADE 6"
60  PRINT 91
70  END
```

Notice that the HOME statement was placed after the REM statements. It is good programming practice to place, at the beginning of the program, the REM statements that generally describe the program.

Example

Write a program to draw a box made of asterisks (*) on the screen.

As with any programming problem, the first step is to understand and then analyze the problem in order to arrive at an algorithm to solve it. The BASIC statement we may use to place output on the screen is the PRINT statement. By using a series of PRINT statements to output the * symbol to the screen, we should be able to write a program to perform the required task. An algorithm to accomplish this task follows:

1. An algorithm to draw a rectangle.
2. Clear the screen.
3. Output a line of fifteen asterisks.
4. Output an asterisk under the first and last asterisks printed out in step 3.
5. Output an asterisk under each of the asterisks printed out in step 4.
6. Output an asterisk under each of the asterisks printed out in step 5.
7. Output a line of fifteen asterisks.
8. End the algorithm.

By tracing through the steps outlined in the algorithm, and perhaps drawing the asterisks on a piece of paper, it is obvious that a computer program written from this logic should produce the desired result. The next step will be to use the algorithm to code the BASIC program. In this instance, each step in the algorithm can be directly translated into a line of BASIC. Compare the algorithm above with the program below.

```
10 REM PROGRAM TO DRAW A BOX
20 HOME
30 PRINT "* * * * * * * * * * * * * * *"
40 PRINT "*                         *"
50 PRINT "*                         *"
60 PRINT "*                         *"
70 PRINT "* * * * * * * * * * * * * * *"
80 END
```

When this program is executed, the desired box appears on the screen.

```
* * * * * * * * * * * * * *
*                         *
*                         *
*                         *
* * * * * * * * * * * * * *
```

The importance of analyzing the problem and arriving at an algorithm before beginning to code a program is often lost on people who are new to programming. This is primarily because of the simplicity of beginning programming problems. Quickly, however, good programming habits, such as problem analysis and algorithm generation, become essential tools as the complexity of the finished computer program increases.

Table 12–1 reviews the information presented so far, as well as selected information from Appendix C on editing and saving programs.

Example	*Function*

Statement

PRINT   10 PRINT "BARBARA"
10 PRINT 125
10 PRINT A
10 PRINT A$ Displays output on the screen or printer.

END   50 END   Stops the computer from executing the program.

REM   10 REM GRADE PROGRAM   Signals a remark.

HOME   20 HOME   Clears the screen and places the cursor in the upper left-hand corner of the screen.

Command

NEW   NEW   Erases the current program in memory.

RUN   RUN   Tells the computer to execute the program in memory.

LIST   LIST   Causes the computer to list the program currently in memory.

SAVE   SAVE MYPROGRAM   Saves the program in memory to disk under the name specified.

LOAD   LOAD MYPROGRAM   Loads a copy of the specified program from disk to memory.

CATALOG   CATALOG   Lists, by name, what is stored on the disk.

To edit the program either retype the entire line, or use the arrow keys to position the cursor where needed on the line you are currently typing and retype as needed.

Table 12–1 Review of Statements and Commands.

EXERCISES

Be sure to generate an algorithm before coding any program you write.

1. Write a program to print your name.
2. Change the program to clear the screen before your name prints.
3. Write a program to draw a triangle on the screen.
4. Write a program to draw a Christmas tree on the screen.
5. Save a program to disk.
6. Catalog your disk.
7. Load a program from disk.
8. Choose a shape and write a program to draw that shape on the screen.

Arithmetic Operations

The following symbols may be used when specifying arithmetic operations in Applesoft BASIC:

( )   Parentheses
^   Exponentiation
*   Multiplication / Division
+   Addition − Subtraction

The order in which operations are performed for a particular expression, such as 5 + 2 * 7, is determined by the order of precedence given in the list above. First, the computer looks through the expression to see if there are any parentheses. If there are, it performs the operation(s) within the parentheses. Next, it looks through the expression again. If there are instances of exponentiation, those are performed. Then the expression is searched once more for any instances of multiplication or division. Because these operations have the same priority, they are performed in order, as encountered. Lastly, the expression is searched for any instances of addition or subtraction. These are performed as they are encountered. At this point the expression has been completely evaluated and the result arrived at.

In the example 5 + 2 * 7 there are no parentheses and no instances of exponentiation, so the computer would first multiply 2 * 7 and the result would leave

$$5 + 14$$

which would be added, yielding

$$19$$

If the expression were changed to

$$(2 + 5) * 7$$

the operation in the parentheses would be performed first, giving

$$7 * 7$$

which would then be multiplied to yield

$$49$$

The expression

$$5 * 6 / 5 - 2 + 1$$

would be treated first by multiplying 5 * 6, giving

$$30 / 5 - 2 + 1$$

Next, the division, 30 / 5, would be performed, leaving

$$6 - 2 + 1$$

Working from left to right, the subtraction operation would yield

$$4 + 1$$

and the last operation, addition, would be performed, giving the result

$$5$$

This order of operations is not unique to computers and is probably familiar to you from previous courses you have taken.

The LET statement is used to assign a value to a numerical or string variable. The BASIC code

```
30 LET A = 240
```

will assign the value 240 to the numerical variable A. The code

```
40 LET AVG = A / 3
```

will cause the computer to evaluate the expression A / 3 and assign the result to the variable AVG. If A is equal to 240, a value of 80 will be assigned to AVG.

String variables may be assigned string values. For example,

```
50 LET NAME$ = "URSULA"
```

assigns the string value URSULA to the string variable NAME$. The PRINT statement can now be used to output the value of NAME$.

```
60 PRINT NAME$
```

This line of code would cause whatever value is currently stored in NAME$ to be printed out. Because URSULA is currently stored in NAME$, URSULA would appear on the screen.

Care must be taken to assign string values to string variables and numerical values to numerical variables. Also, although BASIC will accept A = 240, where the LET statement has been left out, it is better practice to use LET. This tends to make finished programs clearer and more readily understandable. A review of LET and arithmetic operations appears in **Table 12–2**.

	Example	*Function*
Statement LET	LET A = 5 LET C$ = "BOB"	Assigns a value to a string or numerical variable.
Remember:	Assign string values to string variables and numerical values to numerical variables.	
Order of Operations	( ) Parentheses ^ Exponentiation * Multiplication / Division + Addition − Subtraction	
Remember:	Where order of priority is equal (as in multiplication, division, and addition, subtraction) the order of priority is left to right.	

Table 12–2 Review of LET and Arithmetic Operations.

Example

Write a program to compute a student's average and print out the student's name and average. The algorithm is given below.

1. Algorithm to compute and report average.

2. Compute average (grades divided by number of grades).

3. Assign student's name.

4. Output name.

5. Output average.

6. End.

The following BASIC program is written from this algorithm.

```
10 REM PGM TO COMPUTE AVG
20 REM AND PRINT NAME
30 REM AND AVG
40 LET AVG = (75 + 89 + 83 + 81) / 4
50 LET NAME$ = "LYNN"
60 PRINT NAME$
70 PRINT AVG
80 END
```

When this program is run, the output to the screen will be

```
LYNN
82
```

EXERCISES

Write an appropriate algorithm before coding any of the programs below.

1. Write a program that stores your name in the string variable C$ and then prints out the value of C$.

2. Write a program that stores the values ONE, TWO, THREE in three string variables and stores the numbers 1, 2, 3 in three numerical variables. The program should then print out the values stored in all the variables.

3. A student, Bill, has quiz grades of 89, 96, 78, and 88 and test grades of 92 and 87. Test grades count twice as much as quiz grades. Write a program to compute the student's average and output the student's name and average.

4. Change the program you wrote for number 3 to also print out the quiz grades and the test grades.

5. Write a program to compute and print out the average cost per student for a field trip with the following expenses: transportation cost, $150.00; admission, $55.00 for the class; food, $70.00 for the class. There are twenty-five students in the class.

PRINT—One More Time

Suppose a program required output that looked like this:

```
GRADE REPORT
------------
CAROL JONES
SCORES - 97, 86, 96
AVG - 93
```

Reactions and Research

Technology has changed the content of some subjects as they are taught in schools. Mathematics is a good example. The following selection outlines recommendations for changes in the elementary and middle school curricula. Notice the effect that the computer has on the content of the curriculum, as well as the role programming plays in these recommendations. Also, notice the recommendation that computer literacy should not be taught as an addition to the elementary school curriculum. Rather, the suggestion is made that computer literacy should come solely as a by-product of preprogramming activities and computer programming as it is taught within the mathematics curriculum. Many educators would disagree with this view. What do you think?

Applications of calculators, computers, and other electronic information technology are reshaping the fundamental methods of doing and teaching mathematics. When used as tools for arithmetic and for the analysis of graphic or symbolic data, calculators and computers offer powerful new approaches to familiar problems and access to entirely new branches of mathematics. Applications of these same capabilities to instruction are bringing major changes to mathematics classrooms and the roles of mathematics teachers.

The major influence of technology on mathematics education is its potential to shift the focus of instruction from an emphasis on manipulative skills to an emphasis on developing concepts, relationships, structures, and problem-solving skills. Traditional precollege mathematics curricula have stressed the development of a variety of mechanical procedures, including the computational algorithms of arithmetic and the transformation of symbolic expressions in algebra, trigonometry, and analysis. The use of calculators and computers as standard tools in quantitative problem-solving situations, however, has diminished the value of human proficiency in the execution of such procedures. Much of the instructional time currently devoted to acquiring proficiency with paper-and-pencil algorithms should be reallocated to support a range of new or previously neglected topics that have a valid place in the K–12 mathematics curriculum. Moreover, teacher education programs must be modified to reflect these changes in school mathematics content and to model the delivery of instruction through appropriate applications of technology.

The proposals that follow are intended as guidelines for selecting the content of precollege mathematics curricula, for teaching that content in a manner that takes advantage of emerging technology, and for designing teacher education programs that recognize the changing curricular patterns and instructional roles for teachers. The proposals are based on five fundamental assumptions:

1. Coordinated change can take place simultaneously at all levels of mathematics instruction.

2. All students and teachers will have access to calculators and computers for the study of mathematics, in the classroom and at home.

3. All students will experience appropriate application of computers in the study of each school discipline.

4. State/provincial, district, and local mathematics curriculum guidelines and criteria for mathematics textbook adoption will be rewritten to reflect the changing priorities of school mathematics.

5. The publishers of standardized tests and instructional materials will
   a) immediately begin developing products that are consistent with the changing objectives of precollege mathematics;
   b) continue support for that development on a schedule that facilitates the implementation of proposed curricular changes.

TECHNOLOGY AND THE MATHEMATICS CURRICULUM

Today, the computational skills of arithmetic, algebra, geometry, trigonometry, and calculus dominate the K–12 mathematics curriculum. The content and sequences of courses are planned carefully so that students acquire intricate hierarchies of prerequisite skills for each major computational algorithm. Although these well-known mathematical procedures originated as essential aids to efficient problem solving, most of the algorithms of school mathematics have now been programmed for rapid execution by calculators and computers.

To do arithmetic today, mental operations are best for obtaining quick approximations; calculators are the tools of choice for one-time computations; and computers are most appropriate for repetitive calculations. In algebra, trigonometry, and calculus, computers can execute the numerical and symbolic manipulative procedures that students spend countless hours mastering.

As a consequence of this changing environment for mathematical work, the curriculum in grades K–12 needs careful reassessment and revision. Classroom teachers, mathematics supervisors, members of state departments/provincial ministries of education, authors and publishers of textbooks, developers of standardized tests, and other curriculum developers must consider the following recommendations and the questions they raise.

ELEMENTARY SCHOOL LEVEL

The elementary school mathematics curriculum has traditionally focused on developing students' skills in computing with whole numbers, fractions, decimals, and percents. Since computers and calculators can perform such operations more quickly and accurately than can usually be done otherwise, the traditional goals of elementary school mathematics must be reexamined and the predominance of computation-related objectives must be reassessed. Curriculum developers are urged to consider the following recommendations that suggest a broadened view of mathematics appropriate for grades K–4.

- Calculators should routinely be available to students in all activities associated with mathematics learning, including testing. Students should be taught to distinguish situations in which calculators are appropriate aids to computation from situations in which mental operations or paper-and-pencil computations are more appropriate.

- Emphasis should continue to be placed on students' knowledge of basic facts required for proficient mental arithmetic and estimation. However, significant portions of elementary curricula devoted to algorithms for multiple-digit calculations can be eliminated.

- Instruction must shift to emphasize the meaning of arithmetic operations. Such understanding is essential for problem solving.

- Experience with physical manipulatives and other concrete representations of concepts must continue to be an important phase of learning mathematical ideas. Because of the increased instructional emphasis on meaning and understanding, this activity must not be overlooked as the curriculum evolves to take advantage of computers and calculators for instruction.

- Because computers and calculators can be used effectively in teaching mathematical concepts, no a priori assumptions should be made about the appropriateness of any given mathematical topic for elementary students. For instance, decimals, negative numbers, and scientific notation appear naturally when using calculators and can be taught as they arise. Computers facilitate an early introduction to geometric concepts such as transformations, congruence, and vectors; statistical concepts such as randomness; and algebraic concepts such as variable and function.

- Preprogramming activities and simple computer programming in Logo or BASIC can be done by students as early as the kindergarten level to convey both mathematical and computer concepts. Computer literacy should come as a natural byproduct of such experiences rather than as a special addition to the elementary school curriculum.

MIDDLE SCHOOL LEVEL

The mathematics curriculum for the middle school (grades 5–8) must take into account incoming students' knowledge of new topics such as computing, their understanding of topics formerly reserved for the middle grades, and their more limited skills in topics such as arithmetic algorithms. In addition to building on the changes proposed for the elementary grades, curriculum developers for the middle grades should consider the following specific recommendations.

- Mathematics in the middle grades should emphasize the development of "number sense"—the intuitive feeling for the relative sizes of numbers that is essential in skillful estimation, approximation, mental arithmetic, and the interpretation of results for reasonableness.

- Some portion of instructional time should be given to the study of discrete mathematics, including counting, graph theory, probability, and logic, which is important and appropriate for the middle grades.

- Calculators and computers can be used to teach iterative procedures for solving significant problems before traditional formal methods are presented. Such experiences should be part of the middle school mathematics curriculum.

- An introduction to statistics should include extensive gathering, organization, and presentation of data. Important concepts can be developed in the context of real data sets whose manipulation and examination is aided by computer analysis and graphing software.

- Middle school mathematics programs should take advantage of the visual display capabilities of computer graphics that support and underscore the importance of informal geometry objectives. Transformations, mensuration formulas, and spatial visualization can be vividly illustrated by using computer graphics.

- Increased emphasis should be placed on such nontraditional methods of problem solving as organized lists, guess and check, geometrical sketches, and successive approximations, all of which are made feasible by calculators and computers.

- Computer programming experiences that introduce the concepts of variable and function should be provided. These experiences should help prepare students for the study of algebra.

- By the end of grade 6, students should be able to write simple computer programs that require looping and branching concepts. The emphasis in such programming activities should be on problems that convey significant mathematical ideas.

(Corbitt, 1985)

We will assume that the three scores have been previously stored in variables X, Y, and Z, that the average is stored in variable J, and that CAROL JONES is stored in NAME$.

The act of designing the way output will look is called formatting. Often the format for a given set of output is specified within a programming problem. The following segment of code will produce the output specified above.

```
200  PRINT "GRADE REPORT"
210  PRINT "_____"
220  PRINT NAME$
230  PRINT "SCORES - ";X";, ";Y";, ";Z
240  PRINT "AVERAGE - ";J
```

An understanding of how this is accomplished can be gained by going through this segment of code step by step. Line 200 prints the string GRADE REPORT. Line 210 causes a row of dashes to print under GRADE REPORT. The dashes are printed under GRADE REPORT because the computer has automatically issued a carriage return, has gone on to the next line before printing the dashes. In line 220 the string stored in NAME$ (which in this case is CAROL JONES) is printed out on the next line on the screen (again, because the computer has issued another carriage return).

Line 230 uses something new, a semicolon (;), which causes the carriage return to be suppressed. For example, the PRINT statement in line 230 causes the string SCORES – to be printed out. The semicolon after the quotation mark tells the computer to suppress the carriage return, not to go on to the next line. This allows us to continue printing on the same line. Next, because the variable X is specified, whatever is stored in the variable X is printed. Again the carriage return is suppressed by using the semicolon. The string ", " (comma blank) is then printed. Again the carriage return is suppressed and the value of the variable Y is output. The carriage return is suppressed again, a comma and a blank are printed, the carriage return is suppressed one last time, and the value of the variable Z is printed. The effect is to print everything on one line with adequate spacing to make the line legible, as shown below. Notice that in line 230 care is taken to print out a blank both before and after the dash in SCORES – . This allows the first score printed to be preceded by a blank.

```
SCORES - 97, 86, 92
```

Line 240 prints out the string AVERAGE – and then uses the semicolon to suppress the carriage return before printing out the student's average.

By carefully planning the way that output will be formatted, the appearance of information printed by a program can be greatly improved.

INPUT

To this point the only way shown to get data into a program has been through the LET statement. A value may be assigned to a variable using the LET statement and that variable may then be manipulated in some way. The INPUT statement is a way to get data into a program while the program is running. It allows the creation of what are called interactive programs. These are programs that, while running, stop and allow the user to assign values to variables. The general forms of the INPUT statement follow:

```
line number INPUT list of variables separated by commas
line number INPUT quoted string; list of variables
                    separated by commas
```

The first general form is illustrated by the example below

```
10 INPUT X
```

This line of code will cause the computer to pause and place a question mark on the screen followed by the cursor.

?█

The computer will then wait until the person at the keyboard types in something and presses RETURN. In the case above, the computer is waiting for a number to be typed in, since the variable specified in the INPUT statement is a numerical variable. The user might enter the number 45.

```
?45 (PRESS RETURN)
```

It is possible to enter values for multiple variables using a single INPUT statement. For example:

```
10 INPUT X,Y,Z
```

This line will cause the computer to pause in its execution of the program and wait for three numbers to be typed in, separated by commas. The following could be entered to assign the value of 78 to X, 76 to Y and 88 to Z:

```
?78,76,88 (PRESS RETURN)
```

Notice that the numbers are separated by commas.

INPUT may be used to assign values to string variables by specifying a string variable in the INPUT statement. The following code accepts a string value to be assigned to the string variable G$:

```
10 INPUT G$
```

In response to this a person sitting at the keyboard may type

```
?MICHELLE (PRESS RETURN)
```

The string value MICHELLE would then be assigned to the string variable G$. As with numerical variables, values may be assigned to multiple string variables in the same INPUT statement by separating the variables with commas. The program line

```
30 INPUT A$,B$
```

would accept two string constants separated by commas, such as the following:

```
?NANCY,SANDY (PRESS RETURN)
```

In this instance NANCY would be assigned to A$ and SANDY would be assigned to B$.

It is important to give the person using the program an idea of what needs to be typed in as a response to an INPUT statement. Remember, someone using a program may have no idea how the program was written. If confronted with just a question mark on the screen, the person may not know what the program requires in response. For this reason, when using the INPUT statement, always include a brief description of what the user should do. This is called a prompt.

One way of giving the user a prompt is simply to include a PRINT statement in your program to output the prompt just before using INPUT. For example:

```
10 REM PGM TO ASSIGN NAME
15 PRINT "PLEASE ENTER YOUR NAME"
20 INPUT B$
30 PRINT "NICE TO MEET YOU ";B$
40 END
```

This program will first cause the string in line 15 to print. When the program encounters the INPUT statement, it will present a question mark on the screen and wait to receive input.

```
PLEASE ENTER YOUR NAME
?■
```

The prompt has clarified what the user of the program is supposed to do. A name is entered:

```
?DIANE (PRESS RETURN)
```

causing the string DIANE to be assigned to the variable B$. Line 30 causes the message NICE TO MEET YOU, and the name stored in B$ to be printed out as follows:

```
NICE TO MEET YOU DIANE
```

Another way to cause the computer to print out a prompt is by placing the prompt in the INPUT statement. As the second example of the general form of the INPUT statement indicates,

```
line number INPUT quoted string; list of variables
                  separated by commas
```

a prompt can be placed within the INPUT statement as long as it is enclosed in quotes and is followed by a semicolon. For example:

```
10 INPUT "PLEASE ENTER YOUR NAME ";B$
```

This will print out the prompt and allow the user to enter the name on the same line as the prompt. The screen will appear as below. Notice that when this form of INPUT is used, no question mark is printed before the cursor.

```
PLEASE ENTER YOUR NAME ■
```

The user may then enter a name.

```
PLEASE ENTER YOUR NAME JANET (PRESS RETURN)
```

The name will then be assigned to the variable specified (B$ in this instance).

Another example would be

```
10 INPUT "ENTER 4 GRADES ";V,B,N,L
```

The screen would show

```
ENTER 4 GRADES ■
```

And the user would enter four grades as follows:

```
ENTER 4 GRADES 87,78,90,83 (PRESS RETURN)
```

Example

Write a program that will accept as input three student names and a set of four grades for each student. The program should compute each student's average and an average for the group of three students. The heading READING GROUP ONE should be printed, followed by one line each that prints the student's name and average. A last line should be printed with the label GROUP AVERAGE and the group's average.

It is often beneficial to view a programming problem as input, process, and output. In this example, a start may be made by locating the desired output, which in this case is clearly identified as a report including a heading, one line for each student giving the student's name and average, and a summary line stating the group's average. Next, identify what is given or required as input. In this problem the program must, for each of three students, accept as input a name and a set of four scores. Having identified the input and output, all that remains is to decide how the input must be processed to arrive at the output. For this problem, calculations must be done to (a) average each student's score and (b) arrive at a group average.

At this point a general analysis of the problem has been accomplished and may be expressed using a structure chart, as shown in **Figure 12–1**. The intent is to express and record, in a general way, the analysis of the problem accomplished so far. This also isolates the different functions the program will perform into modules that may be worked on one at a time, thereby minimizing confusion.

The next step is to take the structure chart and use it to generate an English-language algorithm. The algorithm will be more specific than the structure chart and will be used as the basis for coding the program. Notice that for this example, each module is identified as to function.

1. Algorithm for group grading.

Input Module

2. Accept three student names and four grades for each student.

Process Module

3. Compute each student's average as sum of grades divided by four.
4. Compute group average as sum of averages divided by three.

Output Module

5. Print heading READING GROUP ONE.
6. Print dashes.

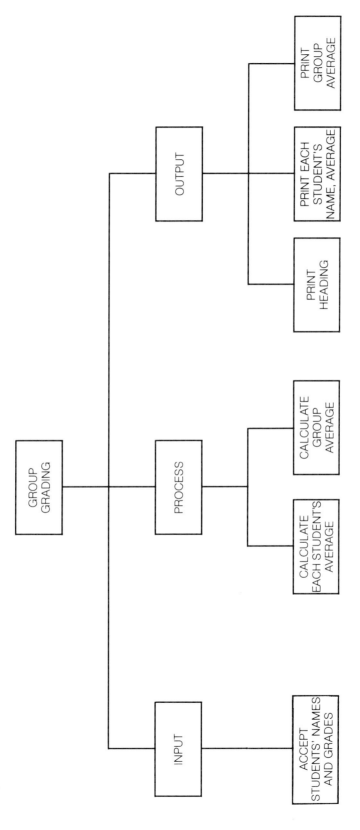

Figure 12–1 Structure chart for "Group Grading".

7. For each student print name, average.

8. Print GROUP AVERAGE followed by average.

9. End.

The following program, coded from the algorithm above, will accomplish the task set forth in the problem. Notice that in the REM statements the variables are identified as to use. This is good programming practice.

```
100  REM GROUP GRADING PROGRAM
110  REM N1$ - 1ST STUDENTS NAME
120  REM A,B,C,D - 1ST STUDENTS GRADES
130  REM N2$ - 2ND STUDENTS NAME
140  REM E,F,G,H - 2ND STUDENTS GRADES
150  REM N3$ - 3RD STUDENTS NAME
160  REM I,J,K,L - 3RD STUDENTS GRADES
170  REM S1 - 1ST STUDENTS AVERAGE
180  REM S2 - 2ND STUDENTS AVERAGE
190  REM S3 - 3RD STUDENTS AVERAGE
200  REM AVG - GROUP AVERAGE
210  REM **** INPUT MODULE ****
230  PRINT "ENTER FIRST STUDENTS NAME"
240  INPUT "AND 4 GRADES ";N1$,A,B,C,D
250  PRINT "ENTER SECOND STUDENTS NAME"
260  INPUT "AND 4 GRADES ";N2$,E,F,G,H
270  PRINT "ENTER THIRD STUDENTS NAME"
280  INPUT "AND 4 GRADES ";N3$,I,J,K,L
290  REM **** PROCESS MODULE ****
300  LET S1 = (A+B+C+D)/4
310  LET S2 = (E+F+G+H)/4
320  LET S3 = (I+J+K+L)/4
330  LET AVG = (S1+S2+S3)/3
340  REM **** OUTPUT MODULE ****
345  PRINT " "
350  PRINT "READING GROUP ONE"
360  PRINT "_____"
370  PRINT N1$;" ";S1
380  PRINT N2$;" ";S2
390  PRINT N3$;" ";S3
400  PRINT " "
410  PRINT "GROUP AVERAGE ";AVG
420  END
```

When this program is run, the screen will appear as shown below, assuming that the names and grades entered for input by the person using the program are those shown.

```
ENTER FIRST STUDENTS NAME
AND 4 GRADES JANE,100,80,90,90
ENTER SECOND STUDENTS NAME
AND 4 GRADES JILL,60,90,80,90
ENTER THIRD STUDENTS NAME
AND 4 GRADES FRED,70,60,70,80
```

	Example	*Function*
Statement		
INPUT	INPUT X INPUT B$ INPUT X,Y INPUT C$,N$ INPUT "ENTER NAME ";H$	Assigns a value to a string or numeric varia- ble while program is running.

Table 12–3 Review of INPUT.

```
READING GROUP ONE
-----------------
JANE 90
JILL 80
FRED 70

GROUP AVERAGE 80
```

Notice that in lines 345 and 400 the statement PRINT " " is used to print out a blank line. Try entering and running the program with different sets of grades.

 # Computers in the Classroom

The activity described in the excerpt below appeared in the Computer Corner section of the Arithmetic Teacher *in October 1984. It gives children the opportunity to predict the outcome of different BASIC statements. This can be a valuable learning experience for students. A similar activity can be created and used as children learn other new statements in BASIC. After presenting a new statement, give children examples of the statement in use and ask them to predict what will happen when the statement is executed. This type of activity can be expanded to include giving children a short program and asking them to predict what will be printed out on the screen when the program is run. Such an exercise requires a knowledge of how the BASIC statements in the program work. It also requires the careful application of logic, as the child plays computer and traces through the logic of the program, step by step, to find out exactly what it does.*

This activity offers students a chance to practice mental computation and judge the effects of various rules for formatting output. Blank computer cards can be held up with different PRINT statements on them, and students can respond on paper (gridded maps of the computer's text screen) or simply explain orally. Practice with both written and oral responses to this activity is important. The ability to predict is an important problem-solving skill that can be practiced by using BASIC and the computer.

Present this program in BASIC:

```
10 LET A = 3
20 LET B = 6
30 LET C = 9
```

Ask the class to describe what will appear if this program is RUN with each of the following PRINT statements:

```
40 PRINT A;B;C
40 PRINT A;" ";B;" ";C
40 PRINT B;C,A
40 PRINT B+A;C
40 PRINT C-A;B-A;A/A
40 PRINT C/A,C-B,A
40 PRINT A:PRINT B:PRINT C
40 PRINT A,B-A,C-B
```

The values of the variables, the combinations of operations, and the punctuation all can be varied to provide many levels of practice. Allow each solution to be discussed and displayed on the chalkboard or computer monitor. The best approach would be to permit students to compare their predictions with the actual output from the computer.

(Hampel, 1984)

EXERCISES

Draw a structure chart and generate an algorithm before coding each program that you write.

1. Write a program that asks for name and address, allows you to input them, and then prints them out on the screen. Use different variables for name and address.

2. Write a program that prints the sum, difference, product, and quotient for any two numbers you input.

3. Write a program that asks for (a) a student's name, (b) the student's teacher, (c) four quiz grades for the student, and (d) two test grades for the student. Tests count twice as much as quizzes. The program should compute the student's average and print it out.

4. A teacher named C$ has a three-year contract that pays P dollars the first year with an R% increase the second and third years. C$, P, and R are to be input. Your program should print out the teacher's name and how much the salary will be for each of the three years.

5. Write a program to calculate the cost of a student's book order. The student will order four books. The student's name and the title and cost of each book should be input. The student receives a 10% discount on the total order. Output the student's name, each book title and cost, the total order cost, and the discount price for the whole order.

Conclusion

In the last example, having to recode the prompts and INPUT statements for the three students is cumbersome and inefficient. Chapter 13 covers a few more BASIC statements that will help to increase the power and flexibility available to you in writing BASIC programs.

Key Terms

command
constant
numerical constant
numerical variable
order of operations
prompt
reserved word
statement
string
string constant
string variable
variable
System Commands
    CATALOG

LIST
LOAD
NEW
RUN
SAVE
Statements
END
HOME
INPUT
LET
PRINT
REM

References/Further Reading

Boillot, Michel. *BASIC: Concepts and Structured Problem Solving.* St. Paul: West Publishing Co., 1984.

Coburn, Edward J. *An Introduction to BASIC: Structured Programming for Microcomputers.* Albany, N.Y.: Delmar Publishers, 1986.

Corbitt, Mary Kay. "The Impact of Computing Technology on School Mathematics: Report of an NCTM Conference." *Arithmetic Teacher* 32, no. 8 (1985):14–18, 60.

Graham, Neill. *Introduction to Computer Science*, 3d ed. St. Paul: West Publishing Co., 1985.

Hampel, Paul J. "Computer Corner: Predict the Outcome." *Arithmetic Teacher* 32, no. 2 (1984):44.

Jones, Richard M. *Structured BASIC.* Newton, Mass.: Allyn and Bacon, 1985.

Millison, Doug. "BASIC's Kemeny and Kurtz Discuss the Language Today." *Computer Language* 2, no. 10 (1985):21–24.

Thompson, Robert G. *BASIC: A Modular Approach.* Columbus, Ohio: Charles E. Merrill Publishing Co., 1985.

13

BASIC: Adding Options

TOPICS ADDRESSED

How are the following BASIC statements used: GOTO, IF-THEN, FOR, NEXT, READ, DATA, RESTORE?

What are relational symbols, and how are they used in BASIC?

How might the GOTO statement be misused?

What are FOR-NEXT loops?

How are FOR-NEXT loops represented on a flowchart?

How can structure charts be used in developing a BASIC program? What are some examples?

OUTLINE

Introduction
GOTO
IF-THEN
  Example One
  Example Two
  Exercises
FOR-NEXT
  Example
  Exercises

READ, DATA, and RESTORE
  Example
  Exercises
Conclusion
Key Terms
References/Further Reading

This chapter introduces more BASIC statements, with examples and practice exercises. Examples of structure charts as they may be used in program development are also included.

GOTO

The GOTO statement is used to transfer control to a particular line number in a program. Unless the program specifies otherwise, such as by using the GOTO statement, instructions in the program are executed sequentially, in the order they appear within the program. GOTO allows this sequential execution of instructions to be changed. The general format of the GOTO statement is

```
GOTO line number
```

Consider the following program:

```
10 REM PROGRAM TO PRINT NEXT INTEGER
20 PRINT "ENTER AN INTEGER"
30 INPUT X
40 LET X = X + 1
50 PRINT X
60 END
```

This program allows a user to enter an integer (line 30). Line 40 adds 1 to the integer and line 50 prints out the result. Each line of the program has executed, one after another, in the order in which it appears in the program. Suppose, however, that instead of printing out the next integer beyond the number the user inputs, we wanted to print out the next five integers. By adding line 55 to the program we can accomplish this.

```
10 REM LOOP PROGRAM
20 PRINT "ENTER AN INTEGER"
30 INPUT X
40 LET X = X + 1
50 PRINT X
55 GOTO 40
60 END
```

In this program an integer will be input in line 30 and increased by 1 in line 40. The result will be output in line 50. If a user had input 5, 1 would be added to it and the result, 6, would be printed out. Next, the program encounters the GOTO statement in line 55. This instructs the program to transfer control to the line specified, in this case line number 40. This means that the next instruction executed will be whatever is on line 40. Because the instruction on line 40 is to add 1 to whatever is the current value of X, 1 is added to 6, giving a result of 7, which is printed out in line 50. Again line 55 is encountered and the program executes the GOTO statement, which sends it back to line 40. X is increased by 1 again, giving 8, which is printed out in line 50. By using the GOTO statement we have created a loop. Control of the program will always loop back to line 40, the program will sequentially execute lines 40 and 50, and then encounter line 55 again, which will send control of the program looping back to line 40. Not only is this a loop, but it is also an infinite loop. Once the program starts to execute, it will enter the loop and never leave it until some outside force acts on it, such as someone turning off the computer or, on an Apple II series computer, pressing the key labeled CTRL or CONTROL and then simultaneously pressing the key labeled C. (This is usually written as CTRL-C.) Try entering and running the program. You will see a stream of numbers pass by on the screen until you intervene to stop the program from executing.

Loops are important in programming, but infinite loops are to be avoided. Therefore, a way is needed to control loops. BASIC provides several ways to do this, two of which are covered later.

One cautionary note about the GOTO statement. There are times in programming in BASIC when it is necessary to use the GOTO statement. It should, however, be used sparingly. It is possible, by indiscriminately using GOTOs in your programming, to create programs that are logically incomprehensible. When GOTO is used in this way, it becomes difficult or impossible to trace through the logic of the program. This leads to a situation in which it is difficult to fix a program if there should be something wrong with it. The unrestricted use of GOTO in this way is not an acceptable practice.

IF-THEN

The IF-THEN statement allows the programmer to control what instructions are executed based on the results of a test of some condition. The general forms of the IF-THEN statement are

```
IF condition THEN one or more BASIC statements
IF condition THEN line number
IF condition THEN GOTO line number
```

A condition in this instance means the comparison of two BASIC expressions using the relational symbols listed below. (It is possible to compare more than two expressions using the logical operators AND, OR, and NOT, but that is beyond the scope of this brief introduction.)

$=$	equal to
$<>$	not equal to
$>$	greater than
$<$	less than
$>=$	greater than or equal to
$<=$	less than or equal to

FUNKY WINKERBEAN by Tom Batiuk. ©Field Enterprises, Inc. 1983. Permission of News America Syndicate.

The following code illustrates the IF-THEN statement:

```
20 IF B = 5 THEN PRINT "OVER LIMIT"
30 LET B = B - 1
```

When line 20 is encountered, the computer will check to see if the condition, B = 5, is true, to see if 5 is currently stored in the variable B. If this condition is true, the program will execute whatever instruction is coded after the THEN. Here the instruction is PRINT "OVER LIMIT", so if B = 5 the string OVER LIMIT will be printed out. Control will then pass to the next line of code, line 30 in our example. If the condition evaluates as false, in this case if B does not currently equal 5, the computer ignores the THEN and any instructions that follow it and control is immediately transferred to the next sequential line number (line number 30 in the code above).

To review: the condition after the IF is tested. If it is true, the instructions after the THEN are carried out and control passes to the next sequential line number. If the condition is false, the THEN is ignored and control passes to the next sequential line number.

Conditional tests may involve any of the symbols cited above and may be done on string or numerical variables.

```
20 IF B$ = "YES" THEN PRINT "CONTINUE"
```

In this case if the string YES is stored in B$, CONTINUE will be printed. Otherwise, it will not be printed.

In either of the following cases, control will be transferred to line 30 if the value stored in A is less than 5.

```
15 IF A < 5 THEN 30
20 IF A < 5 THEN GOTO 30
```

We now have a way to control loops and make decisions. The following code will accept an integer and then print out the next five integers before the program ends:

```
10 REM PRINT NEXT 5 INTEGERS
20 LET A = 0
30 PRINT "ENTER AN INTEGER"
40 INPUT X
50 LET X = X + 1
60 PRINT X
70 LET A = A + 1
80 IF A < 5 THEN 50
90 END
```

Line 20 sets the initial value of A, which will be used as a counter, to 0. Line 30 prints a prompt and line 40 accepts a value to be assigned to X. Line 50 adds 1 to X and line 60 prints the result. In line 70 the variable A, which is used to count the number of integers that have been printed out, is increased by 1. Its current value is then 1, which is as it should be, since 1 integer beyond whatever value was input by the user has been printed.

Line 80 contains the IF-THEN statement that controls the loop. It tests the condition A < 5. If A is less than 5, the program loops back to line 50, X is increased by 1 and then printed out in line 60. The counter is increased again in line 70 and then line 80 tests to see if A < 5. The process of looping back to line 50 will continue until A, the counter, is no longer less than 5, at which point the first five integers beyond the integer originally entered will have been printed out. The program then ends. A run of this program might look like this:

```
ENTER AN INTEGER
?7
8
9
10
11
12
```

How would you change this program to print out the next twelve integers beyond the number input? The next forty?

Example One

Write a program to allow a student's average to be input. The program will print out PASSED if the average is 65 or above and NOT PASSED if the average is below 65.

Figure 13–1 is a structure chart for this program. An algorithm for the program is listed below.

1. Algorithm for pass/not passed program.

2. Accept student's grade.

3. If grade less than 65

   Then print NOT PASSED
       go to step 5.

4. Print PASSED.

5. End.

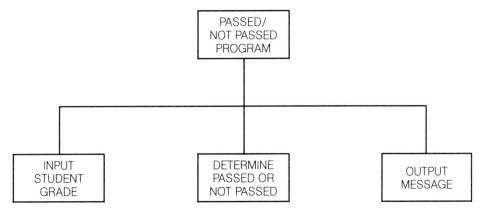

Figure 13–1 A structure chart for the "Passed/Not Passed" program.

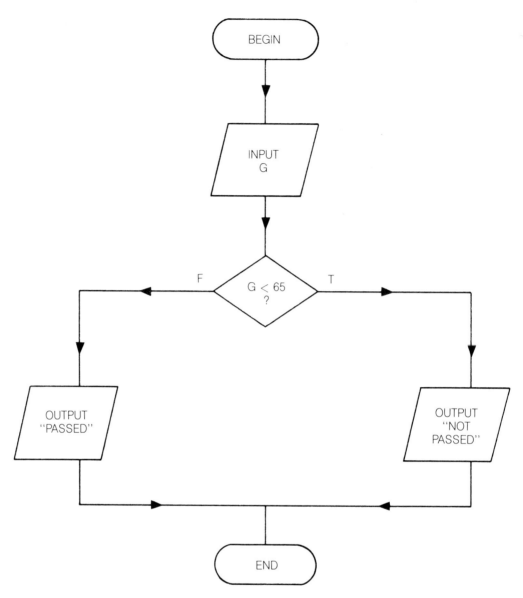

Figure 13–2 A flowchart for the "Passed/Not Passed" program.

Figure 13–2 is a flowchart for this program. Notice that it contains more detail than the algorithm. The program below has been coded from the flowchart.

```
100 REM PASS/NOT PASSED PROGRAM
110 REM G = STUDENTS GRADE
120 INPUT "ENTER STUDENTS GRADE ";G
130 IF G < 65 THEN PRINT "NOT PASSED":GOTO 150
140 PRINT "PASSED"
150 END
```

After accepting a grade as input in line 120, the program uses the IF-THEN statement in line 130 to test if the grade is less than 65. If it is, NOT PASSED is printed out. The colon (:) allows more than one statement to be on one line in BASIC; in this case it allows us to place more than one BASIC statement after the THEN. After NOT PASSED is printed, the GOTO statement sends control of the program to line 150, where the program ends.

If the test G < 65 is false, that is, if G is equal to or greater than 65, the THEN is ignored and control passes to line 140, where PASSED is printed out. The program then ends. When this program is run, the screen would look like this.

```
ENTER STUDENTS GRADE 84
PASSED
```

Although BASIC allows more than one statement to be placed on a line in a program, it is best if this is avoided for the sake of clarity. In a complex program the listing of multiple BASIC statements on one line can cause confusion. Although the previous program is not likely to cause such difficulty because of its simplicity, it is best to get into the habit of not placing multiple commands on a line unless it is absolutely necessary. An alternate way of coding the program above follows:

```
100 REM PASS/NOT PASSED PROGRAM
110 REM G = STUDENTS GRADE
120 INPUT "ENTER STUDENTS GRADE ";G
130 IF G < 65 THEN 160
140 PRINT "PASSED"
150 GOTO 170
160 PRINT "NOT PASSED"
170 END
```

This version of the program still uses the IF-THEN statement in line 130 to test if the grade is less than 65. If it is, control is sent to line 160, where NOT PASSED is printed out. After NOT PASSED is printed, the program ends. If the test G < 65 is false, control passes to line 140, where PASSED is printed out. In line 150 control is sent to line 170, where the program ends. Again in this instance comparison of the structure of these two programs may seem trivial, but in more involved problems the way the program is structured can be of great importance.

Example Two

A teacher earns D dollars per hour at her summer job. Overtime (any time over thirty-five hours per week) pays 1.5 times the regular hourly rate. Write a program to compute gross pay for an H-hour week. D and H should be input while the program is running.

Figure 13–3 is a structure chart for this program. Below is an algorithm for the program.

1. Algorithm for pay problem.

2. Accept input for dollars per hour.

3. Accept input for number of hours worked.

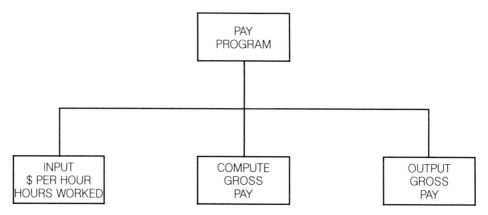

Figure 13–3 A structure chart for the "Pay" program.

4. If regular pay only
   goto step 7.

5. Compute gross pay with overtime.

6. Go to step 8.

7. Compute gross pay, no overtime.

8. Print gross pay.

9. End.

Figure 13–4 is a flowchart for the program. Notice that the flowchart takes the algorithm and makes it more specific. For example, the conditional test that is described in general in step 4 in the algorithm is specifically given in the flowchart. The flowchart is then used to code the program below.

```
100  REM COMPUTE GROSS PAY
110  REM D = HOURLY RATE
120  REM H = HOURS WORKED
130  REM G = TOTAL GROSS PAY
140  INPUT "ENTER PAY RATE (99.99) ==> ";D
150  INPUT "ENTER HOURS WORKED (99.99) ==> ";H
160  IF (H - 35) <= 0 THEN 190
170  LET G = (D * 35) + (H - 35) * (1.5 * D)
180  GOTO 200
190  LET G = D * H
200  PRINT "GROSS PAY IS $";G
210  END
```

In the program above, first the variables are identified as to purpose. D represents hourly rate, H represents hours worked, and G represents total gross pay. Line 140 allows hourly rate to be input and line 150 accepts input for the number of hours worked. The (99.99) in each of the prompts in lines 140 and 150 is an example of the way the numbers should be entered, to two decimal places (i.e., 10.00, 5.50, or 38.75). Line 160 is a test to see if any overtime has been worked. If the hours worked minus 35 is less than or equal to 0, it means

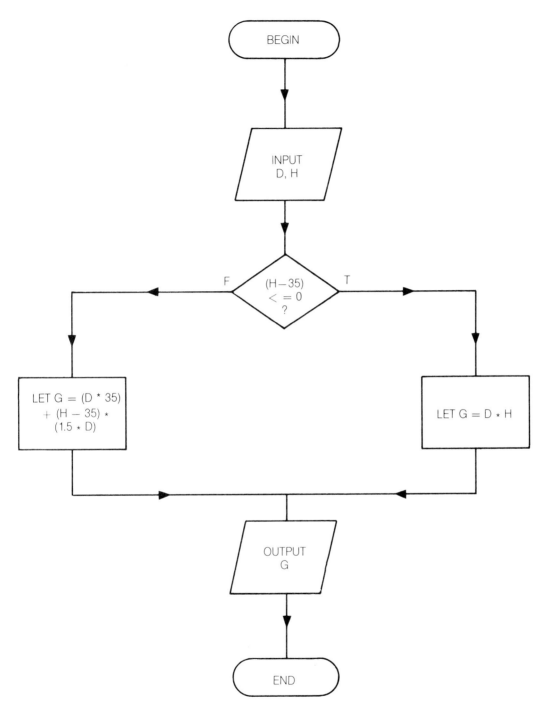

Figure 13-4 A flowchart for the "Pay" program.

that 35 or fewer hours have been worked; therefore, no overtime has been earned. If no overtime has been earned, then control passes to line 190, where gross pay (G) can be computed as G = D * H. G is then printed out in line 200 and the program ends.

	Example	*Function*
Statement		
GOTO	GOTO 80	Transfers control of the program to the line number specified.

IF condition THEN one or more BASIC statements
IF condition THEN line number
IF condition THEN GOTO line number
        IF C\$ = "NO" THEN PRINT "GOODBYE": GOTO 120
        IF A = 5 THEN 150
        IF D > 35 THEN GOTO 90
            If the condition evaluates as true, the instruction(s) following the THEN is (are) done. Allows control of loops and allows decisions to be made.

Table 13–1 Review of GOTO and IF-THEN.

In line 160 if the test evaluates as false, if H minus 35 is not less than or equal to 0, in other words if it is more than 0, then overtime has been earned because H is more than 35. In this case control drops to line 170, where G is computed with overtime. Control then passes to line 180 which sends control to line 200, where G is output. The program then ends. When this program runs, the screen appears as follows:

```
ENTER PAY RATE (99.99) ==> 5.00
ENTER HOURS WORKED (99.99) ==> 35.00
GROSS PAY IS $175
```

Table 13–1 reviews GOTO and IF-THEN.

EXERCISES

For each exercise draw a structure chart, write an algorithm, and draw a flowchart before coding your program.

1. Write a program that prints the squares of all integers from 1 to 100.

2. Write a program that asks for (a) a student's name and (b) four numerical grades for the student and then (c) prints out the student's name and the average of the four grades. The program should then ask if you would like to do the same for another student. If the response is yes, the program should then loop back to allow the new student's name and grades to be input; otherwise, the program should end.

3. Write a program that allows you to enter a number between 1 and 100 inclusive. The program should then print out the remaining integers up to and including 100. (The original number entered should be an integer.)

4. Change Example One to accept the student's name. The program should also ask the user, after one student has been processed, if there are more students to be processed. If the response is yes, the program should loop back to accept another student; otherwise, the program should end.

FOR-NEXT

BASIC offers another way to control loops by making use of the FOR and the NEXT statements. These are called FOR-NEXT loops. Below are two programs

Input/Output

William S. Curran presents a strategy that allows students to learn programming concepts before learning the formal syntax of a programming language. One looping structure introduced in this article is:

```
While Sum is greater than zero Do
End While
```

Instructions placed between these two lines will continue to execute repeatedly while it is true that Sum is greater than zero. For instance, the instruction Subtract 1 from Sum will continue to execute in the following example until Sum is equal to or less than zero.

```
While Sum is greater than zero Do
Subtract 1 from Sum
End While
```

One of the major stumbling blocks for beginning students of computer science is the fact that they must master a new language to write even an elementary program. They often ask why programs cannot be written in ordinary English, and they are stifled by the fact that some of the fundamental aspects of programming cannot be demonstrated until a formal syntax has been grasped.

To a degree, the writers of high-level languages have taken these points into consideration and are trying to achieve more natural constructions, but the great power and range of these languages impose formal constraints which delay the learning process.

This article describes a program which aims at obviating these problems by asking students to write small programs in English, the effects of which are immediately shown on the screen. It is written in BASIC for the Apple computer, making interactive graphics possible and making them available to a large audience. It is designed to function on several levels of sophistication, but requires only a dozen intuitive commands.

The program begins with a robot figure on the screen, seated and facing a wall which is randomly located at *N* steps from the chair. The task is simple: Supply the necessary sequence of commands to get the robot to stand up, walk until it touches the wall, return and sit back down.

On the lowest level of sophistication, the available commands are: stand up, sit down, raise arms, lower arms, turn around and step.

The student or instructor chooses whether to enter and execute the instructions one at a time or to enter several commands (up to 40) and have them executed in sequence. All choices are selected from a menu on the screen; the user simply types the number next to the desired option.

The program will not accept commands not on the list; a command such as "walk" is simply ignored. Neither will it accept synonyms, compound commands or misspellings. The instructor can explain that the reason for this is the robot's computer brain is stupid. (Most beginners love to be told that a computer is really quite dumb.)

With little or no practice, students can make the robot perform the desired task, and in the process they learn a little about formal language constraints as well as sequential processing.

At that point students are ready to move to the next level of sophistication. The instructor explains that the robot has sensors at the ends of its arms and a counter (like those clickers used to count attendance at concerts). The robot can add to and subtract from the counter, and it can sense whether or not it is touching the wall.

The following commands/questions are added to the list of instructions: Add 1 to the counter; subtract 1 from the counter; is the counter equal to zero?; and are you touching the wall? (The robot answers yes or no to the questions.) Now the game is more challenging. The goal is the same, but students are to supply the commands and questions without looking at the screen. The teacher serves as a relay between the student and the machine.

This constraint forces students to use the counter to count the steps to the wall. Otherwise they will not know how many steps it takes to get back to the chair. (Recall that the wall is located at a random distance from the chair; there is no other way to figure out the location of the chair.)

The function of the counter will be obvious to many, but not all, students, so when they do understand, they will have gained an important insight into the use of counters. More important, they learn about conditional action in general.

While students are learning these concepts, they are also growing tired of repeating the same commands over and over for each step taken by the robot. They will search for some means of automatic repetition—and at that point are ready for the next level of sophistication, which adds this looping structure:

```
While the answer is No Do
End While
```

The student can now, without looking at the screen, write a general program for the robot which will work no matter where the chair is placed.

Looping structures are much less intuitive than counters for the beginner, and sometimes require practice. However, the students at this point have seen the need for an automatic repeat mechanism and gladly work for an understanding of the instructions.

In short order they are able to write a program using the all-important concept of looping, and they are immediately gratified by seeing the robot figure following their commands successfully.

Another level of sophistication is available, but this time we do not require additional commands. There are hidden options for the instructor which do not appear on the menu for pedantic reasons.

Most likely, students will write their first programs with the following sequence:

```
Stand Up
Raise Arms
Step
Are you touching the wall?...
```

If the wall is at least one step away, that program will work. If not, it fails. The instructor has a hidden option to locate the wall zero steps from the chair, and it is an eye-opener for most students to find that their working program fails in that case. They must learn to ask, "Are you touching the wall?" *before* taking a step rather than after.

When they resolve that particular oversight, most students are very confident that their program will work in all cases. But another option available to the instructor teaches yet another important idea about initial conditions: It has been tacitly assumed that the counter has an initial value of zero, but that does not have to be the case. When the instructor chooses the hidden option which sets the counter to three, students watch with surprise as the robot crashes into the chair. They have to debug their program to find out why the instructions fail so unexpectedly when they worked so well before. When they realize what the problem is, they must set up an initial loop to set the counter to zero:

```
Is the counter equal to zero?
While the answer is No Do
Subtract 1 from the counter
Is the counter equal to zero?
End While
```

This loop in itself is quite an achievement for beginners, and when it is mastered the student has powerful insights into computer programming.

There are other little features in the program: If the robot runs into the wall, the screen reads, "I just ran into the wall and died," and the command to walk when the chair is in the way elicits a similar response. Other incompatible sequences are also disallowed, analogous to compiler error messages.

Other menu options allow the user to save a program to disk or edit an existing program (insert, delete, modify, list).

All the options in the program can be demonstrated in less than an hour or paced over a longer time at the instructor's discretion, although it is most effective when students are given sufficient time to think about any new concepts presented.

One of the most important and effective features of the program is that it produces a network of reference points for the student. For example, when the concept of looping arises in teaching BASIC (or any other programming language), the teacher may refer back to the robot program and students can relate the new concept to the previous concept. In this way students are led on a painless path from ordinary language commands to more abstract languages and ideas.

Students' reactions to the program have been excellent. They are not threatened by the possibility of getting things wrong, and they enjoy the humorous aspects of the actions and responses of the robot. It is particularly effective with those who have had unpleasant experiences with computers in the past or those who are apprehensive about computers. Young students enjoy it as a kind of video game, permitting a mild level of competition.

Advanced students can modify the code itself to produce different commands and actions, and they can learn a bit about computer graphics in the process....

Note: This program was developed with the idea of maximum effectiveness at a minimum cost. For those with sufficient funding, a voice synthesizer would enable robot responses to be heard; if a voice recognition unit is added, commands can be input by voice.

The program is implemented on an Apple II in two versions: high resolution and low resolution, with no additional memory requirements. Both are in public domain and can be obtained gratis by contacting the author at Loyola University of New Orleans. Listings are available, or send a disk to receive a copy. The author is currently working on a Macintosh version.

[William S. Curran, Box 191, Loyola University, New Orleans, LA 70118. (Curran, 1985)]

---

that will both accomplish the same thing. Each program will print the squares of the integers 1 through 5. The second program uses a FOR-NEXT loop.

```
10 REM PRINT SQUARES OF 1 TO 5
20 LET K = 1
30 LET X = K * K
40 PRINT X
50 LET K = K + 1
60 IF K <= 5 THEN GOTO 30
70 END

10 REM PRINT SQUARES OF 1 TO 5
20 FOR K = 1 TO 5
```

```
30 LET X = K * K
40 PRINT X
50 NEXT K
60 END
```

In the first program, K is assigned the initial value of 1 in line 20. Line 30 squares K and assigns the result to X. In line 40, X is printed out. Line 50 increases K by 1. Line 60 tests to see if K is less than or equal to 5. If it is true that K is less than or equal to 5, then control is transferred to line 30, where K is squared and the result assigned to X. The looping continues until K is no longer less than or equal to 5 (until K is greater than 5). The program then ends.

The second program uses a FOR-NEXT loop to accomplish the same result. In this program the loop is controlled by the FOR statement in line 20 and the NEXT statement in line 50. These two statements define the boundaries of the FOR-NEXT loop. All the lines of code within these boundaries, whether 1 line, 100 lines, or whatever number of lines of code, are called the body of the loop. The FOR statement

```
FOR K = 1 TO 5
```

instructs the computer to initially assign the value of 1 to the variable K and to continue going through the loop until the terminal value, which here is 5, is satisfied. Therefore, when control passes to line 30, the first time through the loop, K is equal to 1 (the initial value assigned to K). In line 30, K is squared and the result assigned to the variable X, which is printed out in line 40. At this point control passes to line 50, which contains the NEXT statement. The statement NEXT K instructs the computer to, in this case, increase the value of the variable K by 1 and then check the FOR statement to see if the value of the variable K is now greater than the terminal value specified in the FOR statement, which, in this example, is 5. Because K is not greater than 5, control is transferred to line 30 and the program goes through the body of the loop with the current value of K, which is 2. In line 30, K is squared, the result assigned to X and, in line 40, X is printed. Once again line 50 is executed, K is increased by 1, becoming 3, and the FOR statement is checked to see if the value of K has exceeded the terminal value specified. Because it has not, the loop is executed again. The loop will continue to be executed until the squares of the integers 1 through 5 have been printed. At that point, when the program executes the NEXT K statement, the value of K will become 6. When the program checks the FOR statement it will see that the value of K has exceeded the specified terminal value and the loop will not execute again. Control will then pass to the line of code in the program that follows the NEXT statement, in this instance line 60, where the program will end.

The general form of the FOR statement follows:

```
line number FOR variable = initial value TO terminal value
                                    STEP value
```

The variable specified is referred to as the control variable. The STEP value refers to how much the control variable will be increased each time the NEXT statement is encountered. If it is omitted, as in the previous example, its value is assumed to be 1. The initial, terminal, and step values can be any number or any numerical variable name.

The general form for the NEXT statement is

```
NEXT variable name
```

where the variable name specified is the control variable identified in the FOR statement.

The following code uses the STEP option to increase the control variable by 2 each time the NEXT statement is encountered. The effect is to print out all the odd numbers from 1 through 21.

```
10 REM PRINT ODD NUMBERS 1 TO 21
20 FOR B = 1 TO 21 STEP 2
30 PRINT B
40 NEXT B
50 END
```

The example below illustrates the use of the STEP option to add a negative number to the control variable each time through the loop. This has the effect of decreasing the control variable by the specified amount each time the NEXT statement is encountered. Notice that the initial value is 50, the terminal value is 1, and the step value is −1. When the NEXT statement is encountered, the computer checks to see if the current value of the control variable is less than the terminal value. If it is not less than the terminal value, the loop is executed again. As soon as the value of the control variable is less than the terminal value, the loop will no longer execute. The following code will cause the integers from 50 through 1 to be printed out in descending sequence:

```
10 REM PRINT NUMBERS 50 TO 1
20 FOR Z = 50 TO 1 STEP −1
30 PRINT Z
40 NEXT Z
50 END
```

The program below will print out the integers 1 through 10. It makes use of a variable to specify the terminal value for the loop. Notice that in line 20 the value of N is set to 10; therefore, the terminal value for the loop will be 10, since the FOR statement FOR X = 1 TO N specifies that the terminal value will be whatever the value of the variable N is when the loop is executed. To print out all integers from 1 through 1,000, how would you change the following program?

```
10 REM PRINT INTEGERS 1 TO 10
20 LET N = 10
30 FOR X = 1 TO N
40 PRINT X
50 NEXT X
60 END
```

Example

A teacher wants to total book order amounts for her students. Each student may have ordered any number of books. Write a program that will accept the student's name, the total number of books the student has ordered, and the price of each book ordered. (If the user accidentally enters a number less than 1 for the number of books ordered, the program should end.) The program should print the student's name, the number of books ordered, and the total cost of the order. The teacher should have the option of processing another student's order or ending the program.

Figure 13–5 shows a structure chart for this problem. An algorithm is presented below.

  1. Book order algorithm.

  2. Set order cost = 0.

  3. Accept student's name.

  4. Accept number of books ordered (B).

  5. If number of books ordered (B) is less than 1 go to step 12.

  6. Loop through steps 6 through 9, B times.

  7. Accept book price.

  8. Compute order cost.

  9. End of body of loop.

10. Print name, number of books ordered and order cost.

11. If more students go to step 2.

12. End.

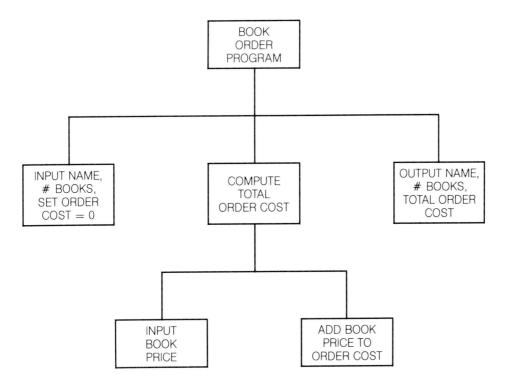

Figure 13–5 A structure chart for the ''Book Order'' program.

Figure 13–6 is a flowchart for the algorithm above. Notice the symbol used to portray the FOR statement, the circle with the control variable in it used to denote the NEXT statement, and the dotted line used to show the boundaries of the loop. This is the way a FOR-NEXT loop is charted. The following program was coded from the flowchart in Figure 13–6:

```
100 REM BOOK ORDER PROGRAM
110 REM N$ = STUDENTS NAME
120 REM B = NUMBER OF BOOKS ORDERED
130 REM P = INDIVIDUAL BOOK PRICE
140 REM C = TOTAL ORDER COST
150 REM Z$ = MORE STUDENTS? RESPONSE
160 REM X = CONTROL VARIABLE FOR-NEXT
170 LET C = 0
180 INPUT "ENTER STUDENTS NAME ";N$
190 INPUT "ENTER NUMBER OF BOOKS ORDERED ";B
192 IF B < 1 THEN 300
195 PRINT " "
200 FOR X = 1 TO B
210 PRINT "ENTER PRICE FOR BOOK #";X
220 INPUT "(99.99) =====> ";P
230 LET C = C + P
240 NEXT X
245 PRINT " "
250 PRINT N$;" ORDERED ";B;" BOOK(S)"
260 PRINT "FOR A TOTAL COST OF $";C
270 PRINT " "
280 INPUT "ENTER Y TO CONTINUE ====> ";Z$
290 IF Z$ = "Y" THEN 170
300 END
```

When this program is run, the screen will appear as follows:

```
ENTER STUDENTS NAME FRAN
ENTER NUMBER OF BOOKS ORDERED 3

ENTER PRICE FOR BOOK #1
(99.99) =====> 2.00
ENTER PRICE FOR BOOK #2
(99.99) =====> 1.55
ENTER PRICE FOR BOOK #3
(99.99) =====> 2.50

FRAN ORDERED 3 BOOK(S)
FOR A TOTAL COST OF $6.05

ENTER Y TO CONTINUE =====> N
```

Notice in this program that line 170 initially sets the variable C, which will store the total cost of the order, to 0. Further, when the program loops back to do another student it loops back to line 170 so that C may be set to 0 before processing the data for another student. If this was not done the old balance would be carried forward and C would no longer contain the total order cost for just one student. Also notice line 192 which will end the program should the user accidentally enter a number less than 1 in response to the prompt ENTER NUMBER OF BOOKS ORDERED.

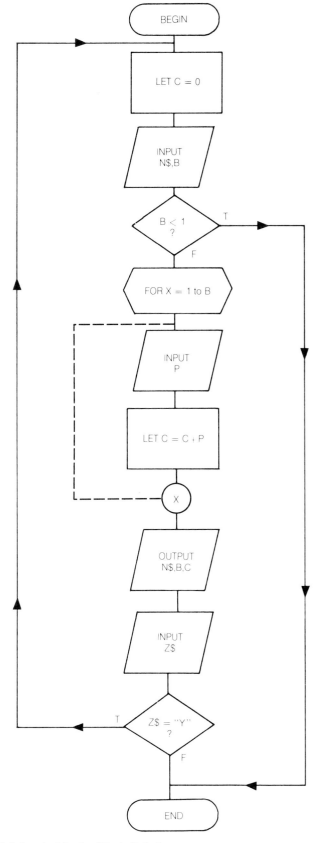

Figure 13–6 A flowchart for the "Book Order" program.

	Example	*Function*
Statement		
FOR	FOR I = 1 TO 5	Controls
	FOR X = 1 TO 20 STEP 2	loops
	FOR T = 55 TO 5 STEP −5	
NEXT	NEXT I	

Table 13–2 Review of FOR-NEXT.

EXERCISES

For each exercise draw a structure chart, write an algorithm, and draw a flowchart before coding your program. Use FOR-NEXT loops in your programs.

1. Write a program to print all the integers from 1 through 100.

2. Write a program to print every third integer from 1 through 99.

3. Write a program to print all the odd numbers from 57 through 107 in reverse order.

4. Write a program that allows you to input an integer and then sums all the integers up to and including that number and prints the sum.

5. Write a program that accepts as input a student's name, the number of quizzes the student has taken, and the number of tests the student has taken. The program should then accept as input each quiz grade and each test grade. The student's average should be computed, with tests counting twice as much as quizzes. The name and average should be printed out, and the user should be allowed to either process more students or end the program.

6. Change the program you wrote for number 5 to also accept the teacher's name and keep track of the overall class average, the class average on tests, and the class average on quizzes. When the program ends, the teacher's name and this information should be printed out.

READ, DATA, and RESTORE

The READ statement instructs the computer to assign a value from a data list to a specified variable. A data list is a list of string or numerical constants (called data elements) contained in a DATA statement.

The general format for a DATA statement is

```
line number DATA one or more data elements
                 separated by commas
```

An example of a DATA statement is

```
100 DATA "LOUIS",89
```

Notice that the elements in a data list are separated by commas. Also, although it is always correct to enclose string constants in quotation marks when they are used as data elements in a data list, they do not have to be quoted unless they start with a leading blank or contain a comma. No double quotation marks (") may appear in strings used in a data list. Examples appear below.

Computers in the Classroom

As the following excerpt points out, games can be an interesting, beneficial way to teach programming. After learning how a number of BASIC statements function, students can be given simple game programs to play, analyze, and perhaps modify.

Inevitably the first, thing elementary school children ask when the teacher announces that they are going to learn some programming is, "Can we make a game?" Almost as inevitable is a response from the teacher such as, "Well ... programming a game is rather complicated. We'll start with something simpler."

But is it really necessary to start off by discouraging students? Game programs do not have to be long or complicated....

PROGRAM 1: SILLY SENTENCE....

Even as short as this program is, it is user friendly, i.e., it includes instructions and prompts. Students should learn that this is an important aspect of most programs. The program itself produces a silly sentence with the structure "The [W1$] kissed the [W2$]" where W1$ is "something that moves" and W2$ is "something that tastes good." The result is a sentence like THE DOG KISSED THE ICE CREAM or THE CAR KISSED THE PIZZA—sentences that manage to produce many laughs from primary grade students. Here is the listing:

```
10  HOME
20  PRINT "LET'S MAKE A SILLY SENTENCE."
30  PRINT "THINK OF SOMETHING THAT MOVES."
40  PRINT "TYPE IT AND PRESS <RETURN>."
50  INPUT W1$
60  HOME
70  PRINT "O.K. NOW THINK OF SOMETHING THAT TASTES GOOD."
80  PRINT "TYPE IT AND PRESS <RETURN>."
90  INPUT W2$
100 PRINT "NOW PRESS ANY KEY."
110 GET A$: IF A$ = " " THEN 110
120 HOME
130 PRINT "THE ";W1$;" KISSED THE ";W2$;"."
```

After students have played the game a few times, have them list the program and ask them about the line commands. How do you think the program works? The HOME and PRINT concepts are not too difficult....

With a game approach, children learn some fairly sophisticated commands very early. One of these is the GET A$ command in line 100. The line holds two commands that form a loop that is only broken when a key is pressed. This is a common loop that enables users to read directions at their own speed or to get ready for some game actions. It is not necessary that students have a complete understanding of this line at this point. Simply explain that this command tells the computer to stop the program until a key is pressed. The actual reason for the IF A$ = " " THEN 110 part of the loop is that the computer polls the keyboard much faster than a human can respond, so the loop forces the computer to poll repeatedly until a response is made....

PROGRAM 2: SPELL-IT

Two students play this game. One looks away while the other enters a word. Once RETURN (or ENTER) is pressed, the word disappears and the other player presses any key to see the word. The word appears on the screen for about a second, then disappears and the computer prompts the child with a "?". The player then spells the word by typing it in and pressing RETURN. If the spelling is correct, the computer prints "YOU'RE RIGHT!!!" If it is incorrect, the message "YOU'RE WRONG—IT'S XXXX" appears, where XXXX is the correct spelling. Here is the listing:

```
10  HOME
20  PRINT "TYPE IN A WORD."
30  INPUT W$
40  HOME
50  PRINT "GET SOMEONE TO TRY TO SPELL IT."
60  PRINT "TYPE ANY KEY WHEN READY."
70  GET A$: IF A$ = " " THEN 70
80  HOME
90  PRINT W$
100 FOR P=1 TO 500:NEXT P
110 HOME
120 INPUT A$
130 IF A$ = W$ THEN PRINT "YOU'RE RIGHT!!!"
140 IF A$<>W$ THEN PRINT "YOU'RE WRONG—IT'S ";W$
```

This program introduces the pause loop. Like the "GET A$" loop, the actual operation of the loop does not have to be explained at this time. All students need to know is that the number 500 determines how long the word will appear on the screen. If you make the number higher, the word will remain longer, and vice-versa. The GET A$ command is used again, as it is in all of these programs.

This program also introduces IF ... THEN and < > (not equal to). These can be explained or deferred until later as the teacher deems necessary.

(Kretschmer, 1984)

```
120 DATA FRED
130 DATA "FRED"
```

Both of the above are correct.

```
150 DATA " FRED"
160 DATA "JONES,FRED"
```

The first example above must be quoted because of the leading blank. The second must be quoted because of the comma contained in the string.

```
200 DATA ""MARY""
```

The above is incorrect because double quotation marks may not appear within a data element.

As mentioned earlier, the READ statement is used to assign values from a data list to specific variables. The general form of the READ statement is as follows:

```
line number READ one or more variables separated by
                          commas
```

Observe the following example:

```
10 REM PROGRAM TO READ AND
20 REM PRINT A DATA LIST
30 READ A$,G
40 PRINT A$;" ";G
50 DATA LOUIS,89
60 END
```

When this program encounters the READ statement in line 30, it will immediately search through each line of code in the program until it encounters a DATA statement. It then starts with the first element in the data list, in this case the string LOUIS, and assigns it to the first variable in the READ statement, A$ in our example. Because there is another variable in the READ statement (G), the program goes on to the next element in the data list and assigns that to the variable G. Because there are no more variables in the READ statement, its task is completed and control passes to the next line of code, which in this instance is a PRINT statement that will cause whatever is stored in variables A$ and G to be printed out on the screen, separated by a space. DATA statements in a program are ignored unless a READ statement is encountered. Therefore, in this example, control now passes to line 60, where the program ends. Because DATA statements are ignored except when a READ statement is encountered, they may be placed anywhere in a program. It is good practice, however, to place them at the end of the program, just before the END statement.

When a READ statement attempts to assign a value to a variable it is important that the data element and the variable be of the same type. For instance, if a READ statement attempted to assign a data element that was a string constant to a numerical variable, an error condition would result. If the READ statement in line 30 below tried to read the data in line 50, an error would result. The error would occur because an attempt had been made to read the string constant LOUIS into the numerical variable G.

```
30 READ G,A$
50 DATA LOUIS,89
```

Unless otherwise instructed, once a program has encountered a READ statement and begun to read through a data list, it keeps track of where it stopped reading in the list by setting a pointer. If another READ statement should be issued, it begins to read at the next data element after the pointer. Take as an example the following portion, or segment, of a program:

```
40 FOR Z = 1 TO 4
50 READ A$,G
60 PRINT A$;" ";G
70 NEXT Z
80 DATA LOUIS,89,ANNE,98
90 DATA BILL,76,LAURA,100
```

When this code is executed it will, the first time through the loop, read the values LOUIS and 89 into the variables A$ and G, respectively, and then print those values. The pointer will be left just before the next data element, ANNE. The second time through the loop, when the READ statement is encountered, the value ANNE will be read into A$ and the value 98 into G. The pointer will be left just before the next data element, allowing the computer to keep track of where it is in the data list. After the second time through the loop the computer will know that the next data element to be read is BILL. Therefore, the third time through the loop the value BILL will be assigned to A$ and the value 76 assigned to G. The last time through the loop the values LAURA and 100 will be assigned to the variables A$ and G, respectively.

If for some reason the computer tried to execute another READ against the data list, an error condition would result. Suppose we changed line 40 in the program segment to be

```
40 FOR Z = 1 TO 5
```

The fifth time through the loop the program would attempt to read data that was not there and the OUT OF DATA error would occur. Specifically, in Applesoft BASIC the message on the screen would be

```
?OUT OF DATA ERROR IN 50
```

The computer would be calling attention to the READ statement in line 50 and telling the person using the computer that an attempt had been made to try and read past the end of the data in the data list.

It should be obvious that a way is needed to control the number of READ statements issued in a program. In the program segment above, a FOR-NEXT loop was used. This is successful if it is known beforehand how many data elements or sets of data elements will be contained in the DATA statements. (Each name and grade in the previous example may be thought of as a related set of data elements.) In the segment above it was known that there were four sets of data elements so the loop was set up to execute the READ statement four times.

Another way to control the READ statements in a program is to use an End of Data tag, sometimes referred to as an EOD tag. This is a handy technique if the number of READ statements to be issued against a data list is unknown.

An EOD tag is simply a meaningless data element, such as the string XXX, that is added to the end of the data list. A conditional test is placed in the program such that when the EOD tag is encountered, control is transferred out of the loop where the READ statement is executed. The following illustrates:

```
100 REM PROGRAM #1 — EOD TAG
105 READ A$
110 IF A$ = "XXX" THEN 180
120 READ G
130 PRINT A$;" ";G
140 GOTO 105
150 DATA LOUIS,89,ANNE,98
160 DATA BILL,76,LAURA,100
170 DATA XXX
180 END
```

In line 105 the READ statement is executed that reads a value into A$. In line 110 a test is performed to see if the value read into A$ is the EOD tag, which in this case is XXX. If it is, control is transferred to line 180 and the program ends. If the EOD tag has not been encountered, control passes to line 120, where a second READ is executed that will read the next data element into G. Line 130 prints the values of A$ and G and line 140 transfers control back to the beginning of the loop. Notice that the program could have been written with one READ statement, as long as two EOD tags were contained in line 170, as below. If the program had been written as follows except with only one EOD tag, such as XXX, an OUT OF DATA error would occur when the last READ statement was executed because there would not be a data element to be read into G.

```
100 REM PROGRAM #2 — EOD TAG
105 READ A$,G
110 IF A$ = "XXX" THEN 180
130 PRINT A$;" ";G
140 GOTO 105
150 DATA LOUIS,89,ANNE,98
160 DATA BILL,76,LAURA,100
170 DATA XXX,999
180 END
```

The pointer in a data list can be reset by using the RESTORE statement, the general format of which is

```
line number RESTORE
```

This has the effect of resetting the pointer from wherever it was in the data list to the beginning of the data list.

Example

This example makes use of the READ, DATA, and RESTORE statements.

A teacher has a data list that contains twelve sets of data. Each set consists of a student's name, the student's reading level, and the student's current average in reading. Write a program that will allow the teacher to input either a student's name or NO. If NO is input, the program should end. If a student's name is input, the program should search the data list to find the student's name and print out the name, reading level, and reading average. If the student's name is not found, a message should be printed out stating STUDENT NOT IN DATA LIST. The teacher should then be able to search for data on another student or end the program, as desired.

Figure 13–7 shows a structure chart for the program. The following algorithm was generated from the structure chart:

1. Algorithm for reading program.

2. Accept input, student's name or NO to end program.

3. If NO entered go to step 13.

4. Loop through steps 4 through 7, 12 times.

5. Read data (name, reading level, average).

6. If input name = name read go to step 10.

7. End of body of loop.

8. Print student not in data message.

9. Go to step 11.

10. Print name, reading level, average.

11. Restore pointer.

12. Go to step 2.

13. End.

Figure 13–8 shows a flowchart derived from the algorithm above. Note the use of the connector symbol to denote movement from one place in the flowchart to another, from the connector symbol labeled 1 to the matching symbol labeled 1 if the decision N$ = "NO" should evaluate as true. Also, notice that DATA statements do not appear in flowcharts. The program written from the flowchart follows:

```
100  REM READING GRADES PROGRAM
110  REM N$ = INPUT NAME OR NO TO END
120  REM S$ = NAME IN DATA LIST
130  REM L = READING LEVEL
140  REM G = READING AVERAGE
150  REM X = LOOP CONTROL VARIABLE
170  PRINT "ENTER A STUDENTS NAME"
180  PRINT "OR ENTER NO IF YOU WISH TO"
190  INPUT "END THE PROGRAM ====> ";N$
200  IF N$ = "NO" THEN 900
210  FOR X = 1 TO 12
220  READ S$,L,G
230  IF N$ = S$ THEN 310
240  NEXT X
250  PRINT " "
260  PRINT "**********************"
270  PRINT "STUDENT NOT IN DATA LIST"
280  PRINT "**********************"
290  PRINT " "
300  GOTO 360
```

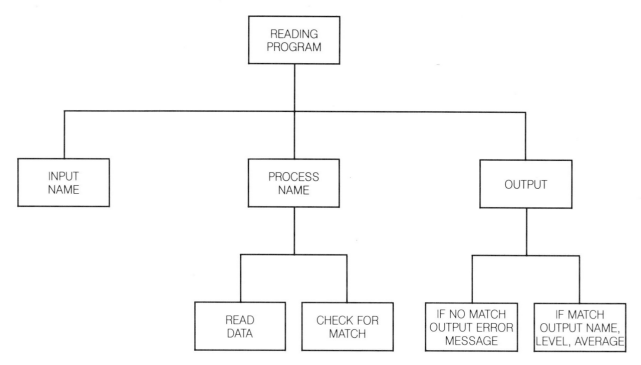

Figure 13–7 A structure chart for the ''Reading'' program.

```
310 PRINT " "
320 PRINT "STUDENT ";N$
330 PRINT "READING LEVEL ";L
340 PRINT "CURRENT AVERAGE ";G
350 PRINT " "
360 RESTORE
370 GOTO 170
500 DATA GERALD CRAFT,7.8,89
510 DATA JOHN MURRAY,6.1,77
520 DATA JILL TORRANCE,8.1,88
530 DATA ALMA CURTIS,6.5,64
540 DATA BOB JACOBS,6.7,78
550 DATA FRED CARLISLE,6.2,79
560 DATA BETTY HENDRICKS,7.4,90
570 DATA ELLEN FONTAINE,7.1,80
580 DATA CATHY JONES,6.2,80
590 DATA TED BATES,7.2,85
600 DATA GRACE GOODWIN,8.2,99
610 DATA BERT ANDERSON,8.1,90
900 END
```

The program begins by prompting the user to enter either a student's name or NO. If NO is entered, the program ends. If a student's name is input, a loop is entered in which the data list is searched to find a match for the name that the user has input. Each time through the loop the program reads one set of data elements and tests to see if the name read matches the name input. If there is a match, control is transferred to line 310, which begins the section of the program where the required information is printed out. The pointer

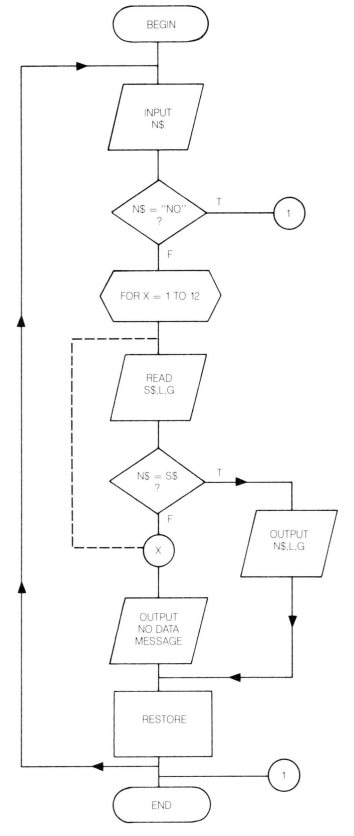

Figure 13–8 A flowchart for the "Reading" program.

is then restored and control is transferred back to line 170 to allow the user to either input another student's name or end the program. If no match is ever found within the FOR-NEXT loop, control falls through to line 250 after the loop has been executed twelve times. The message STUDENT NOT IN DATA LIST is printed out and control is transferred to line 360, where the pointer is restored. The program then goes back to the beginning prompt in line 170 to accept either another student's name or NO to end the program.

The screen display would appear as below when this program is run, given the input data specified:

```
ENTER A STUDENTS NAME
OR ENTER NO IF YOU WISH TO
END THE PROGRAM ====> GRACE GOODWIN


STUDENT GRACE GOODWIN
READING LEVEL 8.2
CURRENT AVERAGE 99


ENTER A STUDENTS NAME
OR ENTER NO IF YOU WISH TO
END THE PROGRAM ====> CINDY BELL


***********************
STUDENT NOT IN DATA LIST
***********************


ENTER A STUDENTS NAME
OR ENTER NO IF YOU WISH TO
END THE PROGRAM ====> NO
```

	Example	*Function*
Statement		
READ	READ A READ A, B, C, READ S$ READ F$, L$, K$ READ S$, B, C	Assigns a value from a data list to a variable.
DATA	DATA "NANCY", 80, 90 DATA DARREN, 90 DATA "JAKE", 99 DATA "CARTER, JOHN"	Lists data elements.
RESTORE	RESTORE	Restores the pointer to the first element in the data list.

Table 13-3 Review of READ, DATA, and RESTORE statements.

EXERCISES

Draw a structure chart, write an algorithm, and draw a flowchart for each program below before you code and test it.

1. Given the data below, write a program to read each student's name and grades, compute the student's average, and then print out the student's name and average.

```
900 DATA FRED,78,65,89,90
910 DATA BETSY,67,78,75,80
920 DATA LARRY,89,96,94,88
930 DATA JAIME,56,89,92,79
940 DATA CHRIS,89,96,98,79
```

2. Write a program to read through the list of numbers given in the data below, compute the average of the numbers, and print out the average. (9999 is used as an EOD tag.)

```
900 12,67,78,45,74
910 34,87,2,10,90
920 62,92,60,16,88
930 9999
```

3. In the example for this section, change the program so that it will process correctly even if the number of sets of data in the data list is not known (i.e., may be any number of sets). (Hint: You may wish to use an EOD tag.)

4. Write a program to read through the data given in exercise 2 and count how many numbers are greater than or equal to 50 and how many are less than 50. This information should then be printed out. The program should then find the sum of all the numbers and print it. Write two versions of your program, one that uses RESTORE and one that does not.

Reactions and Research

In the following selection Ben Shneiderman presents an outline of suggested programming concepts that may be taught to children. Many of the concepts have been introduced in this text. Identify those with which you are already familiar and those you have yet to explore.

PROGRAMMING CONCEPTS

After teaching the concept of a program and its execution, concentrate on various forms of PRINT commands. This gives children an immediate sense of accomplishment in a familiar domain, while allowing the discussion of some control flow issues. Early presentation of loops reveals the power of the computer to print rapidly—most children I worked with got great satisfaction from printing their names 20 times! Meaningful examples and exercises are necessary at every point to adequately anchor the concepts.

It is useful to separate programming concepts into two groups. The initial concepts can be taught to third through sixth graders, while the advanced concepts are appropriate for more advanced students. Third and fourth graders seemed to need a parent or teacher to help overcome some of their problems, but fifth and sixth graders would succeed in learning the initial programming concepts on their own. The list of initial programming concepts includes:

- Command and execution of a command: Program vs. output of the program.

- Formatting: Printing a word, letter, words with embedded blanks, arbitrary string of characters, a blank line. Printing two strings on a line—adjacent or spread out. Printing two or more lines to form a sentence, poem, list of items or shape.

- Sequential execution of one command followed by another. Numeric sequencing of commands.

- Repeated execution of a statement or a group of statements for a fixed number of times.

- Nesting of simple loops—The counter variables go from one to a constant.

- Input a value from the user during execution and use it to control the program, pause in execution to wait for entry, printed prompt.

- Conditional execution: Relational expressions, true or false, execution of consequent command.

- Flow of control: Jumps (forward to skip over, backward to repeat), begin execution, terminate execution.

- **Loops:** Use of counter variable in program—one to a variable, initial values other than one, initial and final values are variables.

- **Values of a variable:** Setting (assignment of a constant), copying (assignment of a variable), printing, using, changing and comparing. Different types of variables such as integers or strings.

- **Counting:** Initialization, incrementation of a value in sequential order, final value.

- **Summing:** Initialization, adding up integer values to form a total.

- **Arithmetic operators:** Infix notation for addition, subtraction, multiplication and division operators.

- **Random numbers:** Generation, conversion to integer ranges, use in programs.

- **Interactive dialogues:** Multiple choice questions, branching based on user input, use of input strings and numbers, adventure stories and games.

My list of advanced programming concepts includes:

- **Advanced Loops:** Decrementation loops, WHILE loops, UNTIL loops, exits, nested loops with interrelated counter variables.

- **Recursion:** Self-invocation as an approach to repetition, stack concept.

- **Complex decision making:** Nested conditionals, decision trees or networks, conditional actions, required actions, backward and forward tracing.

- **Modular design:** Encapsulation of repeated or distinctive functions, argument passing and returning.

- **Data structures:** Collection of values in an array or file, input records, data manipulation.

- **Searching:** Looping through a data structure to locate a given item, count the items, find largest/smallest, determine absence/presence, find first/last.

- **String operations:** Copying, comparison, concatenation, decomposition, substring search.

Programming concepts were carefully chosen to focus on fundamentals and avoid complex mathematics. In teaching the concepts, I began with simple PRINT commands, went on to simple uses of loops and then introduced interactive dialogue design. Arithmetic and conditional commands came later. After ample applications of these concepts, subroutines for modular programming can emerge quite naturally. I recognize that graphics, animation and sound are highly motivating for young programmers, but greatly varying language structures discouraged me from using them. Knowledgeable teachers may wish to include them.

(Shneiderman, 1985)

Conclusion

The more syntax of a language a programmer knows, the more power the programmer has available for creating programs in that language. BASIC has more to offer than we have covered in this introduction. Some sources for further study are given at the end of this chapter. Also, depending on your interests and plans, you may wish to take a full course in BASIC or some other programming language, such as Pascal.

Key Terms

conditional test	Statements
EOD tag	DATA
infinite loop	FOR
initial value	GOTO
loop	IF-THEN
relational symbol	NEXT
step value	READ
terminal value	RESTORE

Bent, Robert J., and George C. Sethares. *BASIC: An Introduction to Computer Programming*, 2d ed. Monterey, Calif.: Brooks/Cole Publishing Co., 1983.

Clark, James F., and William O. Drum. *BASIC Programming: A Structured Approach.* Cincinnati, Ohio: South-Western Publishing Co., 1983.

Curran, William S. "Teaching Programming Made Easy." *The Computing Teacher* 12, no. 8 (1985):32–33.

Ginter, Peter M., and Andrew C. Rucks. *BASIC: Decision Making on the Microcomputer.* New York: Random House, 1985.

Kretschmer, Joseph C. "Teaching BASIC: Why Not Start with Games?" *The Computing Teacher* 12, no. 1 (1984):24–26.

Moriber, Harry A. *Structured BASIC Programming.* Columbus, Ohio: Charles E. Merrill Publishing Co., 1984.

Shneiderman, Ben. "When Children Learn Programming: Antecedents, Concepts and Outcomes." *The Computing Teacher* 12, no. 5 (1985):14–17.

References/Further Reading

14

Computer Resources: Trends and Issues

TOPICS ADDRESSED

What different types of computers are used in schools?

How does cost affect computer resources in schools?

How do the terms stand-alone and networked relate to microcomputers?

What are several ways computer resources may be managed in schools?

What opportunities for instruction does a computer lab offer teachers?

How might teachers make use of computers in the classroom?

What preferences do educators have for managing computer resources?

What role does a computer coordinator play in a school district?

What trends in hardware and software will affect educators in the future?

What practical results from artificial intelligence research will educators benefit from in the future?

What issues related to equity in computer education must educators address?

OUTLINE

Introduction
Types of Computers in the Schools
Computer Education and Cost
Managing Computer Resources: Four Models
  The Computer Lab
  Computers in the Classroom
  Lab/Classroom
  Mobile Lab/Classroom
Which Approach Is the Best?

The Computer Coordinator
Trends and Issues
  Hardware
  Software
  Equity
Conclusion
Key Terms
Questions
References/Further Reading

Introduction

Computer instruction in the schools has taken a firm hold during the 1980s. In this chapter issues related to managing computer resources are addressed. Several trends that will affect computer education in the future are also examined. One important management issue is where should resources be placed and how should they be made available to students and teachers? Several models for managing computer resources are presented. For each model possible implications for teaching are outlined. The role of a computer coordinator is described and analyzed. Lastly, trends related to educational computing are presented, including hardware and software developments and issues of equity in providing computer instruction to all segments of society.

Types of Computers in the Schools

A wide variety of computer hardware and software is available to educators. As covered in Chapter 2, computers have historically been referred to as mainframes, minis, and micros, depending on the capabilities of the particular machine described. Few school systems use mainframe computers for instructional purposes. Some school systems use minicomputers for instruction, especially in junior and senior high school. When minicomputers are used, terminals are placed at various locations throughout the school building, or school district, and are connected to the computer.

Many schools make use of microcomputers for computer education. In fact, microcomputers, as opposed to mainframes and minis, appear to be the catalyst that has made computer education possible for many school districts. From 1983 to 1985 there was significant growth in the number of microcomputers available in schools and the number of teachers and students who used them. Henry Jay Becker, a researcher at the Center for Social Organization of Schools at The Johns Hopkins University, reporting on the preliminary results of a national survey, illustrates this point:

"Well, today we learned to reorder segments on a random-access videodisc through the process of microcomputer interfacing."

Over two years ago I first reported on my national survey of school uses of microcomputers. At that time a majority of U.S. schools had microcomputers, but elementary schools with even five computers were rare. Today, a majority of U.S. elementary schools have five or more computers. Moreover, in 1983 most American secondary schools had fewer than a handful of microcomputers; today, half of U.S. secondary schools have 15 or more computers. In fact, a full one-quarter of all U.S. schools now have enough computers to serve between one-half and one full classroom of students at one time.

Serving 15 students in a school setting that has hundreds or even thousands of students may not sound like much of an accomplishment, but two years ago, countless schools were trying to figure out how to use a single microcomputer with a classroom of students. They could use a single movie projector with a classroom or a single overhead projector, but a single computer was a different story. Only 6 percent of today's schools are still in that predicament. A significant plurality have now entered a second phase of their computer history; now that they have a minimal number of computers, it is time for schools to begin to expect significant improvements in student accomplishment, and it is time to begin to measure the difference that computers are (or are not) making.

Along with a quadrupling of the number of computers in schools in the last two years, there has been a tripling of the number of students using computers and a tripling of the number of teachers supervising students in their use. In the typical school last year, about 150 students used computers during the year. And four to five teachers used computers in their teaching practice. (Becker, 1986, p. 30)

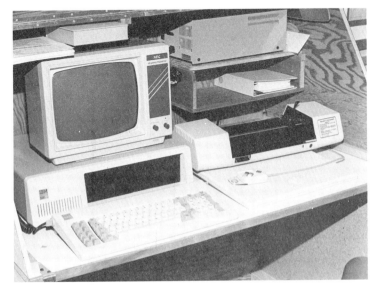

Figure 14–1 A microcomputer work station (above left) and a computer terminal (above right).

The high reliability and relatively low cost of microcomputers, coupled with the ready availability of educational software for micros, have probably led to this trend. Microcomputers may be used in one of two modes: stand-alone or networked. Stand-alone refers to having one computer configuration that operates independently of any other. Perhaps a computer with a color monitor, two disk drives, and a printer might serve as a stand-alone work station for a student. All processing would be handled by the computer and its peripherals. No resources would be shared with any other computer.

When computers are networked they are set up so that they share resources. This may be done in a variety of ways. For example, suppose that three microcomputers were connected to one printer through a device called a switchbox. Each computer would be assigned a number that would correspond to a number on the switchbox. Each computer would be connected to the switchbox, which would in turn be connected to a printer. If a student at computer number one wanted to use the printer, the switchbox would be set to number one. This would route the output from computer number one to the printer. Similarly, when a student at computer number two wanted to print something, the switchbox would be set to number two and the output from that computer would be routed to the printer.

One advantage of networking is that it can save money. In the example above it would cost less to buy a switchbox to connect one printer to three computers than it would to buy two additional printers to provide each computer with its own printer. Computers may be networked in other ways. Several microcomputers may be connected to a hard disk drive to share the information stored on the drive. A hard disk is a permanently mounted magnetic storage medium that is capable of storing a great deal of information. Typically, hard disks can store millions of bytes of information. It is not unusual—in fact it is becoming increasingly common—to find a hard disk that can store 20 to 30 million bytes of information connected to a microcomputer or networked to several microcomputers.

There are advantages to networking, but there are also disadvantages. The more complex a computer system becomes, the more difficult it may be to run. Also, most of the types of microcomputers used in schools to date were not really designed to be networked. This means that the performance of the machines may be degraded when they are networked. For instance, it may take an inordinately long time to load a program into the computer's memory. Newer-generation microcomputers are being designed with networking in mind.

Micros that are set up to work in a stand-alone mode may also, through the use of additional software and hardware, serve as terminals. In this case the computer may sometimes operate as a stand-alone work station and at other times serve as a terminal hooked up to a more powerful host computer, such as a mini or a mainframe. When operating as a terminal the computer will simply receive information from and send information to the host computer, which does all the processing. So, in a sense, the microcomputer is part of the network of terminals hooked up to the host computer, but it is capable of operating in the stand-alone mode when the user chooses.

The majority of microcomputers currently in use in schools operate in a stand-alone mode. In the discussion that follows we will assume that the computers referred to are operating as stand-alone machines.

Input/Output

It will take most of this book for me to convey some sense of the choices among computers, computer languages, and more generally, among computer cultures, that influence how well children will learn from working with computation and what benefits they will get from doing so. But the question of the economic feasibility of free access to computers for every child can be dealt with immediately. In doing so I hope to remove any doubts readers may have about the "economic realism" of the "vision of education" I have been talking about.

My vision of a new kind of learning environment demands free contact between children and computers. This could happen because the child's family buys one or a child's friends have one. For purposes of discussion here (and to extend our discussion to all social groups) let us assume that it happens because schools give every one of their students his or her own powerful personal computer. Most "practical" people (including parents, teachers, school principals, and foundation administrators) react to this idea in much the same way: "Even if computers could have all the effects you talk about, it would still be impossible to put your ideas into action. Where would the money come from?"

What these people are saying needs to be faced squarely. They are wrong. Let's consider the cohort of children who will enter kindergarten in the year 1987, the "Class of 2000", and let's do some arithmetic. The direct public cost of schooling a child for thirteen years, from kindergarten through twelfth grade is over $20,000 today (and for the class of 2000, it may be closer to $30,000). A conservatively high estimate of the cost of supplying each of these children with a personal computer with enough power for it to serve the kinds of educational ends described in this book, and of upgrading, repairing, and replacing it when necessary would be about $1,000 per student, distributed over thirteen years in school. Thus "computer costs" for the class of 2000 would represent only about 5 percent of the total public expenditure on education, and this would be the case even if nothing else in the structure of educational costs changed because of the computer presence. But in fact computers in education stand a good chance of making other aspects of education cheaper. Schools might be able to reduce their cycle from thirteen years to twelve years; they might be able to take advantage of the greater autonomy the computer gives students and increase the size of classes by one or two students without decreasing the personal attention each student is given. Either of these two moves would "recuperate" the computer cost.

My goal is not educational economies: It is not to use computation to shave a year off the time a child spends in an otherwise unchanged school or to push an extra child into an elementary school classroom. The point of this little exercise in educational "budget balancing" is to do something to the state of mind of my readers as they turn to the first chapter of this book. I have described myself as an educational utopian—not because I have projected a future of education in which children are surrounded by high technology, but because I believe that certain uses of very powerful computational technology and computational ideas can provide children with new possibilities for learning, thinking, and growing emotionally as well as cognitively.

(Papert, 1980, pp. 16–18)

Computer Education and Cost

Running a competent computer education program as part of the curriculum in a school system requires a substantial monetary commitment. Costs include teacher time, training, and equipment. A large part of the monetary commitment will have to be for hardware and software. As pointed out in the quote from Henry Jay Becker, computers are not like movie projectors, in that one movie projector can serve a whole class at a time whereas one computer can serve one student (or in some instances two or three students) at a given time.

An ideal situation would provide enough computer power so that each student had access to a computer when needed and for as long as needed. This could be accomplished by having one computer available for each child throughout the child's school career or by carefully scheduling available computer resources through use of one of the models presented later. The notion of each child having her own computer is often discarded as unrealistic because of the expense. The Input/Output selection for this chapter presents another view, that of Seymour Papert. As covered in Chapter 8, Papert is a staunch advocate of providing children with ready access to computers. His argument for making ample computer resources available to children is not that far-fetched when viewed over the long term, especially when consideration is given to the fact that a growing number of colleges are requiring students to purchase a computer for use during their college career. Ten or fifteen years ago this would not have seemed possible.

Managing Computer Resources: Four Models

At the present time few, if any, school districts are able to provide a computer for each child. The problem is primarily one of money. But it is also related to the newness of computer education. The claims of various proponents of computer education need to be evaluated as, more and more, computers are used with students for a wide variety of purposes. As advances take place in hardware and software, and curriculums and teaching techniques are refined, computers may become as common in schools as pencil and paper.

For the present, however, educators are struggling with limited resources to try and meet students' needs related to computers. Those needs exist across the whole spectrum of what a computer curriculum may be. The models below are some of the ways teachers and administrators have tried to deal with the situation.

The Computer Lab

All of the computers available in a school may be placed together at one location to provide a computer lab for the entire school's use. When this is done all the school's software may be located in the lab, or some software may be kept in the lab while software used primarily by individual teachers may be kept in the teacher's classroom. Lab time is usually scheduled in advance and may be restricted to a maximum length for each lab period, depending on how busy the lab is.

When a computer lab is set up an ideal situation is to have one computer for each child in the largest class that will use the lab. If the largest class has twenty-four students, the ideal number of computers operational in the lab at one time will be twenty-four. In this case a teacher may bring his class into the lab and allow each student full use of a computer for the period scheduled. Instruction in this instance may be the responsibility of the classroom teacher, or a computer teacher.

When fewer computers are available than are needed for a full class, two options are possible. Teachers may schedule smaller groups in the lab to be instructed by a computer teacher, while the classroom teacher works in his classroom. A second option, depending on the size of the computer lab, is for the teacher to bring the whole class into the lab and have one group work on the computers while other groups do related work that does not require hands-on experiences. In this case the classroom teacher or computer teacher alone may manage the entire group of students in the lab or the instructional responsibilities may be shared.

Suppose students were working on Logo. Some students might be on the computer experimenting with or refining their programs. Others might be playing turtle, alone or with others, to debug a program. Still others could be designing a shape to be programmed at a later time. Some students might be looking at listings of their programs to find problems, or might be sharing

Figure 14–2 A student receives help in the computer lab.

listings of their programs with other students. The teacher may be working with one or more students to explain a Logo primitive or investigate a new idea or a bug.

If students are using the computer for instruction in other content areas, the teacher can structure the lesson so that best use is made of both student time and available computer time. One group may need to have concepts reviewed or introduced, while another group works with software at the computer (perhaps a simulation, tutorial, or drill and practice program). Another group of students might be working with ancillary material, such as fact-sheets or worksheets related to the lesson, or might be completing a project that was part of the overall unit being studied.

Aside from bringing a whole class or group of students into the lab, the teacher may schedule time for individual students to go to the lab and work independently.

Computers in the Classroom

If computer resources are not centrally located in a lab setting, sometimes one or more computers are allocated to each classroom (**Figure 14–3**). If there are not enough computers available for each classroom, or if some teachers do not have responsibility for computer education, the teachers most interested in working with students and computers may then be allocated the available resources. In this case some classrooms will have computers while others will not.

It also may be that a certain number of computers are designated for a particular grade level, for example, fifth grade. Teachers at that level will then

Figure 14–3 Sometimes one or more computers are set up in an area within a classroom.

decide, based on curriculum requirements and teacher preference, where the computers will be located. In either of these cases it is most likely that software will be kept in the classroom of the teacher who uses it most often, rather than in a centralized location such as the library. Sometimes, in the absence of a computer teacher or a computer lab, the librarian may have overall responsibility for cataloging and keeping track of the school's software resources, even though the software stays in the teacher's classroom.

Having one or more computers located in the classroom presents a variety of opportunities for the teacher. Teachers may carefully schedule all students for computer time to cover required material in the computer curriculum. Students may also be given extra time at the computer as a reward or when other work is completed. Sometimes the computer area is used as an activity center where software and materials are set up so that students can work independently. Children may be required to spend a certain amount of time in the center each week or to complete a specified set of activities or projects over a period of time. A teacher with a student who has been absent may schedule extra time at the computer to use software aimed at helping the student catch up. Other students may need computer time for review or extra practice with skills software. Such a center may be used by a group of students engaged in a project as part of instruction in another content area, such as social studies. The group may decide that they want to use the computer for word processing or data analysis tasks related to their project, or perhaps to present a demonstration.

When computer resources are available on a permanent or long-term basis in an individual classroom, teachers may initially be frustrated by having twenty or more children and only limited resources. Through careful scheduling and by viewing the computer as a tool that can be incorporated into an activity center, some of this frustration can be alleviated.

Some schools have both a computer lab and computers located in individual classrooms. In such cases whole class or group instruction takes place in the lab, while individual work may be pursued in either the lab or the classroom. Such a situation allows a good deal of flexibility for both teachers and students. In general, the more equipment available, the easier the teacher's job becomes in terms of planning and management. With a good variety of software and ample machine time, a well-trained teacher can offer quality computer instruction.

Lab/Classroom

Computer hardware can easily be made mobile by installing each computer on a rolling cart. Special carts are available so that all of the components of a typical microcomputer system can be installed on the cart and plugged into receptacles built into the cart. Then, there is only one cord from the cart to an electrical outlet that needs to be unplugged each time the cart is moved. Some schools choose to set up a computer lab on mobile carts. This allows the flexibility of moving one or more computers to individual classrooms as needed, or even of temporarily breaking up the computer lab while the computers are moved to different locations throughout the building. Carts may also be used in a situation where no computer lab exists, to rotate computers from classroom to classroom.

Mobile Lab/Classroom

No overall answer to this question exists. Any answer depends on the individual factors of a particular situation. Such factors would include the following: What are the curriculum responsibilities of each teacher and each grade level? How much money and space are available? How much training is available for teachers? How much enthusiasm do individual teachers have? Is a computer teacher available?

Which Approach Is the Best?

Peterson (1984) points out that the way computer resources are allocated can have an effect on the success or failure of computer education. Given scant resources a district may choose to disperse the computers equally among classrooms. This seems fair but may mean that there will be only one computer available for every three or four classrooms. Training may also be spread so thin that teachers do not have the opportunity to become intensely involved in what computers can do and how they can be integrated into their teaching. The lack of enough computers and enough training to accomplish anything meaningful may frustrate teachers and do more harm than good.

Another option is for the district to concentrate the computers in one school where ample resources can be made available to all teachers and adequate training can be offered. Perhaps this might be a school in which teachers are greatly interested in working with computers. This approach offers an advantage to the students of that particular school but is clearly unfair to the rest of the students in the district. Peterson cites the computer lab approach as a middle-of-the-road solution opted for by many districts. The lab allows a more equal dispersion of resources and lets teachers have enough access to computers so that students can do meaningful work. Peterson points out, however, that when the lab is run on a voluntary basis, it is used more frequently by boys and that girls, minorities, and special education children do not gain an equitable share of the resources. He further points out that when the lab is integrated into the curriculum, it tends to be used more for drill and practice, programming, and learning about computers than it does for using computers to learn about other content areas.

Because of scarce resources, teachers and administrators have been struggling with the problem of how to integrate computers into the schools. A feeling for teacher preferences regarding computer placement can be gained from the preliminary analysis of data done on the survey by Becker (1986) mentioned earlier.

Should schools put computers in a laboratory where everyone can get at them or should they give computers to the teachers to put in their own classrooms? From my 1983 data, I had concluded that, on balance, labs were a better placement.

This time I asked teachers for their opinions. I posed the question, "If you had a school with 15 computers, where should they go: one laboratory; one lab with 7 computers and 8 more in different classrooms; divide all 15 into as many classrooms as possible; or rotate them together from room to room?" Nearly half of the secondary school respondents, and one third of the elementary, said, "Put them in one laboratory." The next most common response was to put half in a lab and the others in classrooms. "Only in classrooms" was in third place, but in the elementary schools about one-fourth wanted them only in classrooms. Hardly anyone wanted them to rotate from room to room as a group. (Becker, 1986, p. 33)

These findings provide some indication as to preferences, but it appears that the question is still open for debate at every level. It seems fair to conclude that rotating all the computers from classroom to classroom is not favored. However, that is not the same as keeping the computers mobile so that, on an as-needed basis, one or more computers can circulate from classroom to classroom. As computers become more and more a part of education and different models are tested and evaluated, perhaps some consensus will finally evolve. It is just as likely, however, that a range of models will gain favor, depending on where and by whom instruction is offered.

The Computer Coordinator

In some school districts a new educational role has begun to emerge—that of a full-time computer coordinator. This person is often responsible for the district's academic computing resources as well as for development and monitoring of the computer curriculum. The computer coordinator may also be responsible for arranging and providing training for teachers and administrators within the district. This individual will need to keep in touch with new developments in hardware and software and may be responsible for disseminating such information throughout the district. **Figure 14–4** is a job description for a computer coordinator.

Notice that the qualifications for the position have been stated in fairly general terms. For instance, rather than stating a specific type of classroom teaching experience or a particular type of educational background, the qualifications are left open. What appropriate classroom experience might be or

---

Computer Coordinator—Job Description

A. General Description

The computer coordinator will report directly to the Superintendent of Schools. Responsibilities will include developing, implementing, and evaluating the district's computer education program for grades K through 9.

B. Qualifications

1. Ability to work with teachers as a provider of in-service instruction
2. Appropriate classroom teaching experience
3. Significant background (training and experience) with educational computing
4. Excellent interpersonal and communication skills

C. Specific Responsibilities

1. Work with and provide leadership to appropriate committees engaged in developing, evaluating, and revising the district's computer education plan.
2. Coordinate and disseminate information about computer education to faculty, staff, administrators, parents, area residents, and the Board of Education.
3. Arrange staff development activities for teachers and administrators and provide such activities.
4. Work with appropriate committees and individuals engaged in evaluating and purchasing hardware and software.
5. Maintain and disseminate a list of all software available districtwide.
6. Maintain and disseminate a list of all hardware available districtwide. Arrange for repair and replacement of hardware as needed.
7. Establish and maintain, cooperatively with teachers and administrators, a policy for the ethical use of all copyrighted computer material used in the district.
8. Other duties as deemed necessary by the coordinator's supervisor.

Figure 14–4 A job description for a computer coordinator.

exactly what type of experience or preparation relevant to computer education would qualify as significant is not specified. This is partly because of the developing nature of this type of position. The district did not want to rule out a good candidate who had preparation of a nontraditional type. Indeed, the position is so new in most areas that there is no traditional avenue of preparation. A teacher who has developed her own interest in computers by taking several courses and attending workshops and conferences while integrating computers into her teaching may be an excellent candidate. Because the qualifications are phrased in a general way she would be able to apply for the job.

As you review the duties of the computer coordinator observe that this district wants someone to be a leader in the areas of curriculum development and training. They also want someone to be an ethical leader. Many school districts are anxious to establish and enforce policies related to what they consider the appropriate use of copyrighted software (especially in regard to making copies of software). These policies are still in a state of flux, but this job description is evidence that the district is ready to face the problem and arrive at a concrete policy.

A talented computer coordinator, one who has good people skills as well as good computer skills, can be invaluable to a district. Ideally, this individual will be someone sensitive to the needs of all teachers, especially those charged with using computers in their classroom who are not particularly comfortable with computers. As a focal point for all computer activities within the district, the coordinator can help the district to have a successful, well-articulated, smooth-running computer education program. As a respected professional the coordinator can help individual teachers by suggesting appropriate software and helping teachers, on an individual basis, integrate computers into their teaching.

Trends and Issues

Hardware

During the early 1980s IBM entered the microcomputer market. With their extensive resources they quickly became a dominant force in the microcomputer industry. Given the relative assurance that IBM would be around for some time as a company and the large number of IBM PCs installed, many hardware and software manufacturers followed IBM's lead by developing products compatible with the IBM standard. A period of time set in when the main criteria for introducing a new product seemed to be its compatibility with IBM machines. This tended to stifle the innovation and technological development that had been the hallmark of the microcomputer industry. The tendency toward providing more computer power for less money continued, but few startling changes in technology were successfully introduced.

Also, during the early and middle 1980s a shakeout occurred in the microcomputer industry. Many hardware manufacturers, software houses, retail stores, and periodicals could not stay in business. This may be due in part to IBM's dominance, but to some degree it is also because certain aspects of the market for microcomputers became saturated. Businesses continued to be interested in buying microcomputers, but the market for home computers foundered. Educators maintained a high degree of interest in computers, but budgets in education did not always match aspirations (even though there was a steady growth in the number of computers available in schools). The mid-1980s has been a time for the microcomputer industry to regroup.

Figure 14–5 The IBM personal computer (above left) and the Atari 520ST (above right).

Amid all these changes certain trends can be observed. The historical trend of more computer for less money is continuing. For considerably less than the cost of a 64K Apple II Plus computer system purchased in 1979, a 520K Atari 520ST can be bought today (and an Apple system can be bought today for less than the 1979 price also). While not too long ago some educators were forced to use cassette tape for storage because of the cost of disk drives, disk-based storage is less expensive and therefore more common now. The cost of such secondary storage continues to decline. Developments such as 3½-inch disk drives are increasingly used in new machines. These disks are more durable than the older floppy disks. They are contained in a hard jacket, can fit comfortably in a shirt pocket, and can store twice as much information as a conventional 360K floppy. The cost of hard-disk drives has also decreased significantly.

The cost of good dot-matrix printers has dropped appreciably also. Many of these printers now offer a near-letter-quality mode that is difficult to distinguish from letter-quality print. Daisy wheel printers have dropped in cost, as have monitors, both monochrome and color. The quality of the picture presented by monitors (both color and monochrome) has also improved.

More hardware designed specifically for educational use is becoming available. Specialized input devices, such as the Koala Pad, which allows students to draw on the pad and have the results appear on the screen, are available. Specialized keyboards, such as the Muppet Learning Keys, offer young children easy-to-read keys on a flat membrane surface. Keys include the letters of the alphabet, numerals, arithmetic operators, compass directions, all presented attractively on the keyboard. The Muppet Learning Keys is used with specialized software. Other specialized keyboards and input devices include piano-style keyboards for use with music software.

The overall trend is to provide more computer power for less money, but the type of computer power provided is changing too. Manufacturers and designers are interested in making computers as easy to use as possible. One approach allows the computer user to move a cursor around the screen with a small input device called a mouse (**Figure 14–6**). On the screen are usually icons, or pictures, of desired functions (although a standard menu may be used instead of icons). When the cursor is over the desired icon, the user clicks a button on the mouse and the function represented by the icon is executed. For example, while using a word-processing program it is often desirable to remove (cut) one part of the document being created and move it to another place. A pair of scissors might be the icon that must be chosen to cut out a part of the document while a pot of glue may need to be chosen to perform the function of pasting the section into its new location. Another technique often used in conjunction with icons and a mouse allows different sections of the screen to be divided into windows. Each window, or section of screen, can show the user different information. For instance, if a user is writing a report with a word processor, it is possible to view simultaneously on the screen the report being written and, superimposed on part of the screen, an outline of the report. The term desktop metaphor refers to the use of icons, windows, and the mouse when used in software such as a word processor and is derived from the fact that the computer screen begins to resemble a desktop covered with pieces of paper, scissors, file folders, glue, etc. Although the keyboard may be used instead of the mouse to direct the cursor and make selections, the intent is to relieve the

Figure 14–6 A device called a mouse is often attached to a computer to move the cursor around the screen and choose the functions the computer will perform.

user of typing commands and using the keyboard. Also, icons, windows, and the mouse are software-driven, depend on software as well as hardware to work. However, since the mouse is a hardware device and is often coupled with the use of icons and windows, these approaches are included here under hardware trends.

The intent of such user interfaces is to make it easier for a person to sit at the computer and use it quickly, successfully, and efficiently. Theoretically, it would take less time to learn how to use a program by using icons, windows, and a mouse than it would if a more traditional series of commands had to be learned.

Other trends include the further development and adoption of more sophisticated instructional technologies, such as interactive videodisc technology. By combining the power of a computer and a videodisc, interactive lessons can be produced that present instructional segments using the presentation capabilities of the videodisc and the control capabilities of the computer. Using the videodisc, a student is presented with a lesson on a television monitor. The computer then queries the student about the lesson she has just seen. The computer judges the student's responses and either replays parts of the lesson or branches to more appropriate material, as needed.

We can expect, for both the long and short run, to see these hardware trends continue. Computers will become easier to use, cost less, and offer more power. Special hardware will continue to be developed for educational use. More sophisticated uses of the computer for instruction will develop as a by-product of more powerful machines, better software, and the marriage of the computer with other technologies.

Software

One major problem with introducing computers into the schools has been a lack of quality software. Quite often what computers are capable of accom-

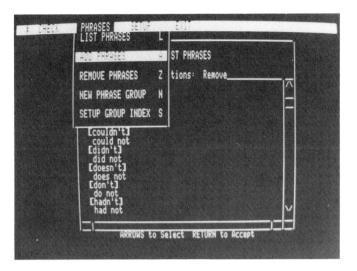 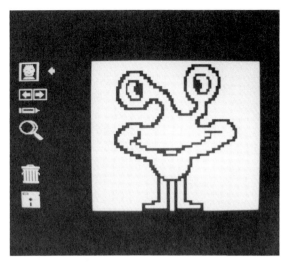

Figure 14–7 Above left, a screen with a window superimposed upon it. Above right, by pointing the cursor at one of the icons shown, the user selects the function desired.

plishing for students and teachers has been oversold. Early software was poorly devised and often poorly executed, sometimes being sold with bugs that the manufacturer knew were there. Modern software still offers no guarantee as to quality, but the proportion of software that has been developed carefully and with sensitivity to educational concerns has increased. Software developers have become sensitive to the needs of students and teachers and have begun to make use of all aspects of the computer, including its powerful sound and animation capabilities. Further, software developers have begun to show concern for the educational issues surrounding software development. It is more likely today than it has been in the past that a piece of educational software will be developed by people who understand both educational issues and issues related to software development. Currently, feedback from practicing teachers is often sought and considered in developing new programs for education.

Although tutor mode computer-assisted instruction has been improving in quality, tool programs, such as word processors, spreadsheets, and data base management systems, as well as graphics programs, have gained wide popularity. This mirrors a trend in business and industry. More and more, individuals are using tool programs to gain ready access to the power the computer offers. A student able to painlessly rewrite and polish a composition because of a word processor, a class using a graphics program to design greeting cards and bulletin boards, or a student using a data base management system to record and analyze data are all using powerful computer applications. This type of tool application will continue to grow as part of what is done with computers in the schools.

The term artificial intelligence (AI) has been used several times in this text. For educators, AI should begin to yield tangible results in the near future. One promising area is that of natural-language processing. The need to make the computer more accessible to all individuals is important. Rather than having to sit and type arcane commands at a keyboard, the goal is to communicate with the computer through spoken natural language. As this goal begins to be realized, the potential of computers in education will expand greatly. Initially, a student will be able to communicate through a keyboard (by typing) using natural language. As work in speech recognition and speech synthesis is refined, the time may come when the computer is simply spoken to and the response from the computer spoken in turn. These developments are not as far-fetched or as far away as they may seem. Commercial software products allowing the user to communicate with the computer through a keyboard using natural language are a reality now. Applications in education will eventually appear. Computers to which a user can freely issue verbal instructions are, however, in the future.

Another area of AI research that will yield benefits for education is that of expert systems. These systems are programmed to make available to a user a specific body of knowledge. Within the confines of the body of knowledge dealt with the computer can act as an expert. Often these systems are used for diagnostic purposes. For example, a physician may consult such a system with questions about a patient. The system will respond by requesting certain facts

Computers in the Classroom

The question of what the world will be like in the future always intrigues students. After all, students will live most of their lives in a future world that may be considerably different from the world they currently know. Constructing a real time capsule can give students a focus for thinking about what computers are, how they are used today, and how they may be used in the future. The computer time capsule will be real in that, once created, it will be carefully stored so that it can be opened at a predetermined time. One simple way of doing this is to use a durable container of plastic or metal that can be filled with the materials students will produce. The container can be sealed (locked or taped shut) with appropriate materials inside and with directions on the outside. The capsule can be given to the librarian to be held in the library until the appropriate date. Depending on grade level, the date for opening the capsule may be ten, twenty, or more years in the future.

Students can begin by gathering examples of how computers are currently used. Pictures, articles, and computer printouts are all valuable candidates for inclusion in the capsule. Students can discuss what they have found and may decide to offer examples from such areas as education, business, government, and science. They should also consider how they expect computers and computer use to change by the time the capsule is

opened. They should further consider how computers might personally affect them as adults. Their observations will be recorded, perhaps as written compositions, artwork, or both. Some students may want to record their speculations on cassette tape. This can lead to an interesting discussion about technology; what if people no longer use cassette tape players when the capsule is opened?

The generation of material for the capsule allows ample opportunity for learning about computers and computer trends. It also provides opportunities for skill development in writing, speaking, and listening. Some students may want to produce materials using the computer. Graphics programs may be used to produce artwork, word processors can be used for writing, even listings of programs that students have completed may be included in the capsule.

Two sets of materials should be selected from all that has been created. One set will show present day computers and how they are used. A second set will predict changes in computers and suggest possible future uses as well as the effects of such uses on society in general and individual students in particular. Directions for care and opening of the capsule will then be written. Students can meet with whomever will be the custodian of the capsule and work out the details of where the capsule will be stored. Directions for opening the capsule will be securely attached to it. A small ceremony commemorating the sealing and storing of the capsule can be held as a culminating activity. Then, all that is left is to come back at the designated time and open the capsule!

about the patient from the physician and will then offer a diagnosis and suggested treatment. **Figure 14–8** shows a portion of a consultation between a doctor and a computer. The computer later goes on to offer a diagnosis and

---

11) Are there any other pending cultures?
No
12) Have there been negative (as opposed to pending) cultures obtained from David King which may be relevant to the present illness?
No
13) Do you suspect David King may have an infection at a site from which you have not obtained culture specimens?
No
14) Is David King currently receiving therapy with any antimicrobial agent?
No
15) During the present illness, has David King been treated with an antimicrobial agent which is no longer being administered?
No
[Considering organisms (other than those isolated from cultures) which might be present...]
16) Has David King recently had symptoms of persistent headache or other abnormal neurologic symptoms (dizziness, lethargy, etc.)?
Yes
17) Has David King recently had objective evidence of abnormal neurologic signs (nuchal rigidity, coma, seizures, etc.) documented by physician observation or examination?
Yes
The CSF cultures will be considered to be associated with MENINGITIS.
18) Please give the date on which clinical evidence (symptoms, signs, or laboratory tests) of the meningitis first appeared.
23/JUNE/84 7:00
19) Does David King have an abnormal chest X-ray?
No
20) Does David King have one or more of the following risk factors for tb: a) positive intermediate strength PPD, b) history of close contact with a person with active tb, c) a household member with a past history of active tb, d) apical scarring on chest x-ray, e) history of granulomas on biopsy of liver, lymph node, or other organs?
No
21) Does David King have any cutaneous lesions or rash on physical examination?
No
22) Does David King have evidence of ocular nerve dysfunction?
Why
[i.e. WHY is it important to determine whether PATIENT-1 has evidence of ocular nerve dysfunction?]
[4.0] This will aid in determining the organisms (other than those seen on cultures or smears) which might be causing the infection.
It has already been established that
[4.1] the infection which requires therapy is meningitis
Therefore, if
[4.2] David King has evidence of ocular nerve dysfunction
then
there is weakly suggestive evidence (.2) that Mycobacterium-tb is one of the organisms (other than those seen on cultures or smears) which might be causing the infection
Author: Yu
[RULE366]
[back to question 22...]

(Harmon and King, 1985, pp. 65–66)

Figure 14–8 An example of a consultation with the expert system MYCIN. The human part of the dialogue is in italics. Notice that when the computer is asked why question 22 was raised, it responds with an explanation.

Reactions and Research

Issues of equity regarding access to computer equipment and training are becoming increasingly important. There is a growing perception that knowledge about computers and information-processing technology will become more and more a necessity. Individuals who are comfortable with and master the new technology will be afforded opportunities for economic, intellectual, and social growth that others will not. The danger exists that minority groups, women, and low-socioeconomic-status (SES) groups will not gain equal access to the skills necessary to thrive in a society increasingly dependent on computer technology.

Hess and Miura (1983), two researchers from Stanford University, report the results of a survey study aimed at investigating the perception that computer literacy is more often sought by boys than girls and by students of middle-SES backgrounds. Computer literacy for this study was defined as gaining knowledge of programming. Questionnaires requesting data on individual students were sent to the directors of thirty-five summer camps, workshops, and classes that offered training in computer programming. Responses were gathered from twenty-three directors, who reported on a total of 5,533 students. Data was provided on enrollment (primary, grades K through 4; middle school, grades 5 through 8; high school, grades 9 through 12), SES characteristics of students (low, middle, and upper), level of difficulty of programming classes (beginning and intermediate, advanced, assembly language), program sponsorship (private/corporate, public school, university), cost, day vs. residential format, and ethnicity (Caucasian, black, Hispanic, Asian, and native American).

It was found that the ratio of boys to girls enrolled was roughly three to one (73.8 percent boys to 26.2 percent girls). More females were enrolled at early grade levels, with the proportion dropping off as grade level increased (30 percent girls in primary grades, 26 percent in middle school, and 24 percent in high school). The proportion of females enrolled as courses increased in difficulty also dropped. Females accounted for 28 percent of those enrolled in beginning and intermediate classes, 14 percent of those taking advanced classes, and only 5 percent of students taking assembly language courses. Other findings include the fact that 91 percent of the students were identified as Caucasian, 5 percent as Asian, 2.5 percent as
black, 1 percent as Hispanic, and 0.5 percent as native American. SES of the students was described as being predominately middle and upper class.

The findings support the perception that males and middle-SES groups are seeking computer literacy. The authors discuss several tentative explanations for the gender differences identified in class enrollment, including the following. One popular explanation is that traditional sex differences in mathematics may transfer to computer programming. The authors note that the sex-typing of school subjects may begin as early as second grade. Also, computers have an image of being associated with science, engineering, and mathematics—traditionally male-dominated professions. Further, even when computers are used for games and other types of educational experiences, much of the software available has male-oriented themes (e.g., adventure and violence). Also, parents tend to encourage and support boys (rather than girls) to use computers.

In analyzing how societal beliefs and conditions influence sex differences in learning about computers, Hawkins (1984) offers some concrete suggestions about what can be done to help change the situation.

As the new technology is introduced into more and more educational settings, it is important to consider the computer as a universal symbolic machine that can be designed and used for a variety of purposes. However, in the absence of a broader perspective, computers tend to be subsumed under math or science curricula and thus take on the already existing stigma of sex differences.

In summary, since the computer can be seen as a flexible tool, attention must be paid to software design and to the organization of children's classroom experience. There are two promising avenues for realizing these goals. First, it is important that computers be used in classrooms as tools for achieving a variety of goals (e.g., word processors, music editors). There need to be opportunities for use that match the goals and interests of individual children, along with appropriate support for learning about the technology. Second, the careful design of software in the areas of math and science may enable girls to view these subjects as personally useful to them. (Hawkins, 1984)

Do you agree with these suggestions? How might you implement them in your classroom?

suggest a course of treatment. This program, called MYCIN, allows the user to question why a computer has asked a question or offered a suggestion. The computer will respond with a reason and perhaps one or more medical references supporting its position. Harmon and King (1985) offer in their book *Expert Systems*, from which this consultation is taken, an excellent overview of what expert systems are and how they are constructed.

There are already available software products called expert system shells (tool software) that allow nonprogrammers to build expert systems even on microcomputers. This promising area of AI may eventually allow educators the benefit of computer consultants in different curriculum areas. Also, when expert systems are teamed with CAI-type software, a student may someday be able to work with a software package, such as a tutorial, that will later provide to the teacher diagnostic information and instructional suggestions related to the student's work.

Two issues related to equity and computers need to be addressed. First, will computers be reserved only for the rich, or will the benefits of computer training and using computers as tools be shared by all segments of society? Few teachers are interested in creating an educational elite and disenfranchising other segments of society because a school or a district cannot afford quality computer education for all students. This topic came up earlier in relation to the different models for managing computer resources. How will such resources be distributed within a district? Who will use computers in a given school? Will remedial students have priority, or will scarce resources be allocated to gifted learners? What about students with exceptionalities? These issues require careful thought if educators are to adequately serve all the constituent groups that make up the school population.

Equity

Second, there is the issue of sexual stereotyping. Turkle (1984) points out the differences in how boys and girls come into contact with computers. Boys tend to exhibit in their interaction with computers those traits historically associated with science; they are systematic, oriented toward planning, interested in controlling the computer. They view the computer objectively. Turkle refers to them as hard masters. Girls tend to be more impressionistic and view the computer subjectively. They interact with the computer more as an artist than as a scientist. They may do something, experiment, look at the results, and try something else. This is called soft mastery. They are less oriented toward planning than are hard masters. Both hard and soft masters are capable of excelling in computer work. Each uses a different style of interacting with the computer. Of course, a boy may be a soft master and a girl may be a hard master. The tendency, however, seems to be for boys to be hard masters and girls to be soft masters. The problem is that teachers must be sensitive to the ways that hard and soft masters use computers. They must be prepared to support the learning that can take place through either style. It is hoped that we are long past the period of sexually stereotyping certain kinds of activities, such as science, as inherently male and other activities as inherently female.

Conclusion

The role of the educator in a technologically sophisticated society must relate to that society's growing and changing technology. This has been illustrated by the reaction of educators to the challenge of providing needed computer education to students. Over the next few decades the computer will continue to revolutionize almost every aspect of our world. Everyone will come into contact with these changes. The individuals prepared to use these new, powerful, exciting tools will flourish and contribute to society. Teachers, by meeting the challenge of preparing students to live and work with computers, do a service to their students and their profession. Citizens who understand technology can make informed decisions about its use. Workers who are able to use technology can make important economic contributions to their families and their country. Individuals who can use technological tools such as the computer to enrich their own lives can enrich all our lives. Teachers who can play a part in offering quality computer education can help students prepare to become fulfilled citizens, employees, and individuals.

Key Terms

computer coordinator
computer lab
desktop metaphor
expert system
expert system shell
hard disk
hard master
icon
interactive videodisc
Koala Pad
lab/classroom

mobile lab/classroom
mouse
Muppet Learning Keys
MYCIN
natural-language processing
network
soft master
stand-alone
switchbox
window

Questions

1. What types of computers are most frequently used in schools? Why?

2. Define the terms stand-alone and networked as they relate to microcomputers. Include an example for each term.

3. How are cost and computer education related? Be specific in naming the factors that affect the cost of implementing a computer curriculum.

4. Cite and react to the "educational utopian" view of Seymour Papert regarding the cost of supplying computers to the schools.

5. Compare and contrast how computer instruction may be managed in a school with one computer lab and no computers in classrooms, and a school with no computer lab but with two computers in each classroom. Which would you prefer?

6. Describe what you consider an ideal distribution of computers in a school with two classrooms at each grade level for grades K through 6. There are approximately twenty children in each classroom. The school can afford to buy forty stand-alone microcomputers and a wide range of software. Include a brief description of how and by whom the computers will be used.

7. What responsibilities would a computer coordinator have in a school district? What qualifications would she need?

8. What trends in hardware and software can educators expect to see in the future?

9. What is natural-language processing, and what are expert systems? How will they affect educators?

10. A parent comes to you concerned that her son and daughter approach their work at the computer differently, yet both seem to be successful. How do you respond?

11. Your school has limited computer resources. Prioritize the following list from most important to least important as to who should have access to those resources. Defend your list. Assume that all three groups will benefit from using the computer.

   - gifted students

   - "average" students

   - special education students

12. Write a short essay expressing your opinions about computers in the schools. Be specific. Have your ideas changed as a result of this course?

References/Further Reading

Becker, Henry Jay. "Our National Report Card: Preliminary Results from the New Johns Hopkins Survey." *Classroom Computer Learning* 6, no. 4 (1986):30–33.

Fuori, William M., and Lawrence J. Aufiero. *Computers and Information Processing.* Englewood Cliffs, N.J.: Prentice-Hall, 1986.

Hess, Robert D., and Irene T. Miura. "Gender and Socioeconomic Differences in Enrollment in Computer Camps and Classes." 1983, ED 237–610.

Harmon, Paul, and David King. *Expert Systems.* New York: John Wiley & Sons, 1985.

Hawkins, Jan. "Computers and Girls: Rethinking the Issues." *Technical Report No. 24,* April 1984, ED 249–922, 16–17.

Peterson, Dale. "Nine Issues. Guide to Computers in Education." *Popular Computing* (special issue), October 1984, 10–18.

Papert, Seymour. *Mindstorms: Children, Computers, and Powerful Ideas.* New York: Basic Books, 1980.

Turkle, Sherry. *The Second Self: Computers and the Human Spirit.* New York: Simon & Schuster, 1984, 101–134.

Appendix A—Relevant Periodicals

The periodicals listed under Education are primarily for educators. Those listed under General are for the general public. Any of those listed under either category may be of value as a resource.

Education

AEDS Monitor
Association for Educational Data Systems
1201 16th Street, NW
Washington, DC 20036

Classroom Computer Learning
2451 E. River Road
Dayton, OH 45439

The Computing Teacher
Department of Computer and Information Science
University of Oregon
Eugene, OR 97403

Educational Computer
P.O. Box 535
Cupertino, CA 95015

Educational Technology
140 Sylvan Avenue
Englewood Cliffs, NJ 07632

Electronic Education
Suite 220
1311 Executive Center Drive
Tallahassee, FL 32301

Electronic Learning
Scholastic, Inc.
730 Broadway
New York, NY 10003

Family Computing
Scholastic, Inc.
730 Broadway
New York, NY 10003

The Journal of Computers in Mathematics and Science Teaching
P.O. Box 4455
Austin, TX 78765

The Journal of Computers, Reading and Language Arts
NAVA
3150 Spring Street
Fairfax, VA 22031

The Logo and Educational Computing Journal
Suite 219
1320 Stony Brook Road
Stony Brook, NY 11790

T.H.E. JOURNAL
Information Synergy, Inc.
P.O. Box 902
Acton, MA 01720

Teaching and Computers
Scholastic, Inc.
730 Broadway
New York, NY 10003

Turtle News
Young People's Logo Association
P.O. Box 855067
Richardson, TX 75085

General

A+
P.O. Box 2965
Boulder, CO 80322
(covers Apple computers)

Byte
70 Main Street
Peterborough, NH 03458

InfoWorld
375 Cochituate Road
Box 880
Framingham, MA 01701

Nibble
Box 325
Lincoln, MA 01773
(covers Apple computers)

PC Magazine
P.O. Box 2443
Boulder, CO 80321
(covers IBM computers)

PC Week
One Park Avenue, 4th Floor
New York, NY 10016
(covers IBM computers)

Popular Computing
70 Main Street
Peterborough, NH 03458

Softside
6 South Street
Milford, NH 03055

TRS–80 Microcomputer News
Tandy Corporation
Fort Worth, TX 76102
(covers Radio Shack computers)

80 Micro
80 Pine Street
Peterborough, NH 03458
(covers Radio Shack computers)

Appendix B—Organizations

The organizations listed below are resources for information about computers and education from a variety of perspectives. Write to any of the addresses listed for information.

Association for Computers in Mathematics and Science Teaching
P.O. Box 4
Austin, TX 78765

Association for Computing Machinery (ACM)
1133 Avenue of the Americas
New York, NY 10036

Association for Educational Communications and Technology (AECT)
1126 Sixteenth Street NW
Washington, DC 20036

Association for Educational Data Systems (AEDS)
1201 16th Street NW
Washington, DC 20036

Association for the Development of Computer-Based Instructional Systems (ADCIS)
ADCIS Headquarters
Computer Center
Western Washington University
Bellingham, WA 98225

International Council for Computers in Education (ICCE)
Department of Computer and Information Science
University of Oregon
Eugene, OR 97403

National Audio-Visual Association (NAVA)
3150 Spring Street
Fairfax, VA 22031

National Council of Teachers of Mathematics (NCTM)
1906 Association Drive
Reston, VA 22091

National Logo Exchange
P.O. Box 5341
Charlottesville, VA 22905

National Science Teachers Association (NSTA)
1742 Connecticut Avenue NW
Washington, DC 20009

Young People's Logo Association
1208 Hillsdale Drive
Richardson, TX 75018

Appendix C—Using an Apple

Operating Systems—DOS 3.3

An operating system is a program or group of programs that allows the computer to control the functions it is required to perform. Examples of such functions are running programs, managing input and output, and controlling peripheral equipment, such as disk drives, printers, and modems. In the past perhaps the most commonly used operating system for Apple II series computers has been DOS 3.3. DOS stands for disk operating system, and 3.3 denotes a version number (the version available before 3.3 was 3.2). A newer operating system, ProDOS, is also available.

Operating system commands are usually referred to as system commands. A few elementary system commands are necessary when beginning to program in BASIC. These will be covered below.

Initializing a Disk, Editing, LIST, and RUN

Before data may be stored on a disk, the disk must be initialized. This is also called formatting the disk. When a disk is initialized the computer automatically divides the surface of the disk into sections where data can be stored. These sections are called sectors. The instructions that follow for initializing a disk are for DOS 3.3. The ProDOS operating system offers a menu-driven utility for initializing a disk. The user simply chooses options from a series of menus.

To initialize a disk, first place the DOS 3.3 System Master disk in the disk drive. Next, turn on the monitor and the computer. The disk drive light will come on and the drive will whir for a few seconds.

Whenever the disk drive light is on, do not try to open the drive door. After the disk drive has whirred for a number of seconds, the disk drive light will shut off and the whirring will stop. A message such as that which follows will appear on the screen.

```
APPLE II
DOS VERSION 3.3 SYSTEM MASTER
JANUARY 1, 1983
COPY. APPLE COMPUTER, INC. 1980, 1982
```

Next, insert a blank disk in the disk drive. Now, type the command NEW and then press the key labeled RETURN. This will have the effect of clearing the computer's memory available for entering programs. The RETURN key is needed to actually enter information into the computer. When you type something on the keyboard, it immediately appears on the monitor. However, what you have typed is not entered into the computer until the RETURN key is pressed.

You will now type in a short program in BASIC called a HELLO program, or a Greeting program. Each time you start (or boot) the computer using the disk about to be initialized, this program will cause a message to be printed on the monitor. We will use the opportunity of entering this HELLO program to learn how to edit, LIST, and RUN BASIC programs.

Type the following program exactly as shown except insert your name where the program has BEV CLARK and the current month and year where the program has 12/86. After you have typed each line, remember to press the RETURN key. If you should make an error when typing the program, you may use the left and right arrow keys to go back and position the blinking rectangle (called the cursor) over your error and retype the line from there on. If you have already left the line (have pressed RETURN) and you notice an error, simply retype the line. This will cause the old line in the computer's memory to be replaced by the line you have just typed.

```
10 REM HELLO PROGRAM
20 PRINT "INITIALIZED 12/86"
30 PRINT "BEV CLARK"
40 END
```

Notice that each line of the program starts with a line number. This is a requirement of BASIC. It is good practice, as you write BASIC programs, to number your program by tens (10, 20, 30, etc.). If you should need to insert more lines of code later, this makes it easy to do so. For instance, in the program above if you needed to add a line after line 20 once the program was typed into the computer, you would simply type the following and press RETURN. Do this now.

```
25 PRINT "FOR COMPUTER CLASS"
```

The computer will automatically insert this line of code after line 20 in the program so that the program stored in the computer's memory would be as below. To see what program is stored in the computer's memory at any given moment, type the BASIC command LIST and press RETURN. A listing of the program will appear on the screen. Try typing LIST and pressing RETURN. The program you typed in should appear on the screen, similar to the program listed below.

```
10 REM HELLO PROGRAM
20 PRINT "INITIALIZED 12/86"
25 PRINT "FOR COMPUTER CLASS"
30 PRINT "BEV CLARK"
40 END
```

To this point you have typed in a BASIC program and learned how to edit and LIST it. There is no guarantee, however, that the program will work. The next step is to tell the computer to run, or execute, the program and see if the program does what is expected. The command to tell the computer to run whatever program is stored in memory (only one program will be in memory at a time) is RUN. In this case we would expect the computer to

print the following on the monitor when the program listed above is run.

```
INITIALIZED 12/86
FOR COMPUTER CLASS
BEV CLARK
```

Type the command RUN and then press RETURN. If you do not get the results expected, your instructor will help you debug, or fix, your program. The process of entering a program into the computer and then debugging it until it produces the correct results is one you will become familiar with as you work through the material on BASIC in this text.

Once your HELLO program performs as it should, it is time to initialize your disk. To do this, type in the command below and press RETURN.

```
INIT HELLO
```

This will cause the computer to initialize your disk and place the HELLO program on your disk. After the disk drive has stopped operation, turn off your computer and then turn it on again. The disk drive will whir for a few seconds and you will then see the message from the HELLO program printed on the screen. Because you now have an initialized disk, you may use it to boot the computer. It also means you can use DOS system commands such as SAVE, LOAD, and DELETE. You should place a label on your disk with your name, the date, and the type of machine on which the disk was initialized. Be sure to write on the label before placing it on the disk. Writing on a label after it is on a disk may damage the disk. After you have labeled the disk, place it back in the disk drive.

CATALOG, SAVE, LOAD, and DELETE

Type NEW and press RETURN to clear the computer's memory. Now type the following program into the computer. Use your name and address in place of the name and address given in the program.

```
10 REM NAME AND ADDRESS PGM
20 PRINT "IVA JONES"
30 PRINT "12 MAIN STREET"
40 PRINT "BATES, IOWA"
50 END
```

RUN the program to be sure it works. If you have a problem, your instructor will help you fix your program. If you have typed the program exactly as shown, only substituting information about yourself in lines 20, 30, and 40, you should not have any trouble.

At this point the program is stored in the memory of the computer. If the computer is turned off, the program will be lost and will have to be retyped in order to be used again. Because this is not practical, it is necessary to save, on disk, programs that have been created. The following command will cause the computer to make a copy on disk of the program stored in memory.

SAVE filename

Each named entry saved on disk is called a file. Whatever file name is specified for the program will be the name that the computer gives to the program that is being saved. You choose the file name. The following will cause the program stored in memory to be saved on disk under the name MYPROGRAM. Type in what follows and then press RETURN. The disk drive will turn on for a few seconds as it saves your program.

SAVE MYPROGRAM

Now type in CATALOG and press RETURN. What will appear on the screen will be a directory of what is stored on your disk, as shown below.

```
DISK VOLUME 254
A 002 HELLO
A 002 MYPROGRAM
```

The two files on your disk are the HELLO program used to initialize the disk and MYPROGRAM, which was just saved to the disk. The letter A indicates that these programs were written in Applesoft BASIC. The number 002 indicates that each program (or file) takes up two sectors of space on the disk. The top line, DISK VOLUME 254, indicates the volume number of the disk, which in this case is 254, the number always automatically generated by the computer when the disk is initialized.

Type LIST and press RETURN. You will see that your program is still in the memory of the computer (there is also a copy on the disk). Type NEW and press RETURN to erase the computer's memory. Now type LIST again and then press RETURN, and you will see that the program is gone from the memory of the computer. To retrieve a copy of MYPROGRAM from disk, use the following command.

LOAD filename

Whatever file name is specified will be loaded from the disk into the computer's memory. Type the following and press RETURN to load MYPROGRAM from disk.

LOAD MYPROGRAM

After the disk drive stops operation, LIST the contents of memory and you will see the program is once again in the computer.

Sometimes it is desirable to erase files from your disk. The command to erase files from disk is

DELETE filename

To delete MYPROGRAM from disk, type in the command below and press RETURN.

DELETE MYPROGRAM

If you now CATALOG the disk, you will see that MYPROGRAM has been erased from the disk. (Because it is still in the computer's memory, you may now save it again if you wish to keep a copy of it.)

You now have an initialized disk and the elementary tools needed to communicate with your computer. This will allow you to begin to write BASIC programs as you progress through that section of the text.

Reserved Words

The following is a list of words already used by
Applesoft BASIC, called reserved words.

ABS	EXP	IF	NOTRACE	RESUME	STOP
AND	FLASH	IN#	ON	RETURN	STORE
ASC	FN	INPUT	ONERR	RIGHT$	STR$
AT	FOR	INT	OR	RND	TAB(
ATN	FRE	INVERSE	PDL	ROT=	TAN
CALL	GET	LEFT$	PEEK	RUN	TEXT
CHR$	GOSUB	LEN	PLOT	SAVE	THEN
CLEAR	GOTO	LET	POKE	SCALE=	TO
COLOR=	GR	LIST	POP	SCRN(	TRACE
CONT	HCOLOR=	LOAD	POS	SGN	USR
COS	HGR	LOG	PRINT	SHLOAD	VAL
DATA	HGR2	LOMEM:	PR#	SIN	VLIN
DEF	HIMEM:	MID$	READ	SPC(	VTAB
DEL	HLIN	NEW	RECALL	SPEED=	WAIT
DIM	HOME	NEXT	REM	SQR	XPLOT
DRAW	HPLOT	NORMAL	RESTORE	STEP	XDRAW
END	HTAB	NOT			

Appendix D—Software Manufacturers

Listed below are selected manufacturers of educational software. Write for information.

Bare Bones Software
5817 Franklin Avenue
LaGrange, IL 60525

Baudville
1001 Medical Park Drive SE
Grand Rapids, MI 49506

Berta-Max Inc.
P.O. Box 31849
Seattle, WA 98103

C & C Software
5713 Kentford Circle
Wichita, KS 67220

CBS Software
One Fawcett Place
Greenwich, CT 06836

Cross Educational Software
1802 North Trenton Street
P.O. Box 1536
Ruston, LA 71270

Davidson & Associates, Inc.
3135 Kashiwa Street
Torrance, CA 90505

DCH Educational Publishing
125 Spring Street
Lexington, MA 02173

DesignWare, Inc.
185 Berry Street
San Francisco, CA 94107

Follett Software Company
4506 Northwest Highway
Crystal Lake, IL 60014

Hartley Courseware
P.O. Box 419
133 Bridge Street
Dimondale, MI 48821

Krell Software
1320 Stony Brook Road
Stony Brook, NY 10803

Logo Computer Systems, Inc.
555 West 57th Street
Suite 1236
New York, NY 10019

Micro Power & Light Company
12820 Hillcrest Road
Suite 219
Dallas, TX 75230

Milliken Publishing Company
1100 Research Boulevard
P.O. Box 21579
St. Louis, MO 63132

Minnesota Educational Computing Corporation
3490 Lexington Avenue North
St. Paul, MN 55112

Radio Shack Education Division
1400 One Tandy Center
Fort Worth, TX 76102

Scott Foresman and Company
1900 East Lake Avenue
Glenview, IL 60025

Sensible Software
210 South Woodward
Suite 229
Birmingham, MI 48011

Springboard Software, Inc.
7808 Creekridge Circle
Minneapolis, MN 55435

Sunburst Communications, Inc.
39 Washington Avenue
Pleasantville, NY 10570

Terrapin, Inc.
222 Third Street
Cambridge, MA 02142

Walt Disney Personal Computer Software
4563 Colorado Boulevard
Los Angeles, CA 90039

Glossary

accommodation: A change in an individual's cognitive structures owing to interaction with the environment.

algorithm: A series of instructions that will carry out a particular task.

artificial intelligence (AI): The branch of computer science engaged in researching ways to make the computer emulate those attributes we classify as human intelligence. Software (sometimes running on specialized hardware) that emulates attributes of human intelligence.

assimilation: The incorporation of new information into existing schemas.

authoring system: Software that facilitates the creation of tutor-mode computerized lessons.

auxiliary storage: Permanent storage on media such as magnetic disk and magnetic tape. Sometimes referred to as secondary storage.

BACK (BK): The Logo command that moves the turtle back a specified number of turtle steps, e.g., BACK 50.

backup copies: Copies made from software to ensure uninterrupted use of the software if something happens to the original.

BASIC: A high-level programming language sometimes used to introduce students to programming. The acronym BASIC stands for *B*eginner's *A*ll-Purpose *S*ymbolic *I*nstruction *C*ode.

binary notation: The use of the binary digits 1 and 0 to represent characters in the computer.

bit: A binary digit, either 1 or 0.

branching: The possibility, in a computer program, of following more than one sequence of instructions based on some condition in the program. For instance, in a tutorial, if the student needed review material, the program would branch to present review material; otherwise, it would go on to the next lesson.

bugs: Errors in computer programs.

byte: A group of adjacent binary digits that are acted on as a unit by the computer. A byte is roughly equivalent to the locations needed to store a character.

C: A programming language used to write both scientific and business programs.

CATALOG: In BASIC (and in Logo) the command that prints on the screen the names of the files on secondary storage.

cell: A location in a spreadsheet where data or a formula can be recorded.

Central Processing Unit (CPU): The component of a computer that controls the operations of the computer. The CPU consists of a Control Unit, an Arithmetic/Logic Unit, and Primary Storage.

CLEARSCREEN (CS): The Logo command that clears the screen and leaves the turtle in its current position.

COBOL: A high-level programming language widely used to write business programs. The acronym COBOL stands for *Common Business Oriented Language.*

command: In general, command may be used to refer to the reserved words in a programming language, although the term statement is often used instead of the term command.

compatibility: The match between computer components, both hardware and software. Two components are compatible if they can work together. For instance, a program written to run on an Apple II series computer is compatible with that computer; it would not be compatible, would not work, on an IBM computer.

computer: A machine that processes data by performing arithmetic or logical operations on it. A device that accepts input (data), processes it, and provides output (information).

computer-assisted design (CAD): The use of a computer in the design of a product. The computer may be used to model or simulate the product being designed.

computer-assisted instruction (CAI): Any use of the computer in instruction, including use in the tool, tutor, and tutee modes.

computer-assisted manufacturing (CAM): The use of a computer in the manufacture of a product, such as the use of industrial robots on an assembly line.

computer-based training (CBT): A term used in business and industry to describe the use of the computer as a vehicle for the presentation of instruction.

computer-controlled interaction: Any instructional interaction between a person and a computer in which the computer controls the interaction more than the person. For example, a drill-and-practice program is highly computer controlled; most of the decisions about the course the instructional interaction takes are made by the computer (or, more appropriately, the program running on the computer).

computer coordinator: The individual in a district who is responsible for any of a variety of functions related to educational computing, including curriculum development, professional development related to computers for staff and faculty, hardware and software acquisition, overseeing one or more computer labs, consulting with teachers, and teaching computer classes.

computer curriculum: The course of study related to computers followed by students in a school system. Such a curriculum will usually include instruction about (a) the history of computing, (b) hardware and software, (c) the social implications of computer use, (d) programming computers, and (e) tutor mode and tool mode software.

computer education: See *computer curriculum.*

computer lab: A centralized area set up with a number of computers to serve the educational needs of students and faculty.

computer literacy: A state where an individual understands what a computer is, how it works, and is comfortable and effective in making a computer accomplish a necessary task.

computer-managed instruction: Using the computer to gather and evaluate data as well as report information about student performance.

computer program: The set of instructions a computer is given that causes it to perform a desired task.

computer revolution: The tremendous growth of computer power and availability that has taken place from approximately 1940 to the present.

computer system: The computer plus all of the attached peripheral devices.

concrete operational stage: The Piagetian stage of cognitive development lasting from about age seven to age twelve during which children use concrete objects to think abstractly.

conditional test: A test that, based on the evaluation of a condition, will effect the flow of logic within a program. For example, in BASIC the statement IF G = 100 THEN PRINT "PERFECT SCORE" will cause PERFECT SCORE to be printed if the condition G = 100 is true; otherwise, it will not be printed.

connector symbol: A flowchart symbol that denotes movement from one place in the flowchart to another.

conservation: The ability to understand that shape is not necessarily related to quantity.

constant: A specific value, either a numerical (for example, 1, 4, 234, and so on) or a string value (for example, Tom, Eileen).

CTRL-D: In Logo, deletes the character under the cursor.

CTRL-K: In Logo, deletes the rest of the line from the cursor position on.

CTRL-N: In Logo, when in the editor, moves the cursor to the next line.

CTRL-O: In Logo, when in the editor, opens a new line.

CTRL-P: In Logo, when in the editor, moves the cursor to the previous line.

Curriculum Alignment Service for Educators (CASE): A service offered by the Educational Products Information Exchange aimed at helping educators match the curriculum and curriculum materials with stated goals and objectives.

cursor: A symbol, usually a rectangle, sometimes a blinking rectangle, that appears on the computer screen and denotes where data will be entered next.

data: The set of facts that can be processed by a computer. For example, the grades for a particular student. Also see *DATA*.

DATA: In BASIC, the statement that lists the data elements contained in the program.

data base: A specialized file made up of a collection of records.

data base management system: Software that manages the data stored in a data base. Such software usually provides for creation of the data base, maintenance of the data by allowing additions and deletions, the generation of reports, and the ability to search (or query) the data base for specific information.

debit cards: A card that, when used, causes the value of a customer's purchase to be subtracted from the balance in a customer's account.

debug: The process of finding and removing all the errors in a computer program.

Decision Support System: A type of computerized system used in business by middle and upper management as an aid in decision making.

decision symbol: A flowchart symbol that denotes that a choice must be made from among two or more conditions.

desktop metaphor: The use of various techniques, such as windows and icons, to make the computer screen resemble an actual desktop both in appearance and function. The aim is to make the computer easier to use.

disk: A type of magnetic storage medium on which data is encoded. Disks may be permanently mounted on a disk drive (such as hard disks on hard disk drives) or be removable (for example, floppy disks).

disk drive: The mechanism that reads data from and writes data to disks.

document symbol: A flowchart symbol that indicates output will be printed on a printer.

documentation: The written material that accompanies either computer hardware or software.

DRAW: The Logo command used to enter DRAW mode (the turtle graphics environment).

drill and practice: An instructional strategy in which exercises are presented in order to provide practice in a skill to a student. For example, a series of addition problems or a series of nouns that end in *y* and must be made into the plural form by the student. Software that presents exercises relevant to a particular skill and that usually provides feedback about how the student does.

editor: When in EDIT mode in Logo, the user is placed in the editor, where various commands are available to easily edit the text of Logo procedures.

Educational Products Information Exchange (EPIE): An independent product evaluation agency supported by consumers.

egocentric: When a child sees the world only in terms of his own perspective, he is egocentric.

Electronic Funds Transfer (EFT): The process of electronically moving money from one account to another. For example, paying bills by phone, where money from the customer's account is transferred electronically to the account of a business.

electronic mail: The use of the computer to send messages electronically from one location to another.

encoding system: A system to represent characters as a series of binary digits.

END: The BASIC statement that signals the end of a program.

EOD tag: End of data tag. A character or series of characters, such as XXX or 999, used in a program to signify that no more data will be input.

ERASE: In Logo, the command that erases the procedure specified from working memory. For example, the command ERASE MOXY would cause the procedure MOXY to be erased from working memory.

ERASEFILE: In Logo, the command that erases from secondary storage the file specified. For example, the command ERASEFILE "STUFF would erase the file named STUFF from the secondary storage.

error handling: The ability of a program to react to errors, either bad data input by the user or errors internal to the program, identify the error, and return control of the program to the user with an explanation.

ESC: In Logo, deletes the character to the left of the cursor.

expert system: A type of computer software that emulates the functioning of a human expert in a particular field of knowledge. An example is a medical diagnosis system related to a particular disease, such as meningitis.

expert system shell: A piece of software used to create specific expert systems.

field: A group of related characters. A student record might consist of the following, each of which is a field: name, address, phone number, father's name, mother's name, teacher, bus route.

fifth generation: The next generation of computer hardware. This generation of hardware is predicted to be much different from the current generation and may make sophisticated artificial intelligence applications a reality.

file: A collection of related records. The student file for a school consists of one record for each student in the school. In Logo, procedures currently in the workspace are stored on disk under whatever filename the user specifies when the save command is used. Thus a file of procedures is created on the disk.

first generation: A period from 1951 to 1958, denoting the first generation of commercially available computers.

flexibility: The degree to which a program offers options to the user of the program.

flowchart: A pictorial representation that makes use of a specific set of predefined symbols to display a sequence of instructions.

FOR: In BASIC, the statement that signals the beginning of a FOR-NEXT loop.

formal operational stage: The Piagetian stage of cognitive development from about age twelve to adult when the individual can use formal logic to reason about the world.

FORTRAN: A high-level programming language used primarily for scientific applications. FORTRAN stands for *For*mula *Tran*slator.

FORWARD (FD): The Logo command that moves the turtle forward a specified number of turtle steps, e.g., FORWARD 55.

FULLSCREEN (CTRL-F): The Logo command that causes the entire screen to be displayed for drawing (graphics).

genetic epistemology: The study of the development of knowledge, both in the individual and in the culture.

GOODBYE: In Logo, the command that clears working memory and restarts Logo.

GOTO: In BASIC, the statement that transfers control of the program to the specified line number. For example, GOTO 100 will transfer control of the program to line number 100.

grade-keeping program: A program that can be used to store, manipulate, and report on grades.

hard disk: A type of secondary storage that makes use of a permanently mounted disk.

hard master: An individual who views the computer objectively, more as a scientist than as an artist. One whose interactions with the computer are systematic, oriented toward planning, and aimed at controlling the computer.

hardcopy: Material presented in printed form on paper, usually output from a printer.

hardware: The physical components of a computer system.

HIDETURTLE (HT): The Logo command that erases the turtle from the screen.

high-level language: A programming language that offers English-like statements to describe tasks to be performed by the computer. Examples include Pascal, Logo, BASIC, and FORTRAN.

HOME: The Logo command that moves the turtle to the home position (the center of the screen). Also, the BASIC statement that clears the screen and places the cursor at the top left-hand corner of the screen.

human-controlled interaction: Any instructional interaction between a person and a computer in which the person is primarily in charge of the interaction. An example is learning to program a computer; the person makes all the decisions about what tasks the computer will perform and what instructions will be given to the computer to perform the tasks.

icon: A symbol portrayed on a computer screen that represents a function available on the computer. For example, a file folder can represent the function of storing a document in a file on secondary storage. By selecting the icon, the function will be performed.

idiot savant: A wise fool. A person with a highly developed talent in one area but who has not developed normal mental ability in other areas. Used to refer to computers as machines capable of performing certain specialized tasks well but incapable of performing any other types of tasks.

IF-THEN: The statement in BASIC that allows for a conditional test. See *conditional test.*

infinite loop: The repetition of one or more statements in a program that will continue without ending unless the programmer or user of the program intervenes.

information: Data that have been processed into a form meaningful to a user. A list of grades for the spring semester for all 1,000 freshman students at a college is data that could be processed into information for a dean. The information might take the form of a report showing a breakdown of student performance by major, highlighting students with grades below 2.0 and above 3.5.

Information Age: The time in which we live; a time when information is generated at a tremendous rate and when vast amounts of information are available. Also, a time when information has come to be seen as a valuable resource.

initial value: In BASIC, the starting value of the control variable in a FOR-NEXT loop.

input: The data accepted by a computer for processing. See *INPUT.*

INPUT: The BASIC statement that allows data to be entered interactively. See *input.*

input/output symbol: A flowchart symbol that denotes data that will be input or output. It may represent output that will be printed on the printer or output that will appear on the screen.

instructional game: A game with rules and a winner, the main purpose of which is learning. Computer software that presents an instructional game.

Integrated Instructional Information Resource (IIIR): A part of the Educational Products Information Exchange's Curriculum Alignment Service for Educators. Specifically, the IIIR helps educators locate particular instructional materials related to specific instructional objectives.

interactive design: A way of creating a computer program that lets the user interact with the program by responding (usually through a keyboard) by entering data such as responses to questions, selections from menus, or any other data the program may require.

interactive videodisc: A method of using a computer and a videodisc to present material by making use of the capabilities of both.

keyboard: A device that allows the user to input data to a computer by pressing keys.

kilobyte: A kilobyte is equal to 1,024 bytes.

Knowledge Explosion: Refers to the tremendous growth of available data and information that has taken place primarily during this century.

Koala Pad: An input device used to enter a variety of information into the computer, including drawings.

lab/classroom: A way of managing a school's computer resources by placing some computers in a lab setting and distributing others to individual classrooms.

LEFT (LT): The Logo command that rotates the turtle in place a specified number of degrees to the left, e.g., LEFT 90.

LET: The BASIC statement that assigns a value to a variable. For example, the statement LET A = 5 assigns the value 5 to the numerical variable A.

LIST: In BASIC, the command that prints a listing of the program currently in memory on the screen.

LOAD: In BASIC, the command that causes the specified program to be loaded from secondary storage into the computer. For example, LOAD PGM1 would cause the program called PGM1 to be loaded into the computer.

logic: The series of unambiguous steps that make up an algorithm are often referred to as the logic of the algorithm (or the logic of the program the algorithm is translated into). The path the reasoning of a solution to a problem takes.

Logo: A high-level programming language designed by Seymour Papert and his colleagues at MIT expressly for educational purposes.

Logo primitive: A command already defined in the Logo programming language, such as FORWARD,

LEFT, BACK, etc. These commands can be used to create new commands as the user desires.

loop: A repetition of one or more statements within a program.

low-level language: A programming language closer to machine language than to the language of people.

machine language: The language in which the computer actually executes programs.

macro-explorer: A student who primarily enjoys the open-ended exploration of procedures and subprocedures without a specific goal in mind. See *micro-explorer* and *planner*.

mainframe computer: Among the most powerful of computers, this class of computers offers large amounts of memory, fast processing speed, and the ability to connect a great many peripheral devices.

management system: A set of computerized options often built in to tutor mode software that allows the teacher to conveniently manage instruction. Options might include keeping track of work completed by the student, selecting from among different instructional levels, changing the content of a lesson, and altering the frequency and content of reinforcers.

megabyte: A megabyte is equal to 1 million bytes of memory.

menu driven: Software that is menu driven presents the user with a list of choices from which one is selected based on what the user needs to do.

microcomputer: A small computer, sometimes referred to as a personal computer. Although microcomputers are not as powerful as minicomputers and mainframe computers, they have ample power and capability to meet the needs of many professionals and small businesses.

micro-explorer: A student who explores Logo in a careful, gradual manner, often experimenting with small pieces of Logo, such as one or several Logo commands, in order to gain assurance about how the Logo environment operates. See *macro-explorer* and *planner*.

microprocessor: A chip that contains all the component circuitry for a computer.

microworld: An environment that is self-contained and operates according to a specific set of consistent laws. The Logo programming language is itself a microworld from which other microworlds can be created.

minicomputer: A class of computer that, in power and capability, falls between microcomputers and mainframe computers.

Minnesota Educational Computing Corporation (MECC): A state-funded organization that provides computer training and support to educators and that publishes educational computer software.

MIT Logo: A version of the Logo programming language. The version of Logo presented in this book.

mobile lab/classroom: A way of managing a school's computer resources by locating some computers in individual classrooms and others on mobile carts. The readily mobile computers may be brought together to form a lab as needed or may be temporarily distributed to individual classrooms as extra resources.

modularized problem solving: The process of generating a solution to a problem by breaking the problem down into modules (subproblems), arriving at a solution to each module, and then putting the modules together to solve the entire problem.

module: A smaller piece of a problem or the solution to a problem. If the problem to be solved was generating student end-of-semester grades, the problem might be broken into the following modules: gather the grades for each student, calculate the end-of-semester grade for each student, and report each student's grade.

mouse: An input device that moves the cursor around the screen by the motion of a ball located on the bottom of the mouse. A button on the mouse is pressed to indicate selection of the option on the screen over which the cursor has been located.

Muppet Learning Keys: A specialized keyboard designed for young computer users.

MYCIN: An expert system designed to be used by doctors to aid in the diagnosis of meningitis and bacteremia infections.

natural-language processing: The potential ability of computers to process, as input, the natural language of humans.

network: A number of computers connected so that they may share information. A number of computers connected so that they may share peripheral devices. A number of computers connected so that they may share both information and peripheral devices.

networking: Connecting two or more computers to share either peripheral devices or primary storage.

NEW: In BASIC, the command that clears the computer's memory of the program currently stored there.

NEXT: The BASIC statement that denotes the lower boundary of a FOR-NEXT loop.

NODRAW: The Logo command that is used to exit DRAW mode.

numerical constant: A specific numerical value, such as 34, 124, 1001.

numerical variable: A storage location for a numerical constant. The name of such a storage location (e.g., in BASIC K, T, and so on).

object permanence: Knowing that an object still exists once it is no longer in view.

office automation: The use of computers and computer technology in the modern office for such tasks as word processing, electronic mail, and data processing.

operations: A mental activity whereby information is combined or transformed.

order of operations: The order in which various arithmetic and logical operations are performed by the computer when encountered in an expression.

output: Information supplied by the computer after data has been processed.

Pascal: A high-level programming language used in education and for business and scientific applications. Named after the French mathematician Blaise Pascal.

PENDOWN (PD): The Logo command that causes the turtle to draw a line as it moves.

PENUP (PU): The Logo command that retracts the pen. The turtle will not draw a line while moving when the pen is up.

peripheral device: Any of a number of devices that may be connected to a computer, such as a printer, disk drive, modem, or voice synthesizer.

personal computer: A small computer. The same as microcomputer.

Piagetian learning: A term used by Papert to describe the high-quality, efficient learning that takes place without formal schooling.

PILOT: An authoring language used to create computerized educational materials.

planner: A student who exhibits a classic programming style by beginning with a coherent plan for a project and proceeding in a methodical way to the completed project. See *micro-explorer* and *macro-explorer.*

playing turtle: The process of acting out, through corresponding bodily movements, the actual or expected movements of the turtle on the screen.

PO: The Logo command that prints on the screen the procedure specified or all the procedures in working memory if ALL is specified. For example, PO MINE would print out the procedure MINE; PO ALL would print out all the procedures in working memory.

Point-of-Sale Terminal (POS Terminal): A terminal located where transactions take place and used to enter data relevant to the transactions. An example is a POS terminal in a department store that is connected to a computer which automatically processes a transaction by totaling the cost of items entered by the clerk, performing a credit check, updating inventory records, and furnishing a receipt.

POTS: The Logo command that causes the titles of all the procedures in working memory to be printed on the screen.

preoperational stage: The Piagetian stage of cognitive development from about age two to age seven during which children begin to use mental symbols and experience a profound period of language development.

PRINT: The Logo command that prints out specified characters. For example, the command PRINT [BOB] will print the word BOB on the screen. In BASIC, the BASIC statement that causes a specified value to be printed. For example, in BASIC the statement PRINT "EXCEL" will cause the value EXCEL to be printed.

procedural thinking: The type of approach to problem solving needed to be able to generate the solution to a problem as a procedure or a series of procedures.

procedure: In general, a specific set of instructions needed by the computer in order for it to perform a particular task. In Logo, a named group of Logo commands.

procedures: Specific sets of unambiguous instructions needed by the computer in order to accomplish particular tasks.

process symbol: The flowchart symbol that denotes that an operation, such as an arithmetic or a logic operation, is to be done.

processing: The arithmetic or logic operations performed by a computer on data in order to turn the data into information.

processing flow symbol: The flowchart symbol that shows the direction, or flow, of logic within a flowchart.

PRO/FILES: A periodically updated set of in-depth analyses and evaluations of educational software offered by the Educational Products Information Exchange.

program: The same as computer program. The set of instructions a computer is given that causes it to perform a desired task.

program shell: The skeleton of a program to perform a certain task, for instance, to present drill-and-practice items to students. In its simplest form, a user simply adds the content that the shell will present and ends up with a completed customized program.

programmer: A person who engages in the act of programming a computer.

programming: The act of writing the instructions needed by a computer to perform a particular task.

programming language: A language in which a computer program (set of instructions) can be written. Examples are Pascal, Logo, BASIC, and COBOL.

prompt: A message placed on a screen to tell the user of a computer program what must be done next.

pseudocode: The presentation of the steps of an algorithm as an English-like narrative description.

READ: The Logo command that reads the specified file into working memory from secondary storage. For example, the command READ "AUTO would cause the file named AUTO to be read into working memory. Also, in BASIC, the statement that causes data to be read from a data list within a program into a variable.

record: A group of related fields. For instance, a student record on a computerized grading system for a classroom might consist of the student's name, assignments completed, date completed, and a grade for each assignment.

recursion: In Logo (and in other programming languages), the ability of a procedure to call itself.

relational symbol: One of the set of symbols used to make comparisons in programming, such as greater than ($>$), less than ($<$), and so on.

REM: In BASIC, the statement that causes the computer to ignore whatever follows REM in the program line. REM is used to place comments that will be of value to the programmer in a program.

REPEAT: The Logo command that causes one or more commands to be repeated a specified number of times. The command REPEAT 4 [FORWARD 50 RIGHT 90] will cause the commands FORWARD 50 RIGHT 90 to be repeated four times.

repetition: One of the three structured programming constructs. Repetition refers to performing the same instruction, or series of instructions, more than once.

reserved word: A word defined in a computer language to perform a particular task.

RESTORE: In BASIC, the statement that places the pointer back at the beginning of the data list.

RIGHT (RT): The Logo command that rotates the turtle in place a specified number of degrees to the right; e.g., RIGHT 90 rotates the turtle 90 degrees to the right.

RUN: In BASIC, the command that causes the program in the computer's memory to execute.

SAVE: The Logo command that causes the contents of working memory (one or more procedures) to be saved to secondary storage under the filename specified. The command SAVE "MYPROCS would cause the contents of working memory to be saved under the filename MYPROCS. In BASIC, SAVE causes the BASIC program currently in the computer's memory to be saved under the specified name to secondary storage. For example, the command SAVE PGM5 in BASIC would cause the program in the computer's memory to be saved to secondary storage under the name PGM5.

schema: Cognitive structures formed through an individual's experience with the environment.

second generation: A period in the development of computers from 1959 to 1964.

selection: One of the three structured programming constructs; refers to choosing from between two or more alternatives.

sensorimotor: The Piagetian stage of cognitive development from birth to about age two during which children come to know about the environment through the use of the senses and motion. During this stage, children gradually see themselves as separate from the environment, develop visual pursuit and object permanence, and the ability to remember.

sequence: One of the three structured programming constructs; refers to the one-after-another execution of instructions in a program (or an algorithm). Instructions are executed in the order they appear unless one of the instructions directs otherwise.

SHOWTURTLE (ST): The Logo command that causes the turtle to reappear on the screen after it has been erased with the HIDETURTLE command.

simulation: A model that closely emulates a real-world situation or occurrence. Software that presents such a model, such as a program that simulates the financial decisions that must be made by a young married couple and the consequences of the decisions.

skeleton program: See *program shell*.

soft master: An individual who views the computer subjectively and interacts with it more as an artist than as a scientist. A soft master may do something when programming the computer, look at the results, and then experiment some more.

softcopy: Output that appears on the screen.

software: The computer programs, or instructions, that make the computer perform particular tasks.

spelling checker: Software that automatically checks the spelling of words within a document and identifies words thought to be misspelled.

SPLITSCREEN (CTRL-S): The Logo command that causes the bottom four lines of the screen to be displayed for text and makes the rest of the screen available for drawing.

spreadsheet: A method of arranging data in rows and columns in order to more readily understand and work with the data for any of a variety of purposes. Commonly refers to software that provides computerized spreadsheets.

sprite: Available in some versions of Logo; objects that may be defined as to shape, size and color and then given velocity and direction in order to animate them on the computer screen.

stand-alone: A computer that is not networked to other computers. A computer configuration that operates independently of any other.

statement: One of the reserved words (commands) in a computer language. Also, a command with a line number.

step value: In BASIC, the amount the control variable is incremented each time through a FOR-NEXT loop.

string: One or more characters. For example, BERT is a string.

string constant: A specific string value. See *string*.

string variable: A storage location where a string may be stored. The name of such a location (e.g., in BASIC A\$, Z\$).

structure chart: A technique for representing, pictorially, the relationship of the modules in an algorithm.

structured design: A set of techniques used to design computer programs and systems of computer programs so that they are understandable and so that their creation will be accomplished efficiently and effectively.

structured programming: An approach to programming a computer that encourages modularized problem solving and makes use of the three structured programming constructs—sequence, selection, and repetition.

structured programming construct: Any one of the three constructs available for use when writing structured programs—sequence, selection, and repetition. See *sequence, selection*, and *repetition*.

subprocedure: A procedure that is called by another procedure is said to be a subprocedure of the calling procedure.

supercomputer: The most highly advanced type of computer available. These computers are usually used for scientific purposes and may have hundreds of megabytes of storage and very fast processing speeds.

switchbox: A device that allows input from one or more sources to be routed to one or more sources. For example, two computers may be connected to one printer through a switchbox. By selecting a 1 or a 2 on the switchbox, the user can control which computer sends output to the one printer connected to the switchbox.

syntax: The exact format the instructions of a given computer language (i.e., BASIC) must take in order for the computer to understand the instructions.

systematic procedure: See *procedures, procedural thinking*.

teacher utility: Educational software that performs any of a number of specialized tasks for teachers, such as creating tests, scoring tests, calculating readability level, and creating customized tutor-mode software.

terminal symbol: The flowchart symbol that signifies the beginning or ending point of the flowchart.

terminal value: In BASIC, the value that will cause a particular FOR-NEXT loop to stop executing.

test: The process of checking to see if a computer program works correctly. This involves finding out if the program will take input data, process it correctly, and provide valid output.

TEXTSCREEN (CTRL-T): The Logo command that displays the entire screen for text.

The Educational Software Selector (TESS): Published yearly by the Educational Products Information Exchange; contains product listings that outline pertinent information about educational software, including sources for reviews of specific software packages and information about software suppliers.

third generation: A period of time in the history of computers ranging from 1965 to 1971.

TO: The Logo command that allows the user to enter the editor for the procedure name specified. The command TO SQUARE would cause the editor to be entered for the procedure named SQUARE. If the procedure SQUARE did not yet exist, it could be created; if it did exist, it could be changed.

tool mode: The mode of computer use where the user's ability in some particular area is enhanced by the computer, such as using the computer for word processing or solving statistical problems.

Total Turtle Trip Theorem: The notion that if the turtle is moved completely around the perimeter of any closed regular figure (such as a circle, square, or star) so that it arrives at the place it started from, the number of degrees the turtle turns during the trip will be 360 or a multiple of 360.

turtle geometry: The presentation of the concepts of geometry in a computational form through the use of turtle graphics, graphics created by moving the turtle around the screen using the Logo programming language.

turtle graphics: Graphics created by moving the turtle around the screen using the Logo programming language. The part of the Logo programming environment that allows the creation of such graphics.

turtle steps: A turtle step is the unit of distance the turtle moves forward or backward on the screen. The turtle may be instructed to move a specified number of turtle steps. For instance, the command FORWARD 50 would cause the turtle to move forward 50 turtle steps.

tutee mode: When the computer is used as an object of instruction, is taught something, it is used in the tutee mode. When a student programs a computer, teaches it the instructions to accomplish something, the computer is used in the tutee mode.

tutor mode: When used in the tutor mode the computer presents material to the student and may query the student for a response based on the material presented. The computer may decide, after evaluating the student's response, to branch to any of several other sets of appropriate material to continue the lesson.

tutorial: Educational software that instructs the student by engaging her in a dialogue related to the material being taught.

universal product code symbol (UPC symbol): A machine-readable code placed on products by manufacturers.

variable: A storage location for a constant. The value stored in a variable may change during the execution of a program.

video display screen: A screen, resembling a TV screen, on which graphics and characters may be displayed.

video display terminal (VDT): A device with a video display screen (VDS) and a keyboard. A VDT is used to communicate with a computer. Data are entered on the keyboard, and text and graphics are displayed on the VDS.

visual pursuit: The ability to follow a moving object with the eyes.

voice synthesizer: A device that emulates the human voice, thus allowing output to be presented as speech rather than text.

window: A section of a screen in which information is displayed. Some software allows several windows to be displayed on the screen at once. This allows the user of the software to look at information from different sources on the same screen at the same time.

word processor: Using a computer to store and retrieve text. Common functions provided by word processors are the creation of a document, the addition and deletion of text to a document, and the rearrangement of text within a document. The software that allows a computer to do this.

working memory: In Logo, the area in the computer's memory where procedures are stored.

workspace: See *working memory*.

Index

Abacus, 28
Arcademic Drill Builders, 139
Accommodation, 226–227
Accounting functions, computers and, 11
Accuracy, as factor in software evaluation, 150
Administrators, management software for, 140
Aiken, Howard, 30
Algorithm(s), 301–304
    characteristics of, 302
American Standard Code for Information Interchange, 54–55
Analysis, software to aid development of, 86, 88–90
Analytical Engine, 29
Antecedent knowledge of programming, 312
Applesoft BASIC, 320–321
    arithmetic operations in, 327–328, 329
Appleworks, 98, 100, 101
Apple Writer II, 99
Arithmetic/logic unit of CPU, 39–40
Arithmetic operations, in BASIC, 327–328, 329
Artificial intelligence, 23, 90, 101, 103
    Logo and, 229
    trends in, 387–390
ASCII system, 54–55
Assimilation, 226–227
Atanasoff, John, 32
Atanasoff-Berry Computer, (ABC), 32
Authoring systems, 138–139
Automatic teller machines, 11
Auxiliary storage, 34, 41

Babbage, Charles, 28–29
BACK, in Logo, 248, 249, 250
Backup copies, as factor in software evaluation, 157–158
Banking, computer uses in, 11
Bank Street Filer, 101
Bank Street Musicwriter, 94
Bank Street Speller, 99

Bank Street Storybook, 94
Bank Street Writer, 99
Bar code readers, 42
BASIC, 53, 67, 101
    Applesoft, 320–321, 327–328
    arithmetic operations in, 327–328, 329
    commands, 322–330, 332–339, 344–369
    instructional software for, 87
    as programming language for teachers, 188, 236
    pros and cons, 300, 324
    reserved words, 321, 322
    statements, 322–323
    syntax, 297, 298
    variables and constants in, 321–322
    variations in, 320
    vs. Logo regarding modularized problem solving, 236
Beginner's All-Purpose Symbolic Instructional Code. *See* BASIC
Berry, Clifford, 32
Binary notation, 34, 54
Bit, 54
Branching, 65
Bugs
    as factor in software evaluation, 157
    in Logo environment, 238
Building Better Sentences: Combining Sentence Parts, 116, 118–123
Building Better Sentences: Creating Compound and Complex Sentences, 116
Bursar, 140
Bus Routes, 140
Business, role of computers in, 11–13
Business programmers, qualifications for, 18
Byte, 47–48, 54

C, 66
CAD. *See* Computer-aided design
CAI. *See* Computer-assisted instruction
CAM. *See* Computer-aided manufacturing

Cardiovascular Fitness Lab, 94
CATALOG
in BASIC, 327
in Logo, 275
Catalogues, as information source for software evaluation, 159–160
Cathode ray tube
as input device, 42
as output device, 44
Cells, 99–100
Central processing unit, 38–46
components, 38–40
peripheral devices of, 40–45
Characters, 247
ChipWits, 94
Class II Reading Testbank, 138
Classmate, 128–135
Classroom Answer, The, 137
Classroom presentations, computer-related, 22, 51–52, 102, 201–202, 261–262, 286, 308, 339, 361, 388
CLEARSCREEN, in Logo, 251, 253
CMI. *See* Computer-managed instruction
COBOL program, example of, 19
Code Quest, 161
Cognitive development in children, Piaget's theory on, 220–225
Color Keys, 161
Commands
for BASIC, 322–330, 332–339
for Logo, 245–260
Compatibility, as factor in software evaluation, 147–148
Compiler, as translator into machine language, 53
Compuserve, 160, 163
Computer-aided design, 12
Computer-aided manufacturing, 12–13
Computer applications, as curriculum component, 199, 200
Computer-assisted instruction
definition of, 63
establishing context for, 60–63
examples of tutor mode, 78–96
modes of, 65–67
Computer-based training materials, 15
Computer-controlled vs. human-controlled interaction, 67–70, 72
Computer coordinator, 382–384
Computer curriculum
See also Computer literacy
components of, 191–194, 199–201
cost of, 377–378
development of, 190–192

evaluation of, 206, 210, 211–213
examples of, 204–206, 207–210
goals, 185–187
sample scope and sequence chart for, 194, 195–198
teacher's role in, 183, 194
Computer instruction
See also Computer-assisted instruction
applications of, 13–15
pros and cons of, 6–9
research on, 97–98, 263–264, 277
value of, in job market, 37
Computerized payroll systems, 11
Computer knowledge. *See* Computer instruction
Computer lab, 378–379, 381–382
Computer Literacy, 91, 92
Computer literacy
definition
for students, 186–187
for teachers, 187–189
development and implementation of curriculum, for, 189–204
educators' philosophies concerning, 184–186, 331–332
in elementary school curriculum, 331–332
importance of, 180–182
in middle school curriculum, 331, 332
need for, 182
software for teaching, 164–167
for students, 183–187, 189
for teachers, 187–190
Computer-managed instruction, 108–116
examples of, 110–116, 118–123
principle of, 109–110
software, 108, 109–110
teacher's role in, 108–109
Computer operations, job responsibilities, 20
Computerphobia, 63–64
Computer programs, 13–14
as algorithms, 301
development of, 296–299
learning to use, as curriculum component, 199, 200
learning to write, as curriculum component, 199, 200
specifications for, 19–20
Computer-related jobs, 18–22
Computer revolution, 4–6, 22–23, 180–182
Computer(s)
in business and industry, 11–13

categories of, 46–50

in education, 13–15. *See also* Education, computer use in

in entertainment, 17

factors affecting initial use of, by teachers, 60–62

fear of, 63–64

function of, 9–10

fundamental concepts about, 200

generations of, 33–37, 103–104

in government, 13

history of, 28–37

as idiot savant, 70

in medicine, 16

new developments in, 23

in office automation, 17–18

in science, 15–16

in the classroom, 22, 51–52, 71–72, 97–98, 117–118, 379–381

in the school, 6–9, 13, 16, 45–46, 153

as tool, 66–67

transition to use of, in teaching, 60–63

as tutee, 67

as tutor, 65–66

types of, in schools, 374–376

Computer sales and service, as job opportunity, 21

Computer science/engineering

as job opportunity, 22

programming as outgrowth of, 296

Computers in Teaching, 79

Computer systems, 37–46, 47, 48

Concrete operational stage of cognitive development, 223, 224

Conditional test, 345–346

Connector symbol, 304, 305

Conservation, 222

Constant

numerical, 321

string, 322

Control unit of CPU, 38–39

Copy-protection policies, 157–158

Cost, as factor in software evaluation, 147

Cost of computer education, 377–378

Courts, computerized management of, in New York, 13, 14

CPU. *See* Central processing unit

Create-a-Base, 87

Creativity, software to aid development of, 87, 88, 94, 95

CRT. *See* Cathode ray tube

Cultural changes, effect of on children, 232

Curriculum Alignment Service for Educators (CASE), 204

Cursor, 246

Daisy wheel printers, 44, 385

Data, 9

DATA, in BASIC, 360, 362–369

Data base, 100–101

instructing students in use of, 87

Data base management system, 100–101

Data elements, 360

Data entry, job responsibilities in, 21

Data entry devices, 42–44

Data list, 360

Data processing, 9–10

Debit card, 11

Debugging, 18, 298

Decision symbol, 304, 305

Delta Drawing, 66, 68, 290

Desktop metaphor approach, 385–386

Difference Engine, 29, 30

Disk drives, 41

Disk storage, 41, 385

Documentation, as factor in software evaluation, 151, 154–155

Document symbol, 304, 305

Dot matrix printers, 44, 385

DRAW, in Logo, 247–248

Drill and practice programs, 78–83

EBCDIC system, 54, 55

Eckert, John Presper, 32, 33

Economic feasibility of computers in schools, 377

EDIT mode in Logo, 246–247, 270–272

Editor, 270–272

Education, computer use in, 13–15, 16, 153

future of, 117–118

modes of, 65–67

research on, 97–98

value judgments related to, 45–46

Educational criteria for software evaluation, 149–152

Educational objectives, as factor in software selection, 149

Educational Products Information Exchange, 160, 163, 202

Educational Software Selector, The (TESS), 160, 163

Educational technology, role of computers in, 153

Educators

philosophies of, concerning computer literacy, 184–186

role of, in changing culture, 232

EDVAC, 33

EFT. *See* Electronic funds transfer

Egocentricity of children, 222

Electronic Discrete Variable Automatic Computer, 33

Electronic funds transfer, 11

Electronic mail, 17–18

Electronic Numerical Integrator and Calculator, 32

Eliza, 252

Encoding system, 54–55

END, in BASIC, 323–325

End of Data tag, 363–364

ENIAC, 32

Entertainment, computer use in, 17

Entrepreneurs in computer industry, 22

Environmental changes, effect of, on children, 226–228, 232

EOD tag, 363–364

Equip, 140

Equity in computer education, 45–46, 390, 391

ERASE ALL, in Logo, 275

ERASE, in Logo, 274–275

ERASEFILE, in Logo, 276

Error handling, as factor in software evaluation, 155–156

Expert system, 23, 103, 388–391

Expert system shells, 390–391

Extended Binary Decimal Interchange Code, 54, 55

Facemaker, 84–85

Fact and Fiction Tool Kit, The, 87

Fear of computers, 63–64

Fifth-generation computers, 103–104

First-generation computers, 33–34

First Letter Fun, as drill and practice example, 79–82

Flexibility, as factor in software evaluation, 151, 152, 154

Flowchart, 121–122, 124–125, 304–308

Formal operational stage of cognitive development, 223, 225, 226

Formatting, 333

Form for software evaluation, 168–172, 173–174

FOR–NEXT, in BASIC, 352, 354–360

FORTRAN, 53, 66, 300

FORWARD, in Logo, 248, 249, 250

Fourth-generation computers, 36–37

FULLSCREEN, in Logo, 257, 258

Fun House Maze, 161

Generation(s) of computer equipment, 33–37, 103–104

fifth, 103–104

first, 33–34

fourth, 36–37

second, 34, 35

third, 34–36

Genetic epistemology, 227

Geography Search, 88

Geometric Supposer: Triangles, 94

Geometry, turtle, 232–233

Glass Computer, The, 87

GOODBYE, in Logo, 275

GOTO, in BASIC, 344–345, 352

Government, computer use in, 13

Grade-keeping program, 123, 127–135

pros and cons of, 126–127

Graphic capabilities, as factor in software evaluation, 154

Graphic tablets, 42, 43

Green Globs, 87

Grouping, as factor in software evaluation, 152

Hands-on experience, as method of evaluating software, 158–172

Hardcopy, 44

Hard disk, 376

Hard master, 391

Hardware, 37–38

trends and issues in, 384–386

HIDETURTLE, in Logo, 255, 256

High-level languages, 53, 297

Hollerith, Herman, 30

Holt Reading Series, software for, 138

HOME

in BASIC, 325

in Logo, 251, 253

Houghton Mifflin Reading Series, software for, 137

Human Physiology Kit, The, 87

IBM. *See* International Business Machines

IBM Automatic Sequence-Controlled Calculator, 30–31

IBOL, 94

Icon, 385

Icon Based Operating Language, 94

Idiot savant, computer as, 70

IF–THEN, in BASIC, 333–336, 338–340

IIIR. *See* Integrated Instructional Information Resource

Illegal duplication of software, 157–158

Incredible Laboratory, The, 87

Industry, role of computers in, 11–13
Infinite loop, 344, 345
Information, as end product of data processing, 9–10
Information Age, 6
Input, 9, 10
Input devices, 42–44
Input/output symbol, 304, 305
Instructional games, 83–86, 88–90
Instructor's System, The, 139–140
Integrated circuits, role of, in third-generation computers, 34, 36
Integrated Instructional Information Resource, 202–204
Integrated software packages, 98, 100
Intelligence, artificial. *See* Artificial intelligence
Interactive design, as factor in software evaluation, 156
Interactive videodisc, 386
International Business Machines, 30
Interpreter, as translator into machine language, 53
Inventory, computerized system for tracking, 12

Jargon, 8
Jenny of the Prairie, 88

K. *See* Kilobyte
Kalamazoo Teacher's Record Book, 128
Kilobytes, 48
Knowledge engineering, 23
Knowledge Explosion, 6
Knowledge goals for computer literacy
    for students, 186
    for teachers, 187
Koala Pad, 385

Laser printers, 45
Learning styles, 288
LEFT, in Logo, 248, 249, 250
LET, in BASIC, 329–330
Light pens, 42
LIST, in BASIC, 327
LOAD, in BASIC, 327
Logic, 297–298
Logic software, 86, 88–90, 91
Logo, 53, 67, 101, 220
    as a learning environment, 229, 230, 231, 232, 233, 235, 236–237
    artificial intelligence and, 229
    basis for, 229, 233, 235
    bugs in, 230, 231, 238
    characteristics of, 235–238

commands, 245–260
    editing commands in, 272
    learning to program in, 230–232, 298
    as microworld, 236–237
    procedures in, 269–274
    as programming language
        for students, 194, 234–235
        for teachers, 188
    reading files in, 276
    research on, 263–264
    saving procedures in, 275–276
    student-teacher interaction with, 238
    teaching, 285, 287–288
    versions of, 244
    working memory in, 274–275
Logo primitives, 272
LogoWriter, 289–290
Looping, 344
    as method of learning programming concepts, 353–354
Lotus 1–2–3, 98, 100
Low-level languages, 53

Machine language, 34, 53
Macmillan Reading Series, software for, 137–138
Macro-explorer, as learner type, 288
Magic Slate, 94
Magnetic core memory, 34
Magnetic disk, as storage medium, 41
Magnetic ink recognition devices, 42
Magnetic tape, as storage medium, 41
Mainframe computers, 47–48, 49
Management system, 109
Mark I, 30–31
Math Blaster, 85–86
Mauchly, John, 32, 33
MB. *See* Megabyte
Medicine, computer use in, 16
Megabyte, 48
Memory, software to aid development of, 84–85
Memory Castle, 161
Menu-driven software, 110
Meteor Mission, 139
Microcomputer, 49–50
    availability of, 36–37
    in mathematics instruction, 68
    role of, in computer revolution, 180–183
    in schools, 374–376
Microcourse Reading, 137
Micro-explorer, as learner type, 288
Microfiche, 44
Microfilm

computer-input, 44
computer-output, 45
Microprocessor, 36
MicroSift, 163
Microworld, 236–237
Microzine, 160, 162–163
Milliken Word Processor, The, 87, 99
Minicomputer system, 48–49, 50
components, 47
Minnesota Educational Computing Corpo-
ration (MECC), 79
in mathematics instruction, 68
microcomputers in, 68
in schools, 374–376
software for, 85–86, 87, 88, 91–92, 93, 94,
95
Minority schools, computer use in, 45–46
MIT Logo, 244
Mobile computer lab, 381
MODEM, 46
Modularized problem solving, 236
Modulator-demodulator. *See* MODEM
Module, 236, 237
Mouse, 385
Muppet Learning Keys, 94–95, 385
Music education, software to aid devel-
opment of, 94
Music synthesizers, 17
MYCIN, 388–390

Natural-language processing, 387–388
Natural Selection, 93, 95–96
Networking of microcomputers, 50, 376
NEW, in BASIC, 327
Newsroom, The, 95
NODRAW, in Logo, 247–248

Object permanence, 221
Office automation, computer use in, 17–18
Operations, 221
Optical character readers, 42, 43
Order of operations, 328
Other Side, The, 95
Output, as end product of data process-
ing, 9–10

Pace, as factor in software evaluation,
150–151
Papert, Seymour, 220, 227–229, 231, 232,
236, 289–290
Parental involvement in computer activi-
ties in school, 175–176
Pascal, 53, 67, 101, 298
Pascal, Blaise, 28
PENDOWN, in Logo, 254–255, 256

PENUP, in Logo, 254–255, 256
Performance goals for computer literacy
for students, 186–187
for teachers, 187–189
Peripheral devices of CPU, 40–45
Personal computer, 49–50.
See also Minicomputer
PFS:File, 101
PFS:Write, 99
Piaget, Jean, 220–222, 225–229
Piagetian learning, 227, 228–229
Pilot, 66, 138–139
Planner, as learner type, 288
Playing turtle, 233, 238, 239
Plotters, 45
PO, in Logo, 274
PO ALL, in Logo, 274
Point-of-sale terminals, 11
POS terminals. *See* Point-of-sale termi-
nals
POTS, in Logo, 274
Practice-theory relationship, 210–212
Preoperational stage of cognitive develop-
ment, 221–222, 223
Prerequisite skills requirement, as factor
in software evaluation, 149
President Elect, 96
Previewing software, 168
Primary storage of CPU, 40
PRINT
in BASIC, 323, 330, 332–333
in Logo, 246–247
Printers, 44–45
Problem solving, steps for, 299, 301
Procedural thinking, as prerequisite for
programming, 199–201
Procedures, in Logo, 269–274
Processing flow symbol, 304, 305
Processing of data, 9–10
Process symbol, 304, 305
PRO/FILES, 160, 164–167
Programmer, job description for, 18–19
Programming
antecedent knowledge for, 312
as career, 18–19
definition of, 7
fundamentals of, 244, 369
procedural thinking as prerequisite for,
199, 201
software to teach concepts of, 94
Teachers and, 188
teaching of, 7, 8, 13–14, 296–315
Programming languages, 13–14, 18
See also specific languages

development of, 34
high-level vs. low-level, 53
teaching, 296–299
Program shells, 139
Prompt, 335
Pseudocode, 20, 304
Punched cards, 29, 30, 31, 44
Purchase, 140

Quill, 88

READ, in BASIC, 360, 362–369
Readability, 139
Readability Estimator, 139
Readability level, computer calculation of, 139
Reading Comprehension: Main Idea and Details, 116
Reading comprehension skills, software to aid development of, 110–115, 116
selection criteria, 136–137
Reading for Meaning with Mother Goose, 2, 110–115
Reading readiness, drill and practice program for, 79–82
Reading Skills Extender, 138
Reasoning, software to aid development of, 86, 88–90
Recursion, 282–284
Relational symbols, 345
REM, in BASIC, 325
REPEAT, in Logo, 259–261
Repetition, as structured programming construct, 309
Research skills, software to aid development of, 88, 90, 102
Reserved words, 321, 322
RESTORE, in BASIC, 364, 365
Reviews, as information source for software evaluation, 160
RICE (Resources in Computer Education), 163
RIGHT, in Logo, 248, 250
Rocky's Boots, 86, 88–91
RUN, in BASIC, 327
SAVE
in BASIC, 327
in Logo, 275
Schemas, 225–227
School Attendance Manager, 140
School Discipline Manager, 140
Schools, computers in the, 6–9, 13, 16, 377–382
See also Education, computer use in.

economic feasibility of, 377
Science, computer use in, 15–16
Science instruction, software for, 87, 94, 95
Scientific programmer, qualifications for, 18–19
Screen design, as factor in software evaluation, 156
Secondary storage, 34
Second-generation computers, 34, 35
Selection, as structured programming construct, 309
Sensible Speller, 99
Sensorimotor stage of cognitive development, 220–221
Sequence, as structured programming construct, 309
SERIES r Instructional Management System, 137–138
SERIES r Vocabulary Comprehension Computer-Assisted Instruction, 137–138
Sexual stereotyping in computer use, 391
Shoot, 237
SHOWTURTLE, in Logo, 255–256
Simulations, 92–93, 95–96
Skeleton programs, 139
Society, impact of computers on, as curriculum component, 199, 200
Socioeconomic factors related to computer use in schools, 45–46, 390, 391
Softcopy, 44
Softmaster, 391
Software
for administrators, 140
review of, by hands-on experience, 158–172
teacher-produced, 80, 82–83, 139
trends and issues in, 386–391
Software evaluation, 146–177
by hands-on experience, 158–172
criteria for reading series, 136–137
form used for, 168–172, 173–174
general criteria, 146–148
specific criteria, 148–152, 154–158
Software protection, 157–158
Sound capabilities, as factor in software evaluation, 154
Spelling checker programs, 99
Spelling skills, software to aid development of, 87, 99
SPLITSCREEN, in Logo, 257, 258
Spreadsheets, 99–100
Sprites, 277, 291

Stages of development, Piaget's theory on, 220–225
Stand-alone, 376
Step value, 355
Stereotypes, as factor in software evaluation, 152
Stored program concept, 32
  in EDVAC, 33
Structure chart, 310–314
Structured design, 309–314
Structured programming, 308–309
  flow charts and, 307–308
  Logo and, 236
Structured programming constructs, 308, 309, 310–311
Student engagement, as factor in software evaluation, 151
Student interaction
  with computer, 67–70, 72, 193
  with other students, 193
Student preparation for computer literacy, 183–187
  knowledge goals, 186
  performance goals, 186–187
Subject area, as factor in software evaluation, 148
Subprocedures, 278–285, 287–288
Supercomputers, 48, 49
Support, as factor in software evaluation, 155
Surge protectors, 46
Survival Math, 88
Switchbox, 376
Syntax, 297–299
System analyst, job description for, 19–20
Systematic procedure, 230–232
System commands, 323

Tabulating Machine Company, 30
Target group, as factor in software evaluation, 148
TAS: Teacher Authoring System, 138–139
Teacher preparation for computer literacy, 187–189
Teacher-produced software, 80, 82–83
Teachers
  as professionals, 60
  as programmers, 188
  role of, in computer-managed instruction, 108–109
  theory-practice relationship and, 210–212
Teacher utility software, 123, 127–135, 138–140

Teaching
  with and about computers, 6–9, 16
    as job opportunity, 21
  transition to, 60–63
Teaching style, as factor in software evaluation, 149–150
Technical criteria for software evaluation, 152, 154–158
Terminal symbol, 304, 305
Test creation/test scoring programs, 139, 140
Testing of program, 18
TEXTSCREEN, in Logo, 257–258
Theory-practice relationship, 210–212
Third-generation computers, 34–36
Tool mode of CAI, 66–67
  examples of, 96, 98–101
Top-down design, 309–314
Total Turtle Trip Theorem, 2, 238
Training of computer personnel, as job opportunity, 21
Turtle geometry, 232–233
Turtle graphics, 230, 233, 247, 291
Turtle steps, 250
Tutee mode
  of CAI, 66, 67
  example of, 101
Tutorials, 90–92
Tutor mode of CAI, 65–66
  examples of, 78–96

Understanding Computers, 164–167
UNIVAC I, 33, 34
Universal product code, entry of, in computer, 42
Usefulness, as factor in software evaluation, 151–152

Variable
  numerical, 321
  string, 322
VDT. See Video display terminal
Videodisc, 386
Video display screen. See Cathode ray tube
Video display terminal, 42
Visual pursuit, 221
Vocabulary, software to aid development of, 87
Voice recognition systems, 42
von Leibniz, Gottfried Wilhelm, 28
von Neumann, John, 32
Voyage of the Mimi, The, 95
Voyageur, 96

Weizenbaum, Joseph, 252
Where in the World Is Carmen Sandiego?, 90
Wiz Works, 139

Word processor, 13, 98–99
Word recognition software, 87–88, 94–95
Word Spinner, 87–88
Word Spinning, 87

Photo and Figure Credits